ACCA

PAPER P3

BUSINESS ANALYSIS

In this June 2007 new edition

- We discuss the **best strategies** for revising and taking your ACCA exams

- We show you how to be well prepared for the **December 2007 exam**

- We give you **lots of great guidance** on tackling questions

- We include **genuine student answers** with BPP commentary

- We show you how you can **build your own exams**

- We provide you with **three** mock exams including the **Pilot paper**

- We provide the **ACCA examiner's answers** as well as our own to key exam questions and the Pilot Paper as an additional revision aid

Our **i-Pass** product also supports this paper.

FOR EXAMS IN DECEMBER 2007

LEARNING MEDIA

First edition June 2007

ISBN 9780 7517 3370 9

British Library Cataloguing-in-Publication Data
A catalogue record for this book
is available from the British Library

Published by

BPP Learning Media Ltd
BPP House, Aldine Place
London W12 8AA

www.bpp.com/learningmedia

Printed in Great Britain by
Hobbs The Printers

We are grateful to the Association of Chartered Certified
Accountants for permission to reproduce past
examination questions. The suggested solutions in the
exam answer bank have been prepared by BPP Learning
Media Ltd, unless where otherwise stated.

Your learning materials, published by BPP Learning
Media Ltd, are printed on paper sourced from
sustainable, managed forests.

Contents

Review form & free prize draw

Question index

The headings in this checklist/index indicate the main topics of questions, but questions often cover several different topics.

Questions set under the old syllabus *Strategic Business Planning and Development* paper are included because their style and content are similar to those which appear in the P3 exam. The questions have been amended to reflect the current exam format.

BPP LEARNING MEDIA

Case studies

Mock exam 1

Questions 42 to 45

Mock exam 2

Questions 46 to 49

Mock Exam 3 (Pilot Paper)

Questions 50 to 53

Planning your question practice

Our guidance from page 25 shows you how to organise your question practice, either by attempting questions from each syllabus area or **by building your own exams** – tackling questions as a series of practice exams.

Topic index

Listed below are the key Paper P3 syllabus topics and the numbers of the questions in this Kit covering those topics.

If you need to concentrate your practice and revision on certain topics or if you want to attempt all available questions that refer to a particular subject, you will find this index useful.

Syllabus topic	Question numbers
Appraisal and performance management	22
Balanced scorecard	3, 21, 29
Benchmarking	6
Corporate governance	11, 28
Corporate social responsibility	13
Critical success factors	29
Culture	14, 35
Ethics	10, 34, 37
Five forces	2, 4
Generic strategies	12
Information strategy	23
International strategy	30, 31, 32, 36
Leadership	26
Levels of strategy	1
Marketing	12, 15, 18, 19, 20, 41
Organisation structure	27, 36
Outsourcing	5, 16, 24
PESTEL	2
Product Portfolio	6
Project management	13, 17, 27
Quality	7
Resource-based strategy and competences	3, 5, 24
Scenarios	8
Software	23
Stakeholders	10, 12, 21, 33
Strategic analysis	7, 8, 9, 25, 33, 34, 35, 37, 38, 39
Strategic failure	26
Strategic options	9, 25, 33, 34, 35, 37, 38, 40, 41
Strategy lenses	1, 31

Using your BPP Practice and Revision Kit

Tackling revision and the exam

You can significantly improve your chances of passing by tackling revision and the exam in the right ways. Our advice is based on feedback from ACCA examiners.

- We look at the dos and don'ts of revising for, and taking, ACCA exams
- We focus on Paper P3; we discuss revising the syllabus, what to do (and what not to do) in the exam, how to approach different types of question and ways of obtaining easy marks

Selecting questions

We provide signposts to help you plan your revision.

- A full **question index**
- A **topic index** listing all the questions that cover key topics, so that you can locate the questions that provide practice on these topics, and see the different ways in which they might be examined
- **BPP's question plan** highlighting the most important questions and explaining why you should attempt them
- **Build your own exams**, showing how you can practise questions in a series of exams

Making the most of question practice

At BPP we realise that you need more than just questions and model answers to get the most from your question practice.

- Our **Top tips** provide essential advice on tackling questions, presenting answers and the key points that answers need to include
- We show you how you can pick up **Easy marks** on questions, as we know that picking up all readily available marks often can make the difference between passing and failing
- We summarise **Examiner's comments**
- We include **marking guides** to show you what the examiner rewards
- We refer to the **2007 BPP Study Text** for detailed coverage of the topics covered in each question
- A number of questions include **Analysis** to show you how to approach them if you are struggling
- We include **annotated student answers** to some questions to highlight how these questions can be tackled and ways answers can be improved.

Attempting mock exams

There are three mock exams that provide practice at coping with the pressures of the exam day. We strongly recommend that you attempt them under exam conditions. **Mock exams 1 and 2** reflect the question styles and syllabus coverage of the exam; **Mock exam 3** is the Pilot paper. To help you get the most out of doing these exams, we not only provide help with each answer, but also guidance on how you should have approached the whole exam.

Passing ACCA exams

Revising and taking ACCA exams

To maximise your chances of passing your ACCA exams, you must make best use of your time, both before the exam during your revision, and when you are actually doing the exam.

- Making the most of your revision time can make a big, big difference to how well-prepared you are for the exam

- Time management is a core skill in the exam hall; all the work you've done can be wasted if you don't make the most of the three hours you have to attempt the exam

In this section we simply show you what to do and what not to do during your revision, and how to increase and decrease your prospects of passing your exams when you take them. Our advice is grounded in feedback we've had from ACCA examiners. You may be surprised to know that much examiner advice is the same whatever the exam, and the reasons why many students fail don't vary much between subjects and exam levels. So if you follow the advice we give you over the next few pages, you will **significantly** enhance your chances of passing **all** your ACCA exams.

How to revise

☑ Plan your revision

At the start of your revision period, you should draw up a **timetable** to plan how long you will spend on each subject and how you will revise each area. You need to consider the total time you have available and also the time that will be required to revise for other exams you're taking.

☑ Practise Practise Practise

The **more exam-standard questions** you do, the **more likely you are to pass** the exam. Practising full questions will mean that you'll get used to the time pressure of the exam. When the time is up, you should note where you've got to and then try to complete the question, giving yourself practice at everything the question tests.

☑ Revise enough

Make sure that your revision covers the breadth of the syllabus, as all topics could be examined in a compulsory question. However it is true that some topics are **key** – they are likely to appear often or are a particular interest of the examiner – and you need to spend sufficient time revising these. Make sure you also know the **basics** – the fundamental calculations, proformas and report layouts.

☑ Deal with your difficulties

Difficult areas are topics you find dull and pointless, or subjects that you found problematic when you were studying them. You mustn't become negative about these topics; instead you should build up your knowledge by reading the **Passcards** and using the **Quick Quiz** questions in the Study Text to test yourself. When practising questions in the Kit, go back to the Text if you're struggling.

☑ Learn from your mistakes

Having completed a question you must try to look at your answer critically. Always read the **Top tips guidance** in the answers; it's there to help you. Look at **Easy marks** to see how you could have quickly gained credit on the questions that you've done. As you go through the Kit, it's worth noting any traps you've fallen into, and key points in the **Top tips** or **Examiner's comments** sections, and referring to these notes in the days before the exam. Aim to learn at least one new point from each question you attempt, a technical point perhaps or a point on style or approach.

☑ Read the examiners' guidance

We refer throughout this Kit to **Examiner's comments**. As well as highlighting weaknesses, Examiner's comments often provide clues to future questions, as many examiners will test areas that are likely to cause students problems. ACCA's website also contains articles by examiners which you **must** read, as they may form the basis of questions on any paper after they've been published.

Read through the examiner's answers to key exam questions and the Pilot paper included at the back of the Kit. In general these are far longer and more comprehensive than any answer you could hope to produce in the exam, but used in conjunction with our more realistic solutions, they provide a useful revision tool, covering all possible points and approaches.

☑ Complete all three mock exams

You should attempt the **Mock exams** at the end of the Kit under **strict exam conditions**, to gain experience of selecting questions, managing your time and producing answers.

How NOT to revise

☒ Revise selectively

Examiners are well aware that some students try to forecast the contents of exams, and only revise those areas that they think will be examined. Examiners try to prevent this by doing the unexpected, for example setting the same topic in successive sittings.

☒ Spend all the revision period reading

You cannot pass the exam just by learning the contents of Passcards, Course Notes or Study Texts. You have to develop your **application skills** by practising questions.

☒ Audit the answers

This means reading the answers and guidance without having attempted the questions. Auditing the answers gives you **false reassurance** that you would have tackled the questions in the best way and made the points that our answers do. The feedback we give in our answers will mean more to you if you've attempted the questions and thought through the issues.

☒ Practise some types of question, but not others

Although you may find the numerical parts of certain papers challenging, you shouldn't just practise calculations. These papers will also contain written elements, and you therefore need to spend time practising written question parts.

☒ Get bogged down

Don't spend a lot of time worrying about all the minute detail of certain topic areas, and leave yourself insufficient time to cover the rest of the syllabus. Remember that a key skill in the exam is the ability to **concentrate on what's important** and this applies to your revision as well.

☒ Overdo studying

Studying for too long without interruption will mean your studying becomes less effective. A five minute break each hour will help. You should also make sure that you are leading a **healthy lifestyle** (proper meals, good sleep and some times when you're not studying).

How to PASS your exams

☑ Prepare for the day

Make sure you set at least one alarm (or get an alarm call), and allow plenty of time to get to the exam hall. You should have your route planned in advance and should listen on the radio for potential travel problems. You should check the night before to see that you have pens, pencils, erasers, watch, calculator with spare batteries, also exam documentation and evidence of identity.

☑ Select the right questions

You should select the optional questions you feel you can answer **best**, basing your selection on the topics covered, the requirements of the question, how easy it will be to apply the requirements and the availability of easy marks.

☑ Plan your three hours

You need to make sure that you will be answering the correct number of questions, and that you spend the right length of time on each question – this will be determined by the number of marks available. Each mark carries with it a **time allocation** of **1.8 minutes**. A 25 mark question therefore should be selected, completed and checked in 45 minutes. With some papers, it's better to do certain types of question first or last.

☑ Read the questions carefully

To score well, you must follow the requirements of the question, understanding what aspects of the subject area are being covered, and the tasks you will have to carry out. The requirements will also determine what information and examples you should provide. Reading the question scenarios carefully will help you decide what **issues** to discuss, **techniques** to use, **information** and **examples** to include and how to **organise** your answer.

☑ Plan your answers

Five minutes of planning plus twenty-five minutes of writing is certain to earn you more marks than thirty minutes of writing. Consider when you're planning how your answer should be **structured, w**hat the **format** should be and **how long** each part should take.

Confirm before you start writing that your plan makes **sense,** covers **all relevant points** and does not include **irrelevant material.**

☑ Show evidence of judgement

Remember that examiners aren't just looking for a display of knowledge; they want to see how well you can **apply** the knowledge you have. Evidence of application and judgement will include writing answers that only contain **relevant** material, using the material in scenarios to **support** what you say, **criticising** the **limitations** and **assumptions** of the techniques you use and making **reasonable recommendations** that follow from your discussion.

☑ Stay until the end of the exam

Use any spare time to **check and recheck** your script. This includes checking you have filled out the candidate details correctly, you have labelled question parts and workings clearly, you have used headers and underlining effectively and spelling, grammar and arithmetic are correct.

How to FAIL your exams

☒ Don't do enough questions

If you don't attempt sufficient questions on the paper, you are making it harder for yourself to pass the questions that you do attempt. If for example you don't do a 25 mark question, then you will have to score 50 marks out of 75 marks on the rest of the paper, and therefore have to obtain 67% of the marks on the questions you do attempt. Failing to attempt all of the paper is symptomatic of poor time management or poor question selection.

☒ Include irrelevant material

Markers are given detailed mark guides and will not give credit for irrelevant content. Therefore you should **NOT** braindump all you know about a broad subject area; the markers will only give credit for what is **relevant**, and you will also be showing that you lack the ability to **judge what's important.** Similarly forcing irrelevant theory into every answer won't gain you marks, nor will providing uncalled for features such as situation analyses, executive summaries and background information.

☒ Fail to use the details in the scenario

General answers or reproductions of Kit answers that don't refer to what is in the scenario in **this** question won't score enough marks to pass.

☒ Copy out the scenario details

Examiners see **selective** use of the right information as a key skill. If you copy out chunks of the scenario which aren't relevant to the question, or don't use the information to support your own judgements, you won't achieve good marks.

☒ Don't do what the question asks

Failing to provide all the examiner asks for will limit the marks you score. You will also decrease your chances by not providing an answer with enough **depth** – producing a single line bullet point list when the examiner asks for a discussion.

☒ Present your work poorly

Markers will only be able to give you credit if they can read your writing. There are also plenty of other things that will make it more difficult for markers to reward you. Examples include:

- Not using black or blue ink
- Not showing clearly which question you're attempting
- Scattering question parts from the same question throughout your answer booklet
- Not showing clearly workings or the results of your calculations

Paragraphs that are too long or which lack headers also won't help markers and hence won't help you.

Using your BPP products

This Kit gives you the question practice and guidance you need in the exam. Our other products can also help you pass:

- **Learning to Learn Accountancy** gives further valuable advice on revision

- **Passcards** provide you with clear topic summaries and exam tips

- **Success CDs** help you revise on the move

- **i-Pass CDs** offer tests of knowledge against the clock

- **Learn Online** is an e-learning resource delivered via the Internet, offering comprehensive tutor support and featuring areas such as study, practice, email service, revision and useful resources

You can purchase these products by visiting www.bpp.com/mybpp.

Visit our website www.bpp.com/acca/learnonline to sample aspects of Learn Online free of charge. Learn Online is hosted by BPP Professional Education.

Passing P3

Passing the P3 exam

The examiner

The examiner for Paper P3 is Steve Skidmore, who is an academic and consultant. He was the Examiner for the old syllabus Paper 2.1 *Information Systems.* This link is evident in the heavy bias in the P3 syllabus towards IT-based topics.

The Examination

It is a good idea to think about the nature of any examination before the day you sit it. You must be sure you know what the Examiner wants from you in terms of number of answers and which questions are compulsory and so on. Paper P3 is quite simple in this respect. You **must do** question 1 and you must answer two questions from Section B.

Note that Section A is crucial. You are highly unlikely to pass on the strength of your answer to Question 1 alone, but **you are highly likely to fail if you do not make a creditable attempt at it**.

You must have a clear view of your overall preference about the order in which you will attempt questions before you enter the exam room. This is something you must do for yourself. Many people will advise that because Question 1 is so important you should definitely answer it first. Other people find that answering a shorter question first builds their confidence, especially if it is on a topic they are confident about. Only you can decide.

However, we would advise you that **it would be very risky to leave question 1 to the end**. This is a recipe for running out of time. While there are certain to be several separate requirements, you cannot deal with them in isolation from each other; you must make sure you do not end up repeating yourself by using ideas too early, for example. So you must allow sufficient time to complete **all** the requirements. If you leave question 1 to the end, you may not manage to do this.

You do not have a lot of choice in this examination. The overall requirements and the likely nature of the questions mean that you will be examined on much of a very wide syllabus. Do not despair if you find you are probing the boundaries of your knowledge. Most of your contemporaries will be in the same boat. Make sure you cover the essentials, use common sense and experience as much as possible, relate your answers to the settings and **do not** ramble or dump theory.

The aim is not to cover pages with ink. Write concisely. This will release time for planning and checking. You **must** allow time to think.

A very important thing to remember in this exam is that there is bound to be more than one way of answering most of the questions: uniquely correct answers are uncommon in a subject like this. If you can analyse data sensibly, apply theory appropriately and reach reasonable conclusions **you will pass**.

Tackling questions

You'll improve your chances by following a step-by-step approach along the following lines.

Step 1   Read the requirement

Identify the knowledge areas being tested and see precisely what the examiner wants you to do. This will help you focus on what's important in the scenario.

Step 2   Check the mark allocation

This shows the depth of answer anticipated and helps you allocate time.

Step 3   Read the scenario/preamble

Identify which information is relevant to which part, also which data will have to be used in calculations. Be careful to select the right alternatives when you're given a choice, and to identify irrelevant information that you won't be using in the calculations.

Step 4   Plan your answer

Marshal the theoretical material that you think is relevant and relate it to the information given in the scenario. Produce a lit of points you will make and decide on a logical order to market them in.

Step 5   Write your answer

Stick carefully to the time allocation for each question, and for each part of each question.

Step 6   Read it through

Most people are very reluctant to do this but it is **very** important. You **will** find errors of grammar, spelling and fact and places were you have not been clear. Put these things right ad press on.

Gaining the easy marks

Not all questions in this exam have easy marks, but most do. Very frequently, easy marks will be found by examining the question scenario in the light of an appropriate theory or model. However, be careful: generally speaking, there are very few marks available for **explaining** those theories and models.

An important aspect of scoring well is to **state the obvious**. Do not assume that the marker will take anything for granted. If, for example, it is very clear that an organisation has neglected its cost control, say so. But do not expect marks for merely reproducing what is in the question: there must be an element of analysis or deduction supporting what you say, even if it is very simple.

Another aspect of scoring the easy marks is time management. Make sure you answer all the parts of a question: the easy marks are not all in part (a). If you are running out of time, you can glean a few marks by writing brief notes – not bullet points, but short paragraphs that demonstrate some thought.

Approaching P3

In this section we will attempt to summarise what the paper is designed to achieve and what you must do to pass it.

1 What the paper is about

Paper P3 is about business strategy. This is not a mainstream accountancy subject and you may be wondering why it forms part of your qualification. The answer to that question is that as a Chartered Certified Accountant you are likely to find yourself dealing with matters that are of strategic importance quite early in your career. You must therefore have a basic understanding of the way business strategy is conducted so that your input may be appropriate and properly considered.

Business strategy is a huge subject and your syllabus can only give you an introduction to it. The syllabus adopts the systems approach to understanding the way organisations work and therefore emphasises the importance of both the internal linkages between the various organisational components and the boundary-spanning links between the organisation and its environment. These two elements are reflected in the two main strategic issues dealt with by the syllabus: the external forces that influence the organisation's strategy and the internal forces and activities that sustain it.

Within this basic vision, the syllabus deals with three interconnected layers.

(a) The top layer is concerned with the overall strategic perspective, moving from the analysis of strategic position through strategic choices to strategic action.

(b) The middle layer expands on the basic idea of strategic implementation. The focus is on three linked aspects of business process management.

- Process improvement
- IS and e-business
- Quality methods

Each of these elements must be financially feasible and requires good project management: project management itself can be of strategic significance.

The middle layer is also a reminder that strategy may emerge from within the day-to-day activities of the organisation.

(c) The bottom layer of the model emphasises the importance of the human resource and, therefore, of effective human resource management

2 The skills you need

The study of business strategy is a work in progress. There is still vigorous debate, not only about how organisations should make their strategies but also about how they actually do make them.

Partly as a result of this, and partly as a result of the complexity of human behaviour there are few, if any, correct answers to business strategy problems. This means that the essence of your exam is not about things you can learn by heart, such as models and procedures; it is about **intelligent argument**: selecting and applying ideas and theories to realistic problems in order to reach sensible conclusions and suggestions.

All of the questions you will encounter in the exam will be of the scenario type. There will almost certainly be some marks for sensible numerical analysis, but there will not be many of them and they will be concentrated in question one. The rest of the marks will be entirely for written argument. The primary skills you must deploy therefore are those that relate to such answers.

(a) Careful reading and analysis of both scenarios and question requirements
(b) Marshalling of scenario facts and relevant theoretical models
(c) Synthesis and clear written expression of reasoned argument

Other papers in your syllabus have required these skills, but few to such an extent as this one. Many candidates find dealing with P3 questions extremely demanding and we can only recommend question practice as an essential part of your preparation.

3   How can you improve your chances of passing the paper?

- Your study must cover the entire syllabus. Question spotting is a very dangerous practice in any advanced exam and particularly so in this one since the clear intention of the Examiner is to set questions that require an integrated knowledge of the whole syllabus.

- Do not be put off by question one. Yes, it is very large and, yes, it is likely to cover a wide range of topics. However, experience shows that candidates who shy away from question one (perhaps leaving it until last) are unlikely to pass. Your BPP Practice and Revision Kit include plenty of practice examples.

- Do not waffle. It is difficult to produce a reasonable answer to a 25 mark question in much under two or three pages of manuscript but this does not mean that a high word count will bring high marks. Markers definitely prefer answers that are complete but brief. Think carefully about what you want to say and do not labour your points.

- Manage your time in the exam hall carefully. We have already referred to candidates who answer question one last – to do this without leaving yourself 90 minutes to answer it is foolish in the extreme.

4   Brought forward knowledge

Paper P3 assumes that you have a good knowledge of the syllabus for Paper F1 *Accountant in Business*. If you were exempt from this exam, you should spend some time considering its syllabus and study guide so as to identify any gaps in your knowledge. Both documents are available on the ACCA web site.

The exam paper

The exam is a three-hour paper consisting of two sections. Fifteen minutes reading and planning time is allowed in addition to three hours writing time.

Section A will be a compulsory case study question with several requirements relating to the same scenario information. The question will usually assess and link a range of subject areas across the syllabus and will require students to demonstrate high-level capabilities to evaluate, relate and apply the information in the case study to the requirements.

Section B questions are more likely to assess a range of discrete subject areas from the main syllabus section headings; they may require evaluation and synthesis of information contained within short scenarios and application of this information to the question requirements.

The paper will have a global focus; no numerical questions will be set.

		Number of marks
Section A:	1 compulsory case study	50
Section B:	Choice of 2 from 3 questions (25 marks each)	50
		100

Analysis of pilot paper

Section A

1   Environmental analysis; financial and sector analysis; assessment of stated options

Section B

2   Principles of internal development, growth by acquisition and strategic alliances; and their application
3   Importance and characteristics of software quality; CMMI levels
4   Drawing a scenario-based value chain and explaining upstream and downstream supply chains

The pilot paper is Mock exam 3 in this Kit.

Useful websites

The websites below provide additional sources of information of relevance to your studies for *Strategic Financial Management.*

- www.accaglobal.com

  ACCA's website. Includes student section.

- www.bpp.com

  Our website provides information about BPP products and services, with a link to the ACCA website.

- www.ft.com

  This website provides information about current international business. You can search for information and articles on specific industry groups as well as individual companies.

- www.economist.com

  Here you can search for business information on a week-by-week basis, search articles by business subject and use the resources of the Economist Intelligence Unit to research sectors, companies or countries.

- www.strategy-business.com

  This website includes articles from *Strategy & Business.*

- www.invweek.co.uk

  This site carries business news and articles on markets from Investment Week and International Investment.

- www.pwcglobal.com/uk

  The PricewaterhouseCoopers website includes UK Economic Outlook.

- www.bbc.co.uk

  The website of the BBC carries general business information as well as programme-related content.

Planning your question practice

Planning your question practice

We have already stressed that question practice should be right at the centre of your revision. Whilst you will spend some time looking at your notes and Paper P3 Passcards, you should spend the majority of your revision time practising questions.

We recommend two ways in which you can practise questions.

- Use **BPP's question plan** to work systematically through the syllabus and attempt key and other questions on a section-by-section basis

- **Build your own exams** – attempt questions as a series of practice exams

These ways are suggestions and simply following them is no guarantee of success. You or your college may prefer an alternative but equally valid approach.

BPP's question plan

The BPP plan below requires you to devote a **minimum of 36 hours** to revision of Paper P3. Any time you can spend over and above this should only increase your chances of success.

Step 1   **Review your notes** and the chapter summaries in the Paper P3 **Passcards** for each section of the syllabus.

Step 2   **Answer the key questions** for that section. These questions have boxes round the question number in the table below and you should answer them in full. Even if you are short of time you must attempt these questions if you want to pass the exam. You should complete your answers without referring to our solutions.

Step 3   **Attempt the other questions** in that section. For some questions we have suggested that you prepare **answer plans or do the calculations** rather than full solutions. Planning an answer means that you should spend about 20% of the time allowance for the questions brainstorming the question and drawing up a list of points to be included in the answer.

Step 4   Attempt **Mock exams 1, 2 and 3** under strict exam conditions.

Syllabus section	2007 Passcards chapters	Questions in this Kit	Comments	Done ☑
Revision period 1				
Business strategy	1	1	Use questions 1 and 2 to drive home the knowledge you have gained on these basic topics. You may answer in note form if you wish, but ensure that you know just what you would write for a full answer. Then tackle question 5 under exam conditions.	☐
The environment	2	2		☐
		5		☐
Revision period 2				
Competitive forces	3	3	Answer in note form. The value of this question lies in the depth of your thinking about how the five forces take effect.	☐
Strategic capability	4	4	Write a full answer taking care to apply the theory to the detail given in the question setting.	☐
Revision period 3				
Corporate appraisal	5	6	This question will reinforce your knowledge of the corporate appraisal. Write a full answer.	☐
		7	This is a vital question. We expect more like it in the Exam	☐
		8	Note from answer only for this rather easy question	☐
Revision period 4				
Corporate appraisal Marketing	6	16	We are now able to move on to the kind of wide ranging question that is usual at this level. Take your time with this question, think about the theory you will use and express yourself clearly.	☐
		19a	Answer in note form only	☐
Strategic options		34	This is your first section A question. Take your time over it, but complete it in one sitting. It will provide wider revision for you.	☐
Revision period 5				
Organisation structure	7	20a	Questions on structure as a single topic are rare. Try this one in note form.	☐
		19b	Wider topics based on relationships are more likely subjects for questions. Note form answer only.	☐
Revision period 6				
Business processes	8, 9	18	This question will help you to acquire some wider expertise in this new syllabus area. Prepare a full answer.	☐
Revision period 7				
E-business	10, 11	29	Prepare a full answer to this question and try to do it in the allowed time of 45 minutes.	☐
IT		38	The link with the syllabus is slight here, but this is a very accessible question on an IT theme, so try it in full – again, in the allowed time of 90 minutes.	☐

Syllabus section	2007 Passcards chapters	Questions in this Kit	Comments	Done ☑
Revision period 8 Quality	12	24	This is a pretty typical exam standard question, and you should be able to deal with it neatly in the 45 minutes allowed.	☐
Revision period 9 Project management	13	29	This question links two important topics: IT and project management. Prepare a full answer in 45 minutes	☐
	6	20b	A more specific project management question.	☐
Revision period 10 Finance	14	35	Finance is most likely to appear as part of the section A case study, rather than forming a specific question topic. Part (a) of this question is probably typical. Complete the other requirements in the 90 minutes allowed in order to gain confidence in dealing with section A.	☐
Revision period 11 HRM	15, 16	30	This question should give you a good workout on the important practical aspects of HR. Produce a full answer.	☐
Revision period 12 Change and development	17, 18	31	This question combines a practical look at leadership with a wider ranging element that will allow you to speculate a little. However, stay focussed and do not waffle.	☐

Build your own exams

Having revised your notes and the BPP Passcards, you can attempt the questions in the Kit as a series of practice exams.

	Practice exams						
	1	2	3	4	5	6	7
Section A							
1	33	34	35	36	39	40	41
Section B							
3	11	14	13	12	28	35	8
4	2	10	12	21	33	4	27
5	5	17	16	18	7	25	24

- Whichever practice exams you use, you must attempt **Mock exams 1, 2 and 3** at the end of your revision.

BPP
LEARNING MEDIA

Questions

THE OVERALL STRATEGIC PERSPECTIVE

Questions 1 to 13 cover the overall strategic perspective, the subject of Parts A, B and C of the BPP Study Text for Paper P3.

1 Preparation question: strategy and strategic management

(a)   Johnson, Scholes and Whittington identify three organisational levels of strategy. What are they?

(b)   Johnson, Scholes and Whittington also identify three main elements of strategic management. Explain them.

(c)   When commenting on the development and management of strategy, Johnson, Scholes and Whittington speak of observing through three different strategy lenses. Explain these lenses

2 Preparation question with analysis: Fancy Packaging

Eddie Lomax is the Marketing Director of The Fancy Packaging Company, a wholly owned subsidiary of the Acme Paper Company plc. Acme is a major industrially integrated European corporation comprising timber interests, pulp and paper production, as well as down-stream consumer focused activities such as publishing and paper products (paper plates, computer paper and note paper). Fancy Packaging was set up in the 1960s when conglomerates and operations in many different industries were popular. The subsidiary concentrates on the European market and produces packaging material, either paper or cardboard, focusing on the fast moving consumer goods sectors. The nature of this packaging is more decorative than protective.

The Fancy Packaging Company is now operating in a much more hostile environment. Firstly, there is increasing competition from other European suppliers, particularly those in eastern Europe that currently have a lower cost base. Secondly, the demand for this decorative type of packaging is falling. There are a number of reasons for this but two stand out. There is an increasing trend to strip out the cost of frivolous packaging that adds little value. There is a growing fashion amongst some consumers to avoid conspicuous wastage and the dissipation of the world's scarce natural resources. Issues such as global warming have had a knock-on effect in alerting consumers to the dangers of resource wastage. A second reason for the decline in the demand for packaging is the increasing price competition within the fast moving consumer goods industries. Manufacturers are now looking for ways to reduce costs and not just differentiate their products. Packaging appears to be one of the areas where cost savings may be found.

Eddie Lomax believes that the potential for growth in Europe is not only limited but that the current level of sales is now threatened. He is convinced that the company must look to other non-European countries for survival. However the company has no experience in sales outside Europe and so he has come to you for guidance.

Required

Prepare a brief report to Eddie Lomax identifying and discussing the key areas of information that would be of importance prior to deciding which overseas markets should be focused upon.

2 Preparation question with analysis: Fancy Packaging

45 mins

SBU, subject to imposed targets	Eddie Lomax is the Marketing Director of The Fancy Packaging Company, a **wholly owned subsidiary** of the Acme Paper Company plc. Acme is a major industrially integrated European corporation comprising timber interests, pulp and paper production, as well as down-stream consumer focused activities such as publishing and paper products (paper plates, computer paper and note paper). Fancy Packaging was set up
Less popular now	in the 1960s when conglomerates and operations in many different industries **were popular**. The subsidiary concentrates on the European market and produces packaging material, either paper or cardboard, focusing
A very specific market	on the **fast moving consumer goods** sectors. The nature of this packaging is more decorative than protective.

Product life cycle?

The Fancy Packaging Company is now operating in a much more hostile environment. Firstly, there is increasing competition from other European suppliers, particularly those from the old Soviet bloc who

A major threat – can it be met?	currently have a **lower cost base**. Secondly, the **demand for this decorative type of packaging is falling**. There are a number of reasons for this but two stand out. There is an increasing trend to strip out frivolous packaging which adds little value. There is a growing fashion amongst some consumers to avoid
Bad publicity	conspicuous wastage and the dissipation of the world's scarce natural resources. This trend has developed as a result of the growing adverse public reaction to the increases in environmental pollution. Issues such as global warming have had a knock-on effect in alerting consumers to the dangers of **resource wastage**. A
Fancy packaging's customers	second reason for the decline in the demand for packaging is the increasing price competition within the **fast moving consumer goods industries**. Manufacturers are now looking for ways to **reduce costs** and not
Bargaining power of customers	just differentiate their products. Packaging appears to be one of the areas where cost savings may be found.

Eddie Lomax believes that the potential for growth in Europe is not only limited but that the current level of sales is now threatened. He is convinced that the **company must look to other non-European countries for survival**. However the company has no experience in sales outside Europe and so he has approached a marketing research consultancy for guidance.

Seems sensible

Required

Explain environmental analysis: PEST, five forces	(a) Prepare a brief report to Eddie Lomax stating the **key areas of information** that would be of importance prior to deciding **which overseas markets** should be focused upon.

(b) Recommend a **methodology** for obtaining the required information by a company (Acme) which has, up to now, had little experience in marketing research.

How to go about solving the problems of lack of information

BPP
LEARNING MEDIA

3 Five forces

45 mins

E, a well known cosmetics manufacturer, obtains worldwide sales for its global branded products. The directors pride themselves on having a clear understanding of E's consumer market which consists of both men and women. Its products mainly comprise deodorants, perfume, after-shave lotions, facial and body washes.

In carrying out an analysis of its competitive environment, the Marketing Director has applied Porter's Five Forces model and analysed the factors which affect E under each heading as follows.

- *Threat of entry:* Little threat as although major competitors exist, the size of E presents a large entry barrier.

- *Power of buyers:* Very important as the customer world wide have much choice from different competitors' products.

- *Power of suppliers:* Little threat as most suppliers of materials are small scale and E could easily source from other suppliers if necessary. Labour is relatively cheap in E's production facilities in developing world locations.

- *Substitute products:* There are many alternative products offered by competitors but there is little by way of a substitute for cosmetics, and therefore this poses little threat.

- *Rivalry among competitors:* There is strong competition in the cosmetics market with new products constantly being developed, and therefore this is a major threat.

The Marketing Director is reasonably confident that he has judged the impact of these competitive forces correctly as they apply to E. However, he would like some re-assurance of this. He has asked you, as Management Accountant, to provide some appropriate indicators by which the strength of the five competitive forces as they apply to E can be judged.

Required

Draft a report to the Marketing Director recommending suitable indicators which could be used to judge the strength of the five competitive forces as they apply to E. Discuss why you consider your recommendations to be appropriate. Include in your discussion consideration of whether or not you agree with his judgement regarding the impact of each force on E.

(25 marks)

4 McGeorge Holdings (3.5, 6/03, amended)

45 mins

McGeorge Holdings plc is a large, international consumer goods company specializing in household cleaning products and toiletries. It has many manufacturing and sales facilities throughout the world. Over several years it has offered an increasingly wide range of products appealing to differing market segments based on both socio-demographic and geographic criteria. However this product spread has not only resulted in increased sales volume but production, marketing and distribution costs have also increased disproportionately. McGeorge's costs are now about 20% higher than those of its nearest competitors. In such a competitive market it is difficult to pass on these extra costs to the customer.

In order to regain a competitive position Adrian Reed, the Managing Director of McGeorge Holdings, has been advised to reduce the range of products and the product lines. Advisors have suggested that a cut back in the product mix by about 20% could increase profits by at least 40%. Reed is keen to implement such a product divestment strategy but he fears that this cutting back could alienate customers. He needs to know which products need to be removed and which products are important to the survival of the company. He is unhappy about the overall performance of his company's activities. Benchmarking has been recommended as a method of assessing how his company's performance compares with that of his competitors.

Required

(a) Using appropriate analytical models discuss how Adrian Reed might select the products to be removed from the portfolio as part of his product divestment strategy. **(10 marks)**

(b) Examine how benchmarking can be carried out and discuss its limitations. **(15 marks)**

(Total = 25 marks)

5 Airtite (3.5, 6/06, amended)　　　　　　　　45 mins

Airtite was set up in 2000 as a low cost airline operating from a number of regional airports in Europe. Using these less popular airports was a much cheaper alternative to the major city airports and supported Airtite's low cost service, modelled on existing low cost competitors. These providers had effectively transformed air travel in Europe and, in so doing, contributed to an unparalleled expansion in airline travel by both business and leisure passengers. Airtite used one type of aircraft, tightly controlled staffing levels and costs, relied entirely on online bookings and achieved high levels of capacity utilisation and punctuality. Its route network had grown each year and included new routes to some of the 15 countries that had joined the EU in 2004. Airtite's founder and Chief Executive, John Sykes, was an aggressive businessman ever willing to challenge governments and competitors wherever they impeded his airline and looking to generate positive publicity whenever possible.

John is now looking to develop a strategy which will secure Airtite's growth and development over the next 10 years. He can see a number of environmental trends emerging which could significantly affect the success or otherwise of any developed strategy. 2006 had seen fuel costs continue to rise reflecting the continuing uncertainty over global fuel supplies. Fuel costs currently account for 25% of Airtite's operating costs. Conversely, the improving efficiency of aircraft engines and the next generation of larger aircraft are increasing the operating efficiency of newer aircraft and reducing harmful emissions. Concern with fuel also extends to pollution effects on global warming and climate change. Co-ordinated global action on aircraft emissions cannot be ruled out, either in the form of higher taxes on pollution or limits on the growth in air travel. On the positive side European governments are anxious to continue to support increased competition in air travel and to encourage low cost operators competing against the over-staffed and loss-making national flag carriers.

The signals for future passenger demand are also confused. Much of the increased demand for low cost air travel to date has come from increased leisure travel by families and retired people. However families are predicted to become smaller and the population increasingly aged. In addition there are concerns over the ability of countries to support the increasing number of one-parent families with limited incomes and an ageing population dependent on state pensions. There is a distinct possibility of the retirement age being increased and governments demanding a higher level of personal contribution towards an individual's retirement pension. Such a change will have a significant impact on an individual's disposable income and with people working longer reduce the numbers able to enjoy leisure travel.

Finally, air travel will continue to reflect global economic activity and associated economic booms and slumps together with global political instability in the shape of wars, terrorism and natural disasters.

John is uncertain as to how to take account of these conflicting trends in the development of Airtite's 10-year strategy and has asked for your advice.

Required

(a) Using models where appropriate, provide John with an environmental analysis of the conditions affecting the low cost air travel industry. **(15 marks)**

(b) Explain how the process of developing scenarios might help John better understand the macro-environmental factors influencing Airtite's future strategy. **(10 marks)**

(Total = 25 marks)

6 Qualispecs

45 mins

Qualispecs has a reputation for quality, traditional products. It has a group of optician shops, both rented and owned, from which it sells its spectacles. Recently, it has suffered intense competition and eroding customer loyalty, but a new chief executive has joined from one of its major rivals Fastglass.

Fastglass is capturing Qualispecs' market through partnership with a high-street shopping group. These shops install mini-labs in which prescriptions for spectacles are dispensed within an hour. Some competitors have successfully experimented with designer frames and sunglasses. Others have reduced costs through new computer-aided production methods.

Qualispecs has continued to operate as it always has, letting the product 'speak for itself' and failing to utilise advances in technology. Although production costs remain high, Qualispecs is financially secure and has large cash reserves. Fortunately, the country's most popular sports star recently received a prestigious international award wearing a pair of Qualispecs' spectacles.

The new Chief Executive has established as a priority the need for improved financial performance. Following a review she discovers that:

(i)   targets are set centrally and shops report monthly. Site profitability varies enormously, and fixed costs are high in shopping malls;

(ii)   shops exercise no control over job roles, working conditions, and pay rates;

(iii)   individual staff pay is increased annually according to a pre-determined pay scale.

Everyone also receives a small one-off payment based on group financial performance.

Market analysts predict a slowdown in the national economy but feel that consumer spending will continue to increase, particularly among 18-30 year olds.

Required

(a)   Produce a corporate appraisal of Qualispecs, taking account of internal and external factors, and discuss the key strategic challenges facing the company.   **(15 marks)**

(b)   Corporate appraisal offers a 'snapshot' of the present. In order to focus on the future, there is a need to develop realistic policies and programmes. Recommend, with reasons, strategies from your appraisal that would enable Qualispecs to build on its past success.   **(10 marks)**

(Total = 25 marks)

7 Question with answer plan: Digwell

45 mins

Eastborough is a large region with a rugged, beautiful coastline where rare birds have recently settled on undisturbed cliffs. Since mining ceased 150 years ago, its main industries have been agriculture and fishing. However, today, many communities in Eastborough suffer high unemployment. Government initiatives for regeneration through tourism have met with little success as the area has poor road networks, unsightly derelict buildings and dirty beaches. Digwell Explorations, a listed company, has a reputation for maximizing shareholder returns and has discovered substantial tin reserves in Eastborough. With new technology, mining could be profitable, provide jobs and boost the economy. A number of interest and pressure groups have, however, been vocal in opposing the scheme.

Digwell Explorations, after much lobbying, has just received government permission to undertake mining. It could face difficulties in proceeding because of the likely activity of a group called the Eastborough Protection Alliance. This group includes wildlife protection representatives, villagers worried about the potential increase in traffic congestion and noise, environmentalists, and anti-capitalism groups.

Required

(a) Discuss the ethical issues that should have been considered by the government when granting permission for mining to go ahead. Explain the conflicts between the main stakeholder groups. **(12 marks)**

(b) Analyse and explain the interest and power of pressure and stakeholder groups in Digwell Explorations. Based on this analysis, identify courses of action that the company might take in order to respond to these groups. **(13 marks)**

(Total = 25 marks)

8 MegaMart (3.5, 6/04)   45 mins

MegaMart plc is a medium sized retailer of fashion goods with some 200 outlets spread throughout the UK. A publicly quoted company on the London Stock Market, it has pursued a growth strategy based on the aggressive acquisition of a number of smaller retail groups. This growth has gone down well with shareholders, but a significant slowdown in retail sales has resulted in falling profits, dividends and, as a consequence, its share price. MegaMart had been the creation of one man, Rex Lord, a high profile entrepreneur, convinced that his unique experience of the retail business gained through a lifetime working in the sector was sufficient to guide the company through its current misfortunes. His dominance of the company was secured through his role as both Chairman and Chief Executive of the company. His control of his board of directors was almost total and his style of management such that his decisions were rarely challenged at board level. He felt no need for any non-executive directors drawn from outside the company to be on the board. Shareholders were already asking questions on his exuberant lifestyle and lavish entertainment, at company expense, which regularly made the headlines in the popular press. Rex's high profile personal life also was regularly exposed to public scrutiny and media attention.

As a result of the downturn in the company's fortunes some of his acquisitions have been looked at more closely and there are, as yet, unsubstantiated claims that MegaMart's share price had been maintained through premature disclosure of proposed acquisitions and evidence of insider trading. Rex had amassed a personal fortune through the acquisitions, share options and above average performance related bonuses, which had on occasion been questioned at the Shareholders' Annual General Meeting. His idiosyncratic and arrogant style of management had been associated with a reluctance to accept criticism from any quarter and to pay little attention to communicating with shareholders.

Recently, there has been concern expressed in the financial press that the auditors appointed by MegaMart, some twenty years ago, were also providing consultancy services on his acquisition strategy and on methods used to finance the deals.

Required

(a) What corporate governance issues are raised by the management style of Rex Lord? **(15 marks)**

(b) Rex Lord has consistently resisted the appointment of independent, non-executive directors to the board of MegaMart plc. What advantages might the company gain through the appointment of such directors? **(10 marks)**

(Total = 25 marks)

9 Preparation question: Westport University

Westport University is a medium-sized educational institution, having achieved university status six years ago. It is located in a large city with a considerable commercial and manufacturing infrastructure. The university has tended to concentrate on vocational courses such as engineering, science and business and management studies. Because of its relative newness it is not a popular university having not yet acquired a strong academic reputation. With a recent growth in university places available, coupled with a small decline in student demand, Westport is currently unable to operate at full capacity. In order to avoid redundancies the university is looking for alternative courses to help them generate both income and students. Bill Loftus is the commercial manager for the business and finance faculty. He recognises that the faculty has a reasonably strong reputation for its degree programmes including an accountancy degree. However this is a full-time programme at undergraduate level. There are currently no postgraduate degrees in accountancy nor any facility for studying professional accountancy qualifications.

Bill realises that accountancy is growing in popularity and that to practice as an accountant and to progress in the profession one has to be a member of one of the professional accountancy bodies. However he also recognises that much of this training is pursued on a part-time basis by students who are already working within a financial environment. Although this area appears to be one with potential, the head of the faculty is unwilling to put resources into offering professional accountancy training until more research has been carried out.

Required

Assuming that the university approves the venture to develop professional accountancy training, identify the main marketing strategies that could be used to attract students to the programmes.

10 Ashkol Furniture (3.5, 6/03, amended)   45 mins

Salim Brommer is the Marketing Director of Ashkol Furniture Supplies, a medium-sized company which specializes in manufacturing office furniture. The company makes its products in India, so benefiting from relatively low labour costs. However it has recently experienced intense competition from suppliers who have even lower cost bases. Salim has decided that his company will benefit if he focuses on those customers who can provide higher profit margins.

He has decided to target domestic customers in Europe. Increasingly private households, particularly those with computers, are converting spare rooms into office-style areas. Additionally there has been a noticeable trend towards working from home. This saves employers incurring the costs of office provision, and also employees save on travel and can also work at times convenient to themselves. However Ashkol has no experience of dealing with these types of customer. The company now needs to develop a suitable marketing strategy to succeed in this new area and maintain a sustainable competitive advantage.

Required

(a)   Using a suitable model of your choice develop a marketing approach which Salim might use to enter this new market.   **(13 marks)**

(b)   Explain how Salim could select appropriate target markets and position his products so as to create and sustain competitive advantage.   **(12 marks)**

(Total = 25 marks)

11 Helen's Cakes (3.5, 6/05, amended)   45 mins

Helen Bradshaw, a recent graduate with a degree in catering management, has spotted a market opportunity during her first job with a large supermarket chain. She knows there is a growing market for distinctive, quality cakes in the bakery sections of the supermarket chains, as well as in supplying independent individual premium cake shops, and also for catering wholesalers supplying restaurants and hotels.

Helen is very determined to set up her own business under the brand name of 'Helen's Cakes', and has bought some equipment – industrial food mixers, ovens, cake moulds – and also rented a small industrial unit to make the cakes. Helen has created three sets of recipes – one for the premium cake shop market, one for the supermarkets and one for the catering wholesalers but is uncertain which market to enter first. Each channel of distribution offers a different set of challenges. The premium cake shop market consists of a large number of independent cake shops spread through the region, each looking for daily deliveries, a wide product range and low volumes. The supermarkets are demanding good quality, competitive prices and early development of a product range under their own brand name. The catering wholesalers require large volumes, medium quality and low prices.

Helen has learnt that you are a consultant specialising in start-up enterprises and is looking to you for advice.

Required

(a)   Acting as a consultant, prepare a short report for Helen advising her on the advantages and disadvantages each channel offers and the implications for a successful start-up.   **(15 marks)**

(b)   How might the marketing mix vary between the three channels Helen is considering using?   **(10 marks)**

(Total = 25 marks)

12 Focus Bank (3.5, 12/04)   45 mins

Focus Bank, a global banking group with operations in some 70 countries worldwide, is facing an interesting dilemma – to what extent should it outsource its customer enquiry service function? Changes in technology have meant it has moved rapidly to set up its own call centres to handle customer enquiries and gain the benefits of increased staff productivity and higher levels of customer service. The increasing competitiveness in banking has meant that increasingly it has to outsource its customer service activities to outsourcing partners in parts of the world with lower labour costs. This in turn is bringing resistance from staff unions to the export of jobs and criticism from customers of poor service as a result of lower understanding and helpfulness from the call centres. The argument is centred around which competences and resources the bank should retain and develop and what activities can be more efficiently outsourced.

Required

(a)   What are the advantages and disadvantages of moving the customer enquiry service to an outside provider?
                    (17 marks)

(b)   What competitive advantage might the bank gain from a better understanding of its core competences?
                    (8 marks)

(Total = 25 marks)

LEARNING MEDIA

13 Preparation question with analysis: global marketing

Kirkbride Weston Inc is a US-based multinational company. It specialises in producing fork-life vehicles and has recently diversified into producing equipment for fully automated warehousing. It has traditionally considered each of its markets (it currently has business in 25 separate countries) as individual and has consequently customised not only the products to suit each market, but also the promotional strategies with localised brand names and distribution networks. As a result the company has been able to increase its share of the world market by appealing to local tastes, but this has been at a cost. This strategy of customisation has meant fragmented production lines, uneconomic distribution networks and a confused corporate image. Despite a regular increase in sales volume, profitability has been falling, as a result of the increased costs brought about by this excessive customisation.

Adrian Green is a new member of the company's marketing department, and having recently qualified from a prestigious business school has written a report for his line manager, basing his findings on work he had done during his studies. His main conclusion is that the company needs to move away from its 'polycentric' strategy and operate a more globally focused 'geocentric' strategy. In essence he is recommending that the company 'thinks globally but acts locally'. Adrian's line manager is impressed with this report and has forwarded it to the Marketing Director who, in turn, has presented the ideas to the main Board. The Board have asked that Adrian should explain his ideas more fully.

Required

(a)   Acting in the role of Adrian Green provide a briefing report for the Board of Kirkbride Weston Inc explaining the different orientations of polycentric and geocentric companies.

(b)   Discuss the major factors which might encourage a company to pursue a policy of customisation.

13 Preparation question with analysis: global marketing

Quality engineering required	Kirkbride Weston Inc is a US-based multinational company. It specialises in producing **fork-lift vehicles** and has recently diversified into producing equipment for **fully automated warehousing**. It has traditionally considered each of its markets (it currently has business in 25 separate countries) as individual and has

consequently **customised** not only the products to suit each market, but also the promotional strategies

with localised brand names and distribution networks. As a result the company has been able to increase its

share of the world market by appealing to local tastes, but this has been at a cost. This strategy of

customisation has meant fragmented production lines, uneconomic distribution networks and a confused corporate image. Despite a regular increase in sales volume, profitability has been falling, as a result of the increased costs brought about by this excessive customisation.

What are the advantages and disadvantages of this approach? The rest of the para sums it up!

Adrian Green is a new member of the company's marketing department, and having recently qualified from a prestigious business school has written a report for his line manager, basing his findings on work he had done during his studies. His main conclusion is that the company needs to move away from its

What is this exactly?

'polycentric' strategy and operate a more globally focused 'geocentric' strategy. In essence he is

recommending that the company **'thinks globally but acts locally'**. Adrian's line manager is impressed with

A well known phrase! Who said it? What did he mean?

this report and has forwarded it to the Marketing Director who, in turn, has presented the ideas to the main Board. The Board have asked that Adrian should explain his ideas more fully.

Required

Text book stuff. You know it or you don't

(a) Acting in the role of Adrian Green provide a briefing report for the Board of Kirkbride Weston Inc explaining the **different orientations of polycentric and geocentric companies**.

(b) Discuss the **major factors** which might encourage a company to pursue a policy of customisation.

The scenario has outlined some reasons for not doing it. When would it be a good idea?

BPP
LEARNING MEDIA

14 Lawson Engineering (3.5, 12/05, amended)   45 mins

Joe Lawson is founder and Managing Director of Lawson Engineering, a medium sized, privately owned family business specialising in the design and manufacture of precision engineering products. Its customers are major industrial customers in the aerospace, automotive and chemical industries, many of which are globally recognised companies. Lawson prides itself on the long-term relationships it has built up with these high profile customers. The strength of these relationships is built on Lawson's worldwide reputation for engineering excellence, which has had tangible recognition in the form of a significant number of patents for its highly innovative products and the award of several prestigious international awards for product and process innovation and quality performance. This in turn reflects the commitment to recruiting highly skilled engineers, facilitating positive staff development and investing in significant research and development.

Its products command premium prices and are key to the superior performance of its customers' products. Lawson Engineering has also established long-term relationships with its main suppliers, particularly those making the exotic materials built into their advanced products. Such relationships are crucial in research and development projects, some of which take a number of years to come to fruition. Joe Lawson epitomises the 'can do' philosophy of the company, always willing to take on the complex engineering challenges presented by his demanding customers.

Lawson Engineering now faces problems caused by its own success. Its current location, premises and facilities are inadequate to allow the continued growth of the company. Joe is faced with the need to fund a new, expensive, purpose-built facility on a new industrial estate. Although successful against a number of performance criteria, Lawson Engineering's performance against traditional financial measures has been relatively modest and unlikely to impress the financial backers Joe wants to provide the necessary long-term capital.

Joe has become aware of the increasing attention paid to the strategic importance of an organisation's resources. He has asked you, as a strategy consultant, to advise him on this concept.

Required

(a)   Using models where appropriate, provide Joe with a report on the significance of the company's resources for its future success and in its search for financial support.   **(15 marks)**

(b)   How useful would it be for Joe to use a balanced scorecard to better assess the overall performance of Lawson Engineering?   **(10 marks)**

(Total = 25 marks)

15 Preparation question with answer plan: grow or buy?

Mark Roberts is the owner of Greenfield Nurseries, a company specialising in growing plants for sale to garden centres and to specialist garden designers. With the growth in home ownership and an increase in leisure time this sector of the economy has seemed recession-proof. The company has grown over the past ten years and now has 30 employees, several glasshouses and a turnover of almost £1 million. The company is located on one site near to a rapidly expanding urban area. The site is relatively large but there is no room for expansion. If the company is to increase its profits as a garden nursery it must either acquire additional land for growing plants or it must direct more of its sales to the ultimate user (the general public) and move away from sales to other intermediaries (the garden centres) and so obtain higher margins.

Mark is annoyed when he sees garden centres putting large margins on his products for re-sale. Why are these profits not coming to Greenfield Nurseries, he wonders? He is now contemplating re-focusing his activities on selling plants and not producing them. It has been suggested that he turns his growing areas into a garden centre, buying in from other specialist nurseries and transforming his glass house space into selling areas. There is a large market nearby, with several new housing developments, all generating a huge demand for horticultural products. Mark has read that the further one moves downstream in the business chain – into dealing directly with the consumer – the greater is the profit margin. He is very tempted by this strategy, but he is not fully convinced of the wisdom of such a move.

Required

(a)   Examine the arguments that may be used to support or reject such a 'buy instead of grow' strategy for Greenfield Nurseries.

(b)   Outsourcing has become a popular strategy for many companies in attempting to reduce their commitment to non-core activities. Identify the main management problems such a policy might generate.

16 Salt and Soap (3.5, 6/04)   45 mins

David Kirk is the recently appointed Sales and Marketing Director of the Salt and Soap Company, a medium-sized business supplying salt and soap products to the major supermarket chains operating in the UK. Salt was bought in bulk and then repackaged into convenient packet sizes using the supermarket's own brand. On the soap side, the company manufactured a range of cleaning materials, including soda crystals and soap flakes, with, again, the majority of its sales coming from supplying the supermarkets with their own label products. The use of soda and soap as 'natural' cleaning materials was now an insignificant part of the UK market for detergents and cleansers dominated by global manufacturers with powerful brand names.

The company's reliance on the supermarket majors was now causing some problems. The power of the supermarkets was such that 70% of the company's products were now for own label brands. The supermarkets were looking to drive costs down and impose price cuts on suppliers such as Salt and Soap. There was little opportunity to add to the product range supplied and one of their major supermarket customers was looking to reduce its cleaning product range by 15%. On the positive side, Salt and Soap now had a virtual monopoly of 'natural' cleaning products in the shape of soap flakes and soda crystals. These cleansing products were environmentally friendly, as they did not cause disposal and other problems associated with household detergents. Soda based products could also be used as safe disinfecting agents in 'commercial catering' where hygiene was of paramount importance; and also in gardens to clean concrete slabs, ponds and ornaments. David was aware that household users were buying these products from hardware stores and garden centres and he could access these new markets and uses through specialist wholesalers and thus reduce Salt and Soda's heavy dependence on own label supermarket customers.

David has commissioned you as a marketing consultant to assess the relevance of marketing to a small company heavily dependent on a small number of large retail customers.

Required

(a)   Provide David with a brief report using appropriate analytical tools assessing Salt and Soap's current position and showing the relevance of marketing to the company.   **(15 marks)**

(b)   What are the advantages of Salt and Soap becoming a 'niche player' in the new markets it is looking to develop?   **(10 marks)**

                                                                                (Total = 25 marks)

17 Lakeside Business School (3.5, 12/04, amended)   45 mins

The senior management team at Lakeside Business School is facing a new challenge. As one of the major faculties within Lakeside University, it has a wide undergraduate and postgraduate portfolio and as one of the new universities it is anxious to improve its position in the national higher education league tables. The problem concerns electronic learning and the challenge it presents to both staff and students. Electronic or e-learning is being encouraged by a number of factors affecting the education environment. The Business School is tasked with increasing its student numbers while, at the same time, facing reduced funding from central government to support such expansion. E-learning, which reduces face-to-face contact with lecturers, offers a means of using staff more effectively. As a result, it increases the independent learning time available to students and provides much more flexibility to the students as to when they choose to learn.

There are a number of disadvantages however. The design and maintenance of e-learning provision requires considerable investment in electronic hardware and software, technician support and academic staff time in converting their material into electronically accessible modules. Commitment to, and conviction about the benefits of e-learning is far from total for both staff and students. The university has committed significant funds to staff development for e-learning, but only the more computer literate members of staff have taken advantage of the courses available. As a consequence, the impact of e-learning is very varied – some modules are at the cutting edge, while others remain largely taught by traditional methods. Student representatives at course committee meetings have already commented critically on this variation. Students themselves vary considerably in their familiarity with and use of electronic learning. Attendance at traditional lectures has dropped significantly as a result of the lecture material being easily accessible on the relevant module's website.

The Business School's senior management team is being pressed by the university authorities to commit to the university's e-learning system. However, they are very wary of imposing e-learning on their staff in the face of known resistance. The impression given to current and prospective students, in an increasingly competitive and international marketplace, is far from impressive. The current partial and unsystematic use of e-learning is becoming a significant competitive disadvantage.

Required

(a)   What approaches could the senior management team use to reconcile the different stakeholders and their views of e-learning?   **(13 marks)**

(b)   What advantages and disadvantages could the balanced scorecard bring to resolving the problem?
                                                                                                                 (12 marks)

                                                                                                          (Total = 25 marks)

18 Fashion retailer   45 mins

Paul Singh operates in the fashion clothing industry, owning 20 retail stores selling mainly to the teenage and youth market. This industry segment, comprising many small firms, each with a few retail stores, has very few large scale competitors. Paul's business has grown at a rapid rate with him acquiring his first store only five years ago. Despite this growth in business there has never been any associated integration of activities. Paul has been too busy growing his company to pay attention to consolidation and efficiency. However, he has now realised that despite this fast expansion his profits have not grown at the same rate as turnover. This part of the fashion business operates with very slim margins. The products are cheap but with the ever changing demand for fashion garments there are few opportunities for individual stores to hold stock for long periods of time. This has prevented Paul from taking advantage of economies of purchasing.

Each of his stores has tended to be run in isolation. He has left his local managers to decide on buying stock and on merchandising. His view has been that these managers are nearer to the customers and therefore they will know the fashion trends better. This appears to have worked with regard to turnover but he now needs to operate in a more cost-conscious manner. His computing system is being used in a old-fashioned way. It focuses on providing store accounts and is really only used by the small financial team (largely unqualified or still studying) located at the Head Office. Paul has been talking to friends who are operating in similar but non-competitive environments, and they have told him how useful they have found the up-to-date computer-based information systems. Several standard software packages have recommended. However, one person has said that it would be more cost-effective to have a standard package modified to fit Paul's particular business operations.

Required

(a) Using a suitable model to support your arguments explain how the strategic use of information systems could provide Paul with a competitive edge in this currently fragmented industry. **(12 marks)**

(b) Acting in the role of a consultant, write a report to Paul discussing packages generally and assessing the two software package options that have been suggested. **(13 marks)**

(Total = 25 marks)

19 Preparation question: La Familia Amable

Ramon Silva is a Spanish property developer, who has made a considerable fortune from the increasing numbers of Europeans looking to buy new homes and apartments in the coastal regions of Mediterranean Spain. His frequent contact with property buyers has made him aware of their need for low cost hotel accommodation during the lengthy period between finding a property to buy and when they actually move into their new home. These would-be property owners are looking for inexpensive hotels in the same locations as tourists looking for cheap holiday accommodation.

Closer investigation of the market for inexpensive or budget hotel accommodation has convinced Ramon of the opportunity to offer something really different to his potential customers. He has the advantage of having no preconceived idea of what his chain of hotels might look like. The overall picture for the budget hotel industry is not encouraging with the industry suffering from low growth and consequent overcapacity. There are two distinct market segments in the budget hotel industry; firstly, no-star and one-star hotels, whose average price per room is between 30 and 45 euros. Customers are simply attracted by the low price. The second segment is the service provided by two-star hotels with an average price of 100 euros a night. These more expensive hotels attract customers by offering a better sleeping environment than the no-star and one-star hotels. Customers therefore have to choose between low prices and getting a poor night's sleep owing to noise and inferior beds or paying more for an untroubled night's sleep. Ramon quickly deduced that a hotel chain that can offer a better price/quality combination could be a winner.

The two-star hotels typically offer a full range of services including restaurants, bars and lounges, all of which are costly to operate. The low price budget hotels offer simple overnight accommodation with cheaply furnished rooms and staffed by part-time receptionists. Ramon is convinced that considerable cost savings are available through better room design, construction and furniture and a more effective use of hotel staff. He feels that through offering hotel franchises under the 'La Familia Amable' ('The Friendly Family') group name, he could recruit husband and wife teams to own and operate them. The couples, with suitable training, could offer most of the services provided in a two-star hotel, and create a friendly, family atmosphere – hence the company name. He is sure he can offer the customer two star hotel value at budget prices. He is confident that the value-for-money option he offers would need little marketing promotion to launch it and achieve rapid growth.

Required

(a) Provide Ramon with a brief report, using strategic models where appropriate, assessing his proposed hotel service.

(b) What are the advantages and disadvantages of using franchising to develop La Familia Amable budget hotel chain?

20 John Hudson (3.5, 12/01, amended)

45 mins

John Hudson is the managing director of ALG Technology, a medium-sized high tech company operating in several geographic markets. The company provides software and instrumentation, mainly for military projects but it also does have civilian interests. It currently has four key projects: (1) a new artillery command, communication and control system, (2) a programme for updating of fighter aircraft avionics, (3) an air traffic control system for a regional airport and (4) radar installations for harbour authorities in the Middle East. All these projects were expected to have a life expectancy of at least five years before completion. However, John Hudson is worried because they are all increasingly falling behind schedule and the contracts have late delivery penalties.

Hudson is convinced that a significant cause of the problem is the way that the company is organised. It has been shown that a competitive advantage can be obtained by the way a firm organises and performs its activities. ALG technology is currently structured on a functional basis, which does not seem to work well with complex technologies when operating in dynamic markets. The functional structure appears to result in a lack of integration of key activities, reduced loyalties and an absence of team work. Hudson has contemplated moving towards a divisionalised structure, either by product or by market so as to provide some element of focus, but his experience has suggested that such a structure might create internal rivalries and competition which could adversely affect the performance of the company. Furthermore there is a risk that such a structure may lead to an over-emphasis on either the technology or the market conditions. He is seeking a structure that will encourage both integration and efficiency. Any tendency towards decentralisation, whilst encouraging initiative and generating motivation may result in a failure to pursue a cohesive strategy, whereas a move towards centralisation could reduce flexibility and responsiveness.

The company is already relatively lean and so any move towards delayering, resulting in a flatter organisation is likely to be resisted. Furthermore the nature of the market – the need for high technical specifications and confidentiality – is likely to preclude outsourcing as a means of achieving both efficiency and rapidity of response.

Required

(a) Provide an alternative organisational structure for ALG Technology, discussing both the benefits and problems which such a structure might bring. **(13 marks)**

(b) Explain how John Hudson should manage the potential slippage and risk associated with his company's projects. **(12 marks)**

(Total = 25 marks)

21 Preparation question: service performance

Michael Medici has just been appointed as the Managing Director of Sun and Sand Travel Ltd, a small package holiday company focusing on cheaper end of the mass market. Travel, accommodation and on-site services are all pre-booked and included in the package price. Company sales have grown at an annual rate of 10% over the past five years but profits have not risen at the same rate. The company has used price as its main competitive tool and the company has been more concerned with bottom-line financial results than with customer service.

Medici has spent the first two months of his work at Sun and Sand Travel Ltd, acting as a 'trouble shooter'. Customer complaints have risen to a record high. Almost 20% of recent customers have registered complaints including poor accommodation, flight delays and time of travel changes. The company is also facing hostile media criticism: both the press and television media are publicising the difficulties of the company. The outlook is not good: advance bookings are 30% lower than a year ago. Medici realises that the obsession with profit at the expense of other criteria has been both foolish and short termist. He recognises that if you do not get the service right then the profits will inevitably suffer.

Medici has set up a working party to advise him on what to do to improve the situation. One of the recommendations of the working party is to use performance indicators other than profit to assess how well the company is performing.

Required

(a)   Identify and discuss the critical success factors for a company operating in this market segment.

(b)   Suggest key performance indicators for Sun and Sand Travel Ltd and explain how they might be combined in a performance measurement scheme.

22 Excalibur Sportswear (3.5, 12/01)   45 mins

Excalibur Sportswear is a United Kingdom marketing firm, selling high quality sports clothing within the UK. The firm has been set up by Simon Smith, who until recently was a world-class athlete. Smith, although selling his products exclusively in the UK, is sourcing production overseas, taking advantage of the cheaper labour costs and materials available elsewhere. Smith has used his reputation and his network of contacts to persuade footballers, tennis and golf professionals to wear his products. The logo and brand name of Excalibur are now becoming well known throughout the world as a result of the famous sports personalities being seen on TV wearing the company's products.

Despite this apparent success Excalibur is facing financial difficulties. In order to achieve the favourable exposure the company has spent heavily on advertising. The biggest expenditure has been the payment of promotional expenses to the world-famous sports stars, so that they will be seen wearing the company's products, particularly at events which are likely to be televised throughout the world. Compared with most of its competitors, Excalibur's costs were too high compared with its revenues. The company needed to sell more. The competitors' revenues were higher because they sold their products on a world-wide basis. Smith has decided that his company should look at its market as a global one and not as a national market. Expanding sales should not prove to be a problem for Excalibur. Most of the production is sub-contracted for foreign manufacturers so an expansion of capacity will have minimal financial impact on the marketing company. Similarly as most of the sales are through independent retail outlets there will be few increased costs for Excalibur as a result of the development of sales on a global basis. Naturally marketing costs, in particular those concerned with advertising, will rise.

Initial marketing research has confirmed the belief that Excalibur's products will be acceptable in many foreign markets. Many of the issues which can frequently threaten companies who decide to move into foreign markets are seen as favourable or at least benign. Trade barriers on such sports clothing products are relatively low. Although the company has no expertise in selling products overseas the fact that key activities – production and distribution – are outsourced, should make the challenge for Excalibur less testing. Finally, when seeking to establish markets overseas a shortage of finance is often a problem. Excalibur's bank is optimistic about the enterprise and is willing to provide market development finance.

Nevertheless Simon Smith is unhappy about relying on outsiders to provide critical inputs into the organisation. He believes that there is an increased risk of poorer quality and control affecting the company's reputation. Although existing suppliers and distributors have performed adequately he believes that a large expansion of Excalibur's activities, as proposed, might be beyond their capacity and any new suppliers may be of a lower standard. He is therefore contemplating setting up his own manufacturing facilities and distribution networks.

Required

(a)   Evaluate the key factors which might encourage Excalibur to become involved in international marketing and even become a 'global' organisation.   **(12 marks)**

(b)   Explain how risk, control and resource commitments might change for Simon Smith's firm as it attempts to take more control of its activities.   **(13 marks)**

(Total = 25 marks)

23 Prestige Packaging (3.5, 12/03)   **45 mins**

David Upton, Managing Director of Prestige Packaging Ltd, a medium sized UK manufacturing company, was faced with an interesting dilemma. The company produced a unique, easy opening packaging process which had found a ready market in Europe with large multinational food and tobacco companies. The packaging process had a significant competitive advantage over its rivals and the company had ensured its technological superiority was protected by patents. However, dealing with global customers meant it was under pressure to become a global supplier with some form of presence in America and the Far East. Having a global presence would help secure its technological leadership and its increased size would help prevent its American and Korean competitors moving into the European market.

Various strategic options were open to the company. Acquiring a similar packaging company in an appropriate location was unlikely, as few companies were for sale. Furthermore, Prestige Packaging's technological advantage meant that a joint venture was not a realistic short term possibility. Eventually the decision was taken to choose some form of internal or organic growth; either a company sales office in a number of key markets, or a manufacturing operation handling the final stages of the manufacturing process and buying semi-finished material from the parent company or, finally, the appointment of an agent or distributor to look after its interests in these distant markets.

David has asked for your assistance in evaluating the risk and benefits associated with these alternative ways of expanding its international operations.

Required

(a)   Evaluate the advantages and disadvantages of the three stated organic options open to Prestige Packaging in its move to become a global company.   **(15 marks)**

(b)   What information should David use in coming to an informed decision?   **(10 marks)**

(Total = 25 marks)

STRATEGIC IMPLEMENTATION

Questions 24 to 32 cover strategic implementation, the subject of Parts D to J of the BPP Study Text for Paper P3.

24 KPG systems   45 mins

KPG systems was set up 10 years ago by its owner, a computer systems engineer, Andy Rowe. Andy is an entrepreneur with a high degree of technical ability and no fear of taking risks in emerging high-tech markets. KPG Systems provides network management systems to medium-sized companies. In the last 10 years the business has grown from Andy's original ideas to one turning over £12 million and employing 100 people. The approach of the business, which has appealed to potential customers, is to recognise that no two information systems are the same and to customise its products and service to meet their individual needs. The company has made a point of exploiting new technology as it became available and has been successful in several linked areas of network technology, including the use of wireless devices. As an adjunct to providing these systems, technical support has become another key business element, although there have been some problems with providing a national network of service support.

KPG systems is a very small player in this market and its success has been due to Andy Rowe's drive, initiative and risk taking. The business is still run on a day-to-day basis by Andy but there are now various functional departments in operation, including manufacturing; sales and marketing; research and development; and administration. Andy has thrived on this challenge, but he now finds that the business is too large for him to do everything that needs to be done. There have been some problems with product quality, time and cost overruns and recruitment. Also, turnover from larger contracts is forming a smaller proportion of the overall total: Business with smaller firms continues to expand but Andy has failed to win several large contracts against competition from larger firms. This has led him to question the continuing validity of his basic approach to the business.

Andy is now concerned that the business is losing focus and he is unsure of where it is going in the future.

Required

(a)   What steps could Andy take to promote the achievement of consistently good quality in KPG's products?

(10 marks)

(b)   Use appropriate models to analyse the current position of KPG systems and recommend how it could develop in the future.   **(15 marks)**

(Total = 25 marks)

25 Preparation question: environmental strategy

Graham Smith is Operations Director of Catering Food Services (CFS) a £1·5 billion UK based distributor of foods to professional catering organisations. It has 30 trading units spread across the country from which it can supply a complete range of fresh, chilled and frozen food products. Its customers range from major fast food chains, catering services for the armed forces down to individual restaurants and cafes. Wholesale food distribution is very much a price driven service, in which it is very difficult to differentiate CFS's service from its competitors.

Graham is very aware of the Government's growing interest in promoting good corporate environmental practices and encouraging companies to achieve the international quality standard for environmentally responsible operations. CFS operates a fleet of 1,000 lorries and each lorry produces the equivalent of its own weight in pollutants over the course of a year without the installation of expensive pollution control systems. Graham is also aware that his larger customers are looking to their distributors to become more environmentally responsible and the 'greening' of their supply chain is becoming a real issue. Unfortunately his concern with developing a company-wide environmental management strategy is not shared by his fellow managers responsible for the key distribution functions including purchasing, logistics, warehousing and transportation. They argued that time spent on corporate responsibility issues was time wasted and simply added to costs.

Graham has decided to propose the appointment of a project manager to develop and implement a company environmental strategy including the achievement of the international quality standard. The person appointed must have the necessary project management skills to see the project through to successful conclusion.

You have been appointed project manager for CFS's 'environmentally aware' project.

Required

(a)   What are the key project management skills that are necessary in achieving company-wide commitment in CFS to achieve the desired environmental strategy?

(b)   How could pursuing a corporate environmental strategy both add to CFS's competitive advantage and be socially responsible?

26 Question with analysis: Apex culture (3.5, 6/02)   45 mins

Carol Brindle is the Managing Director of Apex Finance Ltd, a company specialising in financial services. The company has thirty offices in different geographic locations within the United Kingdom. The company acts for a variety of local businesses in the preparation of accounts and managing the raising of finance for capital investment and it has recently become involved in helping to provide venture capital. These offices also offer tax planning and investment advice to the general public. The culture of the company is rather aggressive and most of the staff are young, ambitious and recently qualified. There is a strong tendency towards centralisation with procedures and policies being imposed from a central management function. The company sought not only to standardise work outputs but also the working practices within its operations, leaving little discretion to its employees.

Recently, in pursuing a strategy of growth, Apex has bought a group of companies, offering similar types of services but in geographic areas where Apex is not represented. The style of management within the purchased group is dissimilar to that operating within Apex. In the acquired group the culture is more relaxed, with staff encouraged to manage and motivate themselves. Most staff have considerable experience and can be trusted to use their own initiative. Carol is naturally concerned that the acquisition might not be successfully integrated..

Required

(a)   Identify the major problems which may occur if this acquisition is not managed carefully.   **(12 marks)**

(b)   Assess the factors which need to be taken into consideration if the new acquisition is to be successfully incorporated into the group.   **(13 marks)**

(Total = 25 marks)

26 Question with analysis: Apex culture (3.5, 6/02)   45 mins

Highly technical; great competence required; subject to regulation

Very similar to the subjects of Herzberg's original study: highly qualified professionals

Carol Brindle is the Managing Director of Apex Finance Ltd, a company specialising in financial services. The company has thirty offices in different geographic locations within the United Kingdom. The company acts for a variety of local businesses in the **preparation of accounts** and managing the **raising of finance** for capital investment and it has recently become involved in helping to provide **venture capital**. These offices also offer **tax planning** and **investment advice** to the general public. The **culture of the company is rather aggressive** and most of the staff are **young, ambitious and recently qualified**. There is a strong tendency towards centralisation with procedures and policies being imposed from a central management function. The company sought not only to **standardise work outputs** but also the **working practices** within its operations, leaving little discretion to its employees.

Because of the need for accuracy and consistency

Synergy

Recently, in pursuing a strategy of growth, Apex has bought a group of companies, offering similar types of services but in **geographic areas where Apex is not represented**. The style of management within the purchased group is dissimilar to that operating within Apex. In the acquired group **the culture is more relaxed**, with staff encouraged to manage and motivate themselves. Most staff have **considerable experience and can be trusted to use their own initiative**. Carol is naturally concerned that the **acquisition might not be successfully integrated**.

Contrast

Many mergers fail over culture

Consider all aspects of the business, not just the staff

Change management

Required

(a)   Identify the **major problems** which may occur if this acquisition is not managed carefully. **(12 marks)**

(b)   Assess the **factors which need to be taken into consideration** if the new acquisition is to be successfully incorporated into the group.   **(13 marks)**

(Total = 25 marks)

27 Supaserve (3.5, 12/05)   45 mins

Chris Jones is Managing Director of Supaserve, a medium-sized supermarket chain faced with intense competition from larger competitors in their core food and drink markets. They are also finding it hard to respond to these competitors moving into the sale of clothing and household goods. Supaserve has a reputation for friendly customer care and is looking at the feasibility of introducing an online shopping service, from which customers can order goods from the comfort of their home and have them delivered, for a small charge, to their home.

Chris recognises that the move to develop an online shopping service will require significant investment in new technology and support systems. He hopes a significant proportion of existing and most importantly, new customers, will be attracted to the new service.

Required

(a)   What bases for segmenting this new market would you recommend and what criteria will help determine whether this segment is sufficiently attractive to commit to the necessary investment?   **(12 marks)**

(b)   Assess the likely strategic impact of the new customer delivery system on Supaserve's activities and its ability to differentiate itself from its competitors.   **(13 marks)**

(Total = 25 marks)

28 Preparation Question: Global Imaging

Global Imaging is a fast growing, high tech company with some 100 employees, which aims to double in size over the next three years. The company was set up by two professors at a major university hospital who now act as joint managing directors. They are likely to leave the company once the growth objective is achieved.

Global Imaging's products are sophisticated imaging devices that are in growing demand from the defence and health industries. These two markets are very different in terms of customer requirements but share a related technology. Over 90% of sales are from exports and the current three-year strategic plan includes the establishment of a foreign manufacturing plant. Management positions are largely filled by staff who joined in the early years of the company when there was heavy reliance on research and development to generate the products to grow the business. Further growth will require additional staff in all parts of the business, particularly in manufacturing and sales and marketing.

Paul Simpson, HR manager at Global Imaging is annoyed. HR is the one management function not involved in the strategic planning process shaping the future growth and direction of the company. He feels trapped in a role traditionally given to HR specialists, that of simply reacting to the staffing needs brought about by strategic decisions taken by other parts of the business. He feels even more threatened by one of the joint managing directors argument that HR issues should be the responsibility of the line managers and not a specialist HR staff function. Even worse, Paul has become aware of the increasing number of companies looking to outsource some or all of their HR activities.

Paul wants to develop a convincing case why HR should not only be retained as a core function in Global Imaging's activities, but also be directly involved in the development of the current growth strategy.

Required

What advantages and disadvantages might result from outsourcing Global Imaging's HR function?

29 IT project

45 mins

The organisation for which you work is about to evaluate a proposal for a major upgrade in its information technology support for office administration staff. Currently the work of these staff is fragmented, lacking integration and cohesion. The proposed upgrade will enable information transfer to be more readily achieved and should improve both the efficiency and effectiveness of the office administration. The suggestion is for each of the fifty staff members to have a high specification personal computer (PC) with associated software (word processing, spreadsheets etc.). All PCs will be linked into a local area network comprising several fileservers to handle shared applications, plus network links into Internet services. At the present time about thirty staff have access to PCs of a variety of types and specifications which are running a number of stand-alone applications. There is limited access on some machines to networked shared services. The capital cost of this proposed upgrade is estimated to be in the region of £250,000.

The Finance Director has asked you to take charge of the proposed project. He wishes the project to focus on two main issues: the cost justification of the expenditure in relation to competing IT project proposals and, if a go-ahead is given, and the achievement of a smooth transition in moving staff and applications to the new office support system. However, he is worried that the review might concentrate exclusively on monetary considerations, such as discounted cash flow, and he feels that this approach would be both simplistic and unsuitable.

Required

(a)   The new office support system is believed to be technically feasible but has not yet been cost justified. Explain how you might undertake a non-technical evaluation of the proposed investment of £250,000 in office information technology. Your evaluation should cover the treatment of both financial and non-financial criteria.   **(15 marks)**

(b)   Outline an approach which you might propose to adopt in planning for and executing an implementation of the new office support system.   **(10 marks)**

(Total = 25 marks)

30 Connie Head (3.5, 6/04, amended)

45 mins

Connie Head was the recently appointed HR manager in a medium sized accounting firm. Her appointment was a belated recognition by the senior partners of the firm that their ambitious corporate growth goals were linked to the performance of the individual business units and the accountants working in those units. Connie was convinced that performance management and an appraisal system were integral elements in helping the firm achieve its strategic objectives. This reflected her experience of introducing an appraisal system into the corporate finance unit for which she was responsible. The unit had consistently outperformed its growth targets and individual members of the unit were well motivated and appreciative of the appraisal process.

However, the senior partner of the firm remained unconvinced about the benefits of appraisal systems. He argued that accountants, through their training, were self-motivated and should have the maximum freedom to carry out their work. His experience of appraisal systems to date had shown them to lack clarity of purpose, be extremely time consuming, involve masses of bureaucratic form filling and create little benefit for the supervisors or their subordinates. Certainly, he was resistant to having his own performance reviewed through an appraisal system. Connie, however, was convinced that a firm-wide appraisal system would be of major benefit in helping the achievement of growth goals.

Required

(a)   Evaluate the extent to which an effective appraisal system could help the accounting firm achieve its goals.   **(15 marks)**

(b)   Using models where appropriate, assess the contribution, if any, of performance management to the strategic management process.   **(10 marks)**

(Total = 25 marks)

31 Rameses International (3.5, 12/02, amended)   45 mins

Jeanette Singh was recently appointed Chief Executive of Rameses International, which is a long-established, family run export house specialising in buying manufactured goods from Western Europe and the USA for re-sale in Africa and in the Middle East. Jeanette Singh was previously Marketing Director of one of Rameses International's biggest suppliers. She is the first CEO appointed from outside the family.

Rameses International had been very successful for many years, but has begun to suffer from increasing competition in its chosen markets, particularly from strong manufacturing companies expanding downstream to capture more of the value in the supply chain.

Rameses designed and initiated a number of strategies over the last three years in order to minimise their problems. These strategies have included seeking a wider range of products to re-sell from a broader supply-base (more suppliers), attempting to have closer collaborative agreements with major suppliers to minimise any potential conflict, and attempting to operate in more markets. None of these strategies has been particularly successful and turnover has stagnated.

Jeanette Singh

Required

(a)   Explain why even carefully considered strategies may not be successful.   **(13 marks)**

(b)   Explain the role of leadership in achieving strategic success.   **(12 marks)**

(Total = 25 marks)

32 Preparation question: Sykes Engineering

Jerome Sykes is the grandson of the founder of Sykes Engineering Group plc. This company is now a publicly quoted company with 2,000 employees, and although Jerome, the Chairman and Managing Director, only owns less than 2% of the equity of the Group he behaves as if it is his personal possession. His behaviour is becoming increasingly autocratic, involving himself in all levels of decision-making. This personalised decision-making has not brought consistency, clarity or rationality to the strategy process. Instead the company has suffered from confused improvisation, uncertainty and wild swings in corporate direction. Unfortunately this culture appears to have influenced many managers below Board level.

The Board of Directors has now been forced into action after extensive media coverage has criticized the company for a number of accounting irregularities over several years, the bribing of key foreign customers and sexual and racial harassment. This has inevitably adversely affected the share price. The key financial institutions who have invested in the Group are now demanding the removal of Jerome Sykes from office.

Required

Discuss actions which might have been taken earlier to have prevented such a situation from developing within the Sykes Engineering Group.

CASE STUDIES

The 50 mark case study is compulsory. It is likely that it will always include a part-question on mainstream strategy, plus two or three other part-questions that could come from almost any part of the syllabus.

33 Question with student answer: Bethesda Heights (3.5, 6/02, amended)

90 mins

The Management Committee of the Bethesda Heights Memorial Hospital was meeting under crisis conditions. The Hospital had moved into a financial deficit and most of the key participants in the decision making process could not agree on the best way to resolve the crisis.

The Hospital was located in the less affluent part of a North American city. It was a large general purpose hospital which served a stable population. Its revenue came mainly from the central government in the form of a grant, based on the size of population served and the actual surgical and medical work carried out. Central government grants accounted for about 65% of total revenue, and the remainder was almost equally split between two other funding bodies. Firstly, the local city council provided about US$ 20 million of grants and secondly, private medical insurance companies paid a similar amount for treatment of their insurance holders. This gave a total annual revenue of some US$ 115 million but costs had risen to US$ 125 million with all parts of the cost structure, including medicines, salaries and materials, seeing increases above the level of inflation. Unfortunately, the outlook did not look good for the Hospital. Revenue from central government was under pressure as the government sought to reduce public expenditure in order to fund significant tax cuts. Grants from the city council were linked to the level of the central government grant and consequently revenue from this source was not expected to increase. Even more depressing for the Hospital was its failure to attract private healthcare patients. They were choosing to go to a neighbouring hospital with a better reputation for patient care and more attractive facilities. Consequently income from medical insurance was likely to decline further. (The current financial and comparative performance data for the two hospitals can be seen in Table 1.)

The Management Committee estimated that if the situation did not improve the Bethesda Heights Memorial Hospital would have a deficit of US$ 75 million within three years. Action needed to be taken urgently. The Management Committee was made up of a number of coalitions. One was led by Michael Gonzales, the Chief Executive of the Hospital. He was an administrator and an accountant by training. His concern was that Bethesda Heights should be run efficiently. To him, and his fellow administrators on the Management Committee, it was important that the Hospital should be financially viable. However efficiency and effectiveness are not always the same thing. In fact some of the actions taken may also lead to further ineffectiveness or inefficiencies elsewhere. An indication of this dilemma was the administrators. wish to reduce the length of time patients spent in hospital so as to reduce costs. However sending patients home early could result in them requiring home visits from nursing staff for up to four or five extra days and in some circumstances this early release might require a re-admission to the Hospital. Consequently initial savings might be eroded by further unanticipated costs. Furthermore some medical staff suspected that these administrators were more concerned with short-term financial concerns than with medical ones. Certain medicines may be rationed or withheld to reduce costs and patients might be denied treatments such as physiotherapy or occupational therapy in a similar drive for cost savings.

Another group was represented by Stefan Kopechnik, a consultant surgeon. He was in favour of developing 'leading edge' micro-surgery. For Stefan and his fellow surgeons the Bethesda Heights Memorial Hospital was losing out to its rival hospital because it was seen as old-fashioned and out of touch with modern medicine and surgery. This was affecting its ability to attract the affluent private healthcare patient. Unfortunately the Hospital would require substantial capital investment to implement such a high-tech medical strategy.

A third group was influenced by the Mayor of the city, Elizabeth Fuller. This group was made up mainly of councillors (local politicians) who sat on various Hospital committees and were anxious to see the Hospital kept open and effectively serving the city's medical needs. Surprisingly, the city council had recently threatened to cut back its funding as a means of avoiding an increase in local taxes. The local news media had attempted to embarrass the local ruling party about this policy but the councillors involved, led by Mrs Fuller, were in no mood to give in to media pressure. There was a real fear that strategy might now be formulated in response to media headlines rather than rational argument.

Naturally the local population within the catchment area of the Hospital wanted it to continue its function as a viable concern and even invest in more modern facilities. Unfortunately this stakeholder group had little power or influence. The residents were socially disadvantaged and were unable to bring concerted pressure to bear on the Hospital's decision-makers.

There was one other important pressure group who were very vocal in their support of the Hospital. These were the employees, including the nurses and the general medical and support staff (not the high-ranking surgeons). Their interests were not political or financial, or even professional, unlike the surgeons who were looking to expand their power and influence. This employee grouping was primarily concerned with the maintenance of an efficient and effective hospital for the local population who could not afford private medical insurance and who relied mainly on government funded healthcare provision.

As one might have expected with these divisions, the Management Committee found it difficult to agree upon an acceptable strategy to solve the financial crisis. Eventually the one chosen reflected the power wielded by the surgeons. These senior medical staff (the surgeons) had threatened to resign if the Committee did not agree to a capital investment programme designed to enhance the Hospital's surgical reputation. The Hospital would effectively cease to function without its surgical teams. Unfortunately the trade-off for this investment was to reduce the number of beds within the Hospital. It was argued that this reduced provision reflected the current utilisation patterns. Unfortunately this did not reflect the latent demand within the community. There were a significant number of patients who were not being given the treatment they needed as they did not have private healthcare insurance. Furthermore, waiting times for seeing the appropriate consultant surgeon or for being admitted to the Hospital were lengthening for this disadvantaged group of patients.

Table 1

Comparison of Statistical Data between Bethesda Heights Memorial Hospital and the

Neighbouring Hospital for calendar year 2001 (figures for 2000 in brackets)

(unless otherwise stated figures are in US$'000)

	Bethesda Heights Hospital		Neighbouring Hospital	
Income from central government	76,000	(76,000)	85,000	(85,000)
Income from local government	20,000	(19,000)	22,000	(21,000)
Income from medical insurance	19,000	(23,000)	63,000	(60,000)
Total income	115,000	(118,000)	170,000	(166,000)
Labour costs	55,000	(53,000)	57,000	(55,000)
Medical equipment	20,000	(19,000)	28,000	(25,000)
Drugs	25,000	(22,000)	30,000	(28,000)
Other variable costs: catering, laundry	10,000	(9,000)	13,000	(12,000)
Fixed costs	15,000	(15,000)	17,000	(16,000)
Total costs	125,000	(118,000)	145,000	(136,000)
Surplus/deficit	−10,000	(0)	+25,000	(+30,000)
Further referrals required % (need for re-admittance)	17	(14)	9	(7)
Mortality % (% of patients dying in hospital)	0·05	(0·03)	0·007	(0·003)
Number of staff (actual)	1,000	(970)	1,100	(1,150)
Number of beds (actual)	350	(350)	450	(450)
Waiting time (days)*	95	(90)	35	(40)
Post-operation time in hospital (days)**	7	(8)	10	(10)
Day surgery operations*** (actual numbers)	1,500	(1,150)	7,000	(1,500)
Number of patients treated annually residentially	10,650	(10,900)	12,700	(12,500)
Ratio outpatients to those committed to hospital****	3:1	(3:1)	5:1	(4:1)

*   from seeing doctor to hospital admittance

**   number of days kept in hospital after an operation

***   minor operations which require no overnight stay

****   number of patients dealt with as external patients (excluding day surgery) compared with those committed to hospital for one night or longer

Required

(a)   It is apparent that the goals and objectives of the senior medical staff have profoundly influenced the chosen strategy. Discuss the factors which have enabled this group to dominate the other stakeholders. What are the main arguments which the other groups might have used to promote their objectives?   **(15 marks)**

(b)   Using the quantitative data provided, identify the major problems facing the Bethesda Heights Memorial Hospital. Examine the extent to which the proposed high-tech strategy will address these problems.

(20 marks)

(c)   Assess the other strategic options open to the Management Committee.   **(15 marks)**

(Total = 50 marks)

34 Hair Care (3.5, 6/03, amended)   90 mins

Sam and Annabelle Burns own and manage the firm Hair Care Ltd, based in the United Kingdom. The firm was formed in 1998 when Sam and his wife re-mortgaged their house and borrowed heavily from the bank to buy out the company from a conglomerate organization who were disposing of non-core businesses. Sam had been a senior salesman with the hair-care subsidiary of the conglomerate. This subsidiary bought hair care products, mainly small value items and consumables – scissors, brushes, combs, hair nets, curlers and hair driers, from manufacturers and resold them to wholesalers and large retail chemist chains within the United Kingdom, mainly for use in hairdressing salons. The new business has continued in this direction. The manufacturers are almost entirely non-UK suppliers, many based in Hong Kong but with manufacturing facilities in mainland China, Taiwan and Malaysia. However about 30% of the products are sourced in Europe – Italy and Germany predominantly.

The company has met with success very quickly and the initial loans have already been repaid ahead of schedule. The company now owns the freehold of a large warehouse/distribution centre which is five times the size of the original depot, leased when the company first started trading five years ago. Sales turnover, now in excess of £5 million, has increased by more than 50% each year and shows little sign of slowing down. Despite this apparent rapid growth Hair Care Ltd only accounts for about half of the current market, leaving some potential for growth. The company is run cost effectively, with minimum staffing. Sam, as Managing Director is solely concerned with the marketing side of the business. He spends most of his time in the selling role and in customer care which he rates as a major contributor to the company's success. The only other key manager is his wife who is responsible for managing the warehouse staff, arranging distribution, general administration and financial management. The company started with six employees, in addition to Sam and Annabelle, and now has 15. Staff rarely leave the company. The staff is almost entirely employed in the distribution and packaging function, although there are two other sales people apart from Sam, but they only deal with the smaller buyers. With the continued growth in turnover it is inevitable that the number of employees will have to increase. It is expected that there will have to be a total of about 30 staff, all non managerial, in two years if sales continue to increase at the current rate.

The success of Hair Care Ltd can be accounted for by a number of factors. Sam is a very good salesman who is responsible for looking after all the major accounts. He is popular and much of the business is built on his personal relationship with the key clients. There is a considerable amount of customer loyalty which is mainly attributable to Sam, and both he and his wife are always accessible to customers and they go out of their way to provide a first class service. Even on vacation the two owners are in daily contact with the office. The company has been able to manage its purchases wisely. Most of the products, being purchased abroad, require payment in a foreign currency. Hair Care has been able to benefit from the relative weakness of the euro against sterling for its European supplies. Although most of the products sourced in the Far East are priced in US dollars, the relative strength of that currency has enabled Hair Care Ltd to negotiate lower purchasing prices. However it is questionable as to how long this situation concerning foreign exchange can be held. The situation may change should the United Kingdom join the euro in the near future and much, of course, will depend upon the level at which sterling enters the euro exchange.

Sam has also developed strong links with his suppliers and he has, until recently, attempted to trade with only a few so that his lines of communication and control are kept as simple as possible. Most of his current suppliers have been with him since the start of the company in 1998. This has provided the company with reliable and good quality products. In fact Hair Care Ltd often has exclusive access to certain products. For example it has the sole rights to

distribute an Italian hair-dryer which is generally recognized to be the best on the market. This product strength has enabled the company to build on the customer loyalty. However, it is inevitable that as demand has increased, existing suppliers have not been able to keep up with the necessary volumes and Sam has had to look for, and buy from new manufacturers.

The company has benefited from a period of relatively steady growth in the economy and even in the current economic down-turn Sam has argued that demand for hair care products is usually recession-proof. Furthermore Hair Care Ltd has currently no near competitors. Many of the small competitors in the wholesale market place have chosen to concentrate on other areas of the hair care business – salon furnishings and the supply of cheap, low-value items such as towels, razors etc, leaving much of this basic business (sales of other relatively low-value and mainly disposable products) to Sam's company. Additionally quite a number of the small firms have even left the market. All this has helped to contribute to the overall growth rate of Hair Care Ltd. There are some major international companies who make shampoos, conditioners and other cosmetic type products who also buy-in consumer hairdressing products such as the ones sold by Hair Care Ltd. They then sell these mainly to the retail trade for domestic use by consumers and not directly to the hairdressing salons as does Hair Care Ltd. Furthermore these are large companies and Sam believes that they do not currently see his company as a major threat.

The company has registered a brand name for its main products which it re-packages, rather than using the individual brands of the original manufacturers. This has enabled Hair Care Ltd to generate even greater loyalty from its customers and often to obtain a price premium from these products. Sam believes that part of the company's success stems from the fact that he has an organization with minimal administrative overheads. He outsources all of his products, adding value mainly through branding and the maintenance of customer care. He believes that strategy is not mainly about beating the competition but in serving the real needs of the customer. The company has also been able to develop a strong relationship with the country's leading retail chemist chain, providing it with good quality, low-cost disposable products such as hair nets and brushes to be sold under an own-brand label. Although the margins are inevitably small, the volumes involved more than compensate for this. The company has had to incur increased investment as a result of the large growth in turnover. The building of the warehouse, the increased stock-holding costs, capital expenditure on items such as computing systems, fork-lift trucks and automated stock control and retrieval systems could not be financed out of current earnings, but the company's bank was only too ready to lend the company the necessary money considering that the original loan had been repaid ahead of schedule.

All the success which Hair Care Ltd has achieved has not diminished Sam's appetite for growth. He now seems to be driven more by seeking power and influence than acquiring wealth. He questions the ability of the company to continue its current growth in the prevailing environment and therefore he is looking for ideas which may facilitate corporate expansion. He has asked his accountant to provide some options for him to consider.

Table 1: Details of Performance of Hair Care Ltd: 2000–2003
(unless otherwise stated, figures are in £'000)

	2000	2001	2002	2003 (forecast)
	£'000	£'000	£'000	£'000
Sales	2,300	3,500	5,010	7,500
Cost of Sales	1,450	2,380	3,507	5,250
Marketing Costs	200	250	290	350
Distribution Costs	300	400	430	500
Administration	50	55	80	120
Interest Payments	0	80	220	700
Operating Profit	300	335	483	580
Loans	0	850	2,400	5,000
Number of suppliers (actual)	15	20	30	50
Range of products (actual)	35	85	110	130
Total staff including Sam and Annabelle	12	14	15	23
Stocks	230	400	700	1,400
Fixed assets	500	1,500	2,700	6,300
Return on Sales (%)	13.0	9.6	9.6	7.7

Required

(a)   Assuming the role of Sam's accountant, prepare a report for Sam, evaluating the current position of Hair Care Ltd and highlighting any financial and strategic issues concerning future developments which you feel should be brought to his attention.   **(20 marks)**

(b)   As his accountant, prepare a short report for Sam, identifying and assessing the strategies which he could consider in attempting to further the company's development.   **(20 marks)**

(c)   Sam currently appears to have a successful formula for growth. Using the concept of the value chain, demonstrate how he has been able to achieve this success.   **(10 marks)**

(Total = 50 marks)

35 Polymat Tapes (3.5, 12/03, amended)   90 mins

Introduction

Richard Johnson, Managing Director of Polymat Industrial Tapes Limited (PIT), was worried. The global economic slowdown following the events of 11 September 2001, and subsequent Stock Market falls had meant 2002 had been a difficult year for the company. The company manufactured a range of industrial tapes for sale to a wide range of customers, from masking tape used by individual Do-It-Yourself (DIY) enthusiasts through to high performance tapes for the major automotive and aerospace companies. The origins of the company were in the late 1920s when PIT set up as a private company making tapes for use by cable manufacturers who were meeting the growing needs of the National Grid (a Government owned electricity supply network). The technology for making its products was, therefore, reasonably mature though breakthrough products did occasionally occur – as witnessed by the explosive demand for optic fibre cable and PIT's hi-tech cable jointing tapes. The tapes were mainly produced by a process that coats adhesive on to a variety of materials, including PVC, textiles and paper.

Product range and competitive environment PIT had grown up in close proximity to some of its much larger cable manufacturing and automotive customers. There were currently three factories manufacturing its product range. Its original factory concentrates on cable jointing products supplied to the large UK cable manufacturers. These manufacturers are exerting strong pressure for price reductions on their suppliers in order to prevent entry into the market by large US global cable manufacturers. PIT's products need to respond to any significant product developments by the UK cable manufacturers and by its US tape competitors. Johnson is very aware of the global brand recognition of one of its major US competitors, which has a strong consumer products division and a reputation for aggressive product innovation.

BPP
LEARNING MEDIA

At its second factory PIT produces PVC tapes, mainly standardised products with a typical 30-year product life cycle. Distribution is primarily through electrical wholesalers with an extremely wide customer base. PIT's main UK competition is of a similar size and not regarded as being particularly innovative. PIT has also had some success in meeting the particular tape needs of car makers in their new car model programmes. PIT has had to satisfy the demanding quality standards required by each car manufacturer of their suppliers. The main competition comes from low cost base manufacturers from Europe and the Far East.

At its third factory PIT produces paper masking tape. The move into paper masking tape is a more recent move aimed at the apparently ever-increasing market for masking tape with particularly heavy demands by the car industry for use in paint spraying and in the domestic market by DIY customers. The technology to produce the tape was imported from the USA under licence with a very modern factory being built to manufacture these products. Unfortunately, PIT's masking tape capacity became available just as there was a significant slow down in global car sales. Tape manufacturers such as PIT are faced with the dual problem of excess industry capacity and sales of low priced tape in Europe by low cost North American producers. The main competitor is an American company with access to lower cost raw materials and a 35% share of the UK market compared to PIT's 20% share. PIT's difficulties were further exacerbated by its inability to achieve efficient low cost operation, partly due to a high level of fixed overhead cost for the company as a whole. The fixed overhead had been significantly increased by an investment in, and operation of, a centralised warehouse facility. This warehouse and distribution facility had been designed to alleviate major space problems at the factories and improve service to all of the key clients, but in practice has merely added to overhead costs and working capital levels with little added value to the company's activities. Safety stocks of finished products continue to be held at the three factories. Distribution to the customers is through the company's own transport system.

Current situation and financial performance

PIT had been acquired by one of the UK's largest cable manufacturers during the Second World War. However, the recession of the early 1990s had seen the parent company look to concentrate on its core product – cable manufacture – and dispose of non-core activities including PIT's industrial tapes. Thus an opportunity was presented to the three senior directors to buy out the company. The subsequent buyout had, to use Richard Johnson's words, given them 'a company with a mature product range produced by outdated equipment'. Each of the directors has spent the majority of their careers in the industry and recognises the challenge of competing in markets that are dominated by large customers looking to drive prices down and rationalise their supplier base. The directors are committed to securing the future of the business and saving as many jobs as possible.

PIT is very much a product led as opposed to a marketing led company. The nature of its products mean that it employs a significant number of chemistry graduates at its three factories and each factory pursues a separate R & D strategy. Recognition of the changing marketplace had come with the appointment of Paul Wright, an economics graduate, as Marketing Manager. Paul soon recognised that the company lacked key information on its customers, the products they bought and which were profitable. To use Paul's words, there were some 'little gems' where the product was generating good margins from a small number of industrial customers. But identifying them is the problem. Many of its customers are small DIY retailers and information on the profitability of such orders was less than impressive. Equally worrying is the lack of any process through which the ideas for new or improved products brought back by its sales force are effectively considered in terms of PIT's ability to develop, make and then sell them at a profit. The dominance of the company by technologists means that there is a real gap between understanding market opportunities and the products developed in the company. There is also a failure to identify the key decision makers in their larger cable manufacture and automotive customers and little external recognition of the technological advances made by PIT's R & D activity.

Table 1: Information on PIT's current sales and financial performance
(£'000) (where appropriate)

	2001/02 £'000	2002/03 £'000	2003/04 (forecast) £'000
Product group			
Cable Jointing Tapes			
Sales	4,000	4,510	5,100
Cost of sales	2,400	2,593	2,805
Gross profit	1,600	1,917	2,295
Transport costs	120	135	153
R & D	High	High	High
Market share	25%	25%	25%
Sales volume index	100	110	121
Product range	Narrow	Narrow	Medium
PVC Industrial Tapes	£'000	£'000	£'000
Sales	3,000	3,100	3,200
Cost of sales	1,650	1,705	1,760
Gross profit	1,350	1,395	1,440
Transport costs	150	155	160
R & D	Low	Low	Low
Market share	10%	9%	8%
Sales volume index	100	103	106
Product range	Wide	Wide	Wide
Paper Masking Tapes	£'000	£'000	£'000
Sales	2,500	2,400	2,300
Cost of sales	1,625	1,680	1,725
Gross profit	875	720	575
Transport costs	150	192	230
R & D	Moderate	Moderate	Moderate
Market share	20%	20%	20%
Sales volume index	100	106	112
Product range	Narrow	Medium	Medium
Company	£'000	£'000	£'000
Sales	9,500	10,010	10,600
Cost of sales	5,675	5,978	6,290
Gross profit	3,825	4,032	4,310
Transport costs	420	482	543
Other fixed costs	3,080	3,270	3,500
Operating profit	325	280	267
ROS	3.4%	2.8%	2.5%

Retardon

Indicative of the problems PIT faces, is its one and only breakthrough product 'Retardon'. This tape had been developed some five years earlier and offered significant fire resistant properties over the normal tapes supplied to cable manufacturers installing their cables in high risk environments, such as underground railway systems, airports and high rise buildings. Environmental conditions are favourable for a product with the ability to both reduce the risk of fire and the toxic fumes given off should a fire occur. However, despite significant R & D investment, the lack of adequate patent protection, a deficient product design and a failure to stimulate the market means that the threat of competition from more effectively organised competitors is increasingly likely.

Outlook for the future

Richard is sympathetic to Paul's concern over the lack of marketing information and the consequent failure to generate new products. Equally concerning is the speed at which many of its products are becoming commodity products in which price is the key factor influencing supplier choice. Certainly there are opportunities to work with the large automotive companies in their development of new models, but such projects were typically of five years duration and PIT's lack of market presence is not helping it secure these long-term contracts. Richard has now decided to get an external assessment of the company's position.

Required

(a)   Assuming the role of an external consultant, prepare a report for Richard evaluating the performance of the three product groups and their contribution to overall company results. Use appropriate models to support your analysis.   **(25 marks)**

(b)   Assess the main strategic options open to PIT and recommend a preferred strategy.   **(15 marks)**

(c)   Explain how PIT might change from a technology driven culture to a marketing led one.   **(10 marks)**

(Total = 50 marks)

36 Elite Plastic Packaging (3.5, 12/04, amended)   90 mins

Introduction

Jeff Wainwright is Managing Director of Elite Plastic Packaging (EPP), part of the Print and Packaging Division, which, in turn, is part of the Sigma Group plc, a diversified company with other separate product divisions in building materials, flooring products and speciality chemicals. The group had emerged during the 1970s as Sigma, like other companies, tried to compensate for the slowdown in internal growth by moving into different industries mainly through merger and acquisition. The grouping into product divisions was largely one of administrative convenience rather than compelling industrial logic and the Print and Packaging Division contained a number of companies which operated largely independently of one another.

Sigma Group corporate headquarters

The Sigma Group headquarters (HQ) is dominated by accountants who Jeff regards as reacting to, rather than anticipating, rivals. Risk is to be avoided wherever possible and projects only approved if they can demonstrate a three year payback – typically a 'one solution fits all' to the companies in the group. This view of risk was reinforced by the Divisional Chief Executive of the Print and Packaging Division, Tim Sterling, also an accountant by background, with whom Jeff had a working but uneasy relationship. There was little confidence that Tim would champion the cause of the companies within the Print and Packaging Division against the wishes of the Sigma Group's domineering Chairman and Chief Executive, Archie Williams.

Archie is convinced that a decentralised management style is the key to maintaining profitable growth in the future. Under him corporate HQ has two key functions, firstly, an executive role carried out by a small team of four – Archie Williams and three Group Directors, collectively known as the Group Executive. Each of the Group Directors takes a special interest in, but not responsibility for, one or more of the divisions and heads up a central support function. Of prime importance are the monthly meetings reviewing, sanctioning, and monitoring each Division's budgets. The process involves the Group Executive and the Division's senior management team and takes a minimum of one week every month generating the information and holding meetings with each of the divisions. Other Group Executive activities include the approval of divisional capital expenditure proposals, policies towards the appointing and remuneration of the top divisional management and planning and managing relationships with the financial world. The second distinct function carried out by corporate HQ are those support activities that were carried out centrally including treasury, financial reporting, tax planning, personnel and legal activities. Fewer than 100 people work at Group HQ.

The Group Executive has a very distinctive view of the relationship between company headquarters and the operating divisions. Archie Williams had been the architect of a recovery plan in the early 1990s which had cut costs and increased profits by getting rid of a number of earlier attempts to reduce geographic dependency on UK markets by moves into Europe, the Middle East and Asia, partly through acquisition. Focus had been placed on growing product areas with the potential for a quick turnaround in results. This on occasion meant reducing sales but improving profitability. The avoidance of earnings dilution was of central importance.

Sigma Group organisation chart

Strategic planning and budgeting in the Sigma Group

Elite Plastic Packaging (EPP)

EPP's main business is advanced plastic packaging where Jeff sees the greatest potential for growth. It manufactures injection moulded plastic packaging primarily for the food, drinks and confectionery markets. Jeff is encouraged by the support of large supermarket customers who have begun to insist that their major suppliers of both food and non-food goods use EPP's packaging. This means that EPP is now a supplier of plastic packaging to global manufacturers. Even more exciting is the development of 'intelligent' packaging where computer chips are built into the packaging allowing companies to 'track and trace' their products all over the world. Such a product has considerable appeal to manufacturers of expensive consumer luxury products such as perfume, alcohol and music discs where counterfeiting is a growing global problem.

EPP's global opportunities

Jeff's frustration with his Divisional Chief Executive and the Group Executive team at Sigma has been brought to a head by their reaction to a major opportunity to move the packaging business on to a global basis. EPP has had five years of fast and very profitable growth in the European market and now wants to exploit the full global market by expansion into both the USA and Asian markets. EPP's share of the European specialist plastic packaging market has reached 50% generating some £50 million in sales revenue. The latest version of the packaging yields significant operating benefits to the manufacturers using it and as a result is generating a 15% net sales margin for EPP. The total world market is estimated at £300 million a year split evenly between the three major regional markets – Europe, the Americas and Asia. Potential competitor packaging companies exist but these have generally failed to invest sufficiently in the new technology to be effective. The issue is how best to enter the American and Asian markets and to convince the risk averse Sigma Group HQ to provide the necessary investment.

Four market entry strategies are available. Firstly, to license the technology to third parties and obtain a royalty of 5% of sales. Secondly, to set up with new green field sites. Net margins would be greater than 15% as the European region would absorb most of the marketing, development and administration costs. Thirdly, subcontracting the manufacturing to a suitable partner. Profits would need to be shared 60:40 in favour of the subcontractor. Finally, by acquisition which would need to be in a related technology and provide access to the relevant sales channels to achieve growth. Each option has its own advantages and disadvantages and capital investment and budgetary consequences.

The HQ philosophy is to devolve and decentralise to the divisions all activities that affect a division's costs and revenues. They want the Divisional Chief Executives to feel that they have complete control over their division's performance. The division's senior management team and the Group Executive at the monthly board meeting critically review each division's performance. These monthly Divisional Executive Boards, in addition to reviewing the division's on-going performance against budget, also considers opportunities and threats and formal plans and budgets. It is the detailed attention and care given to budgeting and performance monitoring that determines the relationship between the Group Executive and its operating divisions. The bottom-up planning process starts with the individual companies in each division developing their own strategy. The financial consequences of this strategy are then built into a divisional budget that is stretching but achievable. This target is designed to be owned by the division and motivate the management team. Budget procedures are formally laid down and extremely comprehensive. Tim Sterling spends a day with each company's MD working on the budget to be presented to the Group Executive. Agreeing the budget is a stressful time as it is the key to Sigma's performance evaluation. Failure to achieve is unacceptable and a divisional management team unable to deliver its promises is under considerable pressure from the Group Executive.

The Group Executive do not get involved with the strategy planning process and see the budget as the tangible evidence of division's strategic planning and in effect a contract to deliver over the coming year. Budgets are typically agreed at the November or December meeting of the Divisional Executive Board and reviewed at subsequent Board meetings, which can last up to half-a-day. The process ensures that the Group Executive are fully aware of each division's performance, where problems are occurring, and able to share thinking on solutions. The Group Executive firmly resists telling a division what to do.

Agreement to significant capital expenditure will be influenced by the previous track record of the division, the fit with their current business, a potential return above that currently being achieved and above all the commitment of the management team. Avoidance of projects with long lead times and in areas not closely connected to existing activities guides approval. Overall, therefore, the Sigma Group has no centrally determined strategy and its broad objectives are aimed at ensuring profitable growth each and every year. Acquisitions, when approved, are focused on the buying of assets rather than incumbent management. Such acquisitions are then left to the divisions to successfully integrate them. Archie Williams firmly believes that the tight budgetary control operated from the centre provides both the incentive and punishment for divisions to achieve profits today and profitable growth tomorrow.

*Table 1: Information on the Sigma Group's current sales and financial performance
(£'000) (where appropriate)*

Year	20X0	20X1	20X2	20X3	20X4
Sigma Group	£m	£m	£m	£m	£m
Group sales	580.2	419.8	382.6	354.6	350.7
Group operating profit	62.9	34.7	23.6	21.9	20.1
Operating margin (%)	10.8	8.3	6.2	6.2	5.7
Print & Packaging	£m	£m	£m	£m	£m
Sales	107.5	87.6	97.4	111.3	117.9
Operating profit	17.2	13.0	11.8	13.5	12.3
Operating margin (%)	16.0	14.9	12.1	12.1	10.4
Elite Plastic Packaging company (EPP)	£m	£m	£m	£m	£m
Sales	28.1	31.5	35.2	45.1	52.3
Operating profit	9.3	10.9	13.2	17.6	21.1
Operating margin (%)	33.1	34.6	37.5	39.0	40.3

Required

Jeff is keen to evaluate the current strategic position and future options facing Elite Plastic Packaging and has asked you to do the following for him:

(a) Prepare a short report evaluating the advantages and disadvantages of each market entry strategy taking into account the Group Executive's short-term performance focus. **(20 marks)**

(b) Examine the value added by the Group Executive to the strategic management of the divisions and the costs and benefits of this style of involvement. **(15 marks)**

(c) Assuming that Jeff is successful in his plan to move EPP into a global operation, discuss which communication, control and co-ordination issues are raised by such a change. **(15 marks)**

(Total = 50 marks)

37 LRP

90 mins

LRP is a division of Stillwell Slim, a large, diversified conglomerate with extensive operations in Europe, North America and the Far East. Originally a UK general engineering business, LRP now operates internationally and specialises in the production of high quality fasteners. Its products range from simple nuts and bolts to complex devices for high stress applications such as submersibles and satellites. The company was sold to Stillwell Slim by its founder, Mr Wingate, when he retired in 1990 and is now managed by Joe Lentaigne, who had joined five years before the sale as Deputy Production Manager.

Stillwell Slim is controlled from a small global headquarters in Lickskillet, Ohio. Its overall strategy may be described as high technology products subject to satisfactory cash flow. Other SBUs include a manufacturer of airliner galleys; an aviation service company whose operations range from engine overhaul to the management of complete airports; a company that builds high capacity trunk telecomms switching nodes; and a design boutique specialising in military standard printed circuits. LRP is a typical Stillwell Slim SBU, having provided a satisfactory return on investment in nine of the past ten years and having funded much of its expansion from its own profits. There is considerable intra-group trade, which is managed by negotiation among the SBUs.

Mr Lentaigne, while essentially a practical engineer, has become accustomed to thinking strategically and globally. LRP has no formal mission statement, but if asked for one, Mr Lentaigne would probably say something along the lines of 'making profit by making very good fasteners'. He feels that the success of the company depends on two main factors: efficiency in production and keeping up with the technology. He has therefore employed Dr Mike Calvert, a recent PhD in metallurgy, to maintain a continuing review of developments in all aspects of the technology. LRP does no research itself, but has developed several new products by applying the research of others, including competitors.

Production efficiency is the responsibility of Jack Masters, the Production Director. His background is in production engineering in the motor components sector. LRP has plants in Ireland, Taiwan and the UK and Mr Masters spends about 180 days a year away from the UK headquarters. He thinks the company has made great progress in both productivity and quality, but does not have the volume of throughput in any of its plants to achieve major purchasing economies. Mr Masters' ambitions for the company include the updating of the machinery in the UK plant, where some machines date back to Mr Wingate's time, and the introduction of computer-based resource scheduling systems to each of the three plants.

Sales and marketing issues are dealt with by Bernard Fergusson, the Sales Director. The market for LRP's more mundane products is very large and competition is tough. Price and delivery are what customers look for, and there is little opportunity to differentiate products. The market is global, but the weight of the products means that airfreight is expensive; on the other hand, intercontinental surface transport inevitably imposes a time penalty on delivery. While the global market is growing at about 4% per annum, historically, the USA has always outstripped the average, and even with the slowdown in the US economy, the lack of a manufacturing facility in North America has always hampered sales.

It has also affected the sale of the more complex, higher value-added products, though not to the same extent, because high and consistent quality is the key to the markets for those products. A more important factor in this market has been the appearance of TIG Products. TIG's production facilities are located in an eastern European country, which combines high technical ability with low costs. Mr Fergusson has recently established that TIG is a joint venture between an established western competitor and a local company, rather than being a wholly owned subsidiary of the competitor. Mr Fergusson made informal contact with the CEO of the eastern European partner company at a recent trade fair and was surprised at a revelation made by him in an unguarded moment late one evening. The CEO stated his belief that the western partner company intends to renege on the joint venture agreement (which was committed to paper but never signed) because it is restructuring its operations. This could lead to major loss for the eastern company. The CEO indicated that he would welcome an approach from LRP to replace the competitor. He went on to explain that such a deal should be very attractive to LRP, since it would enable it to join a price-fixing trade association in a particular regional market that it had never previously been able to penetrate.

Table 1 – Data pertaining to LRP

	1998	1999	2000
Turnover – North America	£7.23m	£7.37m	£7.35m
Turnover – Europe	£27.56m	£28.39m	£29.12m
Turnover – Rest of the world	£14.63m	£15.92m	£17.03m
Profit after capital charges	£4.82m	£6.23m	£6.05m
Market share – basic fasteners	9.76%	9.82%	8.32%
Market share – sophisticated fasteners	4.67%	5.21%	6.83%
Number of employees	147	159	163
Overdraft	£9.78m	£10.24m	£11.02m
WIP*	107%	112%	103%
Finished goods stocks*	98%	115%	121%
Customer returns by value*	57%	87%	124%
Reject rate*	87%	114%	137%
Productivity index*	84%	92%	102%
Average age of machinery	8.6 yrs	9.6 yrs	10.2 yrs

* LRP participates in a confidential benchmarking scheme that includes most major manufacturers of fasteners globally. Industry averages are computed from information provided by member firms; the performance of each member is then assessed against the averages and the results fed back. For example, LRP's productivity index for 2000 means that it achieved 102% of the industry global average productivity.

Required

(a)   As a consultant, prepare a report for the CEO of Stillwell Slim assessing the strategic potential of LRP. (You are not required to undertake portfolio analysis of the Stillwell Slim group as a whole.) Mr Fergusson has not revealed his conversation with the eastern European CEO to you.   **(20 marks)**

(b)   Discuss the usefulness of the diversified conglomerate business model.   **(10 marks)**

(c)   Neither Stillwell Slim nor LRP has any formal policy on business ethics. Discuss the ethical dimension of the TIG partner CEO's proposal.   **(20 marks)**

(Total = 50 marks)

38 Screen Books   90 mins

Jack Benfold Limited is a small independent publisher in London. The management of the business is still dominated by the Benfold family, though several professional managers have been recruited in the last fifteen years. At one time the company specialised in medical text books, but it lost substantial ground in this field during the prolonged illness of the then managing director, George Benfold, the founder's son. The present managing director, Thomas Speight, is George's son-in-law. He brought considerable publishing experience when he joined the company as editorial director twelve years ago and he has succeeded in restoring the company's fortunes by moving into the travel and cookery markets. However, the trend in publishing has been towards the creation of ever-larger companies by amalgamations and takeovers, and independent publishers are tending to become niche operators.

Mr Speight has taken a close interest in the development of Internet commerce as a strategic option for smaller businesses. He formed an alliance with John Rogers Books Limited, a small chain of bookshops in the Midlands. The original plan was to sell books over the Internet, with John Rogers Books providing most of the administrative and logistic facilities and Jack Benfold the capital and Internet technology. A joint venture subsidiary called Screen Books Limited was set up in 1996, with a website called Screenbooks.com.

Screen Books expanded quite successfully and more or less in accordance with its business plan. Its advertising and rapid growth attracted the attention of Rupert Coke, who was at school with Thomas Speight and is now a senior merchant banker. Mr Coke's bank was promoting the dotcom business model heavily in the late 1990's and saw Screen Books as a candidate for heavy capital injection. Mr Speight was enthusiastic about this possibility because he had an idea for a technology-based strategy that would require considerable investment to launch.

Mr Speight proposed the development of a small, portable, liquid crystal display (LCD) screen device dedicated to the presentation of text. The device's memory would be capable of holding the equivalent of up to ten 'blockbuster' novels. It would be inherently Internet-capable, though without a proper browser and it would be programmed to connect automatically to Screenbooks.com. Customers would be able to review Screen Books' catalogue, download books and magazines and pay for them by credit card on line.

Mr Speight felt that such a device would appeal to a wide range of potential customers and suggested that it was particularly attractive because it exploited the main characteristic of the Internet: the high-speed transfer of information in electronic form. It would be independent of warehouses and carriers and other aspects of physical order fulfilment, with consequent benefits for efficiency and quality.

Such devices had already been produced but not on a large scale: there was a need for considerable technical development, which would be expensive. The success of the venture would also depend on the size of Screen Books' own catalogue and permission from other publishers to offer their titles in electronic form.

Mr Coke was sufficiently impressed with the proposal to arrange an initial injection of loan capital in early 1998. Contracts were let with research agencies and marketing staff were recruited. Such was the interest in the proposed product that a flotation on the London Stock Exchange was undertaken in late 1998 and the initial issue of 10p shares was heavily oversubscribed. More research was undertaken, with in-house staff being hired, and a major marketing campaign was planned to launch the new product. To fill the gap until the new device was available, the existing Screenbooks.com website was heavily promoted, with a major advertising campaign and generous discounts. CDs and 'lifestyle' accessories were added to the product range and more marketing, sales and administrative staff were recruited at all levels.

Unfortunately, there are now indications that all is not well. The development of the crucial screen-based device has been held up by fundamental technical limitations. It also seems that the demand for LCD screens has grown to such an extent that prices remain higher than forecast, which will have a major effect on selling price when the device is launched. Expenditure on both research and marketing has been higher than forecast and the marketing director has left the company after only ten months in the job.

There is some doubt about the ultimate demand for the product, as well; research seems to indicate that people are very happy with electronic games consoles, since they offer facilities unobtainable elsewhere, but they do not see the point of the electronic book. A recent article in an influential business newspaper discussed this problem in detail, and some investors are getting cold feet.

Table 1 – Summary data

	1996	1997	1998	1999	2000
Turnover £'000	367	635	1026	2176	4309
Operating loss £'000	42	54	728	1032	1097
Marketing costs £'000	5.5	8.2	198	349	422
Loan capital £'000			500	550	1700
Spending on R&D £'000			204	639	721
Headcount - Marketing	2	4	9	18	42
Headcount – R&D	1	1	17	24	28
Head count - Telesales	4	5	7	16	28
Nominal value of capital at year end £'000	200	200	12498	12498	12498
Share price p high/low	–	–	72/46	85/63	67/17

Required

(a)   Assess the strategy adopted by Screen Books to date.   **(20 marks)**

(b)   Acting in the role of consultant, consider how Screen Books' operations could be developed in the future.

(10 marks)

(c)   Screen Books' plans appear to have been heavily dependent on the new screen-based product. How could it have best managed its technological innovation?   **(20 marks)**

(Total = 50 marks)

39 Universal Roofing Systems (3.5, 6/05, amended) 90 mins

Introduction

Universal Roofing Systems is a family owned and managed business specialising in the design, assembly and installation of low maintenance PVC roofing products for domestic housing. These products include PVC fascia boards and rainwater drainage systems. Set up in 1995 by two brothers, Matthew and Simon Black, the firm has grown year on year, achieving almost £1 million sales by the year 2001. Universal's products, or rather services, are primarily for private house owners, though a significant amount of sales are coming from commercial house owners, mainly local government authorities and housing associations, providing cheaper housing for rent. Universal have recently received central government recognition and an award for their contribution to providing employment in deprived inner city areas. In 2002 and 2003, they were the fastest growing inner city firm in their region.

Origins and competitive environment

Matthew and Simon's decision to go into business owed a considerable amount to the experience and skills they had gained working in their father's local cabinet and carpentry business. At their father's insistence, both were skilled cabinet-makers and shared his commitment to quality workmanship and installation. Their decision to start a business using PVC materials as opposed to wood came as an unwelcome shock to their father. However, the opportunity to install PVC roofing boards on the house of a commercial contact provided the stimulus for them to go into business on their own account.

In the UK there are some 25 million houses, of which 17 million are privately owned and 8 million rented. New housing is now usually built with PVC doors and windows installed, so it is the replacement market of rotten wooden doors and windows in existing houses that the manufacturers and installers of PVC windows and doors focus on. PVC offers some significant advantages to the owner/occupier – it is virtually maintenance free and improves the appearance of the house. Consequently, there is a high demand for PVC replacement doors and windows, estimated at £1·5 billion in the year 2000. This has attracted some large-scale manufacturers and installers. They compete aggressively for market share and use equally aggressive direct sales and promotion techniques to attract house owners to their product.

Although the market for PVC windows and doors is reasonably mature, there has been no significant movement of large companies into the installation of roofing products. Their complex design and location at the top of a house mean that these products are much more complex and difficult to install. Economies of scale are harder to achieve and, as a consequence, the installation of PVC roofing systems is largely in the hands of small businesses able to charge high prices and frequently giving a poor quality service to the house owner. In a market with potential sales of £750 million a year, no firm accounts for more than 3%. It was against this fragmented, but significant market that Universal wanted to offer something distinctively different.

Operational processes

Matthew and Simon looked at the whole process of delivering a quality service in replacement PVC roofing systems. The experience of the PVC door and window installers showed the long-term rates of growth possible through actively promoting and selling the service. Supplies of PVC board and fittings were reasonably easy to obtain from the small number of large UK companies extruding PVC boards in large volumes. However, the unequal bargaining power meant that these suppliers dominated and were difficult to involve in any product development. Sales were generated by door-to-door canvassing, followed by a visit from a company sales representative who tried to complete the sale. Advertising in the press, radio and TV now supported this sales activity. In the early days the opportunity was taken to sell the service at Saturday markets and, being so small, Universal could often pleasantly surprise the house owner by offering virtually immediate installation. Matthew and Simon promoted, sold and installed the systems. One of their key early decisions was to use a new Mercedes van with Universal's name and logo prominently displayed, to carry the bulky PVC materials to their customers' houses. In one move they differentiated themselves from their low cost/low quality competitors and got the company's name recognised.

The skills and experience of the brothers meant that they were able to critically examine the installation process being used by their small competitors to deliver a poor standard of service. Their eventual design incorporated innovative roofing design and parts from Europe and a unique installation stand or frame that provided the installer with quick, easy and safe access to the roofs of the houses being worked on. This greatly improved the productivity of Universal's installation team over competitors using traditional methods. The brothers recognised that without the ability to offer a service that could be packaged, given standard prices and procedures and made as 'installer friendly' as possible they too would be limited to small scale operation and poor service. Being able to replicate a process time after time was the key to delivering an improved service and preventing each job being seen as a 'one-off'. In Matthew's words, 'Whenever the customer can have a predictable experience and you can say that this is what we are going to do, this is the way we are going to do it and this is how much it will cost, the product/service usually goes problem free'.

Ultimately, the installers of the roofing systems determined quality. The brothers quickly built up a team of installers, all of whom worked as sub-contractors and were not directly employed by the company. This gave the company the flexibility to vary the number of teams according to the level of customer demand. Installation took place throughout the year, though it could be affected by winter weather. The two man teams were given comprehensive training in installation and customer care. Payment was by results and responsibility for correcting any installation faults rested with the team doing the particular installation.

Sales and marketing

Marketing and promotion were recognised as key to getting the company's name known and its reputation for a quality installation service established. Comprehensive sales support materials were created for use by the canvassers and sales representatives. Sales representative were able to offer significant discounts to house owners willing to make an immediate decision to buy a Universal roofing system. In addition Universal received a significant income stream from a finance house for roofing systems, sold on extended payment terms.

Universal offered a unique 10-year guarantee on its installations and proudly announced that over 30% of new customers were directly recommended from existing satisfied customers. The growth of the company had led to showrooms being set up in six large towns in the region and the business plans for 2005 and 2006 will see a further nine showrooms opening in the region, each of which costs £30K. Brand awareness was reinforced by the continued use of up-to-date Mercedes vans with the company's logo and contact details prominently shown.

Company structure and performance

By 2005, the organisational structure of the company was in place, based on functional responsibilities. Matthew was now Managing Director, Simon was Operations Director with responsibility for the installation teams, and Matthew's wife, Fiona, was Company Secretary and responsible for the administration and scheduling side of the business. Two key appointments had facilitated Universal's rapid growth. In 2002, Mick Hendry was appointed as Sales and Marketing Director. Mick had 20 years of experience with direct sales in a large installer of PVC windows and doors. Through his efforts, Universal achieved a step change in sales growth, with sales increasing from £1 million in 2001 to £3·3 million in 2002. However, the increased costs involved meant the company made a loss of some £250,000. 2003 saw sales increase to £5·4 million and a profit generated. 2004 saw further sales increase to £6·8 million and a net profit of about £400K. Matthew recognised the increasing pressure on his own time and an inability to control the financial side of the business. 2003 saw Harry Potts appointed as Finance Director and put in much needed financial and management information systems.

Future growth and development

By 2005 Universal had seen 10 years of significant growth and was facing some interesting decisions as to how that growth was to be sustained. Firstly, there was the opportunity to move from a largely regional operation into being a national company. Indeed, the company's vision statement expressed the desire to become 'the most respected roofing company in Britain', based on a 'no surprises' philosophy that house owners all around the country could trust. Economic factors encouraging growth looked fairly promising with a growing economy, stable interest rates and house owners finding it fairly easy to raise additional funding necessary to pay for home improvements. Secondly, there was a real opportunity to develop their share of the commercial housing market. The government had committed itself to a significant improvement in the standard of housing provided to people renting from local authorities and housing associations. Despite the appointment of a Commercial Manager to concentrate on sales into this specialist market, Universal had real difficulty in committing sufficient resources into exploiting this opportunity. In 2002 commercial sales represented over 11% of total sales, but currently commercial sales were around 5% of the total sales. Such were the overall growth predictions, however, that to maintain this share of sales would need commercial sales to more than double over the 2005–7 period. Without the necessary commitment of resources, particularly people, this target was unlikely to be realised. Universal's products also need to be improved and this largely depended on its ability to get into partnerships with its large PVC suppliers. There were some encouraging signs in this direction, but Universal's reliance on PVC opened it to future challenges from installers using more environmentally friendly materials.

Above all, however, the rate of projected growth would place considerable pressures on the senior management team's ability to manage the process. The move towards becoming a national installer was already prompting thoughts about creating a regional level of management. Finally, such had been the firm's growth record that its inability to meet the budgeted sales targets in the first quarter of 2005 was causing real concern for Matthew and Simon.

Table 1: Information on Universal's current sales and financial performance (£'000) (where appropriate)

Universal Roofing Systems Financial information

	2001	2002	2003	2004	2005 Budget	2006 Forecast	2007 Forecast
Domestic sales	854	2,914	5,073	6,451	9,600	15,000	20,500
Commercial sales	36	362	269	324	450	750	1,100
Total Sales	890	3,276	5,342	6,775	10,050	15,750	21,600
Materials	169	589	766	925	1,339	2,105	2,890
Direct Labour	329	1,105	1,941	2,290	3,333	5,125	7,019
Gross Margin	392	1,582	2,635	3,560	5,378	8,520	11,691
Sales commission	20	369	627	781	1,171	1,845	2,501
Canvassers' commissions	74	563	764	962	1,420	2,190	2,993
Marketing	32	171	223	398	657	1,020	1,374
Total sales costs	126	1,103	1,614	2,141	3,248	5,055	6,868
Contribution before overhead	266	479	1,021	1,419	2,130	3,465	4,823
Total overheads	272	723	862	1,140	1,536	2,030	2,627
Trading profit before commission	–6	–244	159	279	594	1,435	2,196
Finance income	0	25	65	115	167	262	342
Net profit	–6	–219	224	394	761	1,697	2,538

Required

(a)   Using an appropriate model, analyse the ways in which Universal has provided a superior level of service to its customers. **(20 marks)**

(b)   Using the information provided in the case scenario, strategically evaluate the performance of the company up to 2004, indicating any areas of particular concern. **(15 marks)**

(c)   Matthew Black is well aware that the achievement of the growth targets for the 2005 to 2007 period will depend on successful implementation of the strategy, affecting all parts of the company's activities.

Required

Explain the key issues affecting implementation and the changes necessary to achieve Universal's ambitious growth strategy. **(15 marks)**

(Total = 50 marks)

40 Datum Paper Products (3.5, 12/05, amended)   90 mins

Introduction and industry background

The current European market for Datum Paper Products (DPP) in 2005 is not encouraging. The company designs and manufactures textile fabrics for use in the paper industry. Its main customers are large European and American paper making companies and while the UK market is fairly stable, over 80% of DPP's products are sold abroad. Its customers use highly expensive capital equipment, with a new paper mill costing £300 million or more. The paper makers supply paper to global newspaper and book publishers who themselves are under pressure to consolidate as a result of the growing competition from alternative information providers, such as TV and the Internet. The industry, therefore, carries many of the signs of a mature industry, the paper manufacturers have considerable overcapacity and are supplying customers who themselves are facing intense competition. Paper makers are looking to reduce the number of suppliers and for these suppliers to meet all their needs. The net result is heavy pressure on suppliers such as DPP to discount prices and improve international service levels, although there is little potential to increase sales volumes to achieve further economies of scale. DPP's response to this more competitive environment has been to attempt to secure higher volumes through increasing their market share and to search for cost reductions in spite of the need to improve customer service levels.

DPP is one of a number of operating companies in the paper and ancillary products division of Park Group Industries plc, a diversified company with other divisions in industrial materials, automotive products and speciality chemicals. The paper and ancillary products division itself is split into the North American Region and the European Region. There are some 30 companies in the division with plants in 13 countries. Within the paper and ancillary products division there is recognition that in order to survive let alone make a profit some industry restructuring is necessary. Currently, DPP has some four UK plants manufacturing different parts of their product range. Any consolidation, including acquisition, is best done on a regional basis and Europe seems a logical place to start.

Strategic options – acquisition or a greenfield site?

Ken Drummond is Managing Director of DPP, and has spent a lifetime in the paper industry but has had little experience in acquiring other companies. The pressures faced by the European industry mean that there are, in reality, two strategic options to achieve the necessary restructuring. Firstly, there are opportunities to buy existing companies available in most European countries. The identification of suitable target companies, the carrying out of due diligence procedures before negotiating a deal and integration of the acquired company typically takes a year to complete. The second option is to move to one of the countries that have entered the European Union in 2004 where operating costs are significantly lower. There are significant government and European Union incentives for firms that move to a new or greenfield site in one of the many economically depressed areas. The greenfield option would take up to three years to get a plant set up and operating.

The acquisition option

Ken is able to draw on the expertise of corporate headquarters that has had some experience with growth by both organic expansion and by acquisition. The initial search for possible acquisition candidates has revealed a French family owned and managed firm, 'Papier Presse', based in the southwest of France, some 800 kilometres from DPP's main plant in the UK. Papier Presse has three manufacturing plants in France, each heavily unionised and controlled by the owner Philippe Truffaud. Papier Presse's markets are exclusively with European paper makers and it has no significant international business outside of the EU. The technology used is more dated than DPP's and manning levels are significantly higher. Papier Presse's product range has some significant overlap with DPP's but there are also some distinctive products. Philippe's son, Francois, is Sales and Marketing Director and his son-in-law, Henri, is Operations Manager. Philippe himself is the third generation of Truffauds to run the firm. Ken recognises the considerable differences between DPP and its potential French partner – language being only the most obvious one.

The sales, service and distribution systems of the two firms are totally distinct but their customers include the same European paper makers. Reconciling the two information systems would be difficult, with customers looking for much higher service levels. Historically, DPP, with its own research and development function, has a better record of product improvement and innovation. However, Papier Presse is better regarded by its customers for its

73

flexibility in meeting their changing demands. In terms of strategic planning DPP contributes to the strategic plans drawn up at divisional level, while the family dominance at Papier Presse means that planning is much more opportunistic and largely focused on the year ahead. Each company has to operate within a climate of heightened environmental concern over toxic by-products of the manufacturing process. There are other similarities in that both companies have felt that product superiority is the route to success but whereas DPP's is through product innovation; Papier Presse's is through customer service. Clearly integrating the two companies will present some interesting challenges and the family ownership of Papier Presse means that a significant premium may have to be paid over the current book value of the company.

The greenfield option

Ken, however, also recognises that the apparent benefits of moving onto a new greenfield site in one of the countries recently admitted into the European Union will itself bring difficulties. One obvious difficulty is the lack of a modern support infrastructure in terms of suppliers, distributors and logistical support. There is also a strong tradition of government intervention in company growth and development. Although there are government agencies looking to attract new companies to set up in these countries, there are considerable bureaucratic and time consuming procedures to overcome. Above all there is continuing government financial support for small inefficient, formerly state-owned, companies making the products for the national paper makers, who themselves are small and inefficient compared to the customers being supplied by DPP and Papier Presse.

Table 1: Financial information on DPP and Papier Presse (£'000,000) for 2005

	Datum Paper Products	Papier Presse
Sales	195.5	90.0
Cost of sales	122.2	67.5
Gross margin	73.3	22.5
Sales and administration	27.4	9.0
Marketing	9.5	1.4
R&D	4.5	0.5
Depreciation	10.0	1.0
Operating profit	21.9	10.6
Net assets	275.0	148.0
Debt	100.0	68.0
Equity	175.0	80.0
Earnings per share	12·5p	13·3p
Dividend per share	5·6p	10·0p
Return on sales	11·2%	11·8%
Employees	1,250	750
Absenteeism (days p.a.)	8	16
Patents – 2004	5	0
Manufacturing facilities	4	3
Sales from products less than 5 years old	20%	5%
Share of major European markets:		
UK	45%	14%
France	10%	60%
Italy	8%	20%
Germany	15%	15%
Spain	10%	25%
Sales outside Europe	50%	5%
North America region	40%	3%
Rest of World	10%	2%

Required

(a)   Using the data provided and models where appropriate, assess the strategic fit between Datum Paper Products and Papier Presse, indicating areas where positive or negative synergies are likely to exist.

(20 marks)

(b)   Assess the advantages and disadvantages to Datum Paper Products taking the greenfield option as opposed to the acquisition of Papier Presse.   **(15 marks)**

There is considerable evidence to suggest that as a result of implementation problems less than 50% of all acquisitions achieve their objectives and actually end up reducing shareholder value.

(c)   Provide Ken with a brief report on the most likely sources of integration problems and describe the key performance indicators he should use to measure progress towards acquisition objectives.   **(15 marks)**

(Total = 50 marks)

41 Churchill Ice Cream (3.5, 6/06)   90 mins

Origins and ownership

Churchill Ice Cream is a medium-sized family owned company, making and selling a range of premium ice cream products. Its origins were in the middle years of the twentieth century, when John Churchill saw an opportunity to supply a growing consumer demand for luxury products. John has been followed into the business by his two sons and the Churchill family has dominated the ownership and management of the company. In 2001 there was recognition of the need to bring in outside management expertise and John reluctantly accepted the need to relinquish his position as chairman and chief executive of the company. Richard Smith, formerly a senior executive with one of the major supermarket chains, was appointed as chief executive. Within one year of Richard's appointment he had recruited Churchill's first sales and marketing director. Richard was consciously looking to reduce the dominance by the Churchill family and make the company a more marketing orientated business able to meet the increased competitive challenges of the 21st century.

Churchill's distinctive strategy

Churchill Ice Cream is in many ways an unusual company, choosing to both manufacture its premium ice cream and sell its products through its own stores. Specialist ice cream stores or parlours had started in the US and soon spread to the UK. Customers can both buy and eat ice cream in the store. John Churchill saw the growing demand for such specialist ice cream stores and created a unique store format, which quickly established the Churchill brand. Most of these stores are owned by the company, but there are also some smaller franchised outlets. By 2005 it had 40 ice cream stores owned by the company and a further 18 owned by franchise holders. Franchise stores typically are in less attractive locations than their company-owned equivalents. All stores are located in and around the London area.

The logic for manufacturing its own ice cream is a strongly held belief that through sourcing its ingredients from local farmers and suppliers it gains a significant competitive advantage. Making its own ice cream also has enabled it to retain control over the unique recipes used in its premium ice cream product range. John Churchill summed up the policy saying 'We are no more expensive than the market leader but we are much better. We use real chocolate and it's real dairy ice cream. Half our expenditure goes on our ingredients and packaging. It's by far our highest cost.' Dairy ice cream, as opposed to cheaper ice cream, uses milk, butter and cream instead of vegetable oils to blend with sugar and flavourings. These ingredients are blended to produce a wide range of products. Churchill has also developed a product range with no artificial additives hoping to differentiate itself from the competition.

Product innovation is a key capability in the ice cream market and 40% of industry sales are made from products less than three years old. Churchill's products are made at a new purpose built factory and supplied quickly and directly to its own ice cream stores and other retail outlets. Unfortunately, detailed and timely information about product and store performance has suffered through a delay in introducing a management information system. Consequently its stores often faced product shortages during the peak summer months.

In 2003 Churchill became the sponsor and sole supplier to a number of high profile summer sporting events held in London. Churchill also supplies eight million tubs of ice cream each year to London based cinemas and theatres. As a consequence, Churchill is now an established regional brand with 90% customer recognition in the London area. It also has major ambitions to become a national and eventually an international brand though facing significant competition from two global chains of US owned premium ice cream stores. Their high profile moves into the UK market was backed with expensive advertising and succeeded in expanding the demand for all premium ice creams.

The UK retail ice cream market

Ice cream is bought in two main ways: either from retail outlets such as supermarkets for later consumption at home or on impulse for immediate consumption from a range of outlets, including ice cream stores such as Churchill's. Impulse sales are much more dependent on the weather and in 2003 sales of take home ice cream and impulse ice cream were roughly equal. Total sales of ice cream in the UK reached £1·3 billion in 2003. Premium ice cream in 2005 accounted for 19% of the UK's take home market, up from 15% in 2002.

Churchill itself does not use advertising. In John Churchill's words, 'There is no point in advertising your product if consumers are unable to buy the product.' Churchill has yet to achieve significant sales into the take home market. Two major barriers exist. Firstly, global manufacturers with significant global brands dominate the industry. Secondly, four major UK supermarket chains dominate the take home market. These supermarket chains account for over 80% of food spending in the UK and have the power to demand that suppliers manufacture their products under the supermarket's own label brand. Supermarkets currently account for 41% of the sales of ice cream in the UK.

However, it is proving difficult to get the Churchill product range into the ice cream cabinets of the supermarket chains. In John Churchill's opinion 'If you want to buy a tub of premium ice cream and you go to a supermarket you have a choice of two American brands or its own label. I think there should be a British brand in there. Our prices are competitive, at least £1 cheaper than our rivals and our aim is to get Churchill ice cream into every major supermarket.' Some limited success has been achieved with two of the smaller supermarket chains with premium ice cream supplied under their own label brands. However, margins are very slim on these sales.

Churchill's international strategy

Churchill, in seeking to increase its sales, has had no success in moving into foreign markets. In the 1990s it tried both setting up its own ice cream stores abroad and acquiring specialist ice cream makers with their own ice cream outlets. Its attempted entry into the US market was by using the established Churchill ice cream store format. Two stores were opened in New York, but the hopes that the emphasis on classic English quality and style and the slogan 'tradition with taste', would prove successful did not materialise and the stores were closed with significant losses – each store took upwards of £100K to fit out.

Acquisition of two established ice cream makers, one in Germany and one in Italy also proved failures. Access to their retail outlets and to complementary product ranges did not overcome differences in taste and customer buying behaviour. Despite attempts to change some of the German and Italian outlets to the Churchill store format the results were less than impressive and the two companies were eventually sold at a combined loss of £5 million.

Table 1 Financial information on Churchill Ice Cream (£'000)

	2002	2003	2004	2005	2006 forecast
Sales	14,100	15,300	16,000	16,400	16,700
Cost of sales	12,790	14,250	14,990	15,360	15,760
Operating profit	1,310	1,050	1,010	1,040	940
Product development	340	530	560	310	500
Net profit	970	520	450	730	440
Fixed assets	10,910	10,400	9,670	8,880	8,320
Net assets	4,810	4,910	4,000	4,300	4,300
Gearing (%)	105	130	111	86	67
Number of UK outlets					
Own stores	39	41	40	40	39
Franchised stores	11	13	16	18	20
Index of UK ice cream sales	106	109	107	104	109

Table 2 Typical product cost breakdown of a Churchill half-litre tub of premium ice cream

	£
Labour	0·63
Ingredients	1·00
Packaging	0·25
Overheads	0·28
Distribution	0·09
Total cost	2·25
Sales price	2·50
Net profit	0·25

Table 3 Sales breakdown for Churchill's premium ice cream

Sales to own stores	60%
Sales to franchise stores	10%
Sales to leisure outlets	25%
Sales to supermarkets	5%
Sales to London region	90%
Sales outside London region	10%

Summary

Overall, Churchill has a distinctive strategy linking the manufacturing of premium ice cream with its distribution through the company's own ice cream stores. This has secured them a regional reputation for a quality product. It has had little success to date in penetrating the major supermarket chains with the Churchill brand and in moving its distinctive ice cream store format into foreign markets. Finally, to complicate both the manufacturing and retail sides of the Churchill business, seasonality is a real issue. Ice cream is still heavily dominated by sales in the summer months. In fact the peak demand in summer is typically five times the demand in the middle of winter. Equally serious is the impact of a cold summer on impulse ice cream sales. This has a number of consequences, which affect the costs of the product and capacity usage at both manufacturing and retail levels.

Despite this, Richard Smith has set three clear strategic goals to be achieved over the next five years. Firstly, to become the leading premium ice cream brand in the UK, secondly, to increase sales to £25 million and finally, to penetrate the supermarket sector with the Churchill product range.

Required

Richard Smith has set three clear strategic goals for Churchill's growth and development over the next five years.

(a)   Using models where appropriate, assess the advantages and disadvantages of the current strategy being pursued by Churchill Ice Cream and its impact on performance up to 2005.   **(20 marks)**

(b)   Using relevant evaluation criteria, assess how achievable and compatible these three strategic goals are over the next five years.   **(15 marks)**

(c)   What changes to Churchill's existing marketing mix will be needed to achieve the three strategic goals?

(15 marks)

Churchill Ice Cream has to date made two unsuccessful attempts to become an international company.

(Total = 50 marks)

Answers

1 Preparation question: strategy and strategic management

Part (a)

Corporate strategy is concerned with the overall purpose and scope of the organisation and how value will be added to the different parts (business units) of the organisation.

Business strategy is about how to compete successfully in particular markets.

Operational strategies are concerned with how the component parts of an organisation deliver effectively the corporate- and business-level strategies in terms of resources, processes and people

Part (b)

Strategic position

The strategic managers must attempt to understand the organisation's **strategic position**. There are three main groups of influences to consider.

(a)   The **environment**, which presents **opportunities** and **threats**

(b)   **Strategic capability**, which is made up of resources and competences. These may be analysed into **strengths** and **weaknesses**.

(c)   The **expectations of stakeholders** concerning the organisation's **purpose**, **responsibilities** and **corporate governance**.

Strategic choice

Strategic choices are made at both the **corporate** and **business unit** level. At the level of the business unit, these choices are about how to achieve **competitive advantage** and are based on an understanding of **customers and markets**. At the corporate level, strategy is primarily about **scope**: this is concerned with the overall product/business portfolio, the spread of markets and the relationship between business units and the corporate centre.

Strategic choices must also be made about the **direction** and **method** of development.

Strategy into action

Strategies must be made to work in practice. Major issues here include **structuring**, **enabling** and **change**.

(a)   **Structuring** includes processes, relationships, organisation structure and how these elements work together.

(b)   **Enabling** is the complex two-way process by which the organisation's resources are managed to both support and to create strategies.

(c)   **Change** is a very common feature of strategic development and the management of change is a most important feature of strategic implementation.

Part (c)

Johnson, Scholes and Whittington suggest **three lenses** through which strategy may be examined.

*   Strategy as **design**
*   Strategy as **experience**
*   Strategy as **ideas**

Strategy as design

There is a widely held view of strategy as a **rational, top-down** process by which senior managers analyse and evaluate strategic constraints and forces in order to establish a clear and rational course of strategic action. This is a traditional view and one that appeals to managers: it is orthodox, logical and supportive of their own view of their role. It also appeals to stakeholders such as shareholders, banks, many employees and public servants.

However, this view makes a number of important assumptions that might be subject to debate. Some of these are given below.

(a) Managers are **rational decision-makers** and the strategic problems facing the organisation are susceptible to **rational analysis**.

(b) There are clear and explicit **objectives**.

(c) The organisation is a hierarchy in which strategy is an **exclusively management responsibility**.

(d) The organisation is also a **rational, almost engineered, system** that is capable of putting management's plans into effect.

The view of strategy as design is useful since it leads to the use of a number of tools and techniques that are both logical and practical. However, it does not describe the whole of strategic management.

Strategy as experience

This view sees strategy as an adaptation and extension of **what has worked in the past**. It is firmly based in the **paradigm, which is to say,** the **experience** and **assumptions** of influential figures in the organisation and the ways of doing things approved by the organisation's cultural norms. This approach tends to lead managers to **simplify** the complexity they face in order to be able to deal with it, selecting and using the elements of their knowledge and understanding that seem most relevant or important.

Where there are choices or disputes about strategic options, these are resolved by negotiation and bargaining. The result is decisions that **satisfice rather than optimise** and strategies that develop in an incremental and adaptive way.

Strategy as ideas

This approach to strategy emphasises **innovation** and the need for **diversity of ideas** in the organisation: strategy can emerge from the way the people within the organisation handle and respond to the changing forces present both in the organisation and in the environment. The role of senior managers is to create the **context and conditions** in which new ideas can emerge and the best ones survive and thrive.

The aim is the achieve an 'adaptive tension' that will keep the organisation functioning without either resorting to machine-like procedure or descending into unproductive disarray. This can be achieved by the use of **simple rules**, which are general principles rather than detailed procedures.

2 Preparation question with analysis: Fancy Packaging

REPORT

To: Eddie Lomax, Marketing Director, The Fancy Packaging Company
From: Market research consultant
Date: December 200X
Subject: Overseas market research

1   I understand that your company is considering expansion into a non-European market sector for your decorative packaging. As you have no experience in non-European markets it is essential that full information is found about potential markets before any decision is made as to which, if any, markets to enter. There are three key areas that you will require information about.

The general environment
Competitors
Customers

2   The general environment

The general environment may be analysed using the **PEST analysis model**, which breaks the environment down into four main parts: political/legal factors, economic factors, social and cultural factors and technological factors.

2.1   Political/legal factors

One of the key issues in this area is the **attitude of the local government** to foreign imports. If a government wishes to protect indigenous businesses, then trade barriers may be an obstacle to entry into the market concerned. These barriers can take more subtle forms than simple tariffs and quotas yet be just as effective at discouraging imports. It is also important to be aware of the nature and extent of legal regulation and how it differs from what you are used to. For example, there may be legal restraints on relationships with agents and distributors; on the amount or type of packaging used; and on the remittance of funds out of the country.

2.2   Economic factors

The **general economy of the proposed new market** will be of prime importance. The **general economic condition** of the country is likely to have a direct effect on demand for your products. You should consider general structural economic factors such as the trend rate of growth, degree of economic stability and current stage of the economic cycle. The current state and prospects for **specific indicators** such as levels of inflation, unemployment and interest rates will be relevant for judging whether the time is ripe for an entry.

2.3   Social and cultural factors

One of the problems you have encountered in the European market has been **environmentally concerned customers'** preference for reductions in conspicuous wastage. You need to be confident that this will not be a major problem in the markets you are considering.

2.4   Technological factors

You will need to consider the technological infrastructure of the proposed markets in terms of **transport** and **communications facilities**, the degree of technical sophistication of the population and whether e-commerce is relevant in these markets.

3   Competitors and customers

Once the general economic climate of the countries you are interested in has been investigated you will require detailed knowledge of conditions in your specific potential markets that you will face. **Customers** and **competitors** will be two of the more important factors: they can be analysed together with other important influences using *Porter's* five competitive forces model.

3.1   Threat of new entrants

You will be the new entrant, presenting a threat to existing suppliers. You need to know the extent to which **effective barriers to entry** exist and the likely response of existing players to the entry of a new supplier.

3.2   Threat of substitute products

The new markets are perhaps unlikely to present any substitute products that you are not already aware of, but it is possible and you should attempt to become familiar with likely local developments.

3.3   *Bargaining power of customers*

Customers' bargaining power is enhanced when suppliers are plentiful and products are commoditised. You need **detailed knowledge of the state of the local packaging industry** and you must be sure that you know how you will impress your customers with the extra value provided by your products. You must obtain quantitative data, such as the number of potential customers, their size, location, buying patterns and purchasing policies. You should also consider qualitative factors, key amongst which is the answer to the questions 'why do these customers buy?' and 'how do they choose who they buy from?' Other relevant concerns will be the quantity in which the customer buys, the number of potential customers, the importance of the product to the customer and the potential customers' own profitability.

3.4   *Bargaining power of suppliers*

The **balance of power** in your relationship with your own suppliers in the potential market will depend upon a number of factors such as their overall number, the threat of new entrants or substitute products, the importance of your purchases to your suppliers' businesses and any differentiation of their products.

3.5   *Rivalry amongst current competitors*

This is an important area for you as it is likely to affect your profitability directly. The more intense the current competitive rivalry, is the **less potentially profitable** the market is.

4   **Conclusion**

The decision to enter a new geographical area is an important and difficult one and it must not be undertaken lightly. Any failure could not only be financially damaging but damaging also to the reputation of the business elsewhere in the world. Before such a decision is taken, therefore, every effort must be taken to ensure that you have as much information as possible about the general environment in which you would be trading as well as detailed information about your competitors and the customers for your particular product.

3 Five forces

Text reference. The topics mentioned in this answer are discussed in Chapter 2 of your BPP Study Text.

Top tips. Explain the model and, as always, apply each element in detail to the question scenario and E's market. This will enable you to establish the relative importance of each force, and indicate and justify appropriate performance indicators, such as customer satisfaction (not just in the current situation, but in the business environment in the future. Customer expectations may be satisfied now, but their needs may change). You must make a conclusion as to whether or not you agree with the Marketing Director.

Easy marks. The question mentions each of the five forces but does not really explain them: a brief explanation is necessary for each one if your recommendations are to make sense. Here are some easy marks.

REPORT

To: Marketing Director
From: Management accountant
Date: May 200X
Subject: Performance indicators – competitive forces

Introduction

CIMA defines the **five competitive forces** as 'external influences upon the extent of actual and potential competition within any industry which in aggregate determine the ability of firms within that industry to earn a profit'. Porter argues that a firm must adopt a strategy that combats these forces better than its rivals' strategies if it is to enhance shareholder value.

If some of these forces are weak, it is easier to be profitable. How can they be applied to E, and their relative strength measured? We shall look at each force in turn and consider some appropriate indicators.

The threat of new entrants (and barriers to entry to keep them out)

A new entrant into an industry will bring extra capacity and more competition. The strength of this threat is likely to vary from industry to industry, depending on the strength of the barriers to entry, and the likely **response of existing competitors** to the new entrant. The **emergence of new competitors** can be easily monitored.

Existing firms in an industry, such as E, may have built up a good brand image and strong customer loyalty over a long period of time. A few firms may promote a large number of brands to crowd out the competition, especially in the cosmetics market. Perhaps for this reason, it could be concluded that this particular competitive force is a low risk, but the situation should be monitored.

The threat from substitute products

A **substitute product** is a good/service which satisfies the same customer needs. There are many companies producing cosmetics, and they invest heavily in research and development. E's own **spend on research and development** is a likely indication of the activity of competitors of a similar size in producing substitute products , such as the use of different ingredients (as in the case of the Body Shop, promoting ethical products) or the possible promotion of a cosmetic-free way of life by other industries. This could be more of a threat than is currently being recognised.

The bargaining power of customers

Customers want better quality products and services at a lower price. Satisfying this might force down the profitability of suppliers in the industry. Just how strong the position of customers is dependent on several factors.

How much the **customer buys**, and the relative importance of each customer in each market served (possibly segmented by location), can be easily measured by **analysis of sales and profit** per product.

There is more to consider than product profitability. Customers have a wide **choice** available to them, and their tastes and fashions will change all the time. This range of choice means the power of customers is a very important one for E's competitiveness.

Variations in customer taste and attitude can be measured using **marketing research**. **Product quality** will be an important consideration and measurement, and its careful control may lead E to conclude that investment in product quality will help to grow sales.

The bargaining power of suppliers

Suppliers can sometimes exert pressure for higher prices. If E had just **one or two dominant suppliers**, able to charge high prices, simple cost analysis will make this clear. However, it is more likely that E is being be served by a multitude of suppliers. The **range of prices charged** by different suppliers can be compared to assess whether E is at the mercy of its suppliers (unlikely, given E's global presence and the fact that most suppliers operate on a small scale) or if it is able to negotiate better terms to ensure consistency and quality of supply.

If some suppliers also supply E's **competitors**, and do not rely heavily on E for the majority of their sales, this will indicate a relative strength. However, the size of E is likely to mean that this competitive force is of less significance. It is more likely to be able to dictate to suppliers what it wants and when it wants it.

The rivalry amongst current competitors in the industry

It is clear that the **intensity of competitive rivalry** within an industry will affect the profitability of the industry as a whole. This is an important force for E. **Competitive actions** to influence customer opinion and increase **market share** can be tracked and might take the form of **price competition, advertising battles, sales promotion campaigns**, introducing **new products** for the market, improving **after sales service** or providing **guarantees or warranties**.

All of these marketing activities can be measured in terms of **cost** and perceived **benefit** (although the relationship between initiatives such as advertising campaigns and subsequent sales levels may be difficult to pin down).

E could employ **market share analysis** to assess whether its cosmetic products are holding their position against competitors, or if new and attractive competitor products can come to the market quickly and establish competitive advantage over E. Products can be assessed using the BCG matrix.

Conclusion

This brief analysis shows that the intensity of competitive rivalry is the most potent force affecting the profitability of E. While it is not strictly necessary to rank the forces in order of influence, it could be concluded that the buying power of customers is also strong (given that they can change their minds, particularly in a fashion-driven industry) and allied to this is the threat from substitute products, which is likely to be stronger than is currently being allowed. Because of E's size, the power of suppliers and the threat of new entrants could rightly be interpreted as lesser threats.

It should be noted that Porter's five forces model has come in for criticism. Perhaps most importantly, it overemphasises the importance of the **wider environment** and therefore ignores the significance of the **individual advantages held by E** with regard to **resources**, **capabilities** and **competence**.

4 McGeorge Holdings

Marking scheme

		Marks
(a)	Use of product life cycle	up to 6 marks
	Use of BCG matrix	up to 4 marks
		Maximum 10 marks
(b)	Methods of benchmarking up to 2 marks for each	
	Internal	
	Competitive	
	Customer	
	Generic	
	Process	**Maximum 10 marks**
	Problems of benchmarking	
	Data availability	up to 2 marks each
	Difficulties in making comparisons	
	Does it add value?	
	Historical tendency	**Maximum 5 marks**
		Maximum for section 15 marks
		Total 25 marks

Part (a)

Text reference. The topics mentioned in this answer are discussed in Chapter 4 of your BPP Study Text.

Top tips. If you follow the example of *Johnson Scholes & Whittington*, you will start off with the product life cycle model. They do not recommend the use of the BCG classification in this context, but do not overlook it when thinking about product portfolios. It is very simple and can give very useful clues about managing a portfolio.

Easy marks. This is a very easy question.

McGeorge Holdings has a diverse range of products that has grown in a rather opportunistic fashion, without a clear vision to guide its structure. Two models can be used to analyse the product portfolio in order to decide which to remove.

The Product Life Cycle

The product life cycle model suggests that a product experiences changes in its revenues and profitability over time. On introduction it Later, it will start to generate profits as it moves through its growth phase and enters its maturity. The length of the maturity phase will vary, but eventually the product will enter its decline: sales will gradually fall, though it will probably remain reasonably profitable to the end.

A **balanced portfolio** is likely to include products at different stages of their lifecycles. Today's mature products will generate the cash needed to launch and build the innovations that will become tomorrow's cash generators. Then, inevitably, one by one, mature products will eventually go into decline.

At the **introduction stage**, a product will have low sales and be loss-making as it pays off its costs of development and absorbs promotional expenditure. It may be that McGeorge Holdings' portfolio includes a disproportionate number of such products as a result of the expansion of its product range and this may account for the disproportionate increase in costs. However, it is these products that will generate profits in the future, so Adrian Reed must be cautious about cutting their numbers. A useful approach might be to look for duplication or near-duplication of customer benefits and cut products so that each of the survivors has its own clearly identifiable and potentially profitable target segment.

In the **growth stage**, the product has gained market acceptance, unit costs are falling and the product should be starting to earn profit. Adrian Reed could usefully examine products in this category for progress and potential: it would be necessary to judge these matters on solidly factual grounds rather than marketing hopes and aspirations.

It is in the **later stages of maturity and decline** that particular attention needs to be focused. It can be hard to determine when decline will start, but it will be signalled by **falling profits**. Some products may go straight from growth to decline. When it is clear that a product has entered this phase, the company needs to decide whether or not to terminate it. However, profitability is not the only criterion to consider. The market consequences and implications of such action must be analysed carefully. For example, though in decline, the product may be particular popular with its remaining customers: any displeasure they feel at its withdrawal could have a negative impact on linked products and may even lead to them switch to competitors. Furthermore, if costs such as marketing and distribution have been **apportioned** over a range of products, withdrawal of some of them may result in a higher allocation of costs to the remainder, making them potentially uncompetitive.

The BCG Matrix

Johnson, Scholes and Whittington do not recommend the use of the BCG matrix for the management of product portfolios, preferring to reserve it for the management of portfolios of businesses by corporate parent companies. However, it has been widely used with product portfolios and can offer useful insights in such contexts.

The BCG matrix assesses a company's products according to their **relative market share** (which is, effectively, a proxy for the extent of economies of scale they enjoy), and the **rate of growth of their market**. Their position in the matrix has general implications for potential cash generation and cash expenditure requirements. This model, while more complex than the product life cycle, may be compared with it

Stars have both high market share and high growth. They may be compared with products in the growth phase of the life cycle model. They require capital expenditure in excess of the cash they generate, in order to maintain their market position, but promise high returns in the future. The strategy for stars is therefore to **build** them and they would not usually be candidates for divestment.

Cash cows have low market growth but high relative market share and generate high levels of cash income whilst needing very little capital expenditure. They are similar to products in the maturity phase of their life cycle. A **hold** strategy is usually appropriate for these products. They are often used to finance other products' development and would not, therefore, be recommended for divestment.

Problem children (or **question marks**) are the opposite of cash cows: they have a low share of a growing market. They may be compared with products at the launch stage of the product life cycle. They would require considerable capital expenditure in order to increase their market share, as, effectively, they are being squeezed out of the market by rival products. A decision needs to be made whether it is worthwhile continuing with these products.

Dogs have a low share of a low-growth market. They may be cash cows that have fallen into the decline stage of their life cycle. They tie up funds, provide a poor return on investment and are, therefore, candidates for withdrawal. Alternatively, they may still have a useful role in completing a product range or keeping competitors out. There are also many smaller **niche businesses** in markets that are **difficult to consolidate** that would count as dogs but which are quite successful.

Adrian Reed needs to look carefully at all of the products in the range, obtain full information about each one and categorise them accordingly. A fully informed, sensible decision can then be made about which products to remove from the portfolio.

Part (b)

Top tips. This question calls for a simple account of the theory of benchmarking, which is, in principle, not a terribly complex idea.

Examiner's comments. Candidates' accounts of the disadvantages of benchmarking were rather rudimentary.

Benchmarking is the establishment, through data gathering, of targets and comparators, through whose use relative levels of performance can be identified. By the adoption of identified best practices it is hoped that performance will improve.

Benchmarking can be carried out in a number of different ways:

Internal benchmarking would compare one operating unit or function with another one within McGeorge Holdings plc. A unit that is particularly effective in one area could be used as an example of best practice and their knowledge and skills transferred to other units within the group.

Competitive benchmarking **would involve gathering information about direct competitors in order to compare products, processes and results and attempt to copy best practice. The obvious problem is the difficulty in obtaining such information.**

Functional benchmarking would compare functions within McGeorge Holdings with similar functions in the best external practitioners, regardless of their industry. Financial indicators such as gearing and liquidity may be easier to obtain than detailed operational information.

Disadvantages of benchmarking

There is an increased flow of information that must be monitored, summarised and assessed. These processes are not cost-free and they can lead to management overload. In a charity, the work involved in benchmarking can be discouraging for volunteer staff.

Overload can also occur when a successful benchmarking exercise produces a large volume of requests to participate from organisations that have themselves little to offer in potential improvements.

Benchmarking usually involves the exchange of information with other organisations. There is a threat to confidentiality, both commercial and personal.

Poor results from a benchmarking exercise can be disproportionately discouraging and demotivating, particularly to managers.

The benchmarking process itself can distract managers' attention from their primary responsibilities. Even when this does not happen, managers may put too much emphasis on improving the efficiency with which they do the things they have always done and fail to ask if new ways of doing things would be better overall.

5 Airtite

Part (a)

> **Text reference.** The topics mentioned in this answer are discussed in Chapter 5 of your BPP Study Text.
>
> **Top tips**. The marking scheme for this question emphasises PESTEL, apparently offering full marks for proper consideration of each of the six factors listed in the mnemonic. This would seem reasonable, given that nearly all of the information in the scenario relates to the general environment. However, the Examiner's suggested solution is largely concerned with a discussion the **nature and process** of environmental scanning and offers little in the way of actual analysis of the data given in the setting.
>
> The message to take away from all this is that this question is not quite as simple as it looks. While you could score quite well with a simple discussion of the PESTEL factors in the scenario, you should also consider **environmental uncertainty**, its implications for **risk** and the potential **impact** of the various environmental factors on Airtite and its operations.
>
> On a different topic, you may find some aspects of the environmental influences given in the scenario rather debatable. A good example would be the potential effects of the demographic changes mentioned in the third paragraph. The way to deal with such a problem is to ignore it: deal with the circumstances as they are given in the scenario.
>
> Of course, if the setting includes unrealistic or one-sided opinions *expressed by a character* within it, it is appropriate to talk about them. This is a fairly common device used by examiners to encourage you to give balanced consideration to a topic. But when the setting is essentially a simple narrative of prevailing conditions, as this one is (despite the identification of John Sykes as a character within it), you should think of it as an **alternative reality with its own rules** and play within them.
>
> Don't forget that all versions of the PESTEL model are fairly arbitrary in the way they analyse the general environment into sectors. It doesn't really matter whether you cover the demographic issues in the setting under the economic heading or the society one, for instance, so long as you cover it.
>
> **Easy marks**. As mentioned above, a reasonably competent discussion of the relevant PESTEL items should score well.
>
> **Examiner's comments**. The important factors in the setting included the key drivers of change.

Marking scheme

		Marks
(a)	PESTEL analysis including:	up to 2 per variable
	Political – increasing government control	
	Economic – trends in disposable income	
	Social – ageing population	
	Technological – more efficient aircraft	
	Environmental – tighter emission control	
	Legal – global agreement on emissions	
	Assessing impact and uncertainty	up to 3
	Maximum for section (a) 15 marks	

(b)   Key features in using a scenario: up to 5
       Identifying high impact/high uncertainty factors in environment
       Identifying different possible futures by factor
       Building scenarios of plausible configurations of factors

       Links to Airtite's strategy   up to 5
                                                                          Maximum for section (b) 10marks
                                                                                          Total 20 marks

Airtite – the general environment

Political and legal factors

Generally, European governments are sympathetic to the idea of low cost air travel, since it has the potential to increase the effective **wealth** of the less affluent. However, the influential green lobby objects to the **environmental effects** of increased air travel. This attitude has now become an aspect of popular journalistic wisdom as a result of climate change and the issue of 'carbon footprints' has become of interest to politicians of all persuasions. In any event, there is a continuing possibility of **increased taxation** or **direct controls** on the growth of air travel.

Economic factors

Fuel is becoming more expensive and this trend is unlikely to change very much because of the increasing demand from China and India as they develop their economies. **Growth** in the European economies varies from country to country. New entrants to the EU tend to have a relatively low GNP per head, while some of the more prosperous countries are finding their growth constrained by their failure to **reform their labour markets**. In both cases, tourism can make a major contribution to national income and economic development. Europe remains a generally wealthy region and the market for air travel is likely to continue to grow, though perhaps at a reduced rate.

Socio-cultural factors

Foreign travel is now accepted as a normal practice by less well off segments of society as a result of the expansion of low-cost airlines.

The incidence of **terrorist activity** aimed air transport seems to be increasing, bringing with it a major increase in security-related costs and, on occasion, a reluctance to travel by air.

Demographic change in Europe may constrain growth in demand for air travel. Aging populations and growth in the number of one parent families are likely to increase the **burden of welfare costs**, leading to increased levels of taxation and reduced disposable income. However, this is a longer-term trend and is unlikely to have much effect over, say, the next five to ten years.

Technological factors

The technology of all aspects of air travel continues to develop, with consequent **increases in safety** and **reductions in cost and emissions**. The spread of broadband access to the Internet increases the size of Airtite's potential market, relying, as it does, on on-line bookings.

Environmental uncertainty

As the analysis above shows, within Europe the general environment for the air travel industry is both **complex** and **dynamic**, with a large number of major factors interacting in complex ways. The effect of this is to create a high level of **uncertainty**. The implication of this for Airtite is that John Sykes and his fellow senior managers must remain alert for developments that might affect them and be innovative and flexible in their policies and plans. **Experience in the industry** is likely to be of great value in assessing the importance of future environmental developments, simply because of the complexity of their interactions.

Part (b)

> **Top tips**. We all know what scenarios are, more or less, but many of us are unsure about both when it would be a good idea to prepare one and how to go about doing it.
>
> The clue to the first problem – when scenarios are a good idea – lies in **environmental uncertainty**. A high degree of uncertainty limits to usefulness of techniques based on extrapolation: the possibility of a transformational change must be considered.
>
> The scenario-writing process then requires a consideration of potential **impact** on the organisation and what it does.

A scenario is an internally consistent view of how the future might turn out to be. Scenarios are useful when there is **high environmental uncertainty** as a result of complexity or rapid change, or both and thus difficulty in forecasting how a range of important influences might affect the future.

Scenario building is not an attempt to foretell the future. It is rather an attempt to **identify critical outcomes or branching points** that may arise at some future time and to work out how to deal with the various possible future states that they imply.

A very large number of factors may influence the way future events develop. *Johnson, Scholes and Whittington* suggest that only a few of them should be considered so as to reduce the complexity that is likely to arise from a large number of assumptions and uncertainties. This can be done by basing scenario development on those factors that display both **high uncertainty** and the **potential for major impact** on the industry in question. Such an approach would concentrate John's mind on the most important environmental features. Fuel prices and taxation are both important in this context, combining a high degree of uncertainty and high potential to disrupt Airtite's budgets.

The chosen factors, or **drivers of change** are assessed for the ways in which they might interact and a small number of different but equally logically consistent scenarios are created. A **time horizon** of perhaps ten years is used, partly to enhance the usefulness of the scenarios that are developed and partly to discourage simple extrapolation from the present. No attempt is made to allocate probabilities to the various future states envisioned: this would lend them a spurious accuracy and would detract from their utility.

The process of writing scenarios depends on an ability to discern patterns and a general awareness of the potential significance of widely disparate data. It can be taken in stages, with the initial production of up to a dozen mini scenarios, each dealing with a restricted set of factors and interactions. These can then be combined into, say, three larger scenarios dealing with all of the drivers.

The preparation and discussion of scenarios would contributes to **organisational learning** in Airtite by developing its senior managers' awareness of the environmental factors influencing the airline's development. This awareness should lead to **more informed environmental monitoring** and prompt the development of appropriate **contingency plans**.

6 Qualispecs

Part (a)

> **Text reference.** The topics mentioned in this answer are discussed in Chapters 4 and 6 of your BPP Study Text.
>
> **Top tips.** In answering this question, you will probably find it best to use a SWOT analysis approach rather than one based on environmental scanning and internal appraisal. There is not really enough data available for you to be able to carry out a thorough external and internal review. The material given is in a significantly summarised form: this is ideal for the SWOT analysis approach.
>
> Take great care in answering part (a) not to leave yourself with nothing to say in part (b). A useful approach would be to confine yourself to more general comments in part (a) and be more specific in part (b).

Qualispecs corporate appraisal

Strengths

- New CEO with good track record in the industry, intimate knowledge of a major competitor and willingness to take vigorous steps
- Reputation for quality products
- Celebrity endorsement
- Strong financial position including large cash reserves

Weaknesses

- Failure to utilise new technology
- High production costs
- Failure to use reward system for motivation
- Over-centralisation

Opportunities

- Fashion 'eye-wear', including designer frames and sunglasses
- Availability of new production technology
- Increased spending among 18-30 year old customers

Threats

- Economic slowdown
- Decline in customer loyalty/increasing competition from innovative rivals

Key strategic challenges

Qualispecs is in danger of being left behind by its competitors. The erosion of its customer base shows that it can no longer allow its product to 'speak for itself'. Unless it takes vigorous steps, its rivals will draw further ahead and its decline will accelerate.

The company has been reluctant to make use of **improved technology**; this is probably linked to its high production costs. Improved technology would almost certainly reduce cost and improve quality simultaneously. There would be important implications for cashflow, production management and training, but these will not be reduced by putting improvements off even longer.

Qualispecs has a rather unimaginative **reward policy** and this is probably having an effect on the productivity of its staff. While *Herzberg* tells us that pay is not a motivating factor, we should be aware that it can be used to enhance the effect of motivational factors. Taking the example of innovation, there are probably people working for Qualispecs who have good ideas that could enhance the company's success. If their ideas were taken up and proved successful, they would probably be disappointed if their reward were confined to praise and a certificate. Something more materially convertible would emphasise the company's appreciation.

The **profitability** of Qualispecs' shops varies enormously. This must be investigated. We know that fixed costs are high in shopping malls; there may be other factors at work, not least the performance of shop managers and staff. This is an area where analysis of performance figures will be useful, if only in highlighting areas for further investigation.

Part (b)

> **Top tips.** This part of the question requires you to recommend specific strategies. A solution might be based on converting threats to opportunities and weaknesses to strengths; matching strengths with opportunities and remedying weaknesses. It would probably also be possible to base an answer on Porter's generic strategies. The product/market vector matrix is perhaps less useful.
>
> **Easy marks.** We have used what the Examiner called a 'freeform' approach, simply identifying areas that are reasonably obviously in need of improvement, based on our discussion of strategic challenges.
>
> Of these, perhaps the most obvious are:
>
> - Computer aided production to cut costs
> - Wide variation in site profitability

Qualispecs is fortunate in that its finances are sound and it has large cash reserves. It would be appropriate to use some of that financial strength to make investments that will improve the company's competitive position. Qualispecs should seek improvements in three main areas of its operations.

- **Innovation**
- **Performance management**
- **Distribution**

Innovation

Two areas are ripe for innovation: products and production methods. In both areas, Qualispecs has to catch up with its competitors. The economic downturn means that growth will be most easily achieved in the 18-30 year old market. Fashion-consciousness is important here, so the design and variety of prescription spectacles and sunglasses must be improved. At the same time, suitable promotion must be undertaken, perhaps making use of sports star endorsement.

Production methods must be examined for opportunities to reduce cost and improve efficiency. The one hour laboratory approach should be considered, as discussed below.

In addition to these two matters, it would be appropriate for Qualispecs to begin to foster a culture of innovation. Given its existing stagnation, there are almost certainly several other aspects of its operation that would benefit from new ideas. Such cultural change is linked to our next area of consideration.

Performance management

We mentioned performance management in our earlier discussion of key strategic challenges. The principle could also be applied in the form of management bonuses based on the overall performance individual shops and regions and individual pay increases and bonuses related to sales and profit performance. Such a change would require greater autonomy for managers at shop level in particular if it were to have significant effect, so there would have to be some delegation of control over such matters as working conditions, job roles and pay rates.

Distribution

Qualispecs must do something about the wide variation in its shops' performance. A careful examination of costs and revenues is needed. There is also a need to look at the shops estate from a marketing point of view. The estate may be in need of renovation or even complete redesign. The company should aim to make its shops pleasant and interesting places to visit. Fastglass has entered into partnership with a high-street shopping group. This may be an innovation that Qualispecs could imitate as part of its attention to product development. A fashion retailer would be a good choice of partner for a new group of in-store shops concentrating on the new designer styles, for example. A partnership approach to costs and revenues may be possible and appropriate.

Qualispecs must also examine the Fastglass mini-lab approach with an open mind. This method may be worth adopting, assuming the technology is not protected, but caution should be employed: a full examination of costs and market prospects should be carried out and implications fully explored.

7 Question with answer plan: Digwell

Text reference. The topics mentioned in this answer are discussed in Chapter 5 of your BPP Study Text.

Top tips. Ethics is the study of concepts of right and wrong. Business ethics is the application of ethical ideas to business. It is doubtful whether this question is actually about *ethics* at all. Looked at objectively, the question is about conflicts of interest rather than notions of right and wrong.

Nevertheless, some pressure groups will always attempt to occupy the moral high ground – and public opinion tends to allow them to do so, often in defiance of rational analysis. Environmental pressure groups are among the worst offenders here, and it is well to be aware of the threat they constitute to some legitimate business operations.

All that being said, you are unlikely to be given any marks for discussing the failings of the question. Proceed as though it made perfect sense.

Easy marks. There are two important areas to consider: environmental protection and the right of communities affected by business externalities to be heard and to have their views considered. However, to obtain a pass mark, you should have to explore the implications of the various points of view in some detail, rather than just asserting a particular opinion.

Answer plan

Part (a)

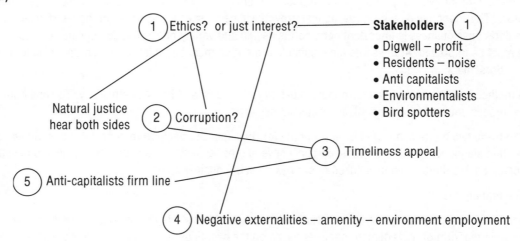

Part (b)

1   Explain Mendelow's map and uses
2   Classify groups and suggest response

A	B Eastborough Alliance Wildlife Anti capitalists Residents Greens
C	D Government

Part (a)

> **Top tips.** Bearing in mind our introductory comments above, it is probably best to avoid too much use of the word 'ethics' here. Think, rather, in terms of 'stakeholder interest'.

This scenario may be summed up as a fairly routine conflict of **environmental amenity against economic activity**. This is a continuing thorn in the side of governments: they are expected both to increase prosperity and to promote environmental improvement. The two goals are not incompatible, but they are difficult to reconcile.

On the one hand we have Digwell proposing to make profit, provide opportunity for the unemployed and generally invigorate the local economy. On the other, we have a loose grouping of interests: local residents afraid of noise, dirt and congestion; wildlife protectors concerned about the effect of the proposed scheme on the rare birds; a vaguer group of presumably all-purpose 'environmentalists' and the lunatic fringe of anti-capitalist activists.

We are not told what matters the government considered when granting permission for mining, nor what representations it heard from those opposed to the mining proposal, but we might hope that it has proceeded in a **transparent** and **even-handed** way.

First and most important, there should be no question that the decision was the result of **corruption**. Some companies and some governments are known to collaborate in a corrupt fashion: money changes hands, favours are done, invoices are adjusted and so on. If there has been any of that sort of thing here, it can be dismissed out of hand as not only unethical but also illegal in all modern jurisdictions.

When considering a decision of this type, a government should apply the basic rules of natural justice and, in particular, **hear both sides**. Extensive opportunities should be given to objectors to state their cases and there should be a right of appeal against the initial decision.

In the UK, the laws relating to planning would cover this matter only too well: the appeals and public hearings could continue indefinitely. We might propose as a matter of principle that the whole process should be not merely impartial and transparent but **timely** as well.

The case for Digwell is that the Eastborough region is suffering from a long-standing **deficit of investment**. Unemployment is high, the infrastructure is poor and there is a general lack of amenity that is hampering the development of tourism. Digwell's scheme will provide jobs and boost tax receipts, making regional improvements easier to finance. Digwell may even undertake to fund some local improvements directly as an incentive to acceptance of its scheme.

The case against Digwell is less clear-cut.

Some local residents are concerned about traffic and noise. These are presumably the ones who have jobs already and can afford to worry about amenity. We might imagine the local long-term unemployed to be less concerned. Nevertheless, the concerned residents have a valid point and one that should be considered. Digwell should be expected to proceed in a way that would **minimise the negative externalities** of their operations.

Wildlife protection representatives are concerned about the rare birds. Their interest is legitimate and can be accommodated in the same way.

The all-purpose 'environmentalists' are a dubious quantity. Such groups tend to object to any development **on principle** and to **manipulate public opinion** unscrupulously. The fact that their position is usually untenable on rational analysis does not deter them. The environmentally undesirable outcome of their interference in the *Brent Spar* problem is a case in point. Such groups can have an impact out of all proportion to their numbers: the validity of their case must be assessed realistically and they must be dealt with firmly.

The views of the anti-capitalist groups may be dismissed without further ado and the advice of London's police sought if they attempt to cause trouble.

Part (b)

> **Text reference.** The topics mentioned in this answer are discussed in Chapter 5 of your BPP Study Text.
>
> **Top tips.** The obvious model here is *Mendelow's* matrix. This is a very simple analysis, but the Examiner remarked that a common error was to fail to relate it to the scenario, with stakeholders being placed in the wrong quadrant. A further common error was to fail to identify how Digwell might respond to the various groups,
>
> We have taken a firm line on this last point, as we did in part (a). Be aware that it would be quite in order to argue for a softer line, but a good answer to this sort of question really requires that you take a position and do not rely on generalities and vague possibilities.

Mendelow classifies stakeholders on a matrix whose axes are **power held** and **likelihood of showing an interest** in the organisation's activities. These factors will help define the type of relationship the organisation should seek with its stakeholders.

Level of interest

	Low	High
Low (Power)	A	B
High (Power)	C	D

(a) **Key players** are found in segment D: strategy must be *acceptable* to them, at least. An example would be a major customer.

(b) Stakeholders in **segment C** must be treated with care. While often passive, they are capable of moving to segment D. They should, therefore be **kept satisfied.** Large institutional shareholders might fall into segment C.

(c) Stakeholders in **segment B** do not have great ability to influence strategy, but their views can be important in influencing more powerful stakeholders, perhaps by lobbying. They should therefore be **kept informed.** Community representatives and charities might fall into segment B.

(d) Minimal effort is expended on **segment A**.

Stakeholder mapping is used to assess the significance of stakeholder groups. This in turn has implications for the organisation.

(a)   The framework of **corporate governance** should recognise stakeholders' levels of interest and power.

(b)   It may be appropriate to seek to **reposition** certain stakeholders and discourage others from repositioning themselves, depending on their attitudes.

(c)   Key **blockers** and **facilitators** of change must be identified.

Stakeholder mapping can also be used to establish political priorities. A map of the current position can be compared with a map of a desired future state. This will indicate critical shifts that must be pursued.

A matrix of this type could be useful to Digwell in analysing its relationships with the various groups concerned with its Eastborough operations.

Shareholders as a body probably have low interest in the Eastborough project. They can probably be kept satisfied by careful public relations effort.

The **government** is a particularly important stakeholder as far as *Digwell's* project is concerned. Permission for mining has been granted, but governments are quite capable of betraying trusts of this type if the environmental alarm is sounded. The UK government's change of heart over the dismantling of US Navy freighters in 2003 is a case in point. The government has almost absolute power and can be provoked into deep interest by bad publicity. It belongs in quadrant D. Digwell must manage its relations with government carefully, paying particular attention to how its project is presented in the mass media: modern governments are unhealthily concerned with short-term image and opinion.

The **Eastborough Protection Alliance** is a classic quadrant B player. Its level of interest is high but it has little power of its own. However, it may exert considerable influence upon government, as outlined above. Digwell's obvious tactic for dealing with this group is to **divide and rule**. If one or more of the member factions can be neutralised, the arguments against Digwell will become less coherent and convincing.

(a)   The **economic benefits** of the project should be emphasised to local residents, perhaps sweetened with the offer of some desirable local facility, such as a general clean up of the beaches and older mine workings. At the same time, a spokesperson might be found to put the case for the improved prospects for the local unemployed and decry the selfishness of those who oppose the project.

(b)   The **wildlife groups** should be treated with respect: Digwell should be prepared to make any modifications to its plans necessary to **protect** the rare birds. This will be rewarded with further public approval.

(c)   The approach to the **environmentalists** will depend on the strength, if any, of their case. If they are the usual doom-mongers, an impartial environmental impact assessment may limit their opposition to nuisance value only. If there are genuine reasons for environmental concern, Digwell should proceed as for the wildlife groups. However, a robust approach is needed to ensure that a kind of creeping veto does not develop.

(d)   Taken by themselves, the anti-capitalists are at the lowest end of the power spectrum. If the local community and wildlife groups can be separated from them, they too will have nuisance value only.

8 MegaMart

Part (a)

> **Text reference.** The topics mentioned in this answer are discussed in Chapter 5 of your BPP Study Text.
>
> **Top tips.** The term 'management style' might put you in mind of models of management behaviour such as those developed by *Blake and Mouton*, *Rensis Likert* or *Tannenbaum and Schmidt*. This was not what the Examiner had in mind. This question is entirely about corporate governance, but it would have been clearer if the words 'management style' had been replaced by the single word 'conduct'.
>
> That said, the scenario gives a pretty clear account of several very significant failures of corporate governance and it should be easy for you to write them up.
>
> Make sure you do not leave yourself with nothing to say about non-executive directors in part (b).
>
> **Easy marks.** Rex Lord's transgressions are pretty blatant, so you should have no difficulty in securing one or two marks at least for each of the main issues we deal with in our answer.
>
> **Examiner's comments.** This was a popular question. Candidates from outside the UK gave particularly good accounts of the issues involved.

Marking scheme

		Marks
(a)	Identification of main issues:	up to 3 marks each
	Chairman and Chief Executive roles combined	
	Remuneration packages	
	Monitoring and control	
	Role and independence of auditors	
	Communication	
		Maximum 15 marks
(b)	Strategic v scrutiny role	up to 3 marks each
	Source of independent thinking	
	Role on executive remuneration	
	Involvement in audit committee	
	'Corporate conscience' on corporate social responsibility	
		Maximum 10 marks
		Total 25 marks

Rex Lord has been using MegaMart plc as a vehicle to **pursue his own ends**, thus depriving the shareholders and other stakeholders of their legitimate expectations. In order to do this he has contravened several well-established **rules of corporate governance** that are incorporated in, for example, the London Stock Exchange Combined Code.

Leading management roles

There are **two leading management roles**: running the Board and running the company. There should be a clear division of responsibilities so that there is a balance of power and no single person has unfettered powers of decision-making. Rex Lord's clear **exploitation of his power** illustrates why this is a good rule.

Non-executive directors

Non-executive directors (NEDs) are dealt with more fully in Part (b). Here it suffices to say that there should be a **strong and independent** body of NEDs with a recognised senior member other than the Chairman. MegaMart does not have this.

Directors' remuneration

Remuneration levels should be sufficient to attract directors of sufficient calibre, but companies should not pay more than is necessary. Directors should not be involved in setting their own remuneration. A **remuneration committee**, staffed by independent NEDs, should determine specific remuneration packages.

Quite clearly, MegaMart has failed to conform with these requirements as far as Rex Lord's remuneration is concerned.

Communication with shareholders

Rex Lord has appears to have failed to abide by the rule that companies should be prepared to communicate directly with **institutional shareholders** and to use the AGM as a means of communication with **private investors**.

Auditors

There are two significant threats to the **independence of the auditors** that should be reviewed both by them and by MegaMart's audit committee (which should be made up of NEDs). The first is that having been in post for 20 years, there is a danger that the auditors have become **complacent and even acquiescent** in their relationship with Rex Lord. In any event, it is necessary that the partner in charge of the audit is changed after a maximum of five years.

The second threat is associated with the provision of services other than audit. This is called **management risk** and is the risk that the auditors effectively act in a management role, doing things that should be reserved to the directors and managers of the company.

Compliance with the Stock Exchange Combined Code

As a quoted company, MegaMart should include in its financial statements a narrative report of how it applied the **principles** of the Combined Code and a statement as to whether it complied with its **specific provisions**. We are not told whether or not this was done, but it was, it must have made interesting reading.

Part (b)

> **Text reference.** The topics mentioned in this answer are discussed in Chapter 5 of your BPP Study Text.
>
> **Top tips.** The Examiner intended you to talk in general terms about the wider role of NEDs in your answer to this part of the question, basing his own suggested solution on an article that had recently appeared in the ACCA magazine.
>
> **Examiner's comments.** It is easy to find yourself repeating points you have already made in your answer to part (a).

Quoted companies such as MegaMart should have a body of NEDs: the **Hampel report** suggested that they should make up at least one third of the board. As already mentioned, these directors should form both the **audit** and **remuneration committees**. All members of the remuneration committee and a majority of the audit committee should be independent NEDs.

NEDs have much to offer the company in addition to these prescribed roles.

They should bring to their role **wide experience of business** and possibly of organisations in other spheres. This should enable them to give **good strategic advice** to the board as a whole and to individual directors, possibly in a mentoring role.

They should be alert for the emergence of problems with an **ethical dimension** or issues of **corporate social responsibility**. Independent NEDs, in particular, should be able to act as a kind of **conscience** for the board as a whole.

NEDs may have a valuable role to play in the **selection and appointment of new board members**, particularly in the case of the Chairman and the Chief Executive.

Recent improvements in corporate governance have led to the emergence of a significant body of NEDs in UK business. There is a common perception that this is something of a **charmed circle** and that many supposedly independent NEDs are in fact nothing of the sort, since they are drawn from the **same pool of senior managers** as their executive director colleagues. There is thus an imperative to widen the bounds of the portion of society from which NEDs are drawn.

9 Preparation question: Westport University

> **Text reference.** The topics mentioned in this answer are discussed in Chapter 3 of your BPP Study Text.
>
> **Top tips.** You may wonder, on examining this part of the question, just what marketing strategy is and how it differs from ordinary strategy. Well, clearly, for 10 marks you don't have to be too abstruse. Nor does the scenario give you enough information to build up an answer in terms of *Porter's* generic strategies, for instance, or *Ansoff's* product market vector. The examiner's suggested solution simply considers the Faculty's proposed project in terms of the 4 Ps of the basic marketing mix. This solution could have been improved by including the other 3 Ps of the extended marketing mix, as we do, since they are relevant to **services** and that is what the Faculty provides, after all.
>
> Don't forget that the elements of the marketing mix must be consistent with one another.
>
> This was originally part of an ACCA exam question set some years ago. It was worth ten marks.

Marketing strategies

Product. Unfortunately, the examining bodies have different syllabuses and, though there is great similarity in total coverage, there is wide variation between individual examinations. We shall thus have to decide whether or not to provide courses for more than one set of examinations to begin with. This will depend in part on the size of the potential markets involved.

Our greatest opportunity to add value probably comes from the provision of lectures, since that is what we are best equipped to do. However, we must carefully consider course design, in the light of our market research. Part time courses, including day release and evening classes, may be most appropriate at first. Commercial providers tend to have two types of short course: teaching and revision. We should aim to do the same.

Place. The location of our courses must also be decided. It would be cheapest to use our own premises, but part-time courses may prove more popular if we can take them to the student by establishing local venues.

Price. We probably need to be competitive in our pricing. Many students fund themselves and employers who pay for training are likely to be equally price-conscious. If we are convinced of our excellence we may be able to justify a price premium, but we will be judged by results. At the moment we do not have much experience of the demands of the examinations.

Promotion. This would be a new venture for us and we would need effective promotion to get it off the ground. We must apply the same standards of decorum and academic appropriateness to this project as to any other of our activities. To be effective, our promotion and the media we use must be carefully targeted. Advertisements in the journals aimed at accountancy students will be a good starting point, supplemented by information on the University website and, possibly, direct mail.

People. People are fundamental to marketing services. The members of our target market are older than our undergraduates and likely to be more demanding of lecturers. If they are not satisfied they will vote with their feet.

Process. Similar considerations apply to processes and particularly to administration. Our existing enrolment system, for example, is used to dealing with a bulge of work before the commencement of the academic year. If we are to run short courses, enrolment queries must be dealt with throughout the year.

Physical evidence. Since education is so very intangible, it may be worth considering the provision of physical evidence. An obvious example would be the provision of course notes. A standard textbook written by a member of our staff would be almost too good to be true.

Conclusion. It is important that decisions about these matters are not taken in isolation. If we are to go ahead with this project, I suggest that a marketing committee be formed and charged with responsibility for ensuring that our plans form a coherent whole.

10 Ashkol Furniture

Part (a)

Text reference. The topics mentioned in this answer are discussed in Chapter 3 of your BPP Study Text.

Top tips. This is an important question simply because it deals with marketing. Students often discount the importance of marketing, possibly because they do not understand how it fits into the wider field of business strategy. Make sure you have read the appropriate sections in your BPP Study Text.

You will notice that we make some comments that are relevant to Salim's particular problems, such as our remarks about shipping in bulk. We have no particular knowledge of the furniture industry, but we are able to make such comments on the basis of general commercial awareness. You must attempt to cultivate this awareness by reading the quality business press. *The Economist* and, in the UK, the *Financial Times* are good places to start.

Easy marks. That very simple model, the marketing mix, would form the basis of a good answer to this requirement.

Examiner's comments. Many candidates were unable to answer in terms of marketing practice at all.

Salim needs to develop a marketing strategy for entry into the domestic market in Europe. This can be achieved by looking at the factors that make up the **marketing mix**: product, price, place and promotion. The design of the marketing mix should be decided on the basis of management intuition and judgement, together with information provided by market research. Elements in the marketing mix partly act as substitutes for each other and they must be **integrated**. The product needs to be positioned to appeal to the target customer. For example, Ashkol would struggle to develop a luxury brand image if they set price at a low, penetration level.

The physical **product** needs to be appropriate for the private household market. Office furniture may have a very different style to household furniture, so a different approach may need to be taken to the design of the product in order to make it appealing for the domestic buyer. For example, it may need to be smaller and made of better quality material. The space available in domestic accommodation is likely to be quite restricted, so some standard items may not sell well simply because they are too large. Multi-purpose items, such as desks that incorporate filing drawers and PC monitor stands may be required.

Place deals with how the product is distributed, and how it reaches its customers. Establishing a suitable distribution system is going to be one of Salim's largest tasks. His products are bulky and will therefore have to be transported by ship from India to Europe, probably in ISO containers, which will impose a minimum economic scale of shipment. Serious consideration will have to be given to how customers will be able to view, order and receive delivery of the products. Furniture showrooms are necessarily large areas and need to be in areas where customers will be attracted. Even if selling is by direct mail or over the Internet, there will probably have to be a warehouse to receive bulk shipments from India, break them down and despatch individual orders. All this has major cost implications, perhaps offsetting the cost savings from cheaper labour. These considerations alone may push Salim towards a co-operative venture with a European agent who knows the market and is prepared to take on the selling and distribution task.

Promotion involves arousing attention, generating interest, inspiring desire and initiating action. Marketing communication involved in this could be advertising, public relations, direct selling or sales promotion. A furniture showroom would be part of this but a wider approach will be needed. The target market is people working from home and the promotional methods used should be appropriate to this market. Direct promotion *via* mailing lists may be appropriate; there are numerous home style magazines in which adverts could be placed; the Internet is a vital part of the life of people working from home and its potential for promotion should be fully utilised, perhaps by setting up a dedicated website. Organising and designing the marketing communication effort will almost certainly require input from someone familiar with the European market

Price is the final element of the marketing mix and is an important signal to customers about the product. It is important that the price should be competitive but also synonymous with the quality of the product. Discounts and payment terms need to be considered as a potential way of attracting customers.

Part (b)

Because of limited resources, competition and large markets, organisations are not usually able to sell with equal efficiency and success to every market segment. It is necessary to select **target markets**. A target market is a particularly attractive segment that will be served with a distinct marketing mix.

While Salim's products may have some application for commercial users, he intends to sell them to consumers, who will view them as **shopping goods**. These goods have a higher unit value than convenience goods and are bought less frequently, usually after some thought and consideration have been expended. Salim should try to **specify the segment** of the customer market into which he wishes to sell his products with some care, since this will influence important decisions about all the elements of the marketing mix, including such things as product design, marketing communications, price, and distribution methods.

Kotler identified six steps in segmentation, targeting and positioning .

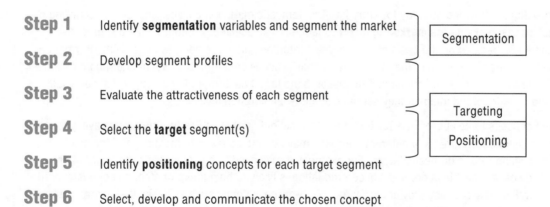

Step 1	Identify **segmentation** variables and segment the market
Step 2	Develop segment profiles
Step 3	Evaluate the attractiveness of each segment
Step 4	Select the **target** segment(s)
Step 5	Identify **positioning** concepts for each target segment
Step 6	Select, develop and communicate the chosen concept

Segmentation variables fall into a small number of categories. Geographical segmentation is very simple, but can usefully be combined with socio-demographic segmentation.

Psychographic segmentation is not based on objective data so much as how people see themselves and their **subjective** feelings and attitudes towards a particular product or service, or towards life in general. The **behavioural** approach segments buyers into groups based on their attitudes to and use of the product, and the **benefits** they expect to receive. Both of these methods are most useful for convenience goods and are not, therefore likely to be very useful to Salim.

Probably the best segmentation approach for Salim is **socio-demographic** segmentation, which is based on social, economic and demographic variables such as education, income, occupation, family size and social class. Much work has already been done on this approach, in the ACORN system, for example, and Salim would be able to buy in the basic information he needs.

A market segment will only be valid if it is worth designing and developing a **unique marketing mix** for that specific segment. Salim will have to be sure of several things about his chosen target market. Is it large enough to be profitable? Can communicate with the potential customers? Will it enable him to build on the company's strengths?

It is important to assess company strengths when evaluating attractiveness and targeting a market. This can help determine the appropriate strategy, because once the attractiveness of each identified segment has been assessed it can be considered along with relative strengths to determine the potential advantages the organisation would have. In this way preferred segments can be targeted.

It is unlikely that Salim will be able to identify a market segment where there is no direct competitor, so it will be necessary to **position the product** line in such a way as to create of some form of **product differentiation**. The aim is to make the customer perceive the product as different from its competitors. An aid to this is to try to **identify gaps in the market** by considering the mix of product attributes such as price, applications, users, occasions for use and specific aspects of quality. may be drawn to refine knowledge of product position.

11 Helen's Cakes

Part (a)

Text reference. The topics mentioned in this answer are discussed in Chapter 3 of your BPP Study Text.

Top tips. It is a general principle of Paper P3 that you do not need any industry-specific technical knowledge to be able to answer any examination question that might be set. However, you do need an **understanding of the way a modern economy works** and an intelligent **awareness of the main characteristics of its more visible industries**. You can achieve this awareness and understanding from your own economic interactions and from the **business pages of the quality press**.

It should not be difficult for you to make sensible remarks about the **consumer interface** with most industries, in particular, and so in a question like this, you should be aware, for example, of how supermarkets operate and the way they use their purchasing power to dominate their suppliers.

The question asks for a short report. There is unlikely to be more than one mark available for report format (if that) so do not waste time on an ornate layout for your answer.

Easy marks. Your basic knowledge about batch sizes, branding and costs should enable you to say something relevant about each of the options.

Examiner's comments. Do not end a report with your own real name! Your exam script must be anonymous.

Marking scheme

		Marks
(a)	Market entry strategy: advantages and disadvantages	
	Premium cake shop market	up to 6 marks
	Supermarkets	up to 6 marks
	Catering wholesalers	up to 6 marks
		Maximum 15 marks
(b)	Marketing mix: premium market	up to 4 marks
	Supermarkets	up to 4 marks
	Catering wholesalers	up to 4 marks
		Maximum 10 marks
		Total 25 marks

Sharpe and Keene
Business consultants

Report: 'Helen's Cakes'

Dear Ms Bradshaw

You have been considering starting to supply cakes to three different types of customer: supermarkets, catering wholesalers and cake shops. You asked us to advise you on the advantages and disadvantages of each potential market from the point of view of your new business.

Supermarkets

In general terms, supermarkets like to sell goods in high volumes. Hygiene and freshness in food products are very important, but long shelf life, uniform attractive appearance and reliability of supply are probably more important than excellence of flavour.

Supplying a supermarket could give excellent visibility to your brand. You would probably be required to deliver to a central depot, which would minimise your distribution costs. However, the supermarket route is probably impractical for a number of reasons.

Generally speaking, supermarkets require supply of branded goods in large volumes: this would offer economies of scale to a large producer, but you do not have the productive capacity necessary to supply on the required scale, even if you severely restrict the range you offer.

Supermarkets are very aggressive on price and aim to cut their suppliers' margins to the absolute minimum. They are also likely to demand extended periods of credit. As a start-up, your business is unlikely to achieve the production efficiencies necessary for survival under such conditions.

The early development of an own-brand range of cakes would put downward pressure on your margins, since the supermarket would aim to sell these cakes at a lower price than your own brand. This would also undermine sales of your own brand cakes. A likely outcome of this scenario is that you would be reduced to being one supplier among many, since the supermarket would demand ownership of the intellectual property rights in their own-brand cakes.

Catering wholesalers

Catering wholesalers will supply both shops and catering establishments such as hotels and tearooms: the former could give **good exposure to your brand**, since they would sell your cakes in their branded packaging, but the latter would not.

Wholesalers are likely to want **large batches of a small number of products**. This may reduce your production costs, though this effect would be limited if your premises and equipment placed a limit on the maximum batch size you could achieve. As with the supermarkets, your **distribution effort** would be limited, but, equally, you may not be able to **produce in the quantities** the wholesalers require.

Also, wholesalers seeking volume sales may not be interested in your **aspirations for a quality brand**: they will be unwilling to pay the necessary price premium and may sell your products into sales outlets that you might not wish them to be seen in. Like the supermarkets, they may be more interested in a long shelf life than in freshness. You may find yourself **trapped into producing an inferior, mass-market product** rather than the distinctive, quality cakes you wish to offer.

Premium cake shops

The premium cake shop market offers you the opportunity to build your brand and add value by combining **differentiation through quality** with **distinctive packaging**. This should enable you to charge higher prices.

You will be able to build up your business in a managed way, operating on a **scale that suits your resources** without pressure to produce in large quantities; this will also assist you in maintaining the high standards you wish to set. However, you may find that your customers require a **wide variety of cakes in small numbers**, which may be challenging in terms of scheduling and the most effective use of your equipment, as well as having the potential to reduce your overall margin if you cannot achieve **economical batch sizes**. You may have to insist on minimum order quantities for some products.

Your **distribution costs** will be higher because you will have to deliver to each shop individually; perhaps the most important aspect of this would be the cost in terms of your own time (assuming you do not employ an assistant, which would, of course be an extra variable cost for your business).

Part (b)

> **Text reference.** The topics mentioned in this answer are discussed in Chapter 4 of your BPP Study Text.
>
> **Top tips.** This part of the question is worth ten marks: it is not very challenging and we need to deal with it briskly. However, using the four elements of the basic marketing mix and considering the three possible market options, we have the potential for **twelve separate small discussions**, some of which may well be more or less identical.
>
> A possible way to proceed here would be to use a **tabulation**, which is, in part, what the Examiner's own suggested solution does. However, you would have to exercise some caution with this approach: if you are to produce a neat and legible table you need to have a good idea of how much writing is going to go into each cell, which might be difficult without trying it out first. This would be unacceptably time consuming, so a simple narrative broken up by headings is probably the best way to present your answer.

Supermarket

Product: hygiene and product integrity are paramount, followed closely by shelf life and consistency and attractiveness of appearance; quality must be good. Volumes required will be large.

Price: is likely to be settled in very unequal bargaining with purchaser.

Promotion for the 'Helen's cakes' brand is likely to be limited to packaging; the supermarket's own brand will benefit from the company's generic promotions.

Place: distribution is likely to be to the purchaser's own depot with their own logistics taking over thereafter.

Wholesalers

Product: as for supermarket, though generally lower quality may be preferred and volumes may be lower.

Price: probably a little less disadvantageous than with supermarkets, especially if 'pull' from catering establishments can be created by promotion.

Promotion: there will probably be opportunities to promote the 'Helen's cakes' brand through packaging and personal selling, but the main sales effort will probably be to the wholesalers' buyers.

Place: as for supermarket.

Premium outlets

Product: all aspects of quality will be of great importance. A wide and innovative range will be an advantage and volumes both overall and for each product are likely to be manageable.

Price: to some extent price can reflect quality, bearing in mind the priorities of the ultimate consumers. Premium cake shops will be pleased to stock expensive products with high margins if they can sell them. If cakes are sold under the Helen's cakes brand, it will be necessary to guard against undermining of brand values by discounting: recommended retail prices should be established.

Promotion: word of mouth may be enough initially, perhaps combined with providing cakes for free trials in the shops. Eventually, a co-operative approach to promotion involving the shops may be appropriate, with the use of discreet point of sale material.

Place: it will be necessary to make individual deliveries to multiple outlets; accuracy of order-taking and delivery will be important if good relations are to be maintained with the shops concerned.

12 Focus Bank

Text reference. The topics mentioned in this answer are discussed in Chapter 4 of your BPP Study Text.

Top tips. Outsourcing and core competences are so closely linked conceptually that it is very difficult to answer the two parts of this question separately. This illustrates the importance of reading all the requirements of a question before starting to answer it. Only in this way can you ensure that you make your points in the correct place.

It is necessary to read the scenario for this question quite carefully. Note that it is Focus Bank's *own* call centres that have been more efficient and given better customer service, while the (presumably not yet complete) process of *off-shoring* call-centre activity has led to complaints of reduced customer service.

Easy marks. In part (b) the Examiner seems to have been looking for evidence of understanding of what core competences are and an appreciation of the resource-based theory of competitive advantage.

Examiner's comments. Candidates found that part (b) of the question was more difficult than part (a).

| Marking scheme |

		Marks
(a)	Advantages of outsourcing customer services:	up to 2 per point
	Cost savings	
	Improved productivity	
	Focus on core competences	
	Service quality improvements	
	Disadvantages of customer services outsourcing:	up to 2 per point
	Loss of control	
	Loss of core competence	
	Bargaining power reduced	
	Reversal of policy difficult	
	Staff morale	
		Maximum 17 marks
(b)	Differentiated customer service	up to 4
	Value chain/process improvement	up to 4
		Maximum 8 marks
		Total 25 marks

Part (a)

Outsourcing has always been a feature of business life. It is the natural way to fit a business into the **upstream supply chain**, for both goods and services. 'Make or buy' is a classic cost accounting problem. Also, it has long been used by businesses too small to be able to establish in-house sources of **highly specialised or expensive goods and services** such as legal services and safety equipment

More recently, in an increasingly competitive and globalised business environment, outsourcing has become popular largely because it holds out the promise of **reduced costs**. Cost reductions become possible for two main reasons. First, the provider may be able to achieve **economies of scale** by concentrating some aspect of the production or service process. Second, particularly in work employing low-skilled labour, a major employer is better placed to exert **downward pressure on wage rates** than are a large number of businesses employing a few staff each, especially when casual, part-time or temporary work patterns predominate.

A further potential advantage is the **increased effectiveness** that can arise from **greater specialisation**. This can be achieved both by the supplier, who concentrates on a particular type of work, and by the purchaser, whose executives are liberated from the management of peripheral activities.

Focus Bank seems to be in the middle of outsourcing its call-centre operation and is wondering how far to take it. It could certainly expect to achieve the **cost reductions** mentioned above. It is now quite common for call centre work to be outsourced to countries with lower labour costs, such as India. However, there have been complaints from customers about **poor service**, so the potential for improved efficiency has not yet been achieved. This may illustrate an important disadvantage of outsourcing, which is the potential for **loss of control** of the work involved.

The significance of this loss extends beyond concerns about quality. There is also a loss of managerial expertise relating to the outsourced function or activity. This means that when changes occur in the market or the environment, it may be much more difficult to plan a suitable response. It will be necessary to consult with the service providers concerned and, naturally enough, they will have their own priorities that affect their stance.

The customer dissatisfaction and staff union resistance illustrate a further disadvantage to outsourcing, which is its potential for generating **stakeholder concern**. It is natural enough that staff union organisers should be opposed to anything that threatens their members' livelihood and their own status. Managing this opposition would be difficult enough; when customers find a reason to be sympathetic to the unions' stand, the Bank is likely to find itself having to adjust its policy.

Stakeholder concern about outsourcing was of particular importance to *British Airways* in 2005, when a dispute arose at *Gate Gourmet*, its Heathrow in-flight catering supplier. Gate Gourmet had, in fact, been spun off from BA some years previously. The dispute caused extensive delays to BA flights out of Heathrow, not merely because of disruption to catering supplies, but because BA's baggage handlers, many of whom were related to Gate Gourmet staff, stopped work in sympathy.

Part (b)

A modern approach to strategic management called **resource based theory** has been widely accepted. Its basic premise is at odd with more traditional theories, collectively known as **positioning theory**, which see strategy as a process of **adaptation to the environment**.

Resource based theory argues that such adaptation is available to all businesses and **cannot, therefore, create a unique competitive advantage**: that is only made possible by the possession of **unique resources**. Such resources include, for example, protected intellectual property or exclusive access to a raw material. More probably in today's complex developed economies, such a unique resource may reside in the **skills and experience** of the people working in the business. *Enron*, in its early days, for example, developed a particular competence in energy trading. Such collective skills and abilities constitute the business's **core competences.**

Hamel and Prahalad suggest that a **core competence** must have three qualities.

- It must make a **disproportionate** contribution to the **value** the customer perceives.

- It must be '**competitively unique**', which means one of three things: actually unique; superior to competitors; or capable of dramatic improvement.

- It must be **extendable**, in that it must allow for the development of an array of new products and services.

A core competence is not a strategy in itself. However, it can form a basis for a strategy. Here it is important to reiterate that a core competence must be difficult to imitate if it is to confer lasting competitive advantage. In particular, skills that can be bought in are unlikely to form the basis of core competences, since competitors would be able to buy them in just as easily.

Focus Bank might therefore benefit from a clear understanding of its own core competences when considering its overall strategy. A particularly fundamental and fairly obvious application of the concept is that no attempt should be made to outsource activities that constitute core competences; that is an obvious way to lose the advantage they confer, both through loss of control and as a result of atrophy of the competence within the organisation.

13 Preparation question with analysis: Global marketing

Text reference. The topics mentioned in this answer are discussed in Chapter 6 of your BPP Study Text.

Top tips. This was a complete question in an early Paper 3.5 exam. It is not sufficiently demanding to be representative of Paper P3. The key to the standardisation/customisation problem is market conditions. We have built our answer to part (b) on the PEST framework. It might be worth considering the extent to which the five forces give some insight as well. For example, in an extremely competitive market, a standardised product simply might not work at all.

Easy marks. Global strategy is a topic that students often neglect. This is actually a very easy question, part (a) dealing with a very basic piece of theory and part (b) looking in a little more detail at its implications. However, you cannot write about even a simple matter if you have never heard of it. The part of the syllabus dealing with global strategy is important and should not be ignored.

Examiner's comments. This was the least popular of the questions in the exam. Part (a) was reasonably well done, but part (b) was generally disappointing.

Part (a)

REPORT

To:	Board of Directors
From:	Adrian Green, Marketing Department
Date:	December 200X
Subject:	International business orientation

Introduction

Perlmutter, identified four different approaches, or **orientations**, in the management of international business: ethnocentrism, polycentrism, geocentrism and regiocentrism.

Ethnocentrism

Ethnocentrism is a **home country orientation**; the company focuses on its domestic market and views exporting as a secondary activity. Differences between countries are ignored and the same marketing mix is used both at home and abroad. There is no local market research or local customisation; opportunities in overseas markets may not be fully exploited as a result.

Polycentrism

The principle of the polycentric approach is that it is necessary to **adapt the marketing mix to each local environment**. Each country is viewed as having unique conditions and requirements and, as a result, the product and marketing effort are totally customised. This can lead to increases in turnover, but the process of customisation precludes economies of scale and profits are unlikely to increase in proportion.

Geocentrism

A geocentric approach is based upon the assumption that there are **both similarities and differences between various countries' markets**. It accepts that there are areas where customisation is required but also areas where standardisation does not affect customer satisfaction and can be employed in order to reduce costs. Typical areas suitable for standardisation are research and development, hidden parts of products, such as internal mechanisms and the development of a global brand. This approach **'thinks globally, but acts locally'**. Regiocentrism is very similar to geocentrism, but applied to regions rather than to the whole world.

Conclusion

The key difference between the orientations of polycentric companies and geocentric companies is in the **balance** of their approach to standardisation. A polycentric approach sees localisation and customisation as paramount, whereas a geocentric orientation recognises the need for a balance between customisation and standardisation.

Part (b)

As the experience of Kirkbride Weston Inc has shown, although customisation has its benefits in terms of increased volume of sales, it will tend to reduce profits as additional costs are incurred. Therefore, careful consideration should be given to whether customisation is actually necessary in a given export market. This is really an aspect of **environmental analysis**.

Political factors

Political or legal factors can make customisation necessary. Many regimes have made essentially political demands, such as the requirement in some Arab countries that no mention is made of Israel. Product safety regulations also vary from country to country and can require product modification. Some countries use regulation as a form of barrier to imports.

Economic factors

The economic condition of the country must be considered. In wealthy, advanced countries, a luxury version of a product may be required whereas in less wealthy countries only a basic version of the product would be purchased. Indigenous products also have an effect: if they are very specific to the market, importers may have to customise their own products.

Social factors

Differentiation may be required in order to satisfy local taste and social or cultural needs. Demographic factors may also be important here, such matters as family size and integration and the role of women being very important in some countries.

Technological factors

The technological infrastructure of the country may also need to be taken into consideration. If this infrastructure is basic then products may be required to be longer lasting and more durable as there is less opportunity for servicing or repair. Products may have to be customised to deal with issues such as climatic conditions and the impact of the transportation infrastructure.

14 Lawson Engineering

Part (a)

Text reference. The topics mentioned in this answer are discussed in Chapter 4 of your BPP Study Text.

Top tips. Note the word 'significance' in requirement (a). You are must give a critical appreciation of Lawson Engineering's resources, not just explain what resource-based strategy is about. You can only do this by making regular reference to the facts given in the scenario.

One important point is that no matter how excellent Lawson Engineering's endowment of intangible assets may be, they will be of little importance if the company is not able to use them to generate superior financial results. Making clever, innovative and high performance products is, no doubt, a very good thing, but if it does not produce profits, it is more akin to a hobby than to a business.

Easy marks. Both requirements require an element of explanation of basic theory, which should be easy for the well-prepared candidate.

Marking scheme

		Marks
(a)	Explanation of resource based strategy	up to 3
	Identification and discussion of assets and capabilities	up to 2 per point
	Use of model(s)	up to 5
	Reasoned argument and conclusion	up to 6
		Maximum for section (a) 15 marks
(b)	Explanation and discussion of the balanced scorecard	up to 2 per point
		Maximum for section (b) 10 marks
		Total 25 marks

The importance of resources

The **positioning** approach to strategy is based on managing the business so as to best respond to the conditions existing in the business environment. This approach has been criticised for two main reasons.

(a)   Many business environments are **too complex and dynamic** to permit timely and effective analysis and response.

(b)   Once a market offering has been made, it is very easy for competitors to make **similar offerings**, thus rapidly eroding competitive advantage.

These problems lead to the development of a resource-based theory of strategy: this suggests that competitive advantage comes not from the achievement of a close fit with the environment but from the possession of **unique resources**. These resources may be tangible, as in the case of *De Beers* monopoly of diamonds, or, more typically in today's advanced service economies, they may be intangible and exist in such forms as knowledge, reputation and information. **Competences,** according to *Johnson, Scholes and Whittington,* are the activities and processes through which an organisation deploys its resources effectively.

An organisation must achieve at least a **threshold level** of competence in everything it does. Its **core competences** underpin its competitive advantage and are difficult for competitors to imitate or obtain. *Hamel and Prahalad* suggest that an important aspect of strategic management is the determination of the competences the company will require in the future in order to provide new benefits to customers. They say a core competence will have three benefits.

(a)   It will make a **disproportionate contribution to the value** the customer perceives.

(b)   It must be '**competitively unique**', which means one of three things: actually unique; superior to competitors; or capable of dramatic improvement.

(c)   It must be **extendable**, in that it must allow for the development of an array of new products and services.

Lawson Engineering seems to be well placed to build a resource-based strategy. It has **important intangible resources** in the form of its reputation for engineering excellence; its (presumably good) long-term relationships with its customers and suppliers; and its 'can do' philosophy. It has a number of patents for innovative products, indicating that its research and development effort is effective. Perhaps most significantly of all, it has made a practice of recruiting and developing **highly skilled engineers**. These factors seem to qualify under Hamel and Prahalad's three headings.

However, the company has a serious problem in that it is **not deploying these resources effectively**: despite continuing growth, its 'performance against traditional financial measures has been relatively modest'. From this statement we may suspect that Lawson Engineering has fallen into the error committed by so many British engineering-based companies. Engineering excellence is not sufficient. Innovative products must be marketed in a way that generates **satisfactory profit**, or the work is wasted. We are told that the company's products command premium prices, so, unless its cost accounting practices are inadequate, we must suspect that its costs themselves are **not under control** and are swallowing up too much of the gross margin.

The classic culprit would be the **cost of research and development**. Overspending on the development of the *RB211* engine led the original *Rolls-Royce* aero engine company into insolvency, for example. It may be that Lawson Engineering's R&D, while **effective**, as pointed out above, is not sufficiently **economical** in its use of resources. This is a failure of management to which Joe Lawson should pay close attention in the future.

A further possibility is that the products themselves are **over-engineered** and **over-specified**. This is another undesirable tradition in British engineering, known colloquially as 'brass plating'. **Value engineering** offers a solution here: products should be analysed to determine how cost could be reduced without affecting performance.

Whatever the actual reasons for Lawson Engineering's poor financial performance, it is the poor performance itself that makes its future uncertain and will worry potential investors. The company certainly has the potential for a successful resource-based strategy, but it has not developed the **core competences** required to exploit them properly. If it continues to be run in its present fashion, it is likely that it will find itself more and more unable to pay its way. Potential backers will only provide funds if they are convinced that Joe is able to manage the company in a way that provides a more acceptable rate of return on investment. If he cannot do this, they will look for other investment opportunities.

Part (b)

> **Text reference.** The topics mentioned in this answer are discussed in Chapter 7 of your BPP Study Text.
>
> **Top tips.** Explaining the four perspectives of the balanced scorecard is not going to be a route to a pass mark. You have to relate the technique to Lawson Engineering's situation.
>
> **Easy marks.** The classic advantage of a balanced scorecard approach is the emphasis it places on aspects of the business that may be under-resourced in the pursuit of return on investment.
>
> **Examiner's comments**. Only the better answers linked the theory of the balanced scorecard to the question setting.

In *Johnson, Scholes and Whittington's* analysis, the balanced scorecard is a direct, output-based control process.

Kaplan and Norton proposed their balanced scorecard approach to performance monitoring and control in order that **proper emphasis** should be laid on **business functions** that build **future performance**: they felt that reliance on a single financial measure such as return on investment was akin to flying an aircraft in cloud using only one instrument. If the four perspectives of the balanced scorecard are all monitored and attention paid to achieving equally good performance in all of them, the business should be well placed for continuing success.

This is not to say that financial performance is in some way discountable against performance in the other perspectives: a **vertical vector** can be seen to link the four perspectives together.

Perspective		*Measures*
Financial		ROCE
Customer		Relationships and loyalty
Internal business		Quality, efficiency and timeliness
Innovation and learning		Skills and processes

The **skills learned** and **processes developed** as a result of attention to the innovation and learning perspective support and enable **high standards of quality**, **efficiency** and **timeliness**, which are measured by the internal business process. These features help to develop the **good relationships** and **loyalty** that are in turn essential if financial performance is to be satisfactory.

Referring back to our discussion of the way things seem to be done at Lawson engineering, we might suspect that not enough attention has been paid to the **efficiency** aspect of the internal business perspective: a balanced scorecard approach, properly implemented might make that clear to Joe Lawson.

A further aspect of the balanced scorecard is the way it sees the organisation in terms of **outcomes** rather than **inputs**. Objectives are set and performance measured not in departmental or functional terms but in ways that **integrate important activities** that cut across traditional boundaries. The customer service perspective at Lawson Engineering ought to be just as relevant to the R&D activity as to the sales office, especially, for example, where customers look to the company to solve technical problems with innovative products. This orientation to outcomes means that there is a potential link between **activity based costing** and the use of a balanced scorecard.

This aspect can be seen as something of a disadvantage, since it can be very challenging for a **traditionally run organisation** such as Lawson Engineering to adjust its ideas about hierarchy and responsibility sufficiently to be able to use a balanced scorecard. Nevertheless, this is not so much a disadvantage of the technique as a disadvantage of running organisations in that kind of way. It does, however, mean that much work can be required in order to implement a balanced scorecard approach. Simply designing the measures to be used can be very difficult and assigning responsibility for the performance they measure even more so.

A further problem can arise when an organisation has a **complex mission**, as is likely to be the case, for example, in a not-for-profit organisation. In such an organisation there may be **several important stakeholder groups**, each with its own interests to promote and defend. The vertical vector described above may be absent and the financial perspective something to be satisfied rather than excelled at.

15 Preparation question with answer plan: grow or buy?

Top tips. This is an actual past exam question from the early days of Paper 3.5. However, it is not sufficiently demanding to qualify as of current exam standard. In today's exam, each of the requirements below might be worth about 8 marks.

Easy marks. The cost and price advantages of the proposed strategy are clear and discussing them would be worth three to five marks. The rest of the question revolves around the idea of competences and resource-based strategy. If you are happy with this, the marks are easy to get; if not, not.

Examiner's comments. Generally, a well answered question, though the phrase 'buy instead of grow' led some candidates to discuss the merits of internally generated growth and growth by acquisition, while part (b) was sometimes answered entirely in terms of outsourcing IT, with irrelevant matters such as data confidentiality being dragged in.

Answer plan

Part (a)

	3D	Investment needed
	2A	Increased profit margin
	1A	Site limits of growth – growth market
	C	Range of suppliers – not dependent on any
	3A	Wider product range
	2D	Capital cost
Poss D1	C	Selling skills – core competences
Conclusion	C	Return to growing

A = advantage D = disadvantage C = wider consideration

Note. This is a typical brainstorming list, supplemented by consideration of how to structure the answer by distinguishing advantages from disadvantages and putting them in a suitable order.

Part (b)

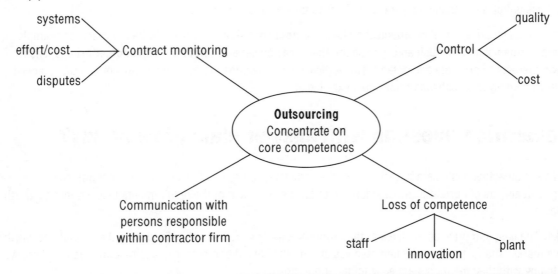

Part (a)

Greenfield Nurseries is currently profitable and growing. However, the **opportunities for additional growth are limited on the current site**. The options are either to acquire new land or to switch from the current strategy of growing in order to sell to distributors to one of buying plants from other suppliers to sell direct to the public. There are arguments both for and against this proposed new strategy.

Arguments for buying instead of growing

Probably the main argument for the proposed switch in strategy would be the **higher profit margins** that would be available. At the moment, Mark is unable to obtain good margins on his output because he is selling to commercial purchasers who will inevitably seek the best value for money they can achieve, squeezing Mark's margins against his production costs. By moving down the value chain, Mark could escape this price pressure, since garden centre products are 'lifestyle' rather than essential purchases and many customers are not particularly price-sensitive when making such purchases.

At the same time, Mark could reverse his current position. He would be buying from a number of specialist nurseries and could seek the best terms available. These could be lower than his own current production costs, especially where large suppliers are achieving greater economies of scale than he can in his existing scale of operations.

At the same time, Mark would have access to a **wider range of products** from general and specialist suppliers. This would enhance the attractiveness of his garden centre at little cost. He would be able to make use of his suppliers' expertise in cultivating delicate or exotic plants in that they would both produce saleable specimens for him and provide advice on how best to keep and display them.

Arguments against buying instead of growing

Perhaps the most persuasive argument against this strategy is that of **core competences**. At the moment, Mark and the Greenfield Nurseries staff have expertise in growing plants; they are not used to the processes involved in buying plants from other suppliers nor in selling to the general public. Not only would **working practices** have to change, but there may also be a **requirement for new staff** with selling rather than horticultural skills.

A further major hurdle is that Mark would have to finance considerable capital investment in order to convert the glasshouses into a suitable garden centre.

By buying plants from other suppliers rather than growing them, Greenfield risks losing a degree of control over the **quality** of the products that it sells. If poor quality products are sold to the public, this will reflect on Greenfield Nurseries rather than on the original supplier.

It could be argued that Greenfield Nurseries risks **disruption to its supplies** if it moves away from growing its own plants. However, as the intention is to buy from a number of suppliers, this is probably not a major problem. There might also be the fear that if Greenfield is not successful in this new retail operation it may not be able to re-enter the production market. However as the expertise, technology and capital cost requirements of production are fairly low, it should not be too difficult a task to re-enter the production market if required.

Part (b)

Outsourcing

Outsourcing enables organisations to concentrate resources on their **value-adding core activities**. Despite the popularity of this strategy, however, there are a number of problems that management may face when outsourcing.

One of the main problems is that of **lack of direct control**. If a function of a business is outsourced, its management lose direct managerial control over it. The danger is that this may result in a poor quality of service, which may require expense and time to remedy.

If outsourcing is to be used successfully, then management must negotiate carefully and set up **systems for review and monitoring** of the contract and the services provided under it. There must also be a system set up for **dealing with disputes** over quality or service.

A further potential problem related to lack of direct control is that of **responsibility**. If an activity is dealt with in-house, then there will be an individual who is directly responsible for that activity who will report to management on it. If there are problems, the individual responsible is clearly identifiable. However, if the activity is outsourced it may be harder to determine who is responsible in the outsourcing agency and therefore **disputes may be harder to settle**.

A further problem is the **loss of internal competences** that accompanies outsourcing. Staff may leave or be transferred, and those who remain will lose their skills. Plant and equipment also will be sold or transferred. Finally, this surrender of competence prevents further improvement in the outsourced function.

16 Salt and Soap

Text reference. The topics mentioned in this answer are discussed in Chapters 3,4 and 6 of your BPP Study Text.

Top tips. This is not a difficult question, though there are two aspects to the requirement in part (a), which complicates it a little. Also, discussing the importance of marketing is complicated by the fact that the term has several different meanings and a range of connotations. For the purpose of this question, it will be best to stick to a simple concept of marketing that emphasises the marketing mix and the importance of the customer.

In part (b), do not be put off by the term 'niche player': it simply means the use, in *Porter's* terms, of a focus strategy. This is an aspect of Porter's model of generic strategy that is easy to gloss over in study: really all it means is doing things on a small scale, most commonly in terms of product range or market served.

Easy marks. The marking scheme for part (a) indicates that there were easy marks for introducing and using very simple models such as the product life cycle and *Ansoff's* matrix.

Examiner's comments. This was a popular and generally well-answered question, though a common problem in part (a) was to fail to assess the relevance of marketing to the company.

		Marks
(a)	Identification of relevant models: Macro-environmental/SLEPT Ansoff's growth matrix Porter's models Product positioning Product life cycle Marketing mix	up to 3 marks each
		Maximum 15 marks
(b)	Advantages of a niche strategy Benefits of specialisation Identifying segment(s) too small to interest major competitors Opportunity to move into emerging markets Create customer goodwill and barriers to entry Ability to charge prices that give better margins Positive approach to market opportunities	up to 2 marks each
		Maximum 10 marks **Total 25 marks**

Part (a)

To: Sales and Marketing Director
Salt and Soap Ltd

From: Marketing Consultant

Date: 1 July 200X

Report

1 Salt and Soap – current position.

1.1 As a supplier of own brand goods to supermarkets, the company is under intense pressure to cut prices, thus eroding its margins. There is really only one way to make a reasonable margin on this basis and that is to achieve scale economies by supplying in extremely large quantities. Salt and Soap, as a medium-sized business would find this difficult to do.

1.2 The ability of the supermarket majors to dictate prices arises from a marked imbalance in what *Porter* calls **the bargaining power of the customers and suppliers** in the industry. The customers really have all the power, for several reasons.

- They take 70% of the Company's output so the Company relies heavily on their business.

- Even so, these purchases represent an insignificant part of their total sales of cleansers: they could manage quite well without stocking them at all.

- The products themselves are entirely generic. This means that the Company can really only add value by breaking bulk and that it would be very easy for other companies to enter the industry.

1.3 The basic products of salt, soap and soda are very mature and may even be regarded as approaching the decline stage of their **product life cycles**: many people are consciously reducing the salt intake in their diet and plain soda crystals and soap flakes have been largely replaced by modern detergents.

All this supports your desire to reshape your business with new products and outlets.

Your principal concern must be to **add value**, because that translates directly into **improved margins**. Porter's **value chain** analysis indicates that value can be added by both **primary activities**, such as, in your case, efficient packaging and delivery, and by **supporting activities**, such as the management of human resources. Salt and Soap will probably find it easiest to pursue the creation of value in its primary operational areas.

The future for Salt and Soap must lie in **product and market development**, as defined by *Ansoff*.

The first step would be to pursue **market development** by selling existing cleaning products through the specialist wholesalers already identified. Following on, it may be possible to develop new products to exploit this market even further.

2 The role of marketing

2.1 Marketing is important to Salt and Soap, both as a concept of the way business should be done and as a group of defined business functions.

Marketing as a concept or model of the way business should work emphasises the **primary importance of the customer**. Business activity can be defined as providing customer satisfaction profitably. The implication is that all members of the business organisation and all of its activities should have as their principal purpose making some contribution to providing customer satisfaction.

Marketing as a function encompasses a range of important activities:

Marketing research will identify potential customers and their needs.

Brand management will build and exploit the company's own brand to enhance both sales and margins.

Marketing communications activities will inform, persuade, reassure and remind both existing and potential customers of the Company.

Customer relationship management will retain existing customers and exploit information about them to expand sales.

Part (b)

If Salt and Soap decides that it wishes to move away from the business of supplying supermarkets, its medium size will still make it necessary for the company to continue with a **focus** generic strategy. That is, it must concentrate its efforts on a fairly small part of the total market, at least to begin with, perhaps defining its chosen segment in terms of geography or type of customer. The current strategy is one of attempting to achieve **cost focus**: this emphasis on price is what makes it vulnerable to the large supermarkets. It may be that the company should aim to move as fast as possible towards a strategy of **differentiation focus**, since that may be the way to improve its margins.

Such a **niche** strategy can have significant advantages.

(a) A small, specialised manufacturer may not attract the attention of **larger competitors** with lower costs and greater resources.

(b) It may be possible to create **high customer loyalty** by building personal relationships and providing good service. This might act as an effective barrier to entry. Also, **word of mouth** is a good form of marketing communication.

(c) **Smaller customers can be targeted**. Such customers may be too small for larger suppliers to take much care over, so healthy margins may be available on sales to them.

The catering and gardening markets that David Kirk has identified are very large overall and may contain some very large wholesalers: such organisations may be potential customers or competitors, or even both. However, both markets also include **numerous small and medium-sized potential customers**, such as garden centres, and small chains of caterers and hardware stores.

Because it will not be constantly seeking the highest possible volumes, Salt and Soap will be able to **develop its product range** for these markets so as to meet a variety of customer needs. Simple additions would include an expanded range of pack sizes, while more complex developments might include convenient, throwaway dispensers and applicators.

There is also great potential for **brand development** as part of the marketing mix, since much more output will be sold under the company's own brand.

17 Lakeside Business School

Part (a)

> **Text reference.** The topics mentioned in this answer are discussed in Chapter 5 of your BPP Study Text.
>
> **Top tips.** A satisfactory answer to this question will have two main elements. The first thing to do is to identify the various stakeholder groups whose opinions are relevant to the e-learning problem. The second is to discuss the techniques that would be useful in dealing with the various groups identified.
>
> **Easy marks.** Whenever you encounter a question on stakeholders, see if it is useful to make use of *Mendelow's* mapping approach. It is certainly appropriate here, since slightly different approaches are probably appropriate to different groups. When using Mendelow's matrix remember that the classification of stakeholder groups will vary according to the specific problem under consideration.
>
> **Examiner's comments.** The Examiner makes two very good points in his model answer about the possible inconsistency of stakeholder motivation. The first is that individual stakeholders, being human, are capable of holding more than one point of view at the same time; the second is that identified stakeholder groups may not be united in their views and may contain factions with divergent or even opposing objectives. This heterogeneity of motivation, operative at both individual and group levels, may make the job of dealing with stakeholders even more complex; alternatively, it may offer good opportunities to proceed by promoting a course of action that has the potential for wide, if less than whole-hearted, acceptability.

Marking scheme

		Marks
(a)	Stakeholder mapping	up to 5
	Change management processes	up to 5
	Education, participation, coercion, manipulation, negotiation	up to 5
		Maximum 13 marks
(b)	Areas of concern: financial and customer perspectives	up to 5
	Internal processes and learning and growth perspectives	up to 5
	Advantages and disadvantages of balanced scorecard	up to 5
		Maximum 12 marks
		Total 25 marks

Mendelow suggests that, in relation to any given issue that might affect them, stakeholders may usefully be classified into four groups according to the extent of their **influence or power** and the extent of their **interest** in the issue.

Stakeholders with high levels of both interest and power are **key players** and must be dealt with carefully. Those with little power but a high level of interest are able to influence more powerful groups and should be **kept informed**. Those with power but little interest are capable of becoming interested and so should be **kept satisfied**. **Minimal effort** is expended on stakeholders with neither interest nor power.

Several stakeholder groups have significance for the e-learning issue at Lakeside Business School (LBS).

Central government is the most powerful stakeholder and its position is clear: student numbers are to be increased while funding is cut. The threat of further cuts in the future if student number targets are not met means that productivity improvements such as an expansion of e-learning cannot be avoided. There may be some small possibility of softening the government's stance through normal processes of consultation, PR and lobbying, but LBS should not count on this.

We are not told very much about the nature of the power relationship between LBS and the **central University authority**, but we know the latter has a strong interest in having their e-learning system taken up by the former. **Negotiation and compromise** are probably the way forward here.

By contrast, we know quite a lot about the attitudes of the **students** and the **staff** of LBS.

Collectively, **the staff of LBS** have a considerable degree of both power and interest in the future of e-learning. However, they are **not a cohesive group**: some are computer-literate and have adopted the new techniques, while others have dragged their feet and are likely to continue to do so. The problem for LBS lies with the latter. Because of their status and significance for the work of LBS, the best approach may be one of **integration and collaboration**. This technique emphasises the importance of the overall mission and the need for individuals to support the overall efforts of the group. This might be combined with a programme of internal co-operation under which the more computer-literate members of each section or discipline might undertake to assist their colleagues with the preparation of e-learning materials.

Like the staff, **the students at LBS** have a significant level of interest in the development of e-learning since it seems to be the only real possibility for maintaining study opportunities under budget pressure. However, like the staff, they seem to vary in their inclination and ability to use the new techniques. This may reflect their varying degree of motivation to work towards their degrees or, indeed, at all. University students can be outspoken and the more activist among them may attempt to agitate on the issue. A programme of **communication and consultation** with student representatives is probably required to handle this tendency. There may also be a need for LBS to provide extra **training** in the use of e-learning materials for students whose computer literacy may leave something to be desired.

Part (b)

> **Text reference.** The topics mentioned in this answer are discussed in Chapter 16 of your BPP Study Text.
>
> **Easy marks.** When the Examiner asks you about a particular model, as he has done in this question, you really have no alternative to discussing it in some detail. However, you may be able to score up to, say, 30% of the available marks for sensible supplementary suggestions involving other relevant models or methods.
>
> In this case we feel that the balanced scorecard is of limited applicability, so we say why and propose a different approach.

The balanced scorecard is much promoted as a robust approach to the measurement of business performance. It is based on four **perspectives**, or views of performance from different standpoints. The **financial** perspective uses traditional financial indicators; the **customer** perspective uses measures that reflect the degree of success in providing customer satisfactions; the **internal** perspective considers the efficiency of business systems and procedures; and the **innovation and learning** perspective looks at the extent to which the business is keeping up with changing circumstances.

The balanced scorecard was devised as an improved way of monitoring continuing, all-round business performance. As such, it can have only **limited relevance** to the e-learning issue at LBS. That issue and the measures appropriate to its resolution have more in common with **project management** than they do with routine business operations: it would be reasonable to think in terms of reaching a satisfactory solution to a problem in a finite period of time rather than of monitoring a continuing process of business activity.

It would therefore be appropriate to use **project management techniques** on the e-learning problem. In very simple terms this would involve the agreement of specific objectives, or 'deliverables'; the creation and monitoring of a project plan and budget; the provision of resources and accounting for them; leadership and management of a project team; management of stakeholder expectations and disputes; an acknowledged formal completion of the project; and a proper post-completion audit of the whole process so that it could be refined for future reference.

That being said, there is no reason why the **perspectives of the balanced scorecard** should not be used to structure thinking about the problem and its resolution. This might be particularly useful in the establishment of **objectives** and the consideration of **resources** and **constraints**.

Thinking about the **financial perspective** would remind the planners of the constraints imposed by the University's financial position and would encourage the creative use of staff time and other existing resources. While the project is intended to improve the productivity of these factors, it is likely to markedly increase the demands made on the time of the staff concerned; indeed, extra temporary staff may have to be provided.

The relevance of the **innovation and learning** perspective is so obvious as to need little further comment: the project is one of learning development and has implications for both staff and students.

The **customer** perspective is an interesting one, in that both students and government might be regarded as customers. This is not a dilemma, however: thinking of them in stakeholder terms would be a proper approach.

Finally, consideration of the **internal** perspective underlines the need to manage the project in an efficient manner

18 Fashion retailer

Text reference. The topics mentioned in this answer are discussed in Chapters 8 and 9 of your BPP Study Text.

Top tips. Fashion retailing is a fairly specialised job. However, we all have some experience of it from the customer's side of the counter. Don't be afraid to make some educated deductions about, for instance, the need for careful stock control when a wide range of goods is moving rather quickly.

An organisation's value-creating activities must be mutually supporting.

Part (a)

Paul's business is in the fashion clothing industry with 20 retail stores but little integration between the stores. This part of the fashion industry operates with very slim margins and with profitability not keeping pace with the increase in turnover, Paul realises that he must operate in a more cost-conscious manner. The computer system is currently underused and is operating in a passive manner or in the 'support' quadrant of the *McFarlan and McKenney* grid.

In order to consider how the IT function can be used to provide Paul with a competitive edge in his business we can use Porter's value chain model to illustrate how this could be done. The firm will be as strong as the weakest link in the chain. The value chain consists of five primary activities and four support activities. The IT investment will be worthwhile if it can be used to reduce costs or to differentiate Paul's business from the others in the industry sector.

Primary activities

Inbound logistics

This relates to the purchasing function and the storage of stock and distribution to the stores. An IT system can help with stock control levels, economic ordering and efficient distribution routings.

Operations

IT can be used to monitor the performance of each store with details being provided about profitability, stock levels, stock turnover, expense levels, staff absences and so on. IT could also be used to analyse the different consumer demand profile in different locations in order to help each store ensure that it has sufficient stocks of the type of sales made in its store.

Outbound logistics

This element of the chain concerns distribution to customers and is more relevant in a manufacturing industry. In Paul's business there will not be much distribution to customers but the system may be able to produce a customer database to assist with marketing and promotions.

Marketing and sales

Paul could use IT to indicate customer purchasing patterns for different stores and to develop databases for promotions. Internet retailing is a possibility, though it would create a fulfilment problem.

Service

This area of the chain is to do with the provision of service to the customers and it is not likely that IT can be of much use here although it could be used to monitor, control and facilitate transfers between stores.

Support activities

Firm's infrastructure

In this area IT can be used to help with the budgeting, finance and management information in order to improve the Paul's company's performance compared to that of his competitors.

Human resources management

As Paul's organisation is quite small and consists largely of retail sales staff, there will not be many very useful applications of IT in this area however it may be used to make recruitment and appraisals more efficient.

Technology development

It is unlikely that the IT function would move from McFarlan and McKenney's support quadrant to the strategic quadrant.

Procurement

This area of support activity is concerned with linking the purchasing system to the sales system. This could be used to automatically update stock records and indicate when new orders should be placed and could also help to minimise times when excessive stock is held in a store. It could also consolidate orders to achieve bulk purchase discounts.

Part (b)

Text reference. The topics mentioned in this answer are discussed in Chapter 9 of your BPP Study Text.

Top tips. The Examiner has co-authored a book on systems development, so make sure you are very familiar with syllabus section D3!

To: Paul Singh
From: A Consultant
Date: December 200X
Subject: Software package options

Introduction

1 You asked for advice on the use of software packages and, in particular on two specific software package options that have been suggested to you.

- Standard package
- Modified standard package

2 In general, standard packages are robust systems that incorporate wide experience of business procedures and their automation. They can provide immediate benefits in the form of improved methods, records and possibilities for analysis of data. They are, however, based on **standardised modules** and are not necessarily optimised for any given commercial application. Claims by vendors that their products can give a competitive edge are questionable: competitors can easily buy the same product. The best that can be said is that a standard package should provide an effective way of doing things. Also, such packages force the organisation to adjust itself to the requirements of the software

3 Standard packages do, however, offer a number of positive qualities.

 (a) While selection may take some time, **installation** should be rapid and there should be no requirement for extensive testing. However, time would be required for staff training and familiarisation

 (b) **Quality** should be guaranteed both by the vendor and, except for launch customers, by earlier installation by other customers.

 (c) **Documentation and training** should be immediately available and of high quality since these are important selling points.

 (d) **Maintenance support** should be good and would normally include help desk service and routine software amendments to correct faults as they become apparent.

 (e) Comprehensive **package evaluation** should be possible. This might include use for a trial period and visits to existing installations.

4 On the other hand, there are problems to note.

 (a) **Property rights** over the software usually reside with the supplier. This has three important potential consequences for the user.

  (i) The supplier controls future development of the software.

  (ii) The supplier controls the support available and may discontinue it, forcing the customer to purchase an upgrade.

  (iii) The supplier may sell the product rights to another supplier, perhaps to the prejudice of the customer.

 (b) The **financial stability** and survival of the supplier is not guaranteed.

 (d) **Inadequate performance** is quite likely: the customer may have to accept restricted functionality or pay for tailored amendments, with accompanying disadvantages discussed below. Further problems may be caused by unwanted standard features: these may cause difficulties in training and implementation.

 (e) **Legal redress** for lack of functionality will almost certainly not be available.

(f) **Changing requirements** can erode a package's functionality. Potential purchasers evaluate a package against their current requirements. These may change as time passes or may not have been properly specified in the first place. In either case, the package fails to provide full satisfaction.

5 Because of the generic nature of standard packages, some clients have them tailored to fit their requirements and their existing systems and procedures. This approach has been recommended to you, but is generally a **mistake**.

- The cost advantage of buying off the shelf is destroyed.
- Introduction is delayed.
- Reliability is reduced.
- New versions of the same software will be useless until they too have been modified.

Generally it is cheaper and more effective to redesign the organisation's processes to fit a standard package than to do the opposite.

19 Preparation question: La Familia Amable

Part (a)

Text reference. The topics mentioned in this answer are discussed in Chapters 3 and 4 of your BPP Study Text.

Top tips. This question is adapted from a Paper 3.5 question.

Easy marks. The most obvious aspect of Ramon Silva's proposed new venture is the specific combination of price and product content he proposes to offer. He thinks he has identified something of a gap in the market.

Examiner's comments. Ramon Silva is following a classic cost focus strategy.

To:	Ramon Silva
From:	Accountant
Date:	December 2005
Subject:	**Proposed new venture**

Creation of value

Your proposed new venture is based on the identification of a gap in the hotel market for an inexpensive but good quality product. You propose to create value by innovative bedroom design and efficient use of a minimal staff. The main source of value would therefore lie in what *Porter* calls **operations**.

I would question your belief that little **marketing** (another of Porter's primary value activities) would be required. You intend that your market offering should be recognised by potential customers as innovative: the launch of a new product of this type should include informative advertising simply to let potential customers know what is available and where. Later, promotion aimed at building the brand would be appropriate. This would be based on the **brand values** of comfort, convenience and moderate cost.

Intensity of competition and new entrants

At the moment, available hotel accommodation is of two general types that are, respectively, cheaper and of lower quality than your concept, or more expensive, but offering extra features that add little extra value. You believe that there is **little direct competition** in your chosen segment. Since much of your ability to combine good quality with low cost depends on room design and construction, building costs should create a **barrier to entry** against potential new entrants seeking to imitate your strategy. However, I would sound a note of caution here.

Currently, the hotel industry in the Spanish holiday areas is somewhat depressed, with overcapacity. While there may be no direct competitors for your new venture, if it is a success, it will attract the attention of the established two star hotel operators and they may start to compete directly by **discounting their own product**. They may do this outside the highest season in the first place, but if they need to do so, they will be able to cut their costs by offering fewer facilities and extend their revised offer into busier periods.

Substitute products

You have identified a gap in the currently available product range provided by hotels. However, there is a **substitute product** that may represent an immediate threeat to your proposed operation. This is **self-catering holiday accommodation**, a well-established alternative to the more expensive type of hotel. There is probably a segment of the market for which this option is not particularly practical, which is the aspiring holiday home purchaser making a short visit of one or two days, for whom the normal booking period of one week would be excessive. However, whether it would be possible to base a business on this presumably rather small segment would remain to be seen.

Part (b)

Text reference. The topics mentioned in this answer are discussed in Chapter 7 of your BPP Study Text.

Easy marks. This is almost an opportunity to write down all you know about franchising, but even so, you must bias your remarks towards the hotel industry.

Examiner's comments. There were some exceptionally good answers to this part of the question.

Advantages of franchising

Ramon Silva's plan to franchise his operation would have **financial benefits** in that he could charge franchisees a substantial initial **premium** and **service fees** subsequently. This would provide a useful positive cash flow that would enable him to expand the business faster than might otherwise be the case.

An important potential advantage of franchising is the **motivation and commitment** that comes from capital participation. A good franchising structure will be fair to both parties and will allow franchisees to benefit in proportion to their input to their businesses.

Franchising should be attractive to franchisees because it should allow them to benefit from a **strong brand** and to run their own businesses with **less risk** then a completely independent venture. However, these aspects are only present when the business model is proven and the brand established: this is not yet the case with 'La Familia Aimable' project. Ramon Silva should set up at least his first hotel and to run it himself for a few years to **prove the concept** and **establish** the brand before seeking franchisees for further expansion.

Disadvantages of franchising

An important potential disadvantage of franchising is the **division of control** between franchiser and franchisee. The franchiser relies on the efforts of the franchisee for the attainment of crucial outcomes such as quality of service, while the franchisee will normally be constrained many operational matters, such as the nature of the services offered and almost any aspect of promotion. The **franchise contract** must be drawn up very carefully, so that both parties to the franchise know what their rights and responsibilities are and, in particular, **how disputes are to be resolved**.

Recruitment and selection of suitable franchisees can be a significant burden for the franchiser, both in terms of **cost incurred** and also as a **distraction** from the overall management of the business. Franchisees can make or break the operation and must be selected with great care. Ramon Silva is considering a chain of hotels, which will probably not grow in the medium term to more than, say, a dozen franchises, if only because of the capital costs involved. The rate at which he needs to recruit is therefore fairly low, but, conversely, the importance of each selection is very high. He will have to spend a lot of time and effort on it.

Training the new franchisees will be as important as selection and for the same reasons. The franchisees will form the organisation's principal point of contact with the customers: they will judge the whole operation by the treatment and quality of service they receive. Ramon Silva will have to provide initial training and motivate the franchisees to work to high standards. He will also have to install a monitoring system to ensure that those standards are maintained.

20 John Hudson

Marking scheme

		Marks
(a)	Definition of project team/matrix structure	up to 2
	Benefits of such a structure	up to 1½ for each point made
	Increased integration	
	More responsive and flexible teams	
	No dominance of a functional area	
	Staff more involved and motivated	
	Good general management training	
	Problems with the structure	up to 1½ for each point made
	Dilution of priorities	
	Conflict and confusion in reporting	
	Complexity of administration	
	Slower decision making	
	Difficult allocation of responsibility	
		Maximum 13 marks
(b)	Slippage solutions	Up to 1 for each solution
	Staged approach to risk	
	Aspects of risk	
	Strategies for dealing with risk	Up to 2 for each well made point
		Maximum 12 marks
		Total 25 marks

Part (a)

Text reference. The topics mentioned in this answer are discussed in Chapters 7 and 13 of your BPP Study Text.

Top tips. A common problem for candidates is the **application** of their theoretical knowledge to question scenarios. In this answer we show in *italics* those parts that constitute application of theory to the specific problems represented by the scenario.

Easy marks. The setting for this question points you fairly clearly towards the matrix and project team approaches. When you get a question that gives you this kind of steer, accept it gratefully and don't waste time trying to think of something different, even if you think you can. However, relevant comment on suitability and potential problems is clearly called for.

ALG Technology might consider a **matrix** *form of organisation structure.* This provides control of activities that overlap functional boundaries, while at the same time maintaining functional departmentation. Senior managers are appointed to oversee activities that span functional boundaries. Lateral lines of communication and authority are thus superimposed on the functional departmental structure. A common example is the appointment of marketing managers with responsibility for all aspects of the marketing of a particular product group. *In ALG, for instance, a manager might be appointed to draw together all the design, manufacturing, financial and promotion efforts relating to the fighter avionics business.*

A related approach is **project team** organisation. This is very similar to matrix management, but is based on *ad hoc* cross-functional teams with responsibility for a defined project. *This might be more appropriate for ALG, since the company is effectively working on specific projects with a defined life cycle rather than steady-state production.* Project team organisation allows for the co-ordination of interdisciplinary effort, with experts in different functions appointed to the team while retaining membership and status within their own functional department.

Advantages of a cross-disciplinary structure

(a)   It offers greater **flexibility**. This applies both to **people,** as employees adapt more quickly to a new challenge or new task, and develop an attitude which is geared to accepting change; and to **task and structure**, as the matrix may be short-term (as with project teams) or readily amended (eg a new product manager can be introduced by superimposing his tasks on those of the existing functional managers). *Flexibility should facilitate efficient operations at ALG by helping it to cope with the complexity of the technology it is deploying and the dynamism of the markets in which it operates.*

(b)   It provides for **inter-disciplinary co-operation** and a mixing of skills and expertise. This should improve **communication** within the organisation and give ALG the **multiple orientation** it needs to integrate its key activities and keep functional specialists from becoming wrapped up in their own concerns.

(c)   It provides a **structure for allocating responsibility to managers for end-results**. A product manager is responsible for product profitability, and a project leader is responsible for ensuring that the task is completed. *This also will promote the integration of effort that ALG needs.*

Disadvantages of a cross-disciplinary structure

(a)   Dual authority threatens a **conflict** between managers. It is important that the authority of superiors should not overlap and areas of responsibility must be clearly defined. *John Hudson must ensure that subordinates know to which of their superiors they are responsible for each aspect of their duties.*

(b)   One individual with two or more bosses is more likely to suffer **role stress** at work. *This is another problem for senior management at ALG to monitor.*

(c)   It is likely to be more **costly**, since additional managers are appointed that would not be required in a simple structure of functional departmentation. *ALG is already quite lean, so it may be able to absorb these costs without great difficulty.*

(d)   It may be difficult for managers **to accept**. It is possible that managers will feel that their authority is being eroded. Similarly, it requires consensus and agreement which may **slow down** decision-making. *John Hudson must monitor managerial attitudes to ensure that managerial conservatism does not seize opportunities to make any new approach fail.*

Part (b)

Top tips. Project management forms an important part of your syllabus.

Project slippage

When a project has slipped behind schedule there are a range of options open to the project manager.

(a) **Do nothing**: after considering all options it may be decided that things should be allowed to continue as they are.

(b) **Add resources**: if capable staff are available and it is practicable to add more people to certain tasks it may be possible to recover some lost ground. Could some work be subcontracted?

(c) **Work smarter**: consider whether the methods currently being used are the most suitable – for example, could prototyping be used.

(d) **Replan**: if the assumptions the original plan was based on have been proved invalid a more realistic plan should be devised.

(e) **Reschedule**: a complete replan may not be necessary – it may be possible to recover some time by changing the phasing of certain deliverables.

(f) **Introduce incentives**: if the main problem is team performance, incentives such as bonus payments could be linked to work deadlines and quality.

(g) **Change the specification**: if the original objectives of the project are unrealistic given the time and money available it may be necessary to negotiate a change in the specification.

Risk management

Projects and other undertakings carry an element of **risk**, for example the risk of an inappropriate system being developed and implemented. Risk management is concerned with identifying such risks and putting in place policies to eliminate or reduce these risks. The identification of risks involves an overview of the project to establish what could go wrong, and the consequences. Risk management may be viewed as a six-stage process:

Stage 1 Plan the risk management approach.

It is appropriate to determine the degree of **risk aversion** that will apply. The general rule is that as risk increases so do potential returns. Minimising risk is expensive, so the degree of risk acceptable to the project sponsor and project board should be considered at an early stage.

Stage 2 Identify and record risks.

Existing plans for time, costs and quality should be examined for risk potential. The critical path, cost estimates and quality assumptions should be examined with particular care. It will be useful for project staff to brainstorm and external advice may be sought: this could come from non-project staff within the organisation or from external sources.

Identified risks are recorded in a **risk register**. *Schwalbe* suggests the detail shown below should be recorded for each risk event in the risk register.

(a) An identification number

(b) A probability

(c) A name

(d) A description

(e) The root cause

(f)   Possible indicators and symptoms: these are factors that tend to increase the chance that the risk event will occur.

(g)   Potential impact

(h)   Potential responses

(i)   An owner: this person monitors the risk event

(j)   Current status: this will change as the project progresses; eventually the risk may become irrelevant.

Stage 3   Assess the risks.

There are two aspects to the assessment of risk.

(a)   The **probability** that the risk event will actually take place
(b)   The **consequences** of the risk event if it does occur

Several quantitative techniques may be useful in assessing risk, including expected values, sensitivity analysis, Monte Carlo simulation and programme evaluation and review technique (PERT). PERT requires the application of probabilities to the time planned for the activities identified in the critical path analysis.

Stage 4   Plan and record risk responses.

Developing a risk **contingency plan** for managing risk events with the highest probability and potential impact should have priority. Following the principle of **management by exception**, the most efficient way of dealing with low probability, low impact risks may be to do nothing unless the risk presents itself. Extra time and finance should be held in reserve for dealing with intermediate contingencies.

Dealing with **risk** involves four strategies.

(a)   **Avoidance**: the factors that give rise to the risk are removed.

(b)   **Reduction** or **mitigation**: the potential for the risk cannot be removed but analysis has enabled the identification of ways to reduce the incidence and/or the consequences.

(c)   **Transference**: the risk is passed on to someone else, perhaps by means of insurance, or possibly by building it into a supplier contract.

(d)   **Absorption**: the potential risk is accepted in the hope or expectation that the incidence and consequences can be coped with if necessary.

Stage 5   Implement risk management strategies.

Stage 6   Review the risk management approach and actions for adequacy.

Risk management is a continuous process. Procedures are necessary to regularly review and reassess the risks documented in the risk register.

21 Preparation question : service performance

Text reference. The topics mentioned in this answer are discussed in Chapter 3 of your BPP Study Text.

> **Top tips.** This question deals with core syllabus ideas. It is based on an actual exam question set for the old syllabus Paper 3.5. The standard is appropriate for your exam, but the question is not worth 25 marks, so we describe it as a preparation question.
>
> **Easy marks.** Any question on performance management is likely to be amenable to an answer using the balanced score card and explaining the framework should be worth a couple of marks.

Part (a)

Critical success factors

It is clear from the information provided that Sun and Sand Travel Ltd has **sacrificed quality and customer service** in order to **compete exclusively on price**. The current unwelcome media comment and fall in bookings show that this is not a good strategy, even in the short term. The continuing longer-term fall in profitability points to the same conclusion. Customers clearly require higher standards from the company, even if it continues to make low prices its main value proposition.

Johnson, Scholes and Whittington define critical success factors in strict market terms: they are **product features that are particularly valued by customers**. In this context, the product is the complex package of tangible and intangible benefits that *Kotler* calls the **augmented product**. This includes branding, quality and, crucially for Sun and Sand Travel Ltd (SSTL), after-sales service. It is likely that SSTL's customers will have a range of views about what they particularly value, but we ought to be able to make some sensible suggestions about what might constitute common ground.

People

In a service industry such as this, good relations with customers are vital: this appears to have been an area where the company has not been succeeding well in the past. The quality and effectiveness of the **holiday representatives** in the resorts is extremely important. They must deploy a range of people skills and work hard for the benefit of the customers. Good **negotiating skills** will contribute to building proper relationships with suppliers.

Dealing with complaints and problems is crucial to the image of the company. If there are problems with flights or accommodation, it will be the representatives' responsibility to solve them. In most cases, if a problem can be solved promptly by the local holiday representative, the customers concerned are likely to feel very positive about the company. On the other hand, if they feel that that their concerns have not been properly addressed, they will form a very negative view.

Administrative skills

The three categories of complaint specifically mentioned in the narrative setting might all arise from events beyond the control of SSTL, but this seems unlikely, given their volume. It seems probable that SSTL has very significant problems with what we might refer to as **administration**. Not unreasonably, customers expect that even a low-cost tour operator such as SSTL should display at least a threshold level of competence in making proper arrangements for travel and accommodation.

Product portfolio

Although many customers may wish to return to the same resort each year, many others will wish to try something new. SSTL must therefore pursue an active policy of **product development**. Novelty could take many forms, including new hotels, new resorts and activity holidays.

Public relations

Part of the reason SSTL has suffered a fall in bookings is the adverse media comment it has received. No doubt this is largely well-deserved. However, in the future, it will be important for the company to ensure that its side of the story is heard. This will require skilled PR management.

Part (b)

Key performance indicators

It is difficult to design effective key performance indicators (KPIs). However, having identified SSTL's critical success factors, we might make some basic suggestions. These would almost certainly require refinement in the light of experience.

Holiday representatives

A common way of assessing quality of personal service is by means of brief, volunteer questionnaires. These aim to establish indices of performance by the use of numerical rating scales. They suffer from the fact that respondents self-select and should, therefore, be supplemented by market research interviews.

Administrative skills

SSTL should monitor rates and extents of travel delays as a matter of routine: this information is extremely valuable since it is a matter of objective fact. Problems in the resort will be more difficult to monitor: representatives may be able to provide objective reports, but they may be biased by their close relationships with such people as hotel managers and coach drivers. Measuring the rate and seriousness of customer complaints is probably a better way of measuring resort problems.

Product portfolio

Assessing the success of product development could be done fairly easily by measuring revenue and profit from new and recently introduced holiday packages. However, this does require a well-developed system of cost accounting.

The balanced scorecard

It would be appropriate to draw indicators such as these and others together by using *Kaplan and Norton's* **balanced scorecard** approach. This uses four 'perspectives' from which the performance of an organisation should be measured:

- The internal business perspective
- The customer perspective
- The innovation and learning perspective
- The financial perspective

Past practice at SSTL has been to concentrate on the financial perspective, but even this has been confined to a single measure. Other financial measures that are likely to be relevant to a service business are those relating to gearing, cash flow, overheads and product costs.

Internal business perspective

The internal business perspective examines matters of routine practice. For SSTL, it might include measures such as the time taken to process a holiday order and the number of errors in booking procedures.

Customer perspective

This perspective is where the administrative matters discussed above will be assessed, together with the assessment of holiday representatives. Measures might include those listed below.

- Number of complaints from customers
- Time taken to deal with complaints
- Number of queries satisfactorily resolved
- Percentage of flights delayed
- Average flight delay time
- Number of schedule changes as a percentage of total holidays
- Number of repeat purchases of holidays
- Number of referrals from satisfied customers

Innovation and learning perspective

This perspective measures the rate and success of innovation in the organisation. Possible performance indicators include:

- Rate of introduction of new destinations
- Sales and profit from new destinations compared to standard destinations
- Availability of new or improved accommodation and activities

Financial perspective

SSTL would measure ROCE and a few other indicators appropriate to its circumstances under this perspective. Other indicators might include measures of liquidity, turnover against budget and prospects for the price of aviation fuel, for instance.

22 Excalibur Sportswear

> **Top tips.** A common problem for candidates is the **application** of their theoretical knowledge to question scenarios. In this answer we show in *italics* those parts that constitute application of theory to the specific problems represented by the scenario.

Marking scheme

		Marks
(a)	Reasons for going international and possibly global and applied to Excalibur	up to 3 for each point
	Customer	
	Company	
	Competitor	
	Currency	
	Country	
		Maximum 12 marks
(b)	Recognition of increasing risk and commitment linked with control examples to relate to Excalibur	
		Maximum 13 marks
		Total 25 marks

Part (a)

> **Text reference.** The topics mentioned in this answer are discussed in Chapter 6 of your BPP Study Text.
>
> **Easy marks.** This first part of this question is best answered using *Ohmae's* **5Cs** model; indeed, the Examiner's own suggested solution was based on this model. Unfortunately, this is a fairly complex theory: the 5Cs themselves do not really give much clue as to what the model is about. On the other hand, if you learn this important theory and a suitable question comes up, you should find it easy to score well. The essence of the theory is given in our answer.

Ohmae suggests that companies *such as Excalibur Sportswear* move towards overseas marketing and eventually to globalisation for five reasons.

(a) **Customers**. Some market segments exhibit a degree of **convergence** across regions and even across the planet. This is particularly noticeable among the young and fashion-conscious and others who are easily persuaded of the importance of major brand names to their personal fulfilment and happiness. *Excalibur Sportswear is operating in such a market segment: its products are well known throughout the world because of its endorsement by those who have achieved fame by being good at games.* Where such transnational market segments exist, it is easy to sell to with a standardised product and brand.

(b) **Company**. Selling globally is likely to bring significant **economies of scale**. In particular, Simon Smith will find that his necessarily heavy spending on promotion can be spread across a higher volume of sales, allowing him to increase his profitability or reduce his prices, whichever seems most appropriate. Similarly, when he increases the size of the orders he places with his suppliers, he will be able obtain lower prices, since increased manufacturing economies of scale are likely to arise.

(c) **Competition**. The effect of the first 2 factors above is that Excalibur Sportswear's competitors have higher turnover and probably higher revenue. Excalibur is driven by competitive pressure to follow them into the global market place. If it fails to do this, it's high costs will erode its ability to compete and may threaten its survival. Ohmae suggests that a further likely result of global competitive pressure is a degree of **strategic co-operation** between competitors. This is seen, for example, in the air travel industry, where co-operate to provide an increased number of travel options to their customers. Excalibur Sportswear may find it appropriate to share distribution systems with one or more competitors, for example.

(d) **Currency**. A company that is essentially based in one country and exports but exports to others has to deal with the problem of **varying exchange rates**. When costs arise mostly in the home country's currency but significant revenues arise in one or more foreign currencies, unfavourable shifts in exchange rates can be extremely damaging. A simple solution to this problem is to manufacture in the countries where sales are made. Costs and revenues are then to some extent matched in currency terms and exchange rate risk is reduced. *Excalibur Sportswear, may find this difficult to achieve, since its products are likely to be sourced in low wage economies but sold in richer countries whose customers will pay the high prices typical of this market.*

(e) **Country**. The company that manufactures and sells in countries across the globe is able to export both **absolute and comparative advantage**. Low wages, mentioned above, are one example of such advantage: cheap and readily available raw materials are another. *If Excalibur sets up its own overseas manufacturing and distribution facilities, it may also find that* local manufacturing status can confer important benefits of an essentially political or social nature. The governments of developing countries may place obstacles in the way of importers in order to defend their balances of payments and, equally, may assist foreign companies prepared to invest in local manufacture. Similarly, locally manufactured goods may be particularly attractive to customers in some markets and confer important selling advantages.

Part (b)

> **Text reference.** The topics mentioned in this answer are discussed in Chapter 8 of your BPP Study Text.
>
> **Top tips.** The Examiner makes the point in his suggested solution that generally, 'risk and resource commitment are positively correlated with control.' This is a very neat encapsulation of what can seem a rather paradoxical situation.

Simon Smith is concerned that expanding his operations by the use of further contract manufacturers and distributors might compromise both his ability to control his operations and the quality of his products. He has to face a dilemma: to achieve greater control of critical inputs into his operations he is contemplating setting up his own manufacturing and distributions operations. Inevitably, this will demand greater investment: greater control implies greater risk.

Generally speaking, any expansion of operations is likely to involve the commitment of extra resources and there fore the acceptance of greater risk. Exploitation of underused indivisible resources to their maximum capacity can limit capital expenditures, but it is almost inevitable that labour and consumable costs will rise.

In the case of Excalibur Sportswear, considerable capital will be required to set up manufacturing facilities. Premises and plant must be acquired, labour hired and raw materials and components purchased. All this must be done before production commences. Part of the labour requirement will be for managers with relevant manufacturing expertise.

The creation of distribution networks is likely to be even more demanding. Vehicles, storage facilities and retail outlets will be needed and all will have to be of a high standard if the current brand image is to be maintained. Skilled management will be just as essential as in manufacturing.

Simon Smith himself and any core associates he has will also find that they have to commit much of their time to the management of these new ventures. We are not told whether the strategic apex of Excalibur Sportswear currently has any skill or experience in these matters: if they do not, they will have to acquire some very able senior managers.

Increased risk is likely to go hand with increased commitment of resources. Risk can be analysed into a number of categories.

- **Environmental risk**. In this category we may include risks inherent in the physical environment, such as earthquake and flooding; political risk, such as the risk of government expropriation; and economic risk arising from the nature of the business cycle. At the moment, Simon Smith holds much of this risk at arm's length, since it is largely absorbed by his manufacturing and distribution contractors. He would be much more exposed if he had extensive operations in a range of foreign countries.

- **Financial risk**. Simon Smith is contemplating using bank finance for his expansion. In the UK, this means an increase in gearing with all that implies for cash flow when times are hard. It also means an effective surrender of some autonomy through the acceptance of restrictive loan covenants.

- **Business risk**. It is not possible for Simon Smith to form a perfectly accurate forecast of the effect his contemplated expansion will have on business risk. There is much he does not know: how his competitors will react; how much of his time will be devoted to overseeing the management of his new facilities; whether he is expanding dangerously beyond his core competences; how his customers will react; and how his costs and revenues will develop.

It is clear, therefore, that the expansion Simon Smith is contemplating is likely to produce significant changes in both the risk profile of his business and the resources it requires. The drive to achieve greater control by doing more may prove impracticable for these reasons.

23 Prestige Packaging

Text reference. The topics mentioned in this answer are discussed in Chapter 6 of your BPP Study Text.

Top tips. Do not ignore the explicit reference in both the scenario and the question to organic options. The firm has ruled out global expansion using either merger and acquisition or joint venture. In the actual exam, many candidates set out to describe the advantages and disadvantages of merger/acquisition and joint ventures – and did not gain any marks. For part (b), there is a distinction between the sort of information that is relevant, and the process by which the information is gained. The question is looking for good sources of information both inside and outside the company.

Examiner's comments. Part (a) was attempted well by most candidates, who showed a real ability to engage with the three organic options facing the firm in its desire to become a more global company. Advantages and disadvantages were clearly and succinctly described.

Part (b) asked for the information which would help in making a choice between the options. Often the information suggested by candidates was derived from a SLEPT analysis, rather than the information to enable a choice to be made. Good candidates were able relate the information needed to the options being considered, and again showed the ability to link their answer to the scenario

Part (a)

Companies can grow **organically** (via internal development), building up their own products and developing their own market. This is the primary method of growth for many companies. Some form of organic growth needs to be chosen by Prestige Packaging: the choice will depend upon the prevailing attitude to **risk**, the **timescale** available and the **opportunities** for growth that each option creates. The preferred strategy should reflect the **long-term goals** of the company. Furthermore, each option will affect the structure and processes within the company, and will have its own implications for staffing and management control.

Overseas sales office

Setting up a sales office in an international location probably involves the **least risk**. The company already has operations in Europe, and this learning may be transferable. Prestige Packaging will need to consider whether it sells to its customers directly, or through a local distributor, after developing its brand sufficiently. Suitable local staff will need to be recruited: but what level of expatriate management and control from head office will be needed?

Manufacturing operation

A manufacturing plant may be the only option in some countries, where governments might be looking for **inward investment and job creation**. Governments may impose **prohibitive tariffs** on imported products to protect local products and jobs.

A manufacturing facility involves **more commitment of finance and other resources**, and a significant alteration to the **value chain**. The required investment may in some cases be prohibitively expensive, and it may be difficult to find enough suitable local staff if there is no local partner in the operation. In Prestige Packaging's case, the **logistics** of getting the semi-finished product to the overseas manufacturing base will also need some thought. The plant may actually end up acting independently, which will affect the **level of control** that can be exercised by Prestige, and may end up increasing the **business risk**.

Quality control will be of importance. Involving another plant may add considerably to quality risks.

Agents and distributors

A major problem here is gaining the **motivation** and **full commitment** of local agents and distributors. They might be carrying the products of several firms, and will be tempted to commit themselves to those products that earn the best return. The question of exclusivity therefore becomes important, and this may be able to be negotiated by Prestige Packaging. **Agents** should be chosen for the **effectiveness of their business networks** and their access to major customers. Regular personal contact with the agent will enable both parties to set out their expectations and any problems that may arise. The provision of attractive commission and other financial incentives will only help the relationship.

A **distributor** typically is used where the company has a large number of small customers that it is trying to service. The distributor buys the product from the supplier and has a greater degree of freedom in deciding price and promotion. Controlling agents and distributors can be difficult, so it is important for Prestige Packaging to set out realistic performance expectations, and contracts should be clear to all parties involved.

Part (b)

The most important requirement of effective international operations is thorough analysis of the market in order to maintain continuous awareness of opportunities, threats and trends. Information can be gathered by Prestige Packaging on:

*   Attractive new markets
*   General packaging market trends
*   Customer needs and preferences
*   Competitor plans and strategies
*   New product opportunities
*   Political, legal, economic, social and technological trends

David should be particularly advised to gather information on the **political** risk associated with operations in different countries. As indicated in the list above, such information could be obtained via a PEST macro-environmental analysis. An industry analysis (such as Porter's Five Forces) would be an important tool in assessing the existing competition, suppliers and key customers. A key issue will be the availability of reliable secondary data, and its ability to generate specific information, but there is always the need to balance the **benefits** of information acquisition against the **costs** (time and money) involved.

24 KPG Systems

Text reference. The topics mentioned in this answer are discussed in Chapter 4 and Chapter 12 of your BPP Study Text.

Top tips. In our answer to requirement (b), we enumerate a number of models that could be used. You will often find in the field of general strategic analysis that any one of several models could be used. If this happens, it is simplest to confine your answer to one model for each aspect of your answer. However, there may be valid extra points that can be made using another model as well. If you want to do this, try to keep the models separate and your reasoning clear. Here there are really two elements: analysis of the current position and recommendations for the future, so we use both SWOT and TOWS.

Easy marks. This question is a good example of a common type, in that it has a very specific and fairly simple task in part (a) and a more open-ended one in part (b). Part (a) is therefore easier, since it requires little more than knowledge, while part (b) requires thought and the careful application of theory to the scenario.

Part (a)

Andy Rowe is right to be concerned about the quality of his products. Purchasers of IS take a great deal on trust, since they rarely understand the nature of the software they purchase or how it works. Poor design and coding produce IS that are difficult to use, maintain and enhance. This leads to excessive costs, undermines user confidence and harms business efficiency.

We do not know the details of Andy's quality problems, but judging by the description of his company and its way of doing things, it seems unlikely that it has progressed beyond a **Capability Maturity Model Level 2**. At this level, success becomes to some extent repeatable and the organisation has some established procedures for project management, such as the use of time and cost plans and development milestones and review points. However, cost and time overruns are still likely, as Andy has experienced. To progress to Level 3, the company would need standard processes that are **defined**, **consistent** across the organisation and subject to **continuing improvement**. The critical distinction from level 2 is that, while standards and procedures may be tailored to suit a project, they are all based on a comprehensive established library rather being largely designed afresh for each project.

There are several approaches to quality improvement that might be of use to Andy. We do not know in detail the procedures his company uses at the moment, but we might suggest an overall quality management system such as **SixSigma** or the **ISO 9000:2000** standards. Also, if he is not already using the V model of IS testing, Andy should probably consider doing so.

The V model

Testing is a major aspect of quality control in the development of IS because of the complexity inherent in them. That complexity also means that testing cannot be regarded as something that is done when all the other aspects of a IS development project are complete: it must be incorporated at each stage of development. This approach is the essence of the **V model** of IS development. Its strength is that it requires the design of both **the testing regime** and of **the system itself** to be run as **two linked and converging streams**.

Quality management systems

If an organisation is to deliver products and services of the necessary level of quality, it must actively manage all the factors that have an impact on quality. The ISO 9000:2000 approach is largely built around the concept of a **quality management system** (QMS). *Tricker and Sherring-Lucas* define this as 'the organisational structure of responsibilities, activities, resources and events that together provide procedures and methods of implementation to ensure the capability of an organisation to meet quality requirements'. Within the QMS, **quality control** is about fulfilling quality requirements, while **quality assurance** is the focussed on providing confidence that quality requirements will be fulfilled.

Thus, **quality control** is about the things the organisation has to do to be sure that the quality of its output is as it should be. It is about activities such supervision, inspection, checks and measurements and applies to all parts of the organisation's value chain. **Quality assurance** is about providing confidence that all the necessary QC activities are operating as they should and that a proper level of quality is being achieved. QA is therefore concerned with the things that make quality control systems and activities effective, such as quality policies; relevant management and training; and documentation such as quality records.

If an organisation's QMS is to provide a proper level of assurance to existing and potential customers, it is necessary for the organisation to achieve **quality certification**. This is an externally provided acknowledgement that the QMS is adequate in its provisions and its operation. Certification can only be provided by **accredited certification bodies**.

Part (b)

There is a variety of models that could be used to assess the current position of KPG Systems, including PESTEL, gap and SWOT analysis; and Porter's five forces model. In this answer we will use a **SWOT analysis**.

A SWOT analysis is a critical assessment of the strengths, weaknesses, opportunities and threats facing the organisation in relation to the internal and environmental factors affecting it, carried out in order to establish its condition prior to the preparation of a long-term plan. Strengths and weaknesses are discovered by internal analysis, whereas opportunities and threats are diagnosed by environmental analysis. The internal analysis should determine strengths that can be exploited and weaknesses that should be improved upon. Opportunities are areas that can be exploited, while threats need to be recognised and assessed for their potential effect on the organisation itself and its competitors.

Strengths

The main strength of the business seems to be the **commitment, enthusiasm and technical ability of the owner**, Andy Rowe, whose efforts are largely responsible for KPG systems' current level of success. Andy has obviously gathered other skilled people about him, since **technical expertise** also appears to be an important strength: in that products are designed to the different requirements of individual customers, which gives the company a competitive edge.

Allied to this is the importance of the **technical support** provided by the company. As technology becomes more complex, it is likely that companies will rely more on specialist technical support rather than on in-house abilities. Technical support is an important aspect of KPG's operations, but it is not an unalloyed success as there have been problems with providing support nationwide.

Weaknesses

One of the major weaknesses of the firm, and one that Andy has recognised, is that it may have **lost its direction**. There is a feeling that the firm is losing ground to larger competitors. Although the technical support activities of KPG are a strength, there is also a problem with **providing support throughout the UK**. Finally, there would appear to be an **over-dependence upon Andy Rowe**, which may mean that there will be senior management problems as the firm grows further.

Opportunities

In this age of high-technology, there is little doubt that KPG's market will continue to grow and expand, though the exact nature of that market in the future is uncertain. It is finding it difficult to win larger customers, though it is doing well with smaller ones. There seems to be an opportunity here for KPG to concentrate on this market segment. In this area there are likely to be many **innovations and advances** that KPG could adapt and embody in its products.

Threats

One major threat to KPG is that it is only a small player in this market with a **small and vulnerable market share**. Many of its competitors are larger companies with heavy investment in market, product and competitor research, which may give them a competitive edge over KPG. **Changes in technology** are considered as an opportunity if KPG has the technical expertise to capitalise on them; however, if KPG cannot keep abreast of changes in technology, the company may fall behind its competitors.

Future development

Weirich suggested that SWOT analysis could form the basis of four groups of strategies.

- SO strategies employ strengths to seize opportunities.
- ST strategies employ strengths to counter or avoid threats.
- WO strategies address weaknesses so as to be able to exploit opportunities.
- WT strategies are defensive aiming to avoid threats and the impact of weaknesses.

One useful impact of this analysis is that the four groups of strategies relate well to different time horizons and levels of available resources. SO strategies may be expected to produce good short-term results, generating profits that can be used to invest in medium-term WT strategies, such as improving areas of weakness. This could lead into a longer-term WO strategy of exploiting opportunities with the remedied weaknesses. ST strategies are relevant to the medium-term and are likely to be resource neutral.

In the case of KPG systems, a suitable SO strategy might be to concentrate effort in the short-term on the smaller business segment in which it is doing well. This could drive enhanced expansion in this segment, generating funds for a WT strategy of investment in capabilities and competences that will enable the company to bid successfully for larger contracts in the medium term. Such capabilities and competences would probably include a comprehensive solution to the service support network problems and a deeper understanding of the reasons for failure (and success) with larger customers.

25 Preparation question: environmental strategy

Part (a)

Top tips. You might think that project management is a rather peripheral topic for this exam; combining it with corporate social responsibility makes for a very unusual question indeed.

Note that the question asks about **skills required to achieve commitment**. You might think that the emphasis here should be on such inter-personal skills as **communication** and **negotiation**. It is clear from the suggested solution and the marking scheme that the Examiner did not wish to be quite so restrictive: marks were available for a wider discussion of project management **activities,** such as planning and post-completion review.

The suggested solution also emphasised the need for a **strategic approach** to such an important development.

Text reference. The topics mentioned in this answer are discussed in Chapters 5 and 13 of your BPP Study Text. This was an actual question in a Paper 3.5 exam, but it is not sufficiently demanding to be representative of the new exam – part (a) only being worth ten to twelve marks and part (b) perhaps worth five.

Easy marks. In general terms, project manager duties are neither complex nor a great deal different from ordinary management duties: it is the context that provides the contrast. If you could remember what you have learned about project management, this should have been a fairly easy question.

Examiner's comments. It seems that not many candidates were, in fact, able to remember very much at all about project management.

Graham Smith is promoting the CFS 'environmentally aware' project for strategic reasons to do with pressure from government and customers. The project manager would ideally have an appreciation of the strategic impact of the project, therefore.

A project is 'an undertaking that has a beginning and an end and is carried out to meet established goals within cost, schedule and quality objectives' (Haynes, *Project Management*). Every project therefore has a finite life and it is possible to identify life-cycle stages through which all projects pass. The activities that project managers undertake and many of the skills they must deploy are related to the different life-cycle stages.

Conception and definition is the first stage and includes problem analysis, assessment of possible solutions and definition of the objectives and scope of the project. This may be the most difficult phase for Graham Smith's project manager to undertake, since we know that several senior people in the organisation are not convinced that a problem exists at all. It is really Graham's role as **project sponsor** or '**project champion**' to gain commitment from his peers within the organisation at this stage. The project manager will be able to support him in this activity by providing details of the advantages the proposed accreditation will bring and the work that will have to be done to achieve it; these facts may be used to oppose to the many vague and imprecise arguments that are likely to be raised against the scheme. The project manager will also undertake an important **communication** and **negotiation role** with his or her own organisational peers.

The second stage of the project life cycle is **planning**. Here the project manager will deploy very specific project management skills, such as work breakdown structure and network analysis. The **project team** will start to form at this stage and the project manager will be responsible for leading and co-ordinating its efforts. An important aspect of this phase is **obtaining and scheduling resources**, so once again, negotiation is likely to be an important part of the project manager's job.

The third stage is **implementation**. Here the project manager must deploy normal managerial skills such as delegating and controlling, and continue to display both **leadership** and **team-building skills**. However, projects always involve dealing with the unexpected, so problem-solving skills will be very important. Also during this phase rescheduling and reassessment of priorities may become necessary, so the ability to **negotiate and balance the interests of the various project stakeholders** comes into play.

The final stage of the project includes the administrative work needed to complete it and to close down the project organisation. This stage should also include an audit or **post-completion review** of methods and achievement so that the organisation can learn from the experience gained and improve its future project management performance.

Part (b)

Corporate social responsibility (CSR) is often regarded simply as a drag on business efficiency, something that imposes cost but brings no tangible benefits in return. However, while costs must always be carefully controlled, CSR spending can be beneficial.

Like much other CSR spending, the CFS 'environmentally aware' project has a great deal of potential to provide competitive advantage in two principal ways. First, it may be a very effective way to **differentiate the company** from its competitors: larger customers are already beginning to show an interest in environmental concerns. Second, it is likely that at some time in the future further government regulation may be imposed. If CFS were already performing to the highest standards, the **impact of such regulation would be minimised**.

A further potential benefit to environmental awareness is the **avoidance of waste**. Policies designed to reduce energy consumption, for example, have an obvious impact on costs. These can include investment in insulation and efficient heating and the use of diesel rather than petrol engine vehicles.

Pressure to meet environmental standards can drive **innovation**, with the introduction of new technology and methods of working. Recycled materials of all kinds can offer cheaper alternatives to traditional options. Similar ideas may be applied to the use of other types of resource so that efficiency and productivity are enhanced.

In order to achieve these benefits, it is necessary that managers embrace the challenge of environmental responsibility, treating it as an opportunity and a challenge rather than as a dead weight loss.

26 Question with analysis: Apex culture

Text reference. The topics mentioned in this answer are discussed in Chapter 5 of your BPP Study Text.

Top tips. This question proved to be particularly difficult, with many candidates misunderstanding the requirement in part (b). The question was intended to be about change management in unpromising circumstances, not what might have been done at an earlier stage to avoid the problems described in the setting.

You should be aware of two things: first, the overriding need to read the question very carefully and answer it as set; and, second, if you do misunderstand the question, the Examiner *may* do what he did here and give you some credit for your efforts. Note, however, that this is **not** an invitation to answer the question you wish had been set!

Easy marks. As is so often the case, part (a) of this question is easier than part (b). This is because the effects of a clash of corporate cultures of the type envisaged are reasonably easy to predict, revolving, as they do, around the stress caused by new ways of doing things.

> **Examiner's comments.** This question was found to be difficult by many candidates. In part (a) a very restricted view of problems was taken, with few candidates mentioning potential effects on customers or the administrative infrastructure. The confusion was worse in part (b), with many candidates explaining how greater care before the acquisition could have avoided problems, rather than discussing ways of managing the problems that would be likely to arise after the acquisition.

Marking scheme

		Marks
(a)	Problems with the acquisition	
	Demotivated staff	up to 2
	Confused culture	up to 2
	Effect on clients	up to 2
	Conflict	up to 2
	Increased labour turnover	up to 2
	Expensive administrative infrastructure	up to 2
	Maximum for section (a) 12 marks	
(b)	Factors to be considered	
	Communication	up to 3
	Participation	up to 3
	Training	up to 3
	Pace of change	up to 3
	Manner of change	up to 3
	Scope of change	up to 3
	Maximum for section (b) 13 marks	
	Total 25 marks	

Part (a)

The clear problem with this acquisition, if it is not managed carefully, is the potential for a **clash of corporate cultures** and the effect this may have on each of the two sets of employees.

The corporate culture of Apex Finance Ltd is one of **centralisation** and **standardisation** of working practices and work outputs, with procedures and policies being imposed from a central management function. If this culture were to be imposed upon the new acquisition group of companies, then their staff, who are used to managing and motivating themselves and using their initiative, would find the atmosphere stultifying and demotivating, which must inevitably generate resentment and opposition.

Alternatively, if the **more relaxed style of management** were introduced throughout the group, it is likely that the original Apex employees would feel that there was a lack of direction and leadership, they may not be able to operate effectively without the centralised management structure that they have been used to.

An alternative might be to try to keep the two cultures separate and to allow each part of the entity to continue with its own management style. However, this is not likely to be successful, as there is likely to be a **degree of leakage**, which may lead to **discontent**. The original Apex employees may desire a degree of independence whereas those who were used to freedom may not always use their initiative and may desire more dependence upon others to give them direction.

If it is decided to impose one culture upon the other part of the organisation, there is likely to be a degree of discontent, probably leading to an **increase in labour turnover**. There may also be an effect on the **clients** of the new amalgamated company who may feel a degree of uncertainty about their relationship with their supplier. Clients will need to know whether they approach individual staff or a centralised management function.

A further problem if the centralised management system is to be continued, is that by its very nature, due to the acquisition, it must become **larger** and **more expensive**. Increased infrastructure will almost certainly add to the overheads of the joint operations. Other considerations are whether there is any possibility of sharing resources and skills between the two entities and the viability of integration of the necessary IT systems.

Part (b)

Carol Brindle is looking at a major **change management** exercise. There are bound to be wide-ranging changes in policy and practice in both halves of the merged company, and the acquisition will only succeed if these changes are undertaken in a proper fashion.

The **scope**, or extent, of any programme of change must be carefully considered. Staff will inevitably be apprehensive about **job security** and also for less specific reasons. Many people are naturally very conservative and dislike change. In extreme cases, severe depression can result. Reaction to change can include passive and active opposition and irrational behaviour: an increase in **conflict** between people and departments is likely. There is a case for keeping change to the minimum in order to, in turn, minimise its undesirable effects; this idea must not be used to justify the avoidance of difficult decisions and adjustments.

A **plan of integration** must be prepared, dealing with such matters as new responsibilities, procedures, structure, appointments and, very critically, the implications for job losses if any. At the same time, the process of **communication** must commence in order to allay the natural sense of apprehension, upset and disturbance that is likely to be present.

The **manner** in which change is introduced is very important. Staff participation in the decision-making process may be useful and provide both an element of motivation and a sense of ownership. However, staff will rapidly detect any tendency to *pseudo-participation*, and its effect will be less desirable than no participation at all. Staff participation in planning the implementation of necessary change is likely to be both less contentious and very useful.

Communication of decisions and developments must be prompt and honest. Resistance must be confronted and any necessary re-training undertaken.

Ms Brindle should also consider the **pace** of the change that is to take place. Slower change is perhaps easier to assimilate and less disturbing for staff. It also allows for review and adjustment of the new ways of doing things. However, there are usually operational imperatives that dictate a minimum acceptable speed and there is something to be said for a brisk approach that gets the upheaval over as soon as possible.

27 Supaserve

Part (a)

Text reference. The topics mentioned in this answer are discussed in Chapter 5 of your BPP Study Text.

Top tips. Segmentation will be most useful to Supaserve in the matter of product mix. This we might reasonably expect to be developed gradually by trial and error and careful sales analysis.

Easy marks. A brief description of segmentation bases in the context of the scenario should provide three or four marks, while an outline of the bases on which the validity of segments is assessed should be worth a couple more.

Examiner's comments. Many candidates did not understand the topic of segmentation.

		Marks
(a)	Bases for segmentation	up to 2 per point
	Significance of segment	up to 4
		Maximum for section (a) 12 marks
(b)	Assessment of impact of new system on internal operations	up to 6
	Assessment of Supaserve's ability to differentiate itself	up to 8
		Maximum for section (b) 13 marks
		Total 25 marks

The practice of market segmentation is based on the idea of creating value by adjusting the marketing mix so as to **satisfy more precisely** the needs and wants of customers. It is part of the move away from a one-size-fits-all mass marketing approach and toward a more targeted system that focuses on smaller market groups without sacrificing the scale economies of the mass market approach. A market segment is only valid if it is worth designing a **unique marketing mix** for it.

In broader terms, Chris Jones seems to have already largely defined his new marketing mix, in the form of his proposed online shopping service. He thus seems to be approaching the segmentation problem from the wrong direction, unless it is his intention to somehow adjust the functionality of his website to provide different service to separately identified different customer segments. This seems unlikely, given that getting just one online shopping website to work well is a major challenge.

Working at a more detailed scale, we might say that probably the only adjustment Supaserve can make to its existing marketing mix lies in the range of products it offers. The company's core products are food and drink. It would be useful to know whether the potential online market would buy the same products in the same proportions as the existing store customers, since this would have immediate implications for buying and stockholding. **Behavioural segmentation** would be the obvious approach here: survey techniques could find existing users of online grocery services and establish their existing preferences. Note that it is a principle of the scientific approach to market research that it is only data about existing behaviour that are worth having. Asking customers about possible future intentions is of little value: it is well-known that interview subjects' responses are affected by their perceptions of what constitutes the 'correct' answer, for example.

Socio-demographic segmentation would not really be useful, since it is linked only loosely to buying practices, and neither would **psychographic** or lifestyle segmentation, since that is really of use only in the development of new products. A basic **geographic** segmentation would presumably be automatically imposed by the imperative of delivery cost: Chris Jones would have to set a maximum radius from Supasave premises that he was prepared to service.

The validity or viability of a segment is determined by asking four questions.

(a) Can the segment be measured? It may be possible to conceive of a segment that cannot actually be measured sufficiently easily.

(b) Is the segment large enough to bother with?

(c) Can the segment be reached, in terms of both promotion and distribution?

(d) Is the segment actually different from existing ones, in terms of requiring a separate marketing mix?

In the case of Supaserve's potential online market, it would be necessary to seek answers to these questions using the survey techniques already mentioned.

Part (b)

> **Text reference.** The topics mentioned in this answer are discussed in Chapter 6 of your BPP Study Text.
>
> **Top tips.** It is clear from the Examiner's answer that you will understand his intention for this requirement better if you mentally insert the word 'internal' between 'Supaserve's' and 'activities' and then think in terms of the value chain. Also, do not be deceived by the reference to 'the new customer delivery system': the Examiner wants you to consider all aspects of the new strategy, not just the delivery of goods to the customer.

The spectacular failure of *Webvan's* attempt to rebuild the grocery business model from the ground up compared with the success of *Tesco's* incremental approach should be enough to convince Chris Jones to proceed by emulating the latter. Supaserve is only a medium-sized operator, so this will mean running the **fulfilment** operation from Supsaserve's existing store premises, probably by having a **dedicated team of in-store shoppers** filling orders from normal display shelf stock. The alternative, of running it from central warehouses, will require breaking bulk at those locations; this would make any unpicked items unusable for normal store deliveries, simply because of the inefficiencies involved in handling small quantities.

We may thus envisage, at best, a website that automatically forwards picking lists to the stores nearest to the customers concerned and produces optimised route delivery lists for the delivery vehicles. Within this basic model we might expect a range of effects on Supaserve's value activities.

Procurement and **inbound logistics** will simply adjust to a slightly different mix and, it is to be hoped, increased volume of purchases.

Operations will be extended to include the order picking activity outlined above and, more dramatically, the maintenance and development of the **sales website**. The quality of this will be critical to success. It must be secure, simple to use and offer access to the full range of Supaserve's stocks. There are likely to be thousands of separate items to be dealt with, so the hardware used will have to be extremely capable.

Outbound logistics will complete the home shopping loop by delivering the orders. Close attention will have to be paid to **requested delivery time slots** if customers are to be satisfied with the online shopping service. It may be possible to outsource this aspect of the operation, but this could only be done with very great care, since it puts the only opportunity for direct personal contact with the customer into the hands of outsiders. It would almost certainly be best to make deliveries in Supasave liveried vans driven by uniformed Supasave employees.

Marketing and sales may be able to obtain important customer information from the details of orders delivered. However, this will not be different in degree or in kind from the information collected by a good loyalty card scheme: the experience of Tesco, the acknowledged UK leader in this field, is that it is difficult to exploit this detailed information simply because of its sheer volume.

Supasave is suffering under intense competition from larger competitors. The scenario does not tell us which country it operates in, but if it is anywhere in the developed world, it seems unlikely that online shopping will provide any degree of differentiation at all. All the large supermarkets in the UK, for example, offer this service.

If Supasave is, in fact, operating in a market where none of its competitors has an online operation, then its new venture would provide a very marked point of differentiation. This is so much the case that we might question the wisdom of a medium size company's implementing such a radical idea. It would probably make better use of its resources if it sought to expand its conventional operation through promotion and opening newer, larger stores in prime locations.

28 Preparation question: Global Imaging

Top Tips. This was originally part of a Paper 3.5 question and was worth eight marks.

Easy marks. This is a fairly simple question: the usual arguments about outsourcing any activity apply, including cost reduction, degree of control and loss of internal competence.

Advantages of outsourcing HR activities

Cost

Outsourcing can be a good way to **reduce costs** since the external supplier should be able to achieve **economies of scale and scope** and achieve higher levels of productivity through **specialisation**. In a properly negotiated outsourcing relationship, some of these cost savings should be passed on to the purchaser.

Expertise

An external agency specialising in HR work should be able to employ a range of full-time HR specialists. This would be prohibitively expensive for a small company such as Global Imaging, which is probably likely to employ only Paul Simpson and one or two assistants. Outsourcing can thus give access to a more **comprehensive range of expertise**. This can be useful for both routine but vital matters such as advice on payroll technicalities and also for more demanding specialist work, such as assessment and selection of candidates.

Focus

Devolvement of generic HR work to an external agency would reduce the demands of routine work on Paul Simpson's time. This would enable him to give greater attention to developing those aspects of HR policy that will make the **greatest contribution to Global Imaging's strategy**.

Disadvantages of outsourcing HR activities

Control

Outsourcing brings the possibility of **loss of control**. This can affect such matters as quality of service and response time. The outsourcing contract must be written carefully to ensure that the potential for loss of control is minimised.

Confidentiality

HR data is particularly sensitive because of the **need to maintain individual privacy**. It is also subject to **data protection legislation** in most Western jurisdictions. An organisation contemplating outsourcing HR services must therefore ensure that it chooses a contractor capable of providing the necessary data security. However, because of the loss of control mentioned above, the ability of the principal to maintain the confidentiality of its data is reduced.

Workforce reaction

Associated with confidentiality is workforce reaction. Employees may object to then release of their data to an outside agency and may be uncomfortable in making use of personal services aspects of HRM such as counselling. On the other hand, some staff may appreciate the extra element of impartiality potentially available from outsourced services.

Loss of expertise

Outsourcing brings with it the possibility of **loss of expertise**. This is particularly apparent in activities that that require regular practice for proficiency or regular updates on current information and practice. HRM is not a core competence for Global Imaging, but, bearing in mind the company's reliance on highly skilled staff, it might well be regarded as an area in which a threshold competence is required.

A problem associated with loss of expertise is that the company may become **over-dependent** on its outside provider, losing its autonomy of action. This is probably not too much of a problem for Global Imaging, since there is no shortage of external HR service providers that would be happy to bid for its work.

29 IT Project

Text reference. The topics mentioned in this answer are discussed in Chapter 10 of your BPP Study Text.

Top tips. Do not be put off by the superfluous word *and* in the third line of the second paragraph of the scenario; minor typos can occur in exam papers; the meaning is clear. Serious errors are rare, but if you have the misfortune to encounter one, report it to the examination staff and ask for guidance.

Easy marks. Many candidates will struggle with questions like this, as they do not fit into a neat category. A little lateral thinking is required. If you feel you have to tackle a question like this, remember that relevance to the scenario is *always* important and use key words like *strategy, organisation structure, competitive advantage, value chain, marketing* and *HRM* to guide your thinking.

Part (a)

The project is to be assessed against 'competing IT project proposals'. Such a comparison should **focus on costs and benefits** and would have two main aspects: matters which could be quantified with some precision, such as capital cost, and more **qualitative factors** such as efficiency of working.

Standard investment appraisal techniques such as NPV should be applied to any **quantifiable costs and benefits**. These should include the capital cost of hardware and software, including physical security measures and any structural work such as enhanced fire precautions and installation of ducts and cables; maintenance costs, including an allowance for contingencies; increased insurance cost; the cost of training; extra telephone costs arising from internet access; and any savings which might arise from staff reductions.

These aspects are probably quite simple to determine and assess. However, it is probable that **such an appraisal will produce a negative NPV** for any project, as costs are fairly easy to establish, but **benefits are likely to be largely unquantifiable.** Nevertheless, a successful IT project can offer benefits which are of major significance for an organisation and they must be taken into account.

It would be normal to attempt to deal with this by **ranking competing projects** by scoring them against **objective criteria**. The scoring could be done by a committee or by several individuals separately, with a moderator combining their scores. This would bring a kind of collective judgement to the process, but would be subject to personal bias, which might break out into acrimony in the later stages of selection.

Projects should be assessed against criteria such as those below.

- Expected improvement in quality of **management information** in such matters as speed of provision and completeness

- **Compatibility** with the existing organisation in terms of structure, responsibilities, personalities, culture and skill levels

- Fit with the current **strategic posture** of the organisation, and, if a commercial organisation, contribution to competitive advantage

- **Risk** associated with the technology: is it proven or groundbreaking? How big is the installed base?
- Extent to which **existing equipment** can be reused

When the financial and qualitative assessments are complete, it will be necessary to integrate them. This should only present a problem if they produce radically different solutions; if that is the case, **rational decision rules** such as minimising the maximum possible loss may help.

Part (b)

The broad objectives of project management are as follows.

Quality. The end result should conform to the project specification. In other words, the result should achieve what the project was supposed to do.

Budget. The project should be completed without exceeding authorised expenditure.

Timescale. The installation should be ready for use by the agreed date.

A typical project has a **project life cycle** and is likely to progress through **four stages**:

- **conception and project definition;**
- **planning;**
- **implementation;**
- **completion and evaluation.**

The first stage may be based on the work already done and described in part (a) above. It will be necessary to define the final objectives and agree fundamental and desirable success criteria.

Project planning breaks the project down into manageable units, estimates the resources required for each and establishes the necessary work schedules. Tools such as critical path analysis and Gantt charts may be used where there are time and sequence constraints.

Implementation must be controlled and progress monitored to ensure that, for instance, quality and financial requirements are being achieved. It is often suggested with IT projects that there should be an extended period of parallel running; it must be remembered, however, that this implies a great deal of extra work by the staff involved and may be impractical for all but the most important elements.

When the installation is complete it should be **appraised for success** in meeting user expectations. With internally managed projects, this provides invaluable opportunities to learn from mistakes.

30 Connie Head

Text reference. The topics mentioned in this answer are discussed in Chapter 15 of your BPP Study Text.

Top tips. This is a quite difficult question, which requires consideration of both performance management and the process of appraisal, together with its potential to assist with strategic management.

Easy marks. The only easy marks were available in part (a), for discussing the uses to which appraisal is put: that is to say, basically, assessment of performance, potential and training needs. To score well, you would also need to discuss how effective implementation of an appraisal scheme can be achieved.

Examiner's comments. This was not a very popular question: part (b), in particular, was not well done overall, a lack of understanding of performance management being very clear.

Marking scheme

		Marks
(a)	Objectives and purpose model of the appraisal process	Up to 5 marks each
	Characteristics of the process	
	Results v activities	
	Frequency of appraisal	**Maximum 15 marks**

(b)   Individual and organisational objectives Up to 3 marks each
      Place in the strategy process
      Feedback and control
      Implementation issues

Maximum 10 marks
Total 25 marks

Part (a)

The Senior Partner and Connie emphasise the aspects of appraisal schemes that **support their own favoured policies**. Such schemes should support the organisation's overall objectives without incurring excessive administrative and management costs.

In an organisation such as an accounting practice, the professional staff should indeed be highly **self-motivated**, able to judge the effectiveness of their own performance and bring to their work a commitment to high professional standards. On the other hand, it is inevitable that their **talents and performance will vary** and they will need **guidance and help with their future development**. Dealing with these issues would be the role of an appraisal scheme.

The overall aim of such a scheme would be to **support progress toward the achievement of corporate objectives** and it would do this in three ways: performance review, potential review and training needs review.

Performance review. Performance review should provide employees with an **impartial and authoritative assessment of the quality and effect of their work**. Individuals should have personal objectives that support corporate goals via intermediate objectives relevant to the roles of their work groups. A reasoned assessment of performance can have a **positive motivating effect**, simply as a kind of positive, reinforcing feedback. It can also provide an opportunity for analysing and addressing the **reasons for sub-optimal performance.**

Potential review. Any organisation needs to make the best use it can of its people; an accountancy practice is typical of many modern organisations in that its people are its greatest asset and its future success depends on managing them in a way that makes the best use of their skills and aptitudes. An important aspect of this is **assessing potential for promotion and moves into other positions of greater challenge and responsibility.**

Training needs review. A further aspect of the desirable practice of enabling staff to achieve their potential is the provision of training and development activities. The appraisal system is one means by which **training needs can be assessed** and training provision initiated.

The appraisal system

An appraisal system must be properly administered and operated if it is make a proper contribution to the organisation's progress.

The appraisal cycle. Formal appraisal, with interviews and written assessments, is typically undertaken on an **annual cycle**. This interval is commonly regarded as too long to be effective because of the speed with which individual roles can evolve and their holders can develop, so the annual appraisal is often supplemented with a less detailed review after six months. Sometimes the procedure is sufficiently simplified that the whole thing can be done at six monthly intervals. Much modern thinking on this topic is now suggesting that any frequency of periodic appraisal is unsatisfactory and that it should be replaced by a **continuous process of coaching and assessment**.

Objectivity and reliability. Appraisal involves an element of direct personal criticism that can be stressful for all parties involved. If the system is to be credible its outputs must be seen to be objective and reliable. This requires proper **training for appraisers**, the establishment of appropriate **performance standards** and, preferably, input into each appraisal from **more than one person**. Having reports reviewed by the appraiser's own manager is one approach to the last point; 360 degree appraisal is another.

147

Setting targets. Past performance should be reviewed against **objective standards** and this raises the question of the type of objective that should be set. Objectives set in terms of **results** or outcomes to be achieved can encourage **creativity** and **innovation** but may also lead to **unscrupulous**, **unethical** and even **illegal choice of method**. On the other hand, objectives designed to maintain and improve the quality of output by **encouraging conformity** with approved procedure and method may stifle the creativity and innovation widely regarded as a vital source of continuing competitive advantage.

Part (b)

Performance management involves the establishment of clear, agreed individual **goals and performance standards**; continuous leadership action to both **motivate and appraise subordinates**; and a **periodic review** of performance at which the goals and performance standards for the next cycle are set.

Performance management is an application of the **rational model** of strategic management, in that individual goals are intended to form the lowest echelon of a **hierarchy of objectives** that builds up to support the **overall mission** of the organisation. It is an essential aspect of the system that individual goals should be **agreed and internalised** so that true **goal congruence** is achieved.

This overall approach was first described (as is so often the case) by *Peter Drucker*, in 1954, and is seen most clearly in the system of **management by objectives** (MbO). MbO as a management system has fallen somewhat from favour with the rise of quality management methods that emphasise processual and procedural conformance rather than the attainment of overall performance goals. Nevertheless, it has much to offer.

Under a formal MbO system, the process of setting goals is part of the **implementation phase** of strategic management and follows consideration of resources, overall objectives and SWOT analysis. Top level subordinate goals are agreed for heads of departments, divisions or functions: these goals should be specific, measurable, attainable, relevant and time-bounded (SMART). It is particularly important that the achievement of a goal can be established by objective **measurement**. There may be different timescales for different objectives, with short-term goals supporting longer-term ones.

Departmental heads then agree SMART goals for their subordinates in discussion with them, that support their own personal goals, and so on down the hierarchy to the level of the individual employee. All members of the organisation thus know what they are expected to achieve and how it fits into the wider fabric of the organisation's mission.

Periodic **performance review** is based on the objective appraisal of success against agreed goals, the agreement of goals for the next period and an assessment of the resources, including training, that the reviewee may require to reach those goals. The MbO system thus closes the **feedback loop** in the corporate control system.

31 Rameses International

Text Reference. The topics mentioned in this answer are discussed in Chapters 1 and 15 of your BPP Study Text.

Top tips. Fairly obviously, not all businesses are equally successful and some of this difference can be traced to strategic failure. It is important to realise that strategy is not a machine that you put money and models into and get growth and profit out of: things can go wrong. An acquaintance with the real world of business will help you to answer questions like this, so make sure you spend a little while reading the business press each week.

Easy marks. Note the use of the word 'may' in the part (a) requirement. This means you are free to speculate on the basis of the brief information given, so apply all your general background knowledge of how things should be done.

Part (a)

The development of successful strategies is a difficult and complex process and there is no guarantee of success. This is particularly true in the conditions of change and increasing competition encountered by Rameses International. Even where conditions are stable, all stages of the strategic process bring opportunities for sub-optimal decision-making.

Johnson, Scholes and Whittington's **strategy lenses** may be used to illustrate this problem.

Using the **strategy as design** lens, which is based on a rational, objective approach, we might suggest failure of analysis, reasoning or implementation as possible sources of strategic failure. For example, in the case of Rameses International, the attempt to move into new markets will have presented many opportunities to get the marketing mix wrong. Similarly, Rameses failed to anticipate its **competitors' reaction** to the strategic changes it made; this made it easier for them to react effectively to the execution of its chosen strategies. Another major reason for the lack of success of Rameses' chosen strategies may have been their **number and variety**. This may led to extensive change within the company in a very short period of time and, in consequence, confusion about priorities and inattention to its core business.

Using the **strategy as experience** lens, in Rameses' case we might be tempted to ask whether this old-established company's **paradigm** was any longer fit for purpose in its changing circumstances. The array of changes indicates a **lack of prioritisation and planning** and has been overly reactive to perceived problems. Rameses appears to be trying to change everything in the hope of getting it right without carrying out appropriate planning and ensuring appropriate resource utilisation. This may be as a result of an **over-rigid approach to business**. Again, the move into new markets might simply have been a case of 'more of the same' rather than a properly considered strategy.

Similar rigidities of thought are likely to apply in other areas. In attempting to carry out so many changes at once, it is likely that the company may have **alienated many of its stakeholders**, including employees and suppliers. For a change of strategy to be successful, it is important that the stakeholders concerned are committed to the change and that they understand the reasons and justifications for them.

The **strategy as ideas** lens suggests that the role of management is to create the context and conditions in which new ideas can emerge and the best ones thrive. An important feature of this role is to avoid relying on either the design approach or the experience approach. The first tends to lead to over-emphasis on control, while the second tends to develop a kind of incremental momentum. In either case, innovation is unlikely and the result is **strategic drift**. While Rameses might just have had a run of bad luck with its ideas, it seems more likely that strategic drift is, indeed what has happened to its strategic management.

Part (b)

Leadership is required for strategic success in any organisation. It must come from the top of the business and it is vital that the senior management are involved in any strategy implementation. Senior management are primarily concerned with the identification, evaluation and selection of strategies, but their involvement must not end there.

Transactional theories of leadership, whether based on traits, behaviour or contingencies are applicable at any level of management and have no specific applicability to the strategic apex. Transactional leaders focus on systems and controls and generally seek improvement rather than change. This kind of leadership is essential for the implementation of existing plans. However, it is not enough.

More recent **transformational theories** are particularly relevant at higher levels of management. Such theories generally accept that the world is a much less stable place than it was and that changes of all kinds are frequent and far-reaching. It is necessary for leaders of all kinds to accept this and to provide leadership that will help their organisations to respond in creative and effective ways. Transformational (or charismatic) leaders energise people and build a vision of the future. Change management is a natural part of what they do.

The applicability of these ideas to Rameses International seems fairly clear. The senior management team have recognised the need for change in what they do, but they have not followed this idea through into its full implications. Instead, they have tried a range of slightly different strategic ploys, all of which have failed. It will be Jeanette Singh's role to counter this strategic drift by fulfilling the five main expectations of modern leaders listed by *John van Maurik*.

- To **change** organisations and systems from within
- To **empower** others
- To work through **teams** in delayered environments
- To provide **clarity of purpose** and direction
- To drive forward adventurous, **visionary strategies**

Achieving this will require the assistance of middle managers. In her pursuit of change, Jeanette Singh may be tempted to see her middle managers as implementers at best and possibly as potential blockers. In fact, their commitment to change is important and they have significant roles to play in change management.

(a) They will be responsible for **implementation** and **control** where change is introduced in a top-down way.

(b) They will have to **translate** of the overall change strategy into forms suited to **specific local contexts**: this may require r**einterpretation** and **adjustment** of strategic factors such as relationships with suppliers and customers.

(c) It will be appropriate for them to provide of **advice** to higher management on requirements for change and potential obstacles.

32 Preparation question: Sykes Engineering

Text reference. The topics mentioned in this answer are discussed in Chapter 4 of your BPP Study Text.

Top tips. This is the first part of a Paper 3.5 question. It was worth ten marks. Take a very high moral stance on any matters of corporate governance and business ethics and do not hesitate to condemn dubious practices. Note, however, that you do not have to endorse the stakeholder view of the corporation if you do not want to: that is not an ethical matter.

Examiner's comments. This requirement was disappointingly answered, with too many candidates putting their trust in a mission statement as an ethical cure-all.

The situation at Sykes Engineering Group is extremely worrying and action should have been taken much earlier to prevent its arising.

Corporate governance

Too much power is **concentrated in one person**, Jerome Sykes. Corporate governance reports have recommended that the roles of Chairman and Managing Director should be held by two different people: this is now a requirement of the London Stock Exchange Combined Code. Also, there should be a strong and independent body of non-executive directors on the board. The role of these non-executive directors should have been to question any dubious policies or actions at an early stage. They would also take charge of executive directors' pay and benefits packages and auditor liaison.

Organisational culture

The autocratic behaviour of Jerome Sykes has influenced the culture of the whole organisation and resulted in sexual and racial harassment. His involvement at all levels of decision-making should have been prevented by a strong organisational hierarchy and control system, with a key role for supervisory management. The non-executive directors would have played an important role here.

BPP
LEARNING MEDIA

Corruption

Bribery is a more difficult issue since it is difficult to define and standards vary from country to country. Nevertheless, a reputation for corrupt practices will seriously harm the reputation of the company. Control procedures and clear guidelines should be in place to prevent corruption and immoral business practice.

Role of the auditors and institutional shareholders

It is surprising that a publicly quoted company has been allowed by the auditors and the institutional shareholders to deteriorate to this extent without intervention. They have a duty to monitor the activities of the company and take action if unacceptable activities are taking place. The auditors, in particular, should have been aware of what was happening and should have taken proper steps.

33 Question with student answer: Bethesda Heights

Text reference. The topics mentioned in this answer are discussed in Chapters 5 and 6 of your BPP Study Text.

Top tips. Part (a) of this question is noteworthy for the way it combines ethical ideas with strategic analysis. As the Examiner has himself said, ethics is not going to go away: expect it to be integrated into the question this way, rather than being examined as a separate topic.

The key to answering this question is to identify the various stakeholder groups. Once you have done this you can identify their interests.

Examiner's comments. Parts (a) and (b) were answered competently, but part (c) was not.

Marking scheme

		Marks
(a)	Factors giving surgeons a powerful negotiating position	
	Scarcity of labour	up to 2
	Status	up to 2
	Single-mindedness and unity of purpose	up to 2
	Power and influence	up to 2
		Maximum 7 marks
	Arguments from other stakeholder groups	
	Patients	up to 3
	Local government	up to 3
	General medical and other staff	up to 3
	Local community	up to 3
		Maximum 8 marks
		Total for section (a) 15 marks

(b) Problems being experienced by Bethesda

Reduced income	up to 3
Increased costs	up to 3
Low income from medical insurance	up to 3
Poor operational efficiencies	
Lower bed capacity usage	up to 2
Higher mortality rates	up to 2
Staff numbers higher	up to 2
Re-admission rates higher	up to 2
Less use of day surgery	up to 2
Poorer ratio of out-patients to residential care	up to 2

Maximum 14 marks

Unlikely to solve the problems of Bethesda

Fewer beds	up to 3
Increased costs of investment (scarce resource)	up to 3
Does not address the real problems – falling revenue etc	up to 3

Maximum 6 marks

Total for section (b) 20 marks

(c) Other strategies including evaluation

Improve internal efficiencies	up to 5
Collaborative strategies	up to 5
Use of generic strategies – focus differentiation etc	up to 7

Maximum for section (c) 15 marks

Total 50 marks

Student answer

> The student starts well by identifying a key theorist to help provide ideas to answer the question. Many people make the mistake of overlong introductions which simply précis the scenario and therefore score few points. This has been avoided here

(a) Based on the Mendelow's matrix, a company should treat stakeholders according to their power & interests. Key players, those with high interest in the company & high power, are the most important & so their opinions prevail.

Senior medical staff is a key player for the Hospital, as the Hospital could not function without then, whereas this staff has no burdens to leave the Hospital if their needs are not met/opinion accepted. Their interest in the Hospital is significant as they longed to expand their power & influence.

However, investment in modern surgery could be a competitive advantage for the Hospital & enhance the Hospital's surgical reputation. Better representation could attract private healthcare patients & thus increase the Hospital's revenues. This would be viewed in a positive way by some other stakeholders including CEO of the Hospital, Mayor of the Coty going to cut back its funding & government not able to increase its funding

Better reputation itself would also be welcomed by the Mayor. Further, modern surgery centre would be appreciated by well off patients.

> The student fairly clearly states the surgeons' position in the matrix and therefore their level of influence as the question requires.

On the other hand, the Mayor group, government and CEO were against this investment as the Hospital is currently in a deficit and should stay in a deficit within next 3 years. Neither government nor Mayor is willing to cover increase of the Hospital costs (-) operational costs or capital investments. However, although power of both government & local council is high its interest in the Hospital is low. Therefore, the hospital preferred fulfilment of senior surgeons' staff.

> This paragraph has some good ideas but makes sweeping unexplained statements in terms of the level of power and interest of the government saying that the government and local council has low interest in the hospital with out explaining why the candidates thinks this is the case.

A series of subheading for each major stakeholder would have improved the ease of marking of the question and may have earned the candidate more marks.

Local population is really interested in the Hospital but it has little power. Therefore, the Hospital just needs to keep them informed but may not have to follow their requirements. This group is even not likely to achieve more power in future even if not satisfied.

This is a good clear well explained paragraph which would score two marks. The points could have been made slightly more briefly to leave time for more points later.

Employees of the Hospital have little power. This lask power results from he fact that they represent only general staff that is easy to replace & they are not supported by unions (if there is any) so far. Therefore the Hospital could afford to overlook their requirements although they showed interest in the efficient & effective hospital treatment of population that could not afford private insurance. This group can increase its influence in future if unions become involved or if high ranking doctors enters this group demanding not only for modern medical centre but also for modern & effective run of the whole Hospital.

The other groups could have stated that trade-off for these investment in surgical reputation is too low. Reduced number of beds will result in additional home visits & re-admission to the Hospital, i.e. in additional costs & potential problems with available beds. Longer waiting times can hurt the Hospital's general reputation & as well as insufficient treatment of the disadvantaged group.

The local government could argue that it could not finance the capital investment into surgical centre.

> The structure of the answer is reasonable as it works through the major stakeholders mentioned in the question stating the objectives and arguments of each.
> Overall this part of the answer would score a strong pass.

Again the candidate gets straight to the point of answering the question and avoids time wasting. A good point for this part of the question will pick out a clear difference in the numbers and then discuss why it is a problem to Bathesda hospital.

(b)   Compared to neighbouring hospital, the BH Hospital has lower income from central & local government due to less population served & less work carried out. However, the most significant difference is in income from medical insurance. This is a result of bad reputation of the BH Hospital. The new surgical centre will attract more private - insured patients & increase BH Hospital's reputation. Thus it should help increase income from medical insurance.

The most important problem is mortality of the BH Hospital's patient. This should be decreased by the new surgical centre.

> This question is in two clear parts i.e. what is the problem and how will the high tech approach overcome this. In this paragraph the student is attempting to answer the parts of the question but does so with little explanation and therefore would score a maximum of one mark for this point.

Due to lower number of beds, the BH Hospital should concentrate on day surgery operations especially based on the number of these operations being approximately 5 times higher on the neighbouring hospital. This would also decrease costs related to tome patients spent in hospital. This is also supported by ratio outpatients to those committed the hospital that is managed but the neighbouring hospital as 5:2 compared to 5:51 in the BH hospital.

Another problem of BH Hospital is long waiting time. This is nearly, 3 times longer then in the neighbouring hospital and is a fact that discourages patients to visit BH Hospital. The new surgical centre could improve the significantly in respect to patients that are admitted to hospital for surgery and not other long-term healthcare treatment.

Although fixed as well as variable costs are lower in the BH Hospital, this indicates a problem with level of healthcare offered by the BH Hospital which is one of its main weaknesses. The new surgical centre would result in an increase of BH Hospitals costs, but, on the other hand, also in more attractive facility & more patients.

Overall, the key problem in the BH hospital is worse healthcare service. Improving it, the BH Hospital needs to increase the costs but, thanks to increased number of patients due to better reputation, it would increase the BH Hospitals income from grants & private medical insurance companies.

> This point is quite well explained but only answers part of the requirement.

> This is a good well explained point which answers the question set and so would score two marks.

> Overall the volume of ideas here is too low for 20 marks and so this part of the question would be a borderline pass.

(c) Management assess committee could have concentrated on improval of the Hospital's efficiency & effectiveness via investing in modern facility overall, not specifically, to the surgical centre. This should improve the Hospital's reputation and attract more patients, including private healthcare patients. Such an investment could have been finances by a bank loan of local community loan/bonds.

Alternatively it could fiancé investment in new technology using leasing/ hire-purchase agreements.

Further, it could introduce special treatment programs that patients could partially cover themselves. This may include some alternative medicine programs, examination not covered by the insurance company or only covered over certain time or no/minimal waiting time (if it was not against the local medical legislation) or physiotherapy/occupational therapy that CEO wishes to withheld.

To support treatments of the disadvantaged group of patients, it could (possibly together with the local government) set up a public collection or a foundation voluntary financed by the local community.

Alternatively, it could share some modern healthcare instrument/surgery rooms with other hospital. In such cases no one-one big investment would be required, waiting time & expenses & reputation of the Hospital may be improved. Although this could result in higher operational costs, these would arise only during the time then the hired technology was effectively used by the Hospital's patients.

> This part of the answer gives a good volume of specific ideas but the overall answer lacks theoretical content and structure.

> Many of these points are too brief and lack explanation.

> The student has chosen not to use a theoretical approach to this question. This may mean that the volume of ideas generated may not be sufficient. However the points are well related to the scenario and specific to the situation.

> Overall this part of the answer would be a borderline pass.

BPP answer

Part (a)

As in most organizations, within Bethesda Heights Hospital there are several **stakeholder groups**, each with different objectives, varying levels of power and differing degrees of willingness to involve themselves in the future strategy of the hospital. The senior medical staff stand out as having both power and the willingness to use it. Using the *Mendelow* matrix, which classifies stakeholders according to the extent of their power and their willingness to become involved, the senior medical staff are 'key players'. However, their use of their power is ethically questionable as they have threatened to withdraw their services to patients if their demands are not met.

The power of the senior medical group comes from both their status and their importance to the hospital. Consultant surgeons have been respected both for their high degree of professional skill and their dedication to their patients' interest. This respect gives them a degree of **referent power** and extends to their opinions generally, even in areas outside their professional expertise.

The senior medical staff have also exercised **resource power** in their threat to resign; the hospital cannot function without them. Their main power lies in their importance to the hospital which stems from the **scarcity of their skills**. In economic terms, the supply of senior medical staff is inelastic. Some of the staff in a hospital are more easily replaced than others. The administrative staff, cleaners, caterers and so on could easily be recruited from other sectors. Skilled staff, such as nurses, are more problematic but there is likely to be a steady supply of such staff if required. However, skilled specialist surgeons are in short supply and would be extremely difficult to replace. Without their skills the hospital could not operate at all. The surgeons have relied on this fact to put pressure on the Management Committee to agree to their strategy.

There are a number of other stakeholder groups in Bethesda: the administrators, the local politicians, the local population and the general medical staff. Each of these groups has its own potential strategies and arguments that they could have used to promote their objectives.

As far as the **administrators** are concerned, their aim is an efficiently run hospital with cuts in costs. The efficiency drive might not be in the best interests of patients as it is pointed out in the scenario that efficiency is not the same thing as effectiveness. However the **administrators'** strongest argument would be the **financial consequences of the surgeons' strategy**. The requirements of the surgeons' strategy are twofold. First, **substantial capital investment** would be required and as a consequential trade-off, there would be a **reduction in the number of beds** within the hospital. The hospital is currently forecasting a deficit of $75 million dollars in three years' time; if this deficit is not substantially improved, then the survival of the hospital must be in doubt. Not only would the capital investment further increase the deficit, but the reduction in the number of beds (and therefore treatments) will inevitably lead to less government funding and a further increase in the deficit. Many stakeholders in the hospital will be unwilling to acknowledge the primacy of financial considerations but with a reduction in revenue from funding it would seem unlikely that the hospital could survive.

The local **politicians** appear to have two **conflicting objectives**. They are anxious that the hospital should be kept open to service the medical needs of the city, but they also wish to cut back the hospital's funding in order to avoid increasing local taxes. They cannot have it both ways: **they must choose** between a properly funded hospital and tax cuts. As the objectives of this group are confused, it would be difficult for them to prepare any coherent arguments If the local politicians accept that it is necessary politically to keep the hospital open, then they can use the media to illustrate the dangers of the surgeons' approach, which will inevitably lead to fewer beds and less treatment for the local population.

The **local population** themselves are the current and potential patients of the hospital and it is in their interest that there should be no curtailment of the hospital's activities. However, even though they are a large group, they are unorganised and it is unlikely that they will be able to exert any significant influence.

The **general medical staff** have possibly the strongest argument on their side: the **ethical argument**. They are primarily concerned with the maintenance of an efficient and effective hospital for the local population who could not afford private medical insurance. This is a strong argument as it is clear that those with medical insurance have the neighbouring hospital to go to but those without would be severely disadvantaged without the Bethesda Hospital in something like its current form.

ANSWERS

Part (b)

> **Easy marks.** You are told clearly to make use of the quantitative data in this part. This is often an easy way to score well, since simple arithmetic is usually all you need to detect important facts such as the significant differences in the two hospital's insurance income movement year on year and their readmission rates. We illustrate both of these points in our answer.
>
> A good way to get started is to work down the table of data, calculating ratios, percentages and simple changes as seems appropriate. Here, the year on year changes are clearly what you should start with.
>
> **Examiner's comments.** Numerical analysis was generally well done, but this good performance was often not extended to using the data to show how the new strategy would improve matters.

Problem areas

It is clear from the quantitative data provided that Bethesda is not run as well as its neighbour institution.

In terms of **income**, the main difference between the two hospitals, other than size (and therefore the amount of government income) is the **income from the medical insurance** sector. Not only is the neighbouring hospital medical insurance income over **three times** that of Bethesda, but it also increased by 5% over the last year, whereas that of Bethesda decreased by 17%. Funding from central and local government would appear to be higher per bed at Bethesda at $274, compared to $238 for the neighbouring hospital. This may be because the medical and surgical work carried out at Bethesda is more complex than at its neighbour, but we have no information to support this supposition.

There are some **areas of cost** that would appear to be beyond the power of the hospital to cut. The costs of labour, medical equipment, drugs and other variable inputs have increased at approximately the same rate in each hospital, indicating that the changes are due to market forces and **must be lived with**. However, the efficiency of the two hospitals does appear to be very different. In particular, the cost per bed at Bethesda is $357 compared to $322 at the neighbouring hospital.

Labour costs are obviously a significant cost in the hospital service; however, Bethesda would appear to be **over-staffed** compared to the other hospital. Not only is the number of staff per bed higher in Bethesda, but its staff numbers have increased since last year, while in the neighbouring hospital staff, numbers were cut.

There are a number of factors that will significantly affect patients' view of Bethesda. Seventeen percent of patients require re-admission, compared to just 9% in the other hospital; this could be caused in part by the **false economies** suggested by the administrative faction on the Management Committee. It could also be related to the time spent in hospital after an operation, which is only 7 days at Bethesda compared to 10 at the other hospital. More concerning are **waiting times** at Bethesda, which is **three times** as long as at the neighbouring hospital, and the **mortality rate** which is over **seven times** higher at Bethesda and increasing. It is, of course, entirely possible that the mortality figures are affected by the type of ailments dealt with at Bethesda, which may be of a more terminal nature than at the other hospital, but we do not have enough information to assess this.

There is obviously a **clear difference in strategy** between the medical treatment in the two hospitals, which may also have adversely affected the efficiency and profitability of Bethesda. The neighbouring hospital has increased the number of **operations that require no overnight stay** by 467%: the equivalent increase at Bethesda has been only 30%. Clearly, an operation that does not require a bed and an overnight stay will be less costly for the hospital than in-patient procedures; such an approach is likely to appeal to the medical insurers as it will be a cheaper option for them.

Similarly, the ratio of the number of patients dealt with as **outpatients** compared to those staying in hospital for one night or more has increased at the neighbouring hospital to 5:1 compared to a constant figure of just 3:1 at Bethesda. Treating outpatients is likely to be a less costly strategy, which although not ignored by Bethesda, does not appear to have been capitalised upon.

The **utilisation of capacity** at each hospital can also be considered from the data provided. For Bethesda with 350 beds, the potential number of bed nights each year is 127,750 (350 x 365 days). With an average stay of 7 nights per patient, this means that potentially 18,250 patients (127,750/7) could be treated in a year. In fact only 10,650 in-patients were treated, which is only 58% of full capacity. The similar figures for the neighbouring hospital indicate that this is operating at 76% capacity. Whereas it is impractical to consider 100% capacity within a hospital system, clearly Bethesda is lagging behind its competitor in this respect.

How the proposed strategy will address these problems

One of the main aims of the surgeons' strategy was to **attract private healthcare patients**. Although the neighbouring hospital is clearly working towards this aim, with substantially more medical insurance income than Bethesda, it must be noted that even at the neighbouring hospital the income from this sector is still only 37% of total income. At Bethesda, such income is significantly lower, currently standing at 16%; it would appear that government payments will remain the most significant element of income despite the surgeons' strategy.

Possibly even more significant in terms of income is the **trade off** for the surgeons' strategy in that the number of beds must be reduced. This will **reduce income** from both central and local government. It would appear unlikely that the move into the medical insurance sector could provide enough income to cover the lost government income and turn the hospital into a profitable venture, particularly considering the natural competition from the established neighbouring hospital. The strategy will also **further increase waiting time** for the non-privately funded patients. It is difficult to see how this will help the hospital.

This strategy will not obviously improve the efficiency of Bethesda or reduce costs. However, it could be argued that with a reduction in beds there could be a drive towards greater efficiency and certainly a reduction in staff numbers, which could serve to improve productivity.

Part (c)

Top tips. This is where you review what you know about strategic options and see how they would fit at Bethesda. You must be logical here and not make irrelevant or impractical suggestions, such as turning the hospital into a hotel. Models are useful here: you will see that we have taken ideas from both *Porter* and *Ansoff*, as well as some simpler thoughts.

Other strategic options

When considering other strategic options open to the Management Committee, we must consider the pressing need in the short term at least to reduce the forecast deficit and improve both effectiveness and productivity. There are a number of strategies that could be considered.

Internal efficiency improvements

From analysis of the quantitative data provided, it is clear that Bethesda does not operate as efficiently as it might. A scheme to improve efficiency might start with a review of staffing requirements in order to improve the staff to bed ratios and costs per bed.

Product development

Analysis of the internal data has also indicated that the neighbouring hospital has made far greater progress with **day surgery**. This could be an area in which Bethesda could concentrate, as it is likely to be less costly and hence more attractive to the medical insurance market.

Similarly, Bethesda could move to increase its **outpatient treatments**: these which have remained static over the past two years in order to improve profitability.

Political pressure

One of the key issues for Bethesda is that its income is largely provided by central and local government. There are both moral and political issues here. The hospital could campaign for greater funding from local government, particularly as it is a hospital that clearly caters largely for individuals who cannot afford private medical insurance.

Focus strategies

A **focus strategy** could might be used by Bethesda, by concentrating on particular areas of healthcare. Such an approach might make better use of the scarce resources available and build up a strong reputation in the chosen specialist areas. This in turn might effectively increase the hospital's catchment area and thus its government and insurance revenue.

Differentiation strategy

Another of *Porter's* generic strategies that could be suitable here is **differentiation.** Bethesda could offer services distinct from those offered by other local hospitals in order to enhance its reputation. Possibilities are improved after care or home support facilities.

Collaborative strategies

In an area such as healthcare it is not necessarily beneficial to society for there to be direct competition between providers. There are a number of areas where collaboration between the two hospitals might be investigated. It could be possible to share key facilities, such as an Accident and Emergency department or maternity ward. The two hospitals could enter into a common purchasing policy in order to try to influence the cost of the drugs and equipment required. The two hospitals could possibly agree to concentrate on separate areas of specialisation.

34 Hair Care

Part (a)

Top tips. You will need to look carefully at the table of data in order to get a good grip on this question. You might find that SWOT would form a good basis for thinking about the information you are given.

Easy marks. The question calls for a report: make sure you write and set out your answer in a suitable way: the marking scheme does not offer any marks for doing this, but the marker will expect it.

It is clear from a glance at the data table that turnover, cost of sales and borrowing have all risen rapidly and are expected to continue to rise. Two minutes with a calculator will reveal the relative rates of increase, which are very significant indeed. A related point, and one that might not have occurred to you, is the change in the rate of interest on borrowings expected in the forecast period.

Examiner's comments. This part of the question was generally well answered, though more attention could have been paid to potential future problems. Too many candidates fail to analyse or apply the quantitative data properly: analysis should extend beyond the calculation of financial ratios.

		Marks
(a)	Analysis of quantitative data	
	Trend in costs	up to 3
	Level of debt	up to 4
	Range of products	up to 3
	Stock levels	up to 3
	Fixed assets	up to 2
	Future developments	
	Exchange rates	up to 2
	Management succession	up to 2
	Relationship with competitors	up to 2
	Supplier rapport	up to 2
	Relationship with customers/branding	up to 2
		Maximum 20 marks
(b)	Market penetration	up to 2
	Product development	up to 3
	Market development	up to 3
	Diversification	up to 3
	Focus	up to 3
	Acquisition	up to 4
	Strategic alliance	up to 4
		Maximum 20 marks
(c)	Primary activities	up to 1·5 marks each to maximum of 7·5 marks
	Support activities	up to 1 mark each to maximum of 4·5 marks
		Maximum 10 marks
		Total 50 marks

To:	Managing Director, Hair Care Limited
From:	Accountant
Date:	June 20X3
Subject:	**Hair Care Limited – current position and prospects**

1   **Current situation**

Trading

The last three years' trading results show **impressive growth in turnover**, which is forecast to continue into 20X3. Unfortunately, **cost of sales**, which is by far the largest expense item, has risen at an even faster rate; this trend is also forecast to continue. The effect of this disproportionate rate of increase has been ameliorated by lower rates of increase in other costs, but has led to **relatively slow growth in profits** as compared to the growth in sales. In fact, the operating profit percentage is forecast to be only 7.7%: in 20X0 it was 13%.

Costs

Cost of sales. The relative rise in cost of sales may be caused, at least in part, by the **expansion of the product range**, the number of lines having more than tripled since 20X0. It might be worth examining the margins achieved on each line to establish whether the product range might be trimmed. This may also have a desirable effect on the amount of capital tied up in **stocks**, which has increased more than 600% since 20X0.

Distribution and marketing. Distribution and marketing costs have risen much more slowly than cost of sales and slower even than turnover. While the level of marketing costs may be regarded as subject to some discretion, holding distribution costs down to an increase of only 67% when sales have more than tripled is a significant achievement.

Finance costs. The expansion of the business has largely been financed by borrowing. Total indebtedness is comfortably lower than the value of fixed assets alone, but the interest payments have risen to 4% of turnover and are expected to rise to 9% of the much increased turnover forecast for 20X3. This is partly because borrowing itself will double, but there is also an **increase in the rate of interest** forecast, presumably reflecting the bank's perception of increasing risk as the company's borrowing expands. This should be borne in mind if further expansion of premises is considered: leasing may turn out to be cheaper.

Administration. Administration remains the smallest category of cost, though these costs are expected to increase in line with turnover, by 50%, presumably as a result of the intended similar **growth in staff numbers**.

2 Issues for the future

2.1 Competition

At the moment, Hair Care is not significantly challenged by **competitor**s: larger hair products companies sell into the consumer market and smaller ones specialise in other product ranges. It would not be wise to plan for the future on the basis that this happy state of affairs will continue indefinitely. Even if the current rate of growth is not maintained, it will not be long before the company is challenged, either by a start-up business or by an established company seeking further growth. The company's relationship with the retail chemist chain will already have brought it to the attention of the larger players.

2.2 Business cycle

You have argued that your market segment is recession-proof. This is unlikely to be the case. You have not so far encountered a downturn. Much of your trade is in superior quality, branded products for which you are able to charge premium prices. In the event of a recession, it is likely that your customers would seek to **contain or reduce their costs by buying cheaper goods**: if you were able to supply them, your margins would be eroded; if you were not you would lose the business all together.

2.3 Suppliers

The expansion of your product range means that you now deal with more than three times the number of suppliers you bought from three years ago. Part of your success has been built on strong relationships with your suppliers: these relationships will be difficult to establish with the new suppliers simply because there are so many of them. This may affect the reliability of your **deliveries**, the **discounts** you receive and your access to newly developed **premium products**. These effects are particularly likely to occur if competitors enter your chosen markets.

2.4 **Management**

The company has expanded to a size many times larger than it was when it was set up, but the **management structure has remained the same**. It seems unlikely that this can continue much longer. The **volume of transactions** alone is likely to generate a scale of managerial work that two people cannot handle; there is also the whole field of **human resource management** to consider. Staff numbers are planned to increase by 50% in 20X3. Payroll administration, recruitment, selection, and other aspects of personnel management are likely to become more and more time consuming. It would also be appropriate to consider the potential for **ill-health** to affect the smooth operation of the business: having greater managerial capacity would provide the organisation with the **flexibility** to deal with absence through ill-health. It is probably time to think about taking on at least one person who can undertake some of the more routine management and administrative functions. This could also have the advantage of releasing some of your own time to allow consideration of **strategic issues** in greater depth.

2.5 **Currency exchange**

Most of your purchases are paid for in foreign currency. The dollar and euro exchange rates have been reasonably stable, but this may not be the case in the future. As the volume of your business expands, it may become practical for you to use your bank's services to **hedge** against unfavourable exchange rate movements.

3 **Conclusion**

Your business continues to expand, but your cost structures might benefit from close attention. This is particularly true of cost of sales and finance charges. Management structure is another matter that needs consideration. There are also a number of possible developments in the business environment that could affect the continuing success of the business. You should give some thought to the possibilities of recession, adverse exchange rate movements and increased competition.

Part (b)

Text reference. The topics mentioned in this answer are discussed in Chapter 6 of your BPP Study Text.

Top tips. This question lends itself to an answer based on the various basic strategic option models that you should be very familiar with. The scenario gives a lot of detail that is relevant when considering the various possible routes to growth, so a fairly careful answer plan would be a good idea here.

There is one aspect of the scenario that may have slightly confused you: we are told in the scenario that the subsidiary that became Hair Care Ltd sold its products 'to wholesalers and large retail chemist chains'. Later, we are told that major international companies sell similar products but 'not directly to the hairdressing salons as does Hair Care Ltd'. We must presume that the later information is more up to date: the Examiner's own answers make it clear that the company does, in fact, sell direct to salons. However, whether it still sells to wholesalers as well is uncertain. It is quite likely that it does and it is probably safest to assume this, though, unfortunately, to do so would rule out one area of market development that you might have been tempted to suggest.

Easy marks. *Ansoff's* product-market vector analysis makes a good starting point for this answer.

Examiner's comments. Far too many candidates failed to discuss longer-term strategies, concentrating instead on quick, tactical courses of action.

ANSWERS

To: Managing Director, Hair Care Limited
From: Accountant
Date: June 20X3
Subject: Hair Care Limited – possible development strategies

1   **Current limitations**

At the moment you have half of your chosen market, which must be accounted a dominant share. While there is still some potential for further organic growth in like-for-like sales, you are probably justified in doubting that this could be a major source of expansion. It is likely that you would have to base such growth on price competitiveness: you may be able to do this reasonably profitably if you can exploit purchasing economies of scale, but you may feel that there are more inviting routes to growth than further **market penetration** based on a **cost-focus**.

However, before leaving this topic completely, it is worth mentioning the possibility of a **differentiation focus** strategy. I have already remarked on the recent rapid growth in the number of products you offer and recommended a **review of profitability**: this might lead you to concentrate much of your attention on the **high margin items** you sell under your own brand. You could aim for a two component business: branded goods selling at high prices and your supply of own brand items in high volumes to your main retail chemist customer.

2   **Product-market options**

2.1   **Product development**

At the moment, you sell a range of hair care items to wholesalers and large retail chemist chains, mostly for salon use, and direct to the salons themselves; your product range includes goods sold both under your company's brand and some sold as own brand items by the country's leading chain of retail chemists. Possible scope for **product development** lies in the category of goods sold into your market by your smaller competitors, such as towels and razors. These items would complement your existing range. However, any future introduction of new products should only be contemplated in the light of the review of profitability already recommended.

It would be inappropriate for you to contemplate a move into **salon furnishings**, since these high-value items are so very different in nature from your existing range. You would probably have to establish **completely new supplier relationships** and the items themselves may incur significant costs in **fitting** and after sales service.

More adventurous product development, such as selling a line of cosmetics, would put you in competition with major international companies. You might be able to source low cost, unbranded supplies, but there could well be **product safety** issues to contend with. This option should not be discarded, but needs careful consideration.

2.2   **Market development**

There are two principal new markets you might consider.

First, you might consider providing other retail chemist chains with goods to sell under their **own brands**. You would, of course have to consider how this might affect your relationship with your existing retail chain customer. This would be low margin business, but you have already found that the volumes make up for this: an expansion should increase your purchasing power and enhance your margins by reducing your purchase costs. This strategy could also be applied to supermarket and department store chains.

Second, you might consider **international expansion**. This would require some careful market research to assess such things as distribution chains, competition and consumer preferences, but there is considerable potential here. Attendance at one of the many European hair care industry trade fairs would be a good way to start.

162 BPP LEARNING MEDIA

2.3 **Diversification**

Diversification is a high risk strategy and none of the options seems appropriate for you. A move into a completely new market with new products would not build on any of your strengths and would expose you to established competition. A **vertical move** up or down the value system has more to recommend it, since you would be able to build on your current market experience, but there would be significant disadvantages to such a move.

A move upstream into manufacturing would put you in competition with your current suppliers. You would not be operating on the same scale as them and therefore you would expect your costs to be higher. It is possible that you could find and exploit a **manufacturing niche**, perhaps producing a small number of similar lines that you currently have difficulty in sourcing, but this does not seem to offer much prospect for achieving your aim of continued substantial growth. If you contemplate manufacturing, you should certainly think in terms of off shore production, perhaps by entering into outsourcing agreements. This would significantly reduce the capital requirement.

A move downstream into **retailing** would be even more difficult. You have no experience of retail operations, so your bank would be unlikely to provide the capital to acquire a chain of outlets; this means that you would have to build the new business by **organic growth**, which would necessarily be a slow process. Such a move would require you to learn all the skills involved in retailing and to source a much larger range of products.

3 **Methods of growth**

3.1 **Acquisition**

I have already mentioned the relatively slowness of organic growth. More rapid growth can often be achieved by the **acquisition** of an appropriate existing business. This might be an attractive option for expansion within your existing markets and as an alternative to the product development route mentioned above. Acquisition could also be a route to rapid implementation of the international expansion and manufacturing niche strategies.

3.2 **Joint venture/strategic alliance**

A joint venture or strategic alliance might be an alternative route to expansion. The difference between the two concepts is that the former involves to creation of a new, jointly owned business entity, while the latter is based on the shared use of an asset, thus spreading its costs and creating scale economies from the increased rate of use. Either of these approaches could be a relatively low risk route to international expansion, for example. A joint venture might be arranged with an existing customer or supplier, while a form of strategic alliance might be created by the use of a foreign commercial agent.

The drawback of these vehicles from your point of view would be that you would have to share control, which might not be an attractive prospect.

4 **Conclusions**

Either a cost focus or a differentiation focus could be a route to further **market penetration**, though growth by these means would probably be slow.

There do not seem to be good prospects for expansion based on **product development**.

You may to look more closely at the two possibilities for **market development** I have described: further manufacturing for own brand retailers and a foreign venture. Acquisition or joint venture might be worth further examination as means to the latter end.

The only diversification strategy that seems worthy of further examination seems to be the development of a manufacturing niche. Acquisition could also be a means of implementing this idea.

Part (c)

Text reference. The topics mentioned in this answer are discussed in Chapter 4 of your BPP Study Text.

Top tips. The question emphasises Sam's success and it would make sense, therefore, to confine an answer to those parts of the value chain that have been managed in a way that contributes to that success. However, the Examiner's answer makes reference to problem areas, such as the lack of succession planning, so it is probably fair to conclude that a balanced picture is required.

This is a good principle to follow: it is often hard to decide just what is relevant in an answer, but the implication here is that an over-strict interpretation of the question requirement is not a good idea. Do not be afraid to add the odd sentence or three that might seem to be marginal to such an interpretation.

There is no need to draw the value chain diagram.

Easy marks. Marketing and sales is an obvious place to start among the primary activities, as Sam is basically, a very successful salesman.

Primary activities

Sam is a very successful salesman and the **marketing and sales** activity of his company, resting in his hands as it does, must be regarded as a major source of the company's success. He has created good relationships with his key customers, not least by his determination to provide excellent service. He has also successfully established both the Hair Care brand, which offers enhanced margins and a bulk, own brand supply to a chain of retail chemists, which gives him volume sales and the advantages of bulk purchasing.

We might consider **operations** and both **inbound** and **outbound logistics** together. Sam has invested substantially in storage and packing facilities and his wife Annabelle has managed the company's staff so as to provide a high quality of service: we must presume that this includes accurate and prompt deliveries. All three of these activities form an important basis for the company's success.

The final primary activity is **service**, in the sense of after sales service. The company's products are generally too simple to require very much of this, but no doubt prompt attention to returns, when required, contributes to its overall reputation.

Secondary activities

Procurement is also an activity into which Sam has put considerable effort and from which the company derives great advantage. Sam sources his products entirely from outside the UK and has overcome problems of foreign exchange, international trade regulation and national culture to do so successfully, having negotiated a number of favourable prices.

Technology development at Hair Care has two aspects. The development of the product range continues apace, possibly to the extent that some rationalisation is required, as discussed earlier. This might be accounted a mixed success for this reason. The continuing development of systems and utilisation of resources (such as those in the warehouse) has allowed the company to expand its operations smoothly and without constraint. However, there is some concern about the level of debt and thus fixed costs that has developed. Overall, this activity continues to need careful management if it is not to become an important weakness.

Human resource management is also an activity worthy of some attention. Staff turnover has been low, which is a good sign, but staff numbers are expected to double over the next two years and it is unlikely that this happy state of affairs will continue. Annabelle will have to pay careful attention to recruitment and training and be prepared for a higher level of turnover as numbers increase. There is also the problem of managerial capacity already discussed: Sam needs increased managerial support of a high calibre.

Firm infrastructure in terms of specialist services such as legal advice is, no doubt, bought in as required. There is however, a growing need for more in-house capacity for such activities as planning, financial control and, possibly, as the scale of operations increases, quality management.

35 Polymat Tapes

Examiner's comments. The compulsory question is the key to passing the examination. Candidates who fail to achieve 30 marks on Question 1 find it difficult to gain sufficient marks from Section B to compensate for a poor performance on the compulsory question. The scenario was of a multi-product manufacturing company supplying a range of industrial tapes to a wide variety of industrial and commercial customers. Many of their customers were large manufacturers themselves. There was therefore an emphasis on business-to-business relationships.

Marking scheme

		Marks
(a)	Evaluation of company performance	Up to 3
	Evaluation of each product group	Up to 6 each
	Use of appropriate models	Up to 5
		Maximum 25 marks
(b)	Source of competitive advantage – generic strategy	Up to 3
	Alternative growth directions	Up to 6
	Alternative methods for growth	Up to 3
	Preferred strategy – justification	Up to 5
		Maximum 15 marks
(c)	Consideration of culture change	Up to 3
	Models for creating change	Up to 3
	Measures for implementing change	Up to 5
		Maximum 10 marks
		Total 50 marks

Part (a)

Text reference. The topics mentioned in this answer are discussed in Chapter 6 of your BPP Study Text.

Top tips. Here is an opportunity to use the BCG model and decide whether the product groups are 'dogs', 'cows', 'question marks/problem children' or 'stars'. Correct use of the financial data provided was essential in locating each product within the grid.

Examiner's comments. The industry structure in the scenario lent itself to an intelligent use of Porter's Five Forces model, and product life cycle analysis was often used to good effect. Candidates also used SWOT analysis which, when it is done well, and not merely as a listing exercise, is revealing about the firm's position.

To: Richard Johnson, Managing Director, Polymat Industrial Tapes Ltd
From: External consultant
Date: December 20XX

Introduction

There is cause for concern at PIT. At company level the return on sales is falling, with a disproportionate increase in fixed costs. Close analysis of the performance of the individual factories and product groups reveals further disturbing developments, as well as some cause for optimism.

Analysis of specific product groups

Cable Jointing Tapes

This product group is registering a sound increase in year-on-year sales, clearly exceeding the increase in the cost of sales with a consequent **improvement of the gross margin** from 40% in 2001/02 to a forecast 45% in 2003/04. There appears to be a link between the consistently high R&D spend and successful development of profitable products that meet customer requirements. **Market share** is high and consistent.

PVC Industrial Tapes

This group seems very stable, with gross margin again forecast at a healthy 45% in 2003/04 and a steady if slow growth in sales. The **decline in market share** does give cause for concern, perhaps reflecting the impact of low cost tapes. In addition, R&D expenditure is low, which seems to indicate that there is little prospect of product innovation to grow the market for the products of this division.

Paper Masking Tapes

Sales are declining and costs are increasing, particularly those associated with transport. **Market share** is being maintained, but costs cannot be allowed to spiral out of control in order to achieve this at any price. Despite the investment in a modern factory, this division is constrained by the terms of the operating licence with the US, and its inability to achieve an efficient low cost operation.

Models that could be used to analyse PIT's performance include the **BCG matrix**, which emphasises the relationship between market share and profitability. A company with a portfolio of products could expect a range of growth profiles in the various industries with which it is associated. There is little evidence however to suggest that PIT has any products in high growth sectors.

In terms of the three product groups, the Paper Masking Tapes group has a respectable market share compared to its main competitor, but it more closely resembles a 'dog' than a 'cash cow' because of its declining profitability and spiralling costs. It is difficult to see how this division could be turned around without radical cost control measures.

Using another model, closer analysis of the tape groups could suggest that PVC Industrial Tapes are reaching the **mature stage** of their **product life cycle**, with stagnant profits and static sales.

A respectable market share together with improving margins, supported by significant R & D, suggests that the Cable Jointing Tapes division has the potential to move into the 'star' category, assuming that market growth can be assured (there is nothing in the scenario however to indicate that this is possible).

Porter's generic strategies

Competitive strategy involves a choice between being the lowest cost producer (cost leadership), making the products different from competitors in some way (differentiation) or specialising in a segment of the market (focus, using cost leadership or differentiation). *Porter* believes that firms must choose one of these, or be regarded as 'stuck in the middle'. It could be said that PIT is 'stuck in the middle', with few if any claims to be a cost leader. Only in its Cable Jointing Tapes division does it have products differentiated to meet the needs of cable manufacturers.

PIT's products are aimed at a wide range of customers – from large multinationals to DIY enthusiasts and, consequently a large range of distribution channels are used. This has promoted inefficiencies: transport costs need to be brought under control and the value chain for each division needs examination for the benefits that are being delivered.

Information for management decision making – organisational knowledge

There is a lack of detailed management information on the **profitability**, or otherwise, of PIT's product range. The links between sales and marketing and the R & D teams seem *ad hoc* and underdeveloped and there is little co-ordination of the overall R & D effort. **Organisational knowledge** is not currently shared.

It should be noted in this context that knowledge and 'knowledge workers' are increasingly recognised as significant factors in the determination of competitive advantage, and PIT should consider the development of a system that encourages the sharing of its significant organisational knowledge. This will eliminate duplication of effort in accessing information, encourage a consistent approach to product management and facilitate employee co-ordination. This will be particularly valuable in the effort to **better understand customer requirements** and **promote innovation**.

Conclusion

Many of PIT's products are **mature**, and suffering from severe **price competition**. A strategy is needed to ensure the survival and growth of the company. The product life cycle is instructive in this regard: opportunities for innovation should be sought out to extend the life of products and create new ones.

Part (b)

Text reference. The topics mentioned in this answer are discussed in Chapter 6 of your BPP Study Text.

Examiner's comments. Part (b) gave the opportunity to discuss strategic options. Here the BCG matrix and the invest/harvest/divest options were relevant, together with a consideration of Ansoff's growth options. Useful consideration was often given to whether the value chain of the firm should stay the same, as there were clear prompts from the scenario to consider whether the centralised warehouse and in-house transport service were really adding value to the company's products. There was often a reluctance to choose a preferred strategy as requested.

Strategies need to be evaluated by PIT according to their **suitability** to the firm's strategic situation, their **feasibility** in terms of resources and competences and their **acceptability** to key stakeholder groups. From the scenario, it appears that radical change to either products or markets is unlikely to occur, but there is a need to establish which products can be developed, and for which customers.

Product market strategies involve the determination of which products should be sold in which markets, by market penetration, market development, product development and diversification. Any analysis of PIT's performance to date should lead to withdrawal from unprofitable markets, divestment of poorly performing products and a closing down of company activities which are adding little value, thereby releasing resources to be redirected to value-adding spheres of activity.

Examining each of the divisions in turn:

Cable Jointing Tape products look to offer the most likely opportunity for improved **market penetration** and **market development**, through links with cable manufacturing customers. There may be an opportunity to **develop PIT's brand** as part of an attempt to stave off aggressive US competition.

Paper Masking Tapes is a product group without much scope for improved performance. Its cost base is higher than its major competitor, it has significantly lower market share and its access to product and process innovation is limited because of the arrangement with the American manufacturer. In addition there is significant overcapacity, and tape supplied to the automobile industry is under **severe price pressure**. **Divestment** would be a sensible option.

PVC tape products look to be a **product group with some potential**, with healthy margins and sales increases. Competition is increasing from competitors with a lower cost base, but PIT has the advantage that its products already meet demanding quality standards so there may be resistance on the part of **satisfied customers** towards moving to a competitor. **Innovation** is likely to be a key differentiating factor in the future for this division, and the way to retain competitive advantage, but the question of whether product innovation in a mature market is a realistic strategy should be asked. Sustained competitive advantage may involve **process** (rather than product) **innovation**. Certainly, PIT needs to look closely at its **value chain** and its customer base.

PIT needs to review the value of operating its own **warehouse and transport system**, which together involve the commitment of significant resources. More evidence is needed on the precise benefit that such an arrangement brings for the company. The scenario indicates that it has merely added to overheads and done very little to add any value for customers or the company.

A range of strategic options is open to the company, but much more information is needed on revenue and costs. From the above analysis however is does appear that an exit from Paper Masking Tapes, closing the warehouse and outsourcing the transport function would contribute to a successful business strategy.
Part (c)

Text reference. The topics mentioned in this answer are discussed in Chapter 17 of your BPP Study Text.

Top tips. Part (c) was looking for ways the culture inside the firm could be changed - the process of change rather than any marketing actions and decisions. Culture and culture change has been a favourite area in previous papers.

Examiner's comments. Parts (c) and (d) were the parts which typically gave the most problems but offered the candidate an opportunity to think creatively about what was required. Lewin's force field analysis and change process was by far the preferred model for explaining how the process might be managed, and there was encouraging evidence of its being better understood and more effectively applied to the problem.

Culture at PIT is production led. This is evidenced by the use of graduate chemists, the organisational structure of the company into factories specialising in their own product range, and separate R & D programmes. There is no overall mechanism for reporting, for example, the performance of the various divisions in terms of customer satisfaction or detailed product/market analysis. R&D should be closely coordinated with marketing because customer needs, as identified by marketers, should be a vital input to new product development.

Favoured models for stimulating change such as is required here include *Lewin's* **force field analysis** and three stage change process (unfreeze, change, refreeze). It is important to recognise that there is likely to be resistance to any change, so the culture shift has to be well thought out and implemented.

Unfreeze is the most difficult stage of this process, concerned mainly with selling the need for a marketing orientation to the staff of PIT, who may regard it as unimportant. They need a **motive** for changing their attitudes – this may be provided by demonstrating the negative effects of a lack of adequate marketing focus for the future of the company. A failure to stimulate the market has certainly had a detrimental effect upon the performance of **Retardon**, and paved the way for competitors.

Change is mainly concerned with identifying the key features of a new marketing orientation, communicating it and encouraging it. The new ideas must be shown to work. **Refreeze** implies the consolidation or reinforcement of the new behaviour. This could involve an **action plan** including timescales for particular activities (such as staff training on how to use a new customer database), milestones and the allocation of responsibilities.

Measures to increase the exposure of all types of staff to marketing, and the setting up of appropriate customer information systems leading eventually to a proper customer database, will help. Marketing has a key role to play in the effective implementation of new products but requires these changes to information provision.

36 Elite Plastic Packaging

Part (a)

Text reference. The topics mentioned in this answer are discussed in Chapter 6 of your BPP Study Text.

Top tips. Unusually, the table of numerical information given in the scenario is very thin. Just about all you can conclude from it is that Elite Plastic Packaging seems to be doing quite well, maintaining steady and profitable growth, while the division and group of which it is part seem to be shrinking and becoming less profitable.

This information is obviously important, but it is available almost by glancing at the table: previous exams incorporated tables that required you to do a little more digging if you were to make full use of the numbers given in a typical Question 1.

By contrast, the Examiner's suggested solution to this part of the question makes it clear that he was expecting candidates to pick up on a number of qualitative factors in the scenario, including management style, business experience and personal judgement.

Easy marks. No marks are allocated for report format in this exam, but it is worth spending a moment on a heading and thinking about report writing style: a little effort here may encourage the marker to be generous.

Marking scheme

		Marks
(a)	Advantages and disadvantages of each option (four options)	up to 5 marks for each option
	Alternative 'hybrid' solutions	up to 3 marks
	Maximum 20 marks	
(b)	Strategic management styles	up to 2 marks per style
	Cost and benefits of each style	up to 3 marks per style
	Maximum 15 marks	
(c)	Use of Mintzberg's organisational configurations	up to 6
	Product v geographic divisions	up to 4
	Centralisation v decentralization	up to 4
	Global co-ordination v local independence and responsiveness	up to 4
	Maximum 15 marks	
	Total 50 marks	

From: A Consultant
To: J Wainwright

ELITE PLASTIC PACKAGING – MARKET ENTRY OPTIONS

You asked me to assess four options for a possible move by Elite Plastic Packaging (EPP) to operations on a global scale.

As well as the usual considerations of business strategy, your freedom of manoeuvre is constrained by the priorities of your Divisional and Group managers. These priorities include a **high degree of risk aversion** and an insistence on **careful and accurate budgeting**.

Current performance

EPP has achieved steady growth averaging six percent between 20X1 and 20X5 and has improved its operating margins from 33.1% to 40.3% over the same period. These leading indicators must be a source of satisfaction to you and ought to impress both Divisional and Group managers, especially as the performance of other parts of the Group seems to have been rather poor overall.

Your success is the result of a strategy that has included both successful **market penetration** and **product development** in the form of your smart packaging. Currently, you have 50% of the European market overall and must therefore probably anticipate some slowing of your company's rate of growth.

The global opportunity

You have identified important market opportunities for your smart packaging in both the Americas and in Asia, since potential competitors in those regions have failed to invest sufficiently in the new technology.

Overall strategic considerations

Sigma Group displays a high degree of risk-aversion generally and takes a short-term view of investment, applying a three-year payback hurdle to investment proposals. The Group Chairman was personally responsible for closing down a previous move towards global operations.

Sigma group thus has little experience of operations outside Europe. The very different **business and cultural conditions** that prevail in those regions must inevitably affect any consideration of potential global expansion.

Global expansion methods

You have identified four possible methods of exploiting your smart packaging on a global scale: licensing, subcontracting, acquisition and establishing your own manufacturing facilities. There is, of course, no reason why you should not employ different methods in different countries.

Licensing

Licensing is a **low-risk option** and would require little investment. It would require care to select a suitable licensee that could be relied on to exploit the technology fully. It would also require the provision of technical assistance to the licensee, at least initially. The financial return on the investment would be good, potentially offering a growing cash flow stream for little input. This would no doubt be attractive to the senior managers of Sigma Group.

The downside of licensing is **loss of control**: you would be in the hands of the licensee for the life of the contract and unable to drive growth by your own efforts. Such a deal would not give clear exposure to your brand and you would gain no experience of wider global management. There would also be **potential for dispute** with the licensee over the terms of the licence, both during the initial negotiations and subsequently.

Licensing should be seen as a long-term option, since a successful licensee will establish competences in all aspects of the business; should you wish at some future time to start up your own operation, you would be starting from scratch and meeting **competition you had yourself created**.

Subcontracting

Subcontract manufacturing would allow you to retain much more control over your operations while avoiding the need for heavy investment in manufacturing plant and staff. You would be able to retain control of the marketing mix and **build your brand** as you wish to.

On the other hand, you would be exposed to the **potential for error** in such matters as logistics and dealing with promotion in a new cultural setting. You would also lose much control over **quality and delivery** since day-to-day management of the production process would be in other hands.

An advantage of this approach is that is might be possible to contract with a privately owned firm that could be taken over after a few years. The owners of such a firm might welcome this as an **exit strategy**. Subcontracting might thus merge into acquisition.

Acquisition

The acquisition of a suitably skilled and equipped packaging company could form the basis for a **very rapid expansion into a new market**. No loss of control over marketing or manufacturing operations would occur. Selection of the target company would be the crucial process.

Acquisition of an efficient company is likely to be expensive as goodwill will have to be paid for: the alternative of buying a company in a distress sale carries a significantly greater degree of risk.

The downside to acquisition is the inherent difficulty of making it work. It is well known that high-profile acquisitions in the past have **consumed rather than created value** and some have brought the companies concerned close to failure. The major problems are **cultural**, but there are also likely to be operational issues relating to the integration of work, management restructuring and system compatibility. The last problem is particularly common with IT systems.

Sigma Group does not seem to be particularly acquisitive and the Chairman led a recovery programme based on unpicking a previous round of acquisitions. However, the accountants who seem to dominate the group might feel at home with a proposal based on **quantifiable costs and benefits**.

The green field option

Building up a business operation from scratch in a new market is a high risk option. It will be extremely expensive and will take a long time to become profitable.

Suitable premises will have to be built, staff engaged and trained and marketing operations started. This will require project management skills of a high order. If you were to take the green field option, you should not contemplate starting operations in both Asia and the Americas simultaneously. The cost would be very large indeed and you would not benefit from any **learning experiences** that might be gained on a single initial project.

The advantage of this option is that complete control is retained over all aspects of the venture. Also, it may be possible to reduce the total cost by taking advantage of government incentives to invest in certain countries and regions.

Conclusion

The four outlines above deal only in generalities and can be no more than a rough indication of initial considerations. I should be pleased to assist with more detailed evaluation of options in due course.

Part (b)

> **Text reference.** The topics mentioned in this answer are discussed in Chapter 7 of your BPP Study Text.
>
> **Top tips.** Any answer to this question needs to be rather heavy on theory. This is for two reasons: there is not a great deal of detail in the scenario to discuss; and there is quite a lot of relevant theory to talk about.
>
> **Easy marks.** It is important to point out that the numerical data indicate that the Group Executive do not seem to be doing a good job.

Sigma Group is a **diversified conglomerate**, owning a number of disparate companies that operate more or less independently of one another. Such groupings are out of favour in the West, largely as a result of unimpressive performance. At one time, taking over an inefficient company and selling off under-utilised assets was a route to quick returns, but such opportunities have now largely disappeared and, anyway, the benefits of such reorganisation can only be achieved once and for all.

Current thinking is that the creation of groups is only appropriate if it can generate extra value through the effect of **synergy**. The argument that diversification **reduces shareholder risk** by creating a ready-made **portfolio** for investors does not impress: such diversification can be achieved by investors themselves through their choice of investments or through an investment trust and without the cost penalty of running a corporate headquarters.

Overall, the top management of Sigma Group do not seem to be doing a particularly good job. Indeed, the Group looks as if it is on the **verge of collapse**. Turnover has shrunk from £580m to £351m over a four year period and operating margins have almost halved from 10.8% to 5.7%. As a result operating profit has fallen from £63m to £20m. Jeff Wainwright of EPP might complain with justification that membership of the group is actually destroying the value his company creates, since EPP's most recent operating profit exceeded £21m.

Goold and Campbell researched the role of the centre in 16 British-based conglomerates. They concentrated on two main activities.

- Determination of overall strategy and the allocation of resources
- Controlling divisional performance

These roles they referred to as **planning influence** and **control influence**. The variation in these roles allowed the identification of eight distinct **strategic management styles**.

Planning influence was exercised in a variety of ways, but a fairly smooth spectrum of styles was observable, ranging from minimal, where the centre is little more than a holding company, to highly centralised, where the managers in the business units have responsibility only for operational decisions.

Control influence was exercised by the agreement of objectives, the monitoring of results and the deployment of pressures and incentives. This gave rise to three distinct categories of control influence: **flexible strategic**, **tight strategic** and **tight financial**.

Of the **eight strategic management styles** they defined, Goold and Campbell found that **three** of them were particularly common; each was associated with one of the three control influence categories mentioned above and with a different degree of planning influence.

Strategic management styles

Strategic planning. The strategic planning style is associated with **flexible strategic control influence** and a **fairly high degree of central planning influence**. The centre establishes extensive planning processes through which it works with business unit managers to make substantial contributions to strategic thinking, often with a unifying overall corporate strategy. Performance targets are set in broad terms, with an emphasis on longer-term strategic objectives. Such organisations build linked international businesses in core areas. Business units tend to follow bold strategies and often achieve above industry average growth and profitability

Strategic control. The strategic control style involves a fairly **low degree of planning influence** but **uses tight strategic control**. The centre prefers to leave the planning initiative to the business unit managers, though it will review their plans for acceptability. Firm targets are set for a range of performance indicators and performance is judged against them. The centre concentrates on rationalising the portfolio. Such companies achieve good profits but are less successful at achieving growth.

Financial control. The centre exercises influence almost entirely through the budget process. It takes little interest in business unit strategy and controls through profit targets. Careers are at stake if budgets are missed. Strategies are cautious and rarely global. Business unit managers tend to sacrifice market share to achieve high profits. As a result, these companies produce excellent profits, but growth comes mainly from acquisitions.

Sigma Group would seem to fit fairly precisely into the **financial controller style**. The Group Executive do not get involved with the strategy planning process, but they impose an extensive and demanding system of budgetary control over performance. However, as pointed out above, the Group's management do not seem to be achieving the excellent short-term results they aspire to.

Part (c)

> **Text reference.** The topics mentioned in this answer are discussed in Chapter 7 of your BPP Study Text.
>
> **Top tips.** It would be possible to answer this question quite well in terms of **organisational and national cultures**, pointing out that whatever method of entry into the new global markets is chosen, issues of the kind identified by *Hofstede*, for example, are bound to affect the way the organisation functions.
>
> The Examiner's suggested solution makes it clear that he was actually thinking about **organisation structure** and, specifically, about structuring a rapidly growing international company.
>
> This is not an unreasonable approach to take, since it is organisation structure that forms the framework upon which systems of communication, control and co-ordination may be hung.
>
> **Examiner's comments.** The Examiner declared that 'structure is the key to implementing chosen strategies'. This will be worth bearing in mind for future exams.

We do not have any detailed forecasts for the size of the expansion Jeff Wainwright (JW) envisages, but we know that he has identified markets in both Asia and the Americas that are similar in size to the existing European market. We might assume that eventually two further businesses might be established, each on a scale similar to that of the current European operation. In other words, JW may be planning to **triple the size of his business by operating in two completely new regions**.

If this is the case, significant issues of control, co-ordination and communication are raised and these in turn make it necessary to consider the basic problems of **organisation structure**.

Organisation structure is the basic mechanism by which organisations are managed. Structure provides the channels of communication and co-ordination and the lines of authority and accountability through which control is exercised.

Archie Williams maintains a strongly expressed commitment to decentralisation as the best way to run Sigma Group. The extensive and complex system of budgetary control he imposes demonstrates that the Group is actually highly centralised, but this does not invalidate the principle.

If EPP does expand on the scale we have assumed, the process of such expansion is likely to impose **severe strains** on the Williams system. The monthly Divisional board meetings are likely to become dominated by the affairs of EPP, as indeed, may the deliberations of the Group Executive. JW will have little time to spare for such matters if he is to drive the planned expansion along and there is a risk that higher management will give only minimal attention to the other Group companies. However, given the current performance of the Group, this may actually be an advantage, freeing operating company MDs to spend more time on running their operations.

The solution to this problem is for EPP to be **allowed much greater freedom of action**, with monitoring restricted perhaps to quarterly reports against outline budget. The Group senior managers cannot be experts in everything, and the changing circumstances of the Group make a policy of decentralisation appropriate.

JW will also have to consider how he wants to run his expanding company. The scale we envisage implies two new operations, each comparable to what exists now, all three being widely separated geographically. If JW is to manage this much expanded structure, he is also likely to find that **decentralisation** will be appropriate. This is because any central system attempting to control the increased scale of operations would be **over-complex and unwieldy**. Regional autonomy would also prevent the emergence of major problems of **language and national or regional culture**.

JW will have to recruit or promote a **replacement for himself** to run the existing European business while he sets up the new global organisation. Eventually, on our assumptions, he will be managing three businesses, each as big as the one he runs now. He will therefore have to find two further managers to head his two new continental operations. The implication of all this for JW himself is that he will have to take an overview and will not be able to spend too much time on any one of his three businesses.

Each of the new companies will require its own internal structure and systems that must reflect local general and managerial culture. There will then be a requirement for an over-arching structure of proper systems of guidance and control for the total expanded business. Creation of this structure will be JW's principal task for the longer term.

37 LRP

Part (a)

> **Text Reference.** The topics mentioned in this answer are discussed in Chapters 2,3 and 4 of your BPP Study Text.
>
> **Easy marks.** It is not unusual for case studies to commence by asking you to analyse and comment on the setting. There are marks available here simply for reading, understanding and summarising. A little thought will then bring you a pass mark in that part of the question.

REPORT

LRP FASTENERS

Introduction

The aim of this report is to discuss the strategic value of LRP as an independent entity.

Background

LRP manufactures a wide range of fasteners, ranging from basic nuts and bolts to more sophisticated devices. It became part of the Stillwell Slim group in 1990. Its turnover in 2000 was £53.5m and its profit was £6.05m. It has plants in Ireland, Taiwan and the UK and sells its products globally.

Strengths and weaknesses

Overall, LRP is a **sound enterprise** and seems **properly managed**. Its average net profit margin over the last three years has been 11%, while turnover has grown steadily at about 4%. Overdraft has increased in line with the growth in turnover.

The company has a record of sensible **product innovation** and maintains a review of technical developments.

There is an appropriate emphasis on **quality** within the company. However, the industry benchmark reports indicate a disturbing upward trend in both **internal reject rate** and **customer returns**. These may be linked to recent productivity gains in that output volume may be being achieved at the expense of quality. This is an important point, especially in the market for the more sophisticated fasteners.

There are opportunities for further improvements to productivity. The average age of the plant is rising as time passes and now stands at 10.2 years. While an average gives no detail, it does indicate that if advantage is being taken of recent technical improvements there must be counterbalancing examples of very old machinery. The UK plant is in **particular need of investment**.

The introduction of **computer-based scheduling systems** (such as MRP2) is another possible route to improved efficiency. The value of WIP is a little higher than the industry average, indicating scope for improvements in **production control**.

The level of WIP, while higher than desirable, is fairly constant. However, over the last two years, there has been a significant **rise in stocks of finished goods**. These are now one fifth higher than the industry average. This rise may be associated with the parallel rise in customer returns, but that possibility is not a proper explanation. Rejected goods should be sold to less demanding customers, reworked or scrapped. They should not accumulate as stock. If they are saleable, with or without rework, their existence should be taken into account in works ordering procedures. This may be further justification for an improved production control system. A review of the saleability of stocks might be an interesting exercise, also.

Opportunities and threats

The **global market for fasteners is growing at about 4% annually** and LRP should be well placed to at least obtain its share of that growth. However, its **market share in basic fasteners has fallen** from almost 10% to less than 8½%. The reasons for this are not clear, but two important possibilities are apparent from the data available. The first is the possible falling-off in quality mentioned earlier. The second is the lack of a manufacturing facility in North America, where growth is higher than elsewhere but sales have remained almost constant over the last three years.

It should also be noted that while turnover growth in the European market has been fairly low at 3% and 2.6% in the last two years, the Rest of the World market has grown strongly in the same period, at 8.8% and 6.7%.

It is possible therefore that LRP's manufacturing facilities are **significantly mis-matched with its markets**, since it has two plants within the EU, none in the NAFTA and only one in the remaining part of the global economy, in Taiwan. Consideration should be given to the possibility of **manufacturing in North America**. The long term future of the two EU plants should also be reviewed.

Sales of higher-value fasteners have been **adversely affected** by the increase in competition resulting from the entry of TIG Products into the market. TIG have a **cost advantage** in that their manufacturing takes place in eastern Europe. Their current success shows that their quality and service must be appropriate. They are in a favourable position to serve the European market, both geographically and in price terms. TIG must be seen as a significant threat to LRP, at least in Europe. However, their ability to compete globally must be constrained by the same factors that hamper LRP, particularly the cost and delay associated with international delivery.

Conclusion

LRP is in reasonably good commercial health, but quality and production planning seem to be areas in which improvements might be possible.

In the longer term, the location of the company's manufacturing facilities should be reviewed in the light of its pattern of trade.

Part (b)

> **Text reference.** The topics mentioned in this answer are discussed in Chapter 7 of your BPP Study Text.
>
> **Top tips.** This part of the question is particularly useful because this organisational form is typical of most large companies. Many aspects of organisational management are drawn together in a consideration of the divisionalised conglomerate.
>
> It is unusual, but not unknown, to be asked to discuss a theoretical topic in the exam.

Chandler showed that the conglomerate form can provide a very large organisation with a suitable compromise between centralisation and decentralisation. Centralised control through functional organisation becomes unwieldy and inefficient as organisations grow geographically or in terms of products and markets. The other extreme, a loosely linked group of independently managed firms owned by a holding company, fails to achieve any advantage or synergy.

The divisionalised conglomerate is based on combining a high degree of autonomy at the operating division (SBU) level with value-adding input from the strategic apex. High divisional autonomy allows the organisation to operate effectively over a wide range of product-markets. Divisional managers can concentrate on their own operations and markets thus becoming more effective in them. Autonomy also promotes a high degree of motivation.

Mintzberg shows that the strategic apex. has a range of roles that contribute to the success of the organisation.

Management of the strategic portfolio. Portfolio analysis is as applicable to SBUs as it is to products. A conglomerate needs a suitable range of product-market operations. The corporate HQ must decide the overall shape of the organisation, buying and selling divisions to achieve a balanced portfolio.

Control of financial resources. Corporate HQ controls major investment in the SBUs. Its detailed knowledge of their operations and prospects enables it to invest more profitably than the most efficient external market. SBUs often have their liquid assets centralised under a corporate treasurer for more efficient short-term investment. The size and stability of the organisation as a whole enhance its creditworthiness and allow it to raise funds in the capital markets more cheaply than the individual SBUs could.

Performance control. Corporate HQ designs and operates a performance measurement system that supports the roles above. The system also permits assessment of the performance of SBU management. The only real method the HQ can use to deal with unsuccessful management is to replace it. The design of the control system must take account of potential manipulation and must not encourage dysfunctional decision making. Members of the corporate HQ supplement the reporting system by making regular **personal visits** to SBUs.

Support services. Some functions may be organised centrally and provided on a charge-out basis to SBUs. Apart from the services of the HQ itself, these typically include R&D, HR, PR and legal services.

Part (c)

> **Text reference.** The topics mentioned in this answer are discussed in Chapter 5 of your BPP Study Text.
>
> **Top tips.**. Always take a firm line and stand by the highest ethical positions.

Ethics is concerned with notions of right and wrong behaviour and is inevitably subject to dispute because of the wide range of cultural, legal, religious and professional influences. The question of price fixing is a common and practical problem for managers.

Johnson and Scholes define an organisation's **ethical stance** as the extent to which it will exceed its minimum obligation to stakeholders. To some extent that minimum obligation is defined by law. However, law and ethics are not congruent; they may in fact be opposed to one another, as is often the case in totalitarian states.

The first comment to make on the CEO's proposal is that collusive price fixing is illegal in most western jurisdictions and is therefore something that responsible managers should not countenance. However, it is a fundamental of economic theory that **oligopolies** rarely compete on price. Industry prices are 'sticky' and even when a price war breaks out, it does not usually last long. It is possible, in fact, for a kind of **non-collusive** price fixing to take place, often when there is an accepted **price leader**. This is not illegal. Whether or not it is ethical is anther question.

The CEO's proposal would be more difficult to deal with if such behaviour were legal in the region in question. Global organisations such as LRP and Stillwell Slim are subject to conflicting pressures from stakeholders in different parts of the world. For example, the use of child labour in developing countries can be seen either as a way for those countries to exploit a form of natural economic advantage, thereby contributing to their economic development, or as a shameful neo-colonialist practice. The water is muddied when it becomes apparent that employers of child labour may be ignoring basic health and safety standards while opponents may merely be seeking to protect domestic employment from competition.

To some extent, the problem of differing national legal standards is being eroded by the modern tendency for **extra-territorial legislation**. The USA has been most prolific with this, particularly in its efforts to promote economic sanctions against Cuba. Generally, such legislation has been limited to major wrongdoing, such as war crimes. However, in 1997, the OECD countries and five others adopted a convention to prohibit the bribery of foreign public officials. This is now making its way into UK law.

While corruption might be seen as more serious wrongdoing than price fixing, it is clear that a trend exists. It would be risky for any international company to behave in a way that was illegal in any of the countries where it has a presence.

A further refinement of LRP's ethical problem would arise if the legal position were different from what was generally acceptable to the ethical notions of the local society. For example, the success of Mr Berlusconi in Italian politics, despite his many brushes with the laws relating to corruption, has been attributed to a belief among the Italian electorate that such behaviour is an unavoidable part of the way their society works.

A very simple test for behaviour is the principle known as the **golden rule**, which is often stated as 'deal with others as you would like them to deal with you'. We are told that LRP has never been able to penetrate the regional market in question. If this has been the effect of trade association action that LRP has condemned as improper, it would clearly be cynical and ethically inappropriate to subscribe to the same behaviour when circumstances changed and it offered an advantage.

A final consideration is a practical one: the effect of bad publicity. Another simple ethical test for individuals is whether a particular course of action would be acceptable to their friends. For companies we might substitute 'stakeholders' for 'friends'. It may be that LRP's current and potential investors, customers, employees and business associates would have differing views on any given ethical question, but giving them due consideration would help to indicate a suitable solution to an ethical dilemma.

38 Screen Books

Text reference. The topics mentioned in this answer are discussed in Chapter 6 of your BPP Study Text.

Top tips. This question is a little dated now, set as it is in the time of the internet bubble, but it is still worth tackling since it brings together basic strategic ideas and the problems associated with innovation.

Part (a)

Screen Books began as a joint venture intended to harness the **direct sales potential of the Internet**. We are told that it was successful initially in that it grew in accordance with its business plan; its operating losses of £42,000 and £54,000 in 1996 and 1997 would fit this assessment, especially as turnover increased from £367,000 to £635,000 in these two years. We may assume both that the joint venture generated some synergistic effects and that the warehousing and distribution part of the business worked satisfactorily. **Fulfilment** was a common problem area for the Internet business model in the early days.

That being said, such a joint venture is not an obvious strategic choice for a publisher such as Jack Benfold Limited to take. In essence, it is an example of **forward vertical integration**, requiring skills in distribution and retailing. The alliance with John Rogers Books made the new venture possible. We gather that Mr Speight is prepared to be **open minded** in his strategic thinking, as indicated when he moved into the travel and cookery markets. From the point of view of John Rogers Books, the Screen Books venture fitted well with their existing business.

The sudden availability of huge amounts of capital in 1998 brought Screen Books into very different territory. There are two important issues here.

(a)   **The band wagon effect of the Internet boom of the late 1990s.** There is no doubt that investing in the Internet became extremely fashionable. For many months, normal business considerations such as profitability, cash flow and prudent investment appraisal seemed no longer relevant. The boom rapidly became a classic bubble, with investors so anxious not to be left behind that they would pour money into any Internet-based venture.

Such profligacy on the part of providers of finance is contagious: managers began to think in more and more grandiose terms and less and less of fundamentals (like profitability and so on). In this atmosphere, the least plausible projects could flourish – for a time.

(b)   **The screen-based device.** The new device was, in fact, quite a plausible idea and no more outrageous in technical or marketing terms than the Internet-connected refrigerators now in production, that are capable of organising their own re-stocking. However, it was a very risky venture.

It is actually quite difficult to classify the new product in terms of *Ansoff's* product-market growth vector matrix.

Penetration. It could be seen merely as a way of bringing more books to the existing market, though this is likely to be a minority view.

Product development. The strategy certainly contains an element of product development, particularly including the risk. 'Considerable technical development' was required, involving both in-house staff and research agencies. The investment in R&D was enormous, rising to a total that exceeded Screen Books' turnover in 1997. It is not possible to assess the inherent practicability of the idea, but it certainly represented a major step.

Market development. It is arguable that the Screen Books joint venture was merely a new way of reaching an existing market; that is, a new form of distribution rather than an example of market development. However, the LCD device would inevitably attract the attention of the particularly gadget-conscious market segment and sales potential might be well be slanted to this segment. It would certainly be appropriate to ensure that books and magazines dealing with computers and the Internet were well represented on Screen Books publications list.

Diversification. It is even possible to see the new device as an example of diversification, being both a new product and aimed at a new market.

This complexity of possible analyses reflects the complexity of the strategy itself. Such a strategy will inevitably make major demands on the top management of the company.

This brings us to **strategic implementation and control**. We are told that expenditure on both marketing and research has been higher than forecast and, indeed, the table of summary data gives the impression of lack of control over expenditure.

In the case of **marketing**, it is fair to comment that turnover has roughly doubled each year and this must inevitably require an increased marketing budget. Indeed, marketing spending *as a proportion of turnover* has fallen in the last three years. However, it still seems rather high. It would be interesting to establish the proportion of the marketing expenditure that was spent on salaries: the marketing headcount has also doubled each year, which would seem rather excessive.

Research and development expenditure seems to have been under greater control. Indeed, it is partly by comparison with the R&D expense that the growth in marketing expenditure seems so high. Nevertheless, spending on R&D has been very high in absolute terms. It is not possible to comment in detail on the R&D effort, but it is somewhat disturbing to hear of 'fundamental technical limitations' after more than £1.5 million has been spent over three years.

The disturbing feature of the Screen Books strategy is its close correspondence with a classic pattern of business failure: that is, escalating commitment to a single, major high-technology project that ultimately proves unworkable. The profligacy of the Internet bubble, mentioned above, appears to have undermined prudence and financial control to the extent that the continued existence of Screen Books appears to depend on the willingness of lenders to finance it. The ability of the basic Internet sales operation to support the current burden of loan finance must be questioned. Also, if the new product fails to materialise and it becomes necessary to write off much of the past development expenditure, lenders may take the first opportunity to salvage what they can by closing the business down.

In conclusion, we may say that Screen Books' strategy appears to suffer from failings in both intent and execution. It is questionable whether the plan for the new product was ever really feasible and it seems likely that its implementation lacked direction and control.

Part (b)

> **Text reference.** The topics mentioned in this answer are discussed in Chapter 6 of your BPP Study Text.
>
> **Easy marks.** A theoretical model helps here. We have based our answer on SWOT: generic strategies or product market vector could also have provided a basis for an answer. We recommend such a use of models because it guides your thinking and allows you to organise both your thoughts and the data given. It will also be worth a mark or two for basic knowledge.

1   **SWOT Analysis**

Strengths

The Internet retailing operation is fundamentally successful and has the crucial fulfilment capacity. While trading at a loss, the company has actually held its losses to not much more than the total of the apparently inflated spending on marketing and R&D. This implies that the basic retailing business is sound.

Extensive experience of both publishing and book retailing is available.

The screen-based device. It is debatable whether this is, in fact, a strength, but if any technical progress has been made it represents a knowledge asset that may have value, if only on disposal.

There would seem to be significant cash reserves. The flotation must have raised more than £12 million and cumulative operating losses amount to less than £3 million.

Weaknesses

The financial position is dubious. There are a number of elements to this.

- The **share price has collapsed**. This may be due partly to market panic, but also reflects the justified doubt about the viability of the new product. This is bound to bring pressure from shareholders and analysts.

- Ability to generate **positive cashflows** is somewhat suspect. While the basic retailing operation is assessed above as probably healthy, it is doubtful that it could generate enough funds to service the existing debt and make a reasonable profit. If it were to be expanded, this would require further marketing expenditure.

- Contracts have been let with external R&D agencies. These may require continuing payments.

The dot com bubble has burst. It will be very difficult for Screen Books to raise capital or even obtain a sympathetic hearing from existing providers. Internet retailing is no longer a fashion statement and has become little more than an alternative to catalogue shopping.

Opportunities

It is difficult to identify opportunities without further information, other than to say that Internet shopping is now accepted as routine by many customers.

Threats

The *Palm Pilot* type of personal organiser is the subject of continuing development and may make the new product unviable, even supposing it can be brought to market.

The current global economic slowdown would prejudice the launch of the new product.

2   **Comment**

Screen Books is subject to major uncertainty over its new screen-based product. If it is ultimately feasible to bring this to market, the company's strategic position will be very different from the one it would find itself in if it proves impracticable. The first priority therefore, is an **authoritative assessment of the project**. This should be carried out externally to ensure objectivity.

If the project is judged to be viable, the next thing to be assessed is whether or not it will be necessary to **raise more finance**. If it is, financial market conditions may mean that it becomes necessary to make an approach to another company in the same field with a view to some form of alliance or even outright sale of the project.

If it is felt that it is possible to bring the product to market with existing resources, it will be necessary to exert **stringent control over progress**.

Should the new product development be shown to be a dead end, Screen Books must **avoid escalating commitment**. It must cut its losses as fast as possible, restricting operations to Internet retailing. This will improve its cash flow position, but it is likely to reveal that the company is under-trading to a dangerous extent. It would be necessary to **expand profitable turnover** significantly in order to service existing debt and satisfy shareholders.

Internet trading may not hold the potential to achieve this. The principals in the joint venture must also consider using their available cash resources to **expand their more traditional operations**. The acquisition of more high street retail outlets is one possibility. There are legal and taxation implications here, relating to the form of the group and the three businesses, that will require detailed attention.

Any retail expansion will require significant **promotional expenditure**.

Part (c)

A research and development project such as Screen Books' must be carefully managed if it is to have the best chance of success. Poor or non-existent planning is a recipe for disaster. In particular, **objectives** must be clearly defined and **time and cost constraints** established. Project management teams often fail to exercise control under changing circumstances. A special problem exists with IT projects: the technical ability of IT staff is no guarantee of management skill.

When an organisation is highly dependent on the success of a single large project, it is particularly important that **effective strategic control** is exercised. In particular, regular performance reviews against planned targets should be held.

All projects are likely to be subject to difficulties that must be resolved.

(a)   **Teambuilding.** The work may carried out by a newly assembled team who must immediately be able to communicate effectively with each other. Arrangements must be made to manage the probable need to cut across functional boundaries within the organisation.

(b)   **Unexpected problems** There should be mechanisms within the project to enable these problems to be resolved during the time span of the project without detriment to the objective, the cost or the time span.

(c)   **Specialists**. Contributions made by specialists are of differing importance at each stage, but must be carefully managed.

(d)   **Unproven technology**. Estimating the project duration can be difficult when it involves new technology or existing technology at its limits. Screen Books' project almost certainly suffered from this.

(e)   **Over-optimism.** Costs are often underestimated by optimistic designers, particularly with new technology. Screen Books may well have suffered from this problem.

A development project often arises out of a perceived problem or opportunity. Screen Books' research arose because of the opportunities presented by the Internet and the availability of finance. Under these circumstances it is important that the **management process should begin immediately**. The problem should be analysed to establish its **precise nature** and to outline possible solutions. When it is determined that technological development is required, the project **objectives** and **success criteria** should be clearly specified and possible routes to achieving them explored.

It should be possible to break the forecast activity down into **stages**. This eases both the assessment of the required **resources** and the establishment of intermediate **objectives**. Subsequent control is greatly enhanced if there is clear understanding of what is to be done, by whom and when. A variety of management techniques may then be used to control projects, including **Gantt** charts and network analysis. Network planning facilitates management by exception by identifying, from the outset, those critical activities that might delay others.

The process of control should include regular **meetings** to review overall progress and undertake financial and quality **audit**. Review will be undertaken at more than one level of management, with those in immediate control of developments meeting perhaps once a week; a higher level review might take place each month and a strategic review perhaps quarterly.

The final stage of control is **post-audit**, which asks two questions.

- Did the project meet its objectives?
- Was the management of the project successful?

Screen Books has been concerned with a single major project. It is possible to make recommendations for organisations that are concerned with broader aspects of innovation.

R&D should **support the organisation's chosen strategy**. To take a simple example, if a strategy of **differentiation** has been adopted, it would be inappropriate to expend effort on researching ways of minimising costs, at the expense of work to create a differentiating feature.

Problems of **authority relationships and integration** arise with the management of R&D. The function will have to liase closely with marketing and with production, as well as with senior management responsible for corporate planning: its role is both strategic and technical.

Pure research or even applied research may not have an obvious **pay off** in the short term. Evaluation could be based on successful application of new ideas, such as patents obtained and the commercial viability of new products.

Research staff are usually highly qualified and profession-orientated, with consequences for the **style of supervision** needed and level of **remuneration** offered to them.

Encouraging innovation means trial and error, flexibility, tolerance of mistakes in the interests of experimentation, high incentives and so on. If this is merely a subculture in an essentially bureaucratic organisation, it will not only be difficult to sustain, but will become a source of immense political conflict. The R&D department may have an academic or university atmosphere, as opposed to a commercial one.

Intrapreneurship is entrepreneurship carried on within the organisation at a level below the strategic apex. The encouragement of intrapreneurship is an important way of promoting innovation. Such encouragement has many aspects.

(a)   Encouragement for individuals to achieve results in their own way without the need for constant supervision
(b)   A culture of risk-taking and tolerance of mistakes
(c)   A flexible approach to organisation that facilitates the formation of project teams
(d)   Willingness and ability to devote resources to trying out new ideas
(e)   Incentives and rewards policy that support intrapreneurial activity

39 Universal Roofing Systems

Part (a)

Text reference. The topics mentioned in this answer are discussed in Chapter 4 of your BPP Study Text.

Top tips. The requirement for this part of question 1 makes an explicit call for your answer to make use of 'an appropriate model'. The **value chain** is the obvious model to use, since providing 'a superior level of service' is just one example of the way in which companies succeed in their fundamental task of creating value for their customers: the value chain model may be used to analyse the ways in which any company does this.

Indeed, the **marking scheme** for this part is heavily biased towards this model, offering up to five marks for each of: primary activities, secondary activities, linking activities and value system. Up to a further five marks are also available for a discussion of the **distinguishing features of service businesses**. This last element of the mark allocation supports the view that a brief and relevant introduction to the subject under discussion is usually worthwhile.

The test for determining whether or not to provide such a technical introduction is to ask yourself how much you could say about the overall question topic that is both **relevant** and **appropriate at this level**. If you have nothing to say, get on with the main part of your answer; if you think there is a lot that could be said and you believe it is both relevant and that it is at an appropriate technical level, you are probably justified in spending a few minutes writing about it. However, do not lose track of time and spend longer on your scene-setting than is justified.

As always at this level, **judgement is required**.

Easy marks. Assuming you are familiar with the value chain and choose to use it, you ought to be able to score a couple of marks each for identifying the things that URS does that correspond to the primary and secondary activities; the links between them; and the value system.

Examiner's comments. The Examiner expected that the value chain would be used here and suggested that the balanced scorecard was a possible alternative. He cautioned that, while there may be no single best model to use in any question, some will be inappropriate and lead to candidates answering their own question, rather than the one actually asked.

As you will see, we do not consider inseparability in the classic sense to be a significant problem for Universal Roofing Systems.

Marking scheme

		Marks
(a)	Value chain analysis:	
	Primary activities	up to 5 marks
	Support activities	up to 5 marks
	Linking activities	up to 5 marks
	Value system	up to 5 marks
	Features that distinguish services	up to 5 marks
		Maximum 20 marks
(b)	Performance analysis:	
	Rate of sales growth	up to 4 marks
	Cost behaviour	up to 4 marks
	Profit margins	up to 4 marks
	Staff	up to 4 marks
	Other measures	up to 4 marks
		Maximum 15 marks

(c)   Implementation:
       Strategy   up to 2 marks
       Structure   up to 2 marks
       Systems   up to 2 marks
       Skills   up to 2 marks
       Staff   up to 2 marks
       Style   up to 2 marks
       Shared values   up to 2 marks
       Other implementation issues   up to 4 marks
                                                        Maximum 15 marks
                                                        Total 50 marks

Universal Roofing Systems (URS) falls into the large category of businesses whose market offering includes both physical product and service elements. Despite the fact that they provide a tangible and significant physical product, Matthew and Simon Black have successfully differentiated their business by establishing superior standards of service. Services differ from physical products in ways that have important implications for how a business is run.

(a)   **Intangibility.** There are no substantial material or physical aspects to a service. As mentioned above, URS provides a mix of tangible product and intangible service. To some extent, the quality of the services provided is reflected in the physical products, such as in the fit and finish of the roofing systems installed, but for other aspects of service, such as the provision of credit facilities, there is **no physical evidence for the customer to contemplate**. The implication of intangibility is that a satisfying purchase experience depends on the quality of the service provided, which in turn has implications for management and for HR practice in particular.

(b)   **Inseparability.** The creation of many services cannot be separated from their consumption: an example is dental treatment. Associated with this is **perishability**: such services cannot be stored. This is not really a problem for URS: the installation service can, in fact, be **scheduled** to suit the convenience of the customer and the availability of supplies and labour, as can the provision of credit facilities, which are arranged during follow up visits by salespeople. The use of a flexible labour force is an advantage here, since the ability exists to trim capacity at periods of low demand, thus maintaining a high rate of **resource utilisation**.

(c)   **Variability** or **heterogeneity.** It may be hard to attain precise standardisation of the service offered. The quality of the service may depend heavily on **who** delivers it and exactly **when** it takes place. For URS, there is a clear link here to the intangibility factor and its implications, which we have already discussed. In particular, the quality of workmanship achieved when roofing products are installed must be of a high and consistent standard.

(d)   **Ownership.** Services differ from goods in that they do not normally result in the **transfer of property**. The purchase of a service only confers **access** to a facility, not **ownership** of it. However, in the case of URS, the company's service revolves around a very substantial and long-lasting physical structure. We might reasonably expect customers to see the improvements made to the roofs of their houses as having very important property implications.

Porter's value chain model provides a useful basis for analysing the way URS carries on its business.

Inbound logistics is the activity concerned with receiving, storing and issuing **inputs to the operational systems**. It deals with physical assets and is therefore of principal importance in relation to physical products as opposed to intangible services. This is not exclusively the case, of course, since the provision of many services depends on physical inputs such as tools, consumables and fuel. In the case of URS, inbound logistics is primarily concerned with the PVC components needed in its roofing systems. These must be made available to the installation teams in the right quantities and at the right times.

Transportation of installers and supplies to sites will be an important aspect of this activity and a significant element of cost. The materials used are bulky rather than heavy, which will tend to extend the service life of the vehicles, so the choice of Mercedes vans for the transport fleet is justified on grounds of long-term reliability (as well as image). We know that URS has six showrooms in its region, with plans for nine more: a similarly distributed approach to stockholding may reduce installers' travelling time and enhance system flexibility.

With less than 1% of the UK PVC roofing market, URS is unlikely to have much influence over its much larger suppliers and will have to base its stock management on traditional lines rather than JIT. It must also be prepared for failures of service on the part of its suppliers, which also implies the holding of a certain level of stock.

Operations is the value activity that converts resources into a final product. This is where URS is able to generate much of the value it offers. In particular, its **standardisation of processes**, **innovative roofing design** and use of a **unique installation** stand increase the productivity of its installers, while the founders' **emphasis on a high quality of service** puts this aspect of value creation at the heart of the company's operations. The financial service offered by the company also falls under this heading and constitutes a significant part of the value it offers.

The value added by both the roof fitting and the financial service aspects of the company's operations is enhanced by effective **human resource management**. *Porter* includes this in the **support activities** of the value chain: we have already mentioned its importance in service provision.

There is no significant **outbound logistics** element in the URS value chain as delivery is part of the **operations** activity.

Marketing and sales provides the interface between the company and the customer. It thus creates value both by informing customers what the company can do for them and by informing the company about what customers need and want. URS has a sophisticated sales operation, making use of canvassers, sales representatives, showrooms and a full range of promotional methods. Discounts for immediate orders can work to the advantage of both customer and company, though they must be carefully controlled so that they do not become routine. The ability to offer credit rounds out the sales service, though it brings training and regulatory burdens under the Financial Services Act.

Marketing and sales also has an important linking role within the company. **Customer satisfaction** is fundamental to survival and growth and it is the marketing and sales people who should be closest to the customer. It is for them to feed **customer comments** on work that has been done back into the operational systems and to take a leading role in considering **possible future market and product developments** in discussion with the other functions.

Service in this context is **after sales service**. This makes a vital contribution to customer satisfaction. The company provides a unique ten year guarantee on its installations. By the nature of its product, URS has little opportunity for repeat selling to the same customer. This is a general characteristic of building services and explains to some extent the poor quality and dissatisfaction typical of the sector. However, good service and customer satisfaction is an important aspect of URS' business model and helps the company attract the 30% of its customers that come from personal recommendation. There are obvious links here with the marketing and operations activities and we would expect that in a company as small as URS the same people would be involved.

Support activities are emphatically not of secondary importance in creating sustainable competitive advantage. However, their significance is not perhaps as obvious in the short term as that of the primary activities. The brothers Black evidently understand this and seem to have given a large measure of attention to these activities.

Firm infrastructure is the activity that, among other things, manages the company's property portfolio, its finances and its vehicles. It is thus fundamental to several of the value-adding features we have identified and must be integrated with them. For example, financial constraints must be balanced against marketing validity in the selection, fitting out and operation of the company's showrooms. The financial and management information systems installed by Harry Potts form an important part of the firm's infrastructure.

We have already mentioned the importance of **human resource management** to a business with a high service content and the importance of linking it effectively with other activities. Selection, training, remuneration and other aspects of motivation must all be managed so as to produce staff who are both willing and able to provide exemplary service.

Technology development has been very important to the company's ability to create value. Despite the difficulty of involving their large suppliers in development, URS has used technology to improve and differentiate its offering: this was discussed earlier, in connection with **operations**.

Procurement as a function is usually distributed within an organisation, with **decision-making units** comprising members of more than one department or team. These people must work together effectively, maintaining commitment to overall goals rather than system goals. Routine re-ordering of supplies and components must be done efficiently, but the real value-adding opportunities in procurement lie in sourcing decisions. URS has found innovative designs and products that distinguish its roofing systems from the competition, while simultaneously keeping its materials costs under control.

Part (b)

Top tips. Questions requiring a strategic evaluation are very common in Part A of your exam. They are often pitched at the level of overall strategy, though the focus is occasionally narrower, as in December 2003, when a product portfolio review was called for.

It can be difficult to know quite where to start with a question of the broader type. Basically, there are two possible approaches.

The first is to run through a few **analytical models** (such as the five forces, the value chain, the competences concept and the various portfolio analysis approaches; the balanced scorecard could also be useful) and see if they are relevant to any of the material in the scenario. It is unlikely that a scenario will fit any of them particularly neatly, but you may find that it can be broken down into manageable chunks like this.

The second basic technique is to **go through the scenario** noting anything that seems to be of strategic significance, then arranging the facts with relevant comments so as to make a reasonable account. This approach is certainly worth using on the table of numerical data that always accompanies the Part A scenario: the computation of a few percentage changes from year to year and a few basic ratios such as gross profit can reveal much of interest.

You can, of course, use both of these approaches sequentially. In any event, you should ensure that you spend ten minutes or so giving careful consideration to the numbers. As indicated above, you will not normally be expected to carry out any complex calculations; the data will be of overall strategic significance.

The marking scheme for this question mentioned sales growth, cost behaviour, profit margins and the contributions made by the management and staff of the company.

Examiner's comments. Candidates seemed to find this part of the question quite difficult. The Examiner wondered if the requirement to 'strategically evaluate' might have been puzzling. He intended it to indicate that there was a need to go beyond a purely financial analysis.

URS is a small company, turning over less than £10m and having less than 1% of the potential national market. Not surprisingly, it has followed a strategy of **focus differentiation**: the company operates in one region only and, as discussed above, differentiates its product in a variety of ways related to service scope and quality. The directors have communicated their ideas about quality and service effectively and the company seems to have achieved the differentiation they sought. URS is now poised to move beyond its home region and build up a national presence.

URS has achieved **impressive growth** since the appointment of Mick Hendry in 2002 and the adoption of a business model based on that used in the PVC replacement door and window industry. The company achieved growth of 27% in total turnover in 2004. Most of this growth has come from the private housing sector; the achievement of commensurate growth in the commercial sector would have required the commitment of substantial extra resources that the company does not possess.

URS seems to have its **costs under control**. Its cost structure has changed markedly since 2002, with **total sales costs** approximately doubling as a proportion of turnover. However, there was also a massive increase in sales, which has continued in subsequent years. At the same time, there was an increase in **gross margin** from 44% in 2001 to 48% in 2002 and 49% in 2003. Gross margin in 2004 was 53% and is expected to remain at that level in the near to medium term future. **Net profit** was negative in 2002 as a consequence of the up front nature of the increased sales costs, but rose to 5.8% in 2004. Continuing increases are forecast, with 11.8% being expected for 2007. **Direct labour costs** seem to be reasonably stable, despite the expansion, which might have been expected to counteract any experience and learning effects.

In the context of labour costs, the company's **policy of using sub-contractors** for its roofing operations is worthy of mention. This practice has certainly helped the company to **manage its costs** but must inevitably limit its ability to achieve its desired standards of service. The sub-contractors work in teams of two, so they must be largely self-motivating and they must take considerable responsibility for the quality of the service provided. The problem is that their somewhat insecure status may **prejudice their commitment** to a high level of service provision.

There is also potential for **problems in after-sales service**. The **potential weakness** of the URS system is that rectification is carried out by the installers, who are paid by results. If these teams are paid to rectify the work they have not done properly, there is an obvious disincentive to getting things right first time. If they are not paid, there is an equally obvious disincentive to getting it right the second time. Managing the implications of this approach is likely to be rather difficult.

Part (c)

Text reference. The topics mentioned in this answer are discussed in Parts C to J of your BPP Study Text.

Top tips. It is not unusual to find current ideas about strategic implementation to be less cohesive than those concerned with strategic analysis and strategic options. This is because **implementation covers such a wide and varied range of business activities**. You could approach this question in either of the ways we outlined in our tutorial note to part (b) above, but it is probably best to start with some ideas about just what is involved in implementation.

Strategic choice

A fundamental issue is whether or not the directors of URS have made **good basic strategic choices**. The industry is highly fragmented, with no firm having more than 3% of the market. URS is unlikely to find its growth constrained by powerful competition for some time, therefore, but the directors should give some thought to the longer term. This raises the question of the continued appropriateness of the differentiation strategy. They may have an opportunity to achieve **cost leadership**, with all its advantages, but if they are to do this they must avoid decisions that would close off the possibility. This means actively seeking economies of scale and, above all, maintaining close control of costs.

A second basic decision concerns the **market** the company has chosen. We must presume that a conscious and reasoned decision has been taken to give higher priority to the domestic housing market and to starve the commercial market of resources. If this is not the case, and the strategy has arisen by default, it would appear to be questionable.

The domestic market requires **intensive sales and marketing effort**: expanding it to a national scale will require major investment in showrooms and in the recruitment, selection and training of canvassers and salespeople. The commercial market, by contrast, appears to require much less marketing effort, since a single sale can cover many houses: the problem has been finding the (presumably operational) resources to exploit the opportunity. We must now ask whether the resources that would be required for significant expansion of domestic house operations would be better employed in the commercial market. This expansion could be within the home region at first, potentially generating cash to finance later national expansion.

Finance

The company's growth to date does not seem to have been hampered by the **working capital shortages that often accompany such rapid expansion**. However, this may not be the case in the future. We are not told very much about the company's financial resources or its relationship with its bank, but it must be remarked that adequate working capital is fundamental to any business operation. There will also be a requirement for significant capital investment in new premises and equipment and in the personnel costs mentioned earlier.

Structure and systems

URS is currently organised along **functional lines** but a **regional structure** is being considered. The functional approach is suitable for the company's current scale of operations and some form of regional structure is probably appropriate for a company operating nationally. The problem is how to move from the one to the other. Effectively, the current directors will have to duplicate the existing structure in each of the new regions they operate in. This will require the recruitment of managers and staff capable of doing the things the directors and their staff do now and the expansion of existing control and administrative systems.

It will also be necessary to provide a **management structure at the national level** to manage the regions. Perhaps the most difficult thing that Matthew and his colleagues will have to do will be to undertake a different and more challenging role themselves as the strategic apex of national operations. They may find this beyond their capacity.

Culture and change management

Matthew and Simon Black have been successful in putting customer service at the heart of their business. To some extent their ability to provide customer satisfaction has been the result of their careful **standardisation of work processes**, but there must also have been the successful development of a **culture of good service**. Such a culture is one of the most important assets a service business can have. It must be nurtured and defended against erosion by the side effects of other management priorities, such as cost reduction. The planned expansion, with its inevitable expansion of staff numbers has the potential to **dilute and even destroy this culture**. Matthew and Simon must make it their business to ensure that this does not happen; they will have to make sure they devote time to communicating their ideas to new and existing staff and make sure that their attention is not diverted by minor operational problems.

This brings us to the issue of **change management**. No specific changes are currently proposed to the way things are done at URS, but growth on the scale anticipated is bound to bring substantial change. New and improved **systems of reporting and accounting** will be required, almost certainly involving major developments in the company's IT systems. This is also likely to be true in marketing, where, for instance, a **national marketing database system** may be appropriate. Such developments imply new staff, new procedures and new problems.

There may be other issues, such as promotion, sideways moves, new responsibilities and even relocation for existing staff. These must be handled with great care if the current successful company is not to be dangerously disrupted. Careful planning will be required, overseen at board level, combined with clear ideas about how the various necessary changes are to be achieved.

40 Datum Paper Products

Part (a)

> **Text reference.** The topics mentioned in this answer are discussed in Chapter 7 of your BPP Study Text.
>
> **Top tips.** Unfortunately, there is no acknowledged model available that you could use as the basis of an answer to this requirement. However, you could make good use of the value chain model to establish relevant duplications, conflicts and complements in the two companies.
>
> It is well established that a majority of acquisitions fail to achieve the synergy they appear to offer. You should be aware of this from your general reading of the business press. Perhaps the most obvious things to say about mergers is that the potential for synergy occurs when the combined business seems likely to create greater total value than its constituents do separately.
>
> One possible approach to producing an answer is to use the suitability-acceptability-feasibility framework. The problem with this is that it begs the question somewhat, as nearly all the material available to us would have to be dealt with under the 'suitability' heading and thus leaves us little closer to getting a grip on the material.
>
> One thing we can recommend is to start with the numerical data. With this sort of table, it takes very little time to analyse the operating statement into percentages of turnover and to calculate simple ratios such as gearing and sales per employee. Carrying out this kind of simple numerical analysis will get your mind moving in the right direction. A careful look at the data table also reveals a high level of dividends and a low charge for depreciation, a combination with clear potential for future decline as a result of a lack of investment.
>
> **Easy marks.** Some things are fairly obvious from the data in the table: the two companies' markets would complement each other quite nicely and DPP is the more innovative of the two. Also, there is also a strong likelihood of problems over cultural matters generally and productivity in particular.
>
> **Examiner's comments.** Caution was necessary here in terms of the number of models used and the depth of analysis.

Marking scheme

		Marks
(a)	Areas of strategic fit: customers, value chains, technology, systems, style etc.	up to 3 per point
	Areas of positive synergy and areas of negative synergy	up to 2 per point
		Maximum 20 marks
(b)	Advantages and disadvantages of greenfield option	up to 2 per point
	Advantages and disadvantages of acquisition	up to 2 per point
		Maximum 15 marks
(c)	Identification of integration problems	up to 2 per point
	Selection of key performance indicators	up to 2 per point
		Maximum 15 marks
		Total 50 marks

Strategic options

An acquisition is a major strategic step and should be evaluated using the same **suitability-acceptability-feasibility** framework as any other potential strategic option. In the case of an acquisition of Papiere Presse (PP) by DPP, the main considerations relate to suitability, or strategic logic, since we must assume that the necessary resources are available to make the purchase and that since DPP is a subsidiary operating company, its stakeholders will themselves be largely concerned with the suitability criterion. There is an obvious further potential acceptability hurdle, which is the reaction of PP's workforce, to which we will return.

Synergy

If the aim of strategy is to **maximise the value created by the business** organisation, the only justification for an acquisition is potential **synergy**: that is to say, a probability that, overall and in the longer term, the combined enterprise will generate greater value than the components would do separately. There are often immediate efficiency improvements that follow the merging of two businesses, but they are once and for all: the aim must be to create an organisation that will enjoy continuing advantages. Research indicates that a majority of mergers and acquisitions fail to do this, so there should be a heavy burden of proof laid on the promoters of such schemes.

Johnson, Scholes and Whittington suggest that there are four categories of difficulty that await the aspiring synergy manager.

- The costs involved in sharing resources
- The impact of self-interest among senior managers
- Incompatibility of systems and culture
- Variation in local conditions

Synergy managers must be determined if they are to achieve their goal of integrating and controlling the parts of the combined operation. They must also be realistic about their ability to leverage the combined resources and competences to achieve synergy. It is very easy to be deceived by the illusion of synergy.

DPP's strategic aims

DPP's medium-term strategic objective would seem to be **to survive the wave of consolidation** that seems likely as a result of falling demand and pressure for price reductions in the industry as a whole. Under these circumstances it will be only the most efficient operators that survive. Major factors will be **market share**, with its associated scale economies; **efficiency**, which means in effect strong downward pressure on costs; improvements in **customer service**; and **innovation**, with its potential for higher margins.

DPP and PP

We must assume that DPP is not planning to buy PP simply in order to take over its order book and then reduce industry capacity by closing it down: PP is quite successful: its operating profit percentage, at 11.8%, is slightly higher than DPP's own and it seems unlikely that all of PP's potential for value creation could be captured in this way. There is not even any guarantee that PP's existing customers would transfer their business to DPP.

DPP must therefore **seek synergy** from an acquisition.

Markets

There is a good fit between the two companies' **markets**. Half of DPP's sales, or almost £100m, are outside Europe, against PP's £4.5m. PP has 60% of the French market and 20% of the Italian, while DPP has only 10% and 8% respectively. DPP has 45% of the UK market, while PP has only 14%.

ANSWERS

Operations

While PP's operating profit is very similar to that of DPP, the breakdown of costs is revealing. PP's gross margin is only 25%, compared to 37.5% for DPP. A major cause of this discrepancy must be PP's **significantly lower productivity**: we are told that its manufacturing manning levels are higher than DPP's; its turnover per person employed is only £120,000, compared with DPP's £156,400; and its absenteeism rate is twice that of DPP.

This is a point of great importance, bearing in mind both our remarks above about the need for efficiency and the French national attitude to productivity and job protection. The potential for damaging disputes seems very significant.

Fixed assets

DPP should look more closely at PP's plant and machinery. We know that **the technology is dated**. This is borne out in the very low figure of 1.1% of turnover charged for depreciation by PP, compared with DPPs 5.1%. This would constitute another obstacle to improved efficiency.

The fixed asset picture is particularly interesting in the light of the **high level of dividends** paid by PP. Dividend cover is only 1.33, while DPP's is 2.23. The Truffaud family are taking money out of PP at a rate that is eroding its ability to continue to operate.

Innovation

DPP's **superior record of innovation** is borne out by its record of patents granted, its sales from products less than five years old and its much higher relative level of R&D expense (2.3% of turnover compared with 0.6%). This would actually provide some synergy in that DPP's strength would compensate for PP's weakness.

Customer service

Philippe and François Truffaud have established for PP a reputation for a level of customer service that exceeds that enjoyed by DPP. This is the single **greatest asset** that PP might bring to a merger of the two companies' operations and the one that has the greatest longer term potential to add value. It is, however, questionable whether this alone would justify an acquisition, since the **language** and **other cultural differences** between the companies may make it very difficult to transfer the PP approach. Ken Drummond might do better to seek a home-grown solution, possibly strengthening his company by recruiting service oriented and experienced managers to supplement his existing team.

IT systems

It would be difficult to reconcile the two companies IT systems. This represents a **negative synergy** that could by itself preclude an acquisition: the cost if integration might be excessive, while to continue to run separate operations would seriously hamper the realisation of any potential synergies.

HRM

PP's three plants are heavily unionised. We are not told of DPP's approach to industrial relations, but it seems almost inevitable that there would be a clash with the French unions over productivity. It simply would not be worth DPP's while to acquire PP unless there were **potential to improve the productivity of the French plants**.

Culture

We have already mentioned the problems of language and working practices at the PP plants. There are also likely to be **significant cultural differences** arising from the contrast between DPP's status as a UK subsidiary of a very large conglomerate and PP's as a privately owned French independent.

Part (b)

> **Top tips.** Interpreting this question is a little tricky: the phrase 'as opposed to the acquisition of Papier Presse' would seem at first glance to be no more than an emphasis on the idea that your assessment should relate to the greenfield option only. This view is borne out by the Examiner's suggested solution, which confines its remarks to matters relevant to that option. However, his marking scheme offers equal marks for the consideration of the each of the two options. What, then, are we to do?
>
> Our advice in puzzling circumstances like these would be this: first, read the question very carefully indeed; second, try to work out what the Examiner really wants; third, ask yourself if he might actually want something rather different and what that might be. The number of marks available may help you here, by giving you an indication of the total size of answer the Examiner has in mind. If you think the 'something rather different' case is a possibility, you have two possible courses of action.
>
> The first would be to start your answer with a clearly expressed **assumption** and then answer it on that basis. So, in the case of this question, you might write:
>
> *Assumption: this question calls for an assessment of the greenfield option only.*
>
> The second possible course of action would be to proceed on the basis of what you *think* the question means but to hedge your bets by allowing a little time to deal with any extra matters you suspect might be relevant.
>
> **Easy marks.** The Examiner has described two important considerations very clearly in the scenario: these are infrastructure and government policy. It is also clear that the main motivation for moving to Eastern Europe would be to achieve cost savings. You should be able to make these points very easily.
>
> **Examiner's comments**. The examiner accepted that the question was ambiguous and said that answers on either interpretation were acceptable.

Advantages of the greenfield site option

Cost savings

The entire paper making industry is under heavy pressure to cut costs. The **operating cost savings** available from moving production to an Eastern European country must be a major reason for DPP to do so. A major element of the potential for cost saving must come from the much lower labour costs prevalent in Eastern Europe. It difficult to forecast how long these countries will retain this advantage as they become more prosperous, but it is likely to last beyond any reasonable strategic planning horizon.

An associated advantage is the generally high level of **educational attainment** in the countries of Eastern Europe, which should assist the recruitment of competent staff.

Financial incentives

In addition to cost savings, there is the prospect of receiving significant EU and government **incentives** for setting up operations in a currently depressed area. Such incentives typically include tax advantages, soft loans, subsidised or nil rental of premises and outright grants. Any of these would help with the inevitable costs of moving a large production operation to another country.

Concentration

DPP currently operates four plants. We are told that each of the four plants manufactures a different part of the total product range but not whether this split is inevitable or even desirable. A move to a greenfield site may offer an opportunity to **consolidate** some aspects of production and other operations and to achieve some **economies of scale**.

Currency

Most new EU members have adopted the euro as their currency. Siting the new operation in such a country would be an advantage for that part of DPP's sales made into the Eurozone, in that currency translation, charges and risks would not be issues. On the other hand, sales into the UK would be made more complicated for the same basic reason. Unfortunately, we do not know how much of the 50% of its sales that go to European markets is broken down between the UK and the eurozone, so we do not know if this would actually represent a net benefit.

IT systems

A new single site operation could be built from the ground up and could include a single, integrated IT **enterprise resource planning** system, with all its advantages for planning, control and knowledge management

Disadvantages of the green field site option

Lack of infrastructure

We are told that potential sites lack suppliers, distributors and logistical support. **Logistics** is likely to be a major concern: as a manufacturing company, DPP will have to obtain its raw materials and other supplies and move its output to its customers all over the world. Reliable **transport links** will be essential for its operations. A related consideration would be the extent of any cost differential caused by the location of the new site: it is likely that average delivery distances would increase if production were moved to Eastern Europe, with consequent increases in transport costs.

The lack of local suppliers may not be a major concern if inputs can be reliably moved from current suppliers to the new site, but here again, transport infrastructure will be very important.

Government policy and practice

DPP will be affected by the extent of **bureaucratic drag** said to be present in potential host countries. Since the company's markets are in the West, it need not be particularly concerned about government intervention in local markets, but the prospect of intervention in its own operations is more worrying. The **stability of government policy** would also be a concern, though all the countries in contention are members of the EU, so a reasonable level of stability could be expected.

Productivity

While Eastern European workers generally have proven themselves to be willing and productive workers, it is likely to take some time to build up the **experience** needed to achieve overall high levels of productivity. It would probably be desirable to relocate at least some of the existing UK supervisory managers, if they could be persuaded to move: there should be no major problem in doing this because of the UK's stand on free movement of labour within the EU.

Existing UK plants

Since the motive for a move to Eastern Europe would be to **reduce costs**, we must assume that most of the UK operation would be shut down. This would involve the company in significant expense associated with **redundancy** and possibly with work involved in closing down existing premises. There is also the possibility of a damaging industrial dispute to consider.

It seems likely that the **design function** would be retained in the UK at least in the short term, as this would probably be the most difficult part to transfer or replace.

Top tips. If you decided to consider the advantages and disadvantages of the French option as well, you might mention low productivity; high cost labour; good infrastructure; good and well-established market relationships; heavy labour market regulation; and the currency issue.

Part (c)

From: Accountant
To: Ken Drummond
Date: June 20X5

Integrating an acquisition

You asked for a report on potential problems with integrating an acquisition. Historically, acquisitions have failed to achieve the benefits forecast for them and this, generally has been because of failures to integrate effectively.

IT systems

IT systems are fundamental to the operations of most companies and critical to many. There can be little synergy if the two parts of the new organisation continue to operate as they did before because of **incompatibility of systems**. **Scale economies** are much more difficult to achieve, **overall control data** is not readily accessible and **knowledge** cannot be pooled effectively. Several approaches can be taken to integration, including the commissioning of a totally new system and extension of one system to cover both elements of the new organisation. Measure of progress are set in terms of system availability and functioning and might include the number of workstations with access to the combined management system and the number of elements of that system in place. These elements would include compatibility of functions such as email and intranet and preparation of routine reports.

Rationalisation of assets and operations

An acquisition is likely to lead to opportunities to rationalise assets such as plant by concentrating work in a reduced number of locations. In the case of an acquisition of PP by DPP, for example, it would seem likely that **productivity** could be improved by closing at least one of the French plants and transferring the work to the more up to date and productive UK sites. Similar consolidation might be carried out with sales teams, transport fleets and stock-holding facilities.

Key measures of progress would depend on the setting of **targets** for what was to be achieved and the creation of a suitable plan for achieving it. In the case of a rationalised field sales force, for example, it might be decided to reduce headcount by a combination of redundancy and natural wastage, while reallocating the remaining staff. This would have to be done in stages and the completion of each stage could be reported in terms of staff numbers remaining, area coverage achieved and, to monitor effectiveness, sales per head of sales staff.

Culture

Organisational culture is often regarded as a source of problems during the integration phase. As already discussed above, DPP and PP have clear differences in culture, most of which arise from the facts of their national origins. Perhaps the most important example of the practical impact of a cultural impact of a cultural difference is the unionisation and rate of absenteeism at PP's sites. The French economy generally is highly productive, but these two elements lead to a suspicion that what might be called a **Theory X culture** prevails within these plants. If this is the case, it will be a difficult task to improve the performance of these establishments. Practical targets might include the negotiation of a suitable agreement with the local unions and simple measure such as those already in place to measure absenteeism and individual productivity.

41 Churchill Ice Cream

Part (a)

> **Text reference.** The topics mentioned in this answer are discussed in Chapter 6 of your BPP Study Text.
>
> **Top tips.** Clearly, the first thing you have to do here is to decide just what you think Churchill's strategy is. Equally clearly, you are not going to find that the way the company has gone about its business can be easily slotted into a single theoretical category, other than, perhaps, focussed differentiation. Remember, strategy has many aspects and Churchill ice cream seems to have had a go at a fair number of them. The Examiner is using the term 'strategy' in its widest sense here and we are interested in any aspect of what the senior management of the company consciously decides to do.
>
> Be prepared to discuss the company's activities from the various points of view presented by the strategic models you are familiar with. You do not have to cover these in an ideal order or discern any pervasive theme. There is plenty to say.
>
> **Easy marks.** You should have noticed that the company displays a significant degree of vertical integration. There are standard text book arguments for and against this approach that lend themselves to Churchill's particular situation.
>
> **Examiner's comments.** This requirement was answered well, generally speaking.

Marking scheme

		Marks
(a)	Advantages of current strategy including:	up to 2 per feature
	Control obtained through vertical integration	
	Value chain linkages	
	Closer to the final customer	
	Strategy difficult to imitate	
	New product innovation easier	
	Reduced buyer power	
	Flexibility in meeting varying demand levels	
	Disadvantages of current strategy including:	up to 2 per point
	Increased level of resource/capabilities needed	
	Internal competition between manufacturing and retail sides of business	
	Increased operation/organisational complexity	
	Growth function of number of ice cream stores	
	Cost implication of varying levels of demand	
	Performance analysis	up to 6
	Use of models where appropriate including:	up to 5
	Value chain/system	
	Five forces analysis	
	Ansoff's growth matrix	
	Maximum 20 marks	

(b)   Suitability   up to 6
       SWOT analysis
       Gap and 'fit' analysis
       Resource/capability analysis

       Acceptability   up to 5
       Risk and return analysis
       Screening process
       Stakeholder analysis – owners v managers

       Feasibility: up to 5
       Funds availability
       Resource/capabilities availability

       Compatibility of three strategic goals   up to 5
                                                                          Maximum 15 marks

(c)   Identification of current marketing mix   up to 2 per element

       Changes to the mix for each goal including: up to 3 per goal
       Becoming leading national brand – product innovation,
       premium pricing strategy, national availability, and national promotion
       sales of £25 million – higher take home sales,
       increasing product range, national availability,
       Increased advertising
       Penetration of supermarkets – own label brands,
       lower prices, national distribution, promotion support

                                                                          Maximum 15 marks
                                                                          Total 50 marks

In **generic strategy** terms, Churchill is a **focussed differentiator**. The company has established a geographical niche in the London area for its outlets and distinguishes itself from its competitors both by its emphasis on the quality of its ingredients and recipes and by its vertical integration of the production and distribution of its ice creams.

Differentiation is the obvious strategy for a company of Churchill's size. **Cost leadership** can only be attempted when there is favoured access to resources or technology or, more commonly, sufficient volume to generate significant **economies of scale**. Churchill has neither of these advantages so, like most small and medium sized enterprises, it has pursued differentiation.

Differentiation by quality is a common ambition, but difficult to achieve, particularly in service businesses, since it requires unrelenting attention to detail. Services cannot be prepared in advance of delivery, so there is no way that they can be subjected to traditional methods of quality control by inspection. The service company's reputation is largely dependent on the performance of its staff.

However, Churchill is only partly a service business. The company appears to have made the use of **high quality ingredients** the main source of differentiation in its manufacturing operation, and there is no reason why this should not be part of a satisfactory strategy, especially as premium ice cream is now a well-established product for adults in the UK.

The company seems to have had some success with its ice cream parlour operation also. In terms of *Lynch's* market options matrix, this constitutes **vertical integration**. This is a subcategory of **diversification** in *Ansoff's* growth vector model.

Diversification is commonly regarded as the **most risky** of the four basic options in the Ansoff model since it involves the greatest degree of new and unfamiliar activity. However, Churchill has established its ice cream parlours alongside its manufacturing operation and they constitute an established part of its business.

Vertical integration may bring **specific strategic advantages**.

In terms of *Porter's* **five forces**, downstream vertical integration may be a way to reduce the bargaining power of customers. It is not necessary to monopolise distribution for this reduction to take place: a large enough volume of profitable sales to consumers may lead other distributors to feel that they must have the product in their sales portfolio.

Marketing may be assisted. Churchill's distribution of its products through its own retail outlets should enable it to establish a closer and more knowledgeable relationship with its customers. This should assist its pursuit of its generic strategy of **focus differentiation**.

Churchill's ice cream parlours extend its **value chain** downstream to the customer, allowing it to capture much of the value created by the various ice cream distribution channels. Seventy percent of its sales are made to its own stores, so this is a very important feature of its strategy.

Synergy may be achieved. A merger or acquisition creates synergy when assets are used more efficiently than they were by the individual organisations separately. Improved efficiency of material assets is probably easier to achieve in horizontally integrated companies than in vertically integrated ones, since there is a greater chance that specific assets will be of use to different parts of the merged organisation. A good example would be shared use of distribution facilities. The points we make above about Churchill's ice cream parlours are all connected to the difficulty of achieving synergy through vertical integration.

There are likely to be some opportunities for the creation of **managerial and administrative synergies**, however, in such areas as IT, HRM and finance. There is also the likelihood that **new product development** will be assisted by the immediate availability of test markets in the owned stores.

There are also reasons to be cautious about a strategy of **vertical integration**.

There is a significant degree of **operational and organisational complexity** in such a strategy. The **management skills** involved in running the stores are significantly different from those required for manufacturing; possibly even to the extent that **competing factions** might develop within the company. The two parts of the organisation are likely to focus **conflict** over resources and a partisan approach might be taken, with managers in the manufacturing and retail elements each regarding the other operation as something of a distraction.

There is also a significant **cost** involved: the outlets themselves must be financed, equipped, stocked, staffed and managed. In the case of franchised stores, these costs are met by the franchisees, but more than two thirds of Churchill's stores are owned by the company. Also, the six to one ratio of sales volume, compared with the forty to eighteen ratio of owned to franchised stores, would seem to indicate that the owned stores must be **significantly larger** operations. The owned stores must achieve at least the same ROCE as the manufacturing operation if they are to be regarded as worthwhile.

Performance indicators

Top tips. The numerical information given in the three tables of the scenario is quite interesting and prompts a number of observations and questions; unfortunately, not all of the latter can be answered.

This need not discourage you from making suitable comment, even if it amounts to no more than pointing out the puzzles and the areas in which more information would be required if they were to be resolved.

Note that 'net assets' would appear on a balance sheet prepared under UK GAAP and would be equal to 'capital and reserves'; it would not appear on a balance sheet prepared under IAS.

We are told that sales of ice cream are both seasonal and heavily influenced by summer temperatures; the table of numerical data shows that total ice cream sales shows no clear pattern of change. Under these circumstances, Churchill has done quite well to increase its sales each year, though it is important to note that the **rate of growth has declined** from 8.5% in 2003 to 2.5% in 2005 and is forecast to decline further to 1.8% in 2006.

Annual growth in cost of sales is also declining, though at a slower rate than the decline in turnover. The actual increases in 2003 and 2004 were greater than the corresponding increases in revenue, and this is forecast to occur in 2006. In 2005, the increases were identical. The company is thus experiencing an **erosion of its operating (gross) profit**, which has declined from 9.3% of turnover in 2002 to 5.6% forecast in 2006. Indeed, gross profit has declined in absolute as well as percentage terms, falling from £1,310k in 2002 to £1,040k in 2005 and £940k forecast in 2006.

The income statement shows only one expense other than cost of sales applied to produce net profit: product development. This seems to be **very expensive**, amounting in total to slightly less than 40% of operating profit for the years 2002 to 2005.

Net profit is itself very low, having declined from 6.9% in 2002 to 2.8% in 2004. It showed a small recovery to 4.5% in 2002, but is forecast to decline again to 2.6% in 2006.

The typical Churchill **product cost card** provided is interesting. It indicates a target profit percentage of just ten percent. We are not told what the cost item 'overheads' includes, but even if it is restricted to variable or factory overheads and the profit figure is thus gross rather than net, it is still ambitious: as discussed above, gross profit has not been as high as ten percent overall in the years for which we have data.

The value of **fixed assets** has declined from £10,910k in 2002 to £8,880 in 2005. Were this trend to continue for more than a few more years, it would represent a possibly damaging decline in the employment of modern technology: as a result, both serviceability and productivity might be expected to suffer.

The data shown as **net assets** is also interesting. This is, presumably, equal to capital and reserves. One would therefore expect to see this value increasing as profits are added to reserves. However, despite a small rise in 2003, it has declined from £4,810k in 2002 to £4,300k in 2005. Such a decline would be expected if the company were making **losses**, as these would be charged against reserves. However, the company is profitable. The only other charge that might be made against reserves would be a write-down of assets that had previously been revalued upwards: in the absence of any information to indicate that this might be a possibility, we are driven to the conclusion that Churchill's directors make a practice of **paying dividends out of reserves**.

Part (b)

Text reference. The topics mentioned in this answer are discussed in Chapter 6 of your BPP Study Text.

Top tips. Both the Examiner's marking scheme and his own suggested solution assume that you will answer this requirement using the well-known criteria of **suitability**, **acceptability** and **feasibility**. These criteria are, of course, primarily used to assess not strategic *goals* but strategic *options;* that is, possible courses of action. However, their use to assess these goals is reasonable, especially as penetration of the supermarket sector might indeed be seen as a strategic option rather than as a goal.

The lesson is that you must think fairly widely when considering a question requirement and be prepared to use the basic models in imaginative ways. Here, because the question asks about strategic goals, you might have been tempted to answer largely in terms of **stakeholder expectations**, perhaps with additional comment on the **compatibility** or otherwise of the three stated goals. This would have been a good start, and might have led you to consider **resource implications**. However, the Examiner's approach has the advantage that it relates the three goals very clearly to the company's general strategic circumstances through the **suitability** criterion.

Easy marks. Obvious points to discuss are the **ambitious nature** of the goals; the **thin margins** to be expected from distribution through the major supermarkets; and the probable **high cost of effective promotion** of the brand.

The five year strategic goals set by Richard Smith are first, to establish Churchill as the leading premium ice cream brand in the UK; second, to build turnover to £25M and third, to penetrate the supermarket sector.

We can use *Johnson and Scholes'* three appraisal criteria of **suitability**, **acceptability** and **feasibility** to structure and guide our further consideration of these goals.

The criteria

Suitability is judged in terms of the **overall strategic situation**. A strategy would achieve a high degree of suitability if it exploited strengths, seized opportunities, avoided threats and overcame weaknesses. It would fit well with existing plans, fill any gaps detected by gap analysis and suit the organisation's culture and way of doing things.

Acceptability lies in the perceptions of key stakeholder groups and is particularly dependent on assessment of **risk and reward**. At the moment, these are the members of the Churchill family that own the company and make a contribution to its management, Richard Smith, who has a significant personal commitment, the new Sales and Marketing Director and the company's bank, since significant finance will be required for the envisaged expansion.

Feasibility is a matter of resources. The fundamental resource is **money**, since it can be used to obtain any other material resources that may be required. It can also be used to obtain skilled labour, but the skill and experience of **human capital** is difficult to buy in: generally, it must be developed in-house over an extended period of time. Richard Smith has set three **ambitious goals**: each of them will require the commitment of significant sums of **money** and the deployment of a considerable degree of **management skill**.

The goals

The aim of becoming the UK's leading premium ice cream brand seems to qualify as **suitable**, though the five year time scale is very optimistic. Actually, this goal might well be a good choice as the company's overall long-term **mission**. It seems likely that a natural emotional commitment to the company will make this goal **acceptable** to stakeholders, but there must be doubts about its **feasibility**.

Churchill has achieved a high level of brand awareness in its region but to extend that awareness to the rest of England alone will require **extensive promotional expenditure**; the cost would be significantly increased if the whole of the UK were the chosen arena. It does not seem likely that the company will be able to finance a major and sustained **marketing communications campaign** from its existing resources. Also, it faces strong competition from its two main competitors. To become market leader will be extremely difficult.

The **turnover target** fits well with the brand target and could be seen as a stage along the route to brand leadership. It represents overall growth of just 50%, but this is **ambitious**, given the current rate of growth in the UK premium ice cream market: that growth has been driven by the advertising of the two US owned chains and they may be expected to seize most of it. Churchill's **reluctance to advertise** and its **logistic failures** will prevent it from gaining much extra market share. It is difficult to regard this goal as either suitable or feasible, even in the medium term, though, in principle, it would be acceptable to stakeholders. Expansion based on 'more of the same' with, perhaps, additional ice cream parlours and an expansion of sales to major public events outside the London region would be a reasonable route to a smaller degree of increased turnover. It might be difficult to finance extra retail outlets, but the company is familiar with the franchise method and could utilise it more extensively.

There is likely to be a general internal consensus on the idea of distribution through **supermarkets**, since John Churchill and Richard Smith seem to be in agreement on it, but this goal is of **questionable suitability and feasibility**. At the moment, Churchill is little more than a **niche player**, differentiated on quality of ingredients. While it might be easy enough to obtain supermarket distribution on a trial basis, permanent stocking would depend on the achievement of **satisfactory volume sales**. This would require not only a major increase in production capacity, but also the ability to deliver at the right place and at the right time. Given the failings of its current production control and logistic systems, Churchill might find this beyond its abilities to achieve. It is likely that it would also find it difficult to finance the major plant expansion that would be required.

A further problem with this goal is that a major supermarket chain would **seek to deprive the company of most of the value it creates**, either by demanding very large **discounts** on Churchill branded ice cream or by insisting that Churchill produce an **equivalent own-brand**.

In general, we may say that stakeholders generally are likely to be sympathetic to the pursuit of expansion, but are likely to look more carefully at the detailed methods chosen. The **problems of implementation** that we have already noted are likely to be of concern to all significant stakeholder groups. In particular, the requirement for extensive new **financial commitments** means that the ability of the company to deliver on its ambitions will be examined very carefully. There is some potential for **conflict between stakeholder groups** here, in that shareholders may be required to provide more capital or accept restrictions on dividends in order to fund the proposed expansion.

Part (c)

Text reference. The topics mentioned in this answer are discussed in Chapter 3 of your BPP Study Text.

Top tips. Questions about the marketing mix tend to be fairly easy because the model is little more than a list of important market-related factors. If you are able to deploy a little business awareness and background knowledge you should be able to tackle such questions with reasonable confidence. Remember the important basic rule that the various elements of any marketing mix should be mutually supporting.

The basic 4Ps and the extra 3Ps for services can usually be applied to a scenario to produce a list of sensible ideas and comments. In fact, the checklist below (which is far from exhaustive) should give you something to say about most question settings.

Product Mix, quality, packaging, enhancements
Price Penetration or skimming for new products, image
Promotion Brand management, integration of media
Place Relationship with distributors, forward integration, discounts, reliability of delivery
People Crucial to quality of service, training, motivation
Processes Efficiency, standardisation, computerisation

Physical evidence Ambience, evidence of ownership

Easy marks. Before you can recommend changes, you really have to establish the important features of Churchill's existing marketing mix. Indeed, the marking scheme offers you up to two marks per element for doing just that. However, it is unlikely that you would receive a pass mark on this question for doing that alone.

Examiner's comments. Some answers were unacceptably vague as a result of failing to relate the various strategic options to the marketing mix as required.

Product

At the moment, Churchill has a **premium product** in its ice cream and, judging by the cost of fitting them out, in its **ice cream parlours** too. The latter might be regarded as an aspect of **place**, or distribution, but they are worthy of consideration under this heading since they form part of the **enhanced product** or total consumer product experience. John Churchill places great emphasis on the quality of the ingredients and packaging used. There is also an additive-free range of products. These are good points of **differentiation** for the company.

Pursuit of Richard Smith's **three strategic goals** has implications for Churchill's products. The brand leadership and turnover targets will certainly require the company to continue with its **product development** effort: we are told that this is a key activity in the ice cream market. A wide range of flavours and sizes will be essential if sales are to be maximised. Supermarket placement would also benefit from this, but the main area for consideration is whether the company wishes to manufacture **own brand** ice cream for the supermarkets. This would provide high volume sales but at the price of losing both control over the product and much of the potential margin. However, this might be a way of building up manufacturing capacity with a view to future expansion of Churchill brand sales.

Price

Churchill's current pricing policy is **curious**. 'At least £1 cheaper than our rivals' is **not consistent** with the long-established policy of providing a superior product. This approach is not only likely to **confuse the customer**, since the price and the quality of the product say different things, it is also **hurting Churchill's revenues and profitability**. Nationally, the luxury ice cream market seems to be an oligopoly and it would be sensible for Churchill, as a relatively small player, to **follow the lead** of the larger ones on pricing. A case could be made for charging a **premium to emphasise the product quality**, but a competitive price is probably the safest policy at the moment. This would work for the brand and turnover objectives and probably for the supermarket objective as well.

Promotion

The company has a great deal of promotional work to do if it is to make significant progress towards any of its objectives. There is no advertising at the moment, the only promotional activity being sponsorship of sporting events in London. As already mentioned, both the brand leadership goal and the turnover goal are likely to require **considerable expenditure** on promotion. Advertising and point of sale promotion will certainly be required. The role of sponsorship is possibly less clear: Churchill really needs the advice of experts in branding if it is to get the best effect from its promotion spending. In brief, it will be necessary to create a positive **brand image** and to **position** the brand relative to the competition by promoting a suitable range of **brand values**. This is very skilled work.

The supermarket distribution objective may complicate the promotion problem. Churchill will need to be sure that its chosen supermarket partners do not undermine the brand values it is trying to create by, for example, using its products as loss leaders or by failing to display them correctly. It will be necessary to achieve a degree of co-operation on such matters and on promotional spending to which both manufacturer and distributor make contributions.

Place

Churchill has a major problem with distribution at the moment, in that its lack of a management information system has led to shortages and delays in delivery to its retail outlets. There can be no prospect of successful expansion until the company has a robust logistic system that is capable of handling the anticipated growth.

A further matter is the provision of branded cold display containers. *Mars* set the standard for this when it introduced its ice cream *Mars* bar in 1988. Branded refrigerators are now common for premium ice cream products and the company will have to decide whether it wishes to go down this route. The expense will be significant and there may be a problem of acceptance by distributors, but such exclusive displays can provide strong enhancement to brand values such as exclusiveness, quality and luxury.

Service aspects

Churchill's products have a high physical content, but the service marketing mix 3Ps are highly relevant to the company's ice cream parlours. If the company wishes this aspect of its business to grow in step with its other activities, it will have to pay significant attention to recruiting, training, motivating and rewarding its **people**, to the **physical evidence** of its ice cream parlours ambience, and to the **processes** it uses in all of its operations.

Mock exams

ACCA
Paper P3
Business Analysis

Mock Examination 1

Question Paper	
Time allowed	
Reading and planning	**15 minutes**
Writing	**3 hours**
This paper is divided into two sections	
Section A	**ONE compulsory question to be attempted**
Section B	**TWO questions ONLY to be attempted**

During reading and planning time only the question paper may be annotated

DO NOT OPEN THIS PAPER UNTIL YOU ARE READY TO START UNDER EXAMINATION CONDITIONS

SECTION A – The one question in this section is compulsory and must be attempted.

Question 1

Introduction

Tony Masters, chairman and chief executive of the Shirtmaster Group, is worried. He has recently responded to his senior management team's concerns over the future of the Group by reluctantly agreeing to appoint an external management consultant. The consultant's brief is to fully analyse the performance of the privately owned company, identify key strategic and operational problems and recommend a future strategy for the company. Tony is concerned that the consultant's report will seriously question his role in the company and the growth strategy he is proposing.

Group origins and structure

Tony's father, Howard Masters, set up Shirtmaster in the 1950s. Howard was a skilled tailor and saw the potential for designing and manufacturing a distinctive range of men's shirts and ties marketed under the 'Shirtmaster' brand. Howard set up a shirt manufacturing company with good access to the employee skills needed to design and make shirts. Howard had recognised the opportunity to make distinctive shirts incorporating innovative design features including the latest man-made fibres. In the 1960s London was a global fashion centre exploiting the UK's leading position in popular music. Men became much more fashion conscious, and were willing to pay premium prices for clothes with style and flair. Shirtmaster by the 1960s had built up a UK network of more than 2,000 small independent clothing retailers. These retailers sold the full range of men's wear including made-to-measure suits, shirts and matching ties, shoes and other clothing accessories. Extensive and expensive TV and cinema advertising supported the Shirtmaster brand.

The Shirtmaster Group is made up of two divisions – the Shirtmaster division which concentrates on the retail shirt business and the Corporate Clothing division which supplies workwear to large industrial and commercial customers. Corporate Clothing has similar origins to Shirtmaster, also being a family owned and managed business and is located in the same town as Shirtmaster. It was set up to supply hardwearing jeans and workwear to the many factory workers in the region. The decline of UK manufacturing and allied industries led to profitability problems and in 1990 the Shirtmaster Group acquired it. Tony took over executive responsibility for the Group in 1996 and continues to act as managing director for the Shirtmaster Division.

Shirtmaster division – operations and market environment

By 2006 the UK market for men's shirts was very different to that of the 1960s and 1970s when Shirtmaster had become one of the best known premium brands. In a mature market most of Shirtmaster's competitors have outsourced the making of their shirts to low cost manufacturers in Europe and the Far East. Shirtmaster is virtually alone in maintaining a UK manufacturing base. Once a year Tony and the buyer for the division go to Asia and the Far East, visiting cloth manufacturers and buying for stock. This stock, stored in the division's warehouse, gives the ability to create a wide range of shirt designs but creates real problems with excessive stock holdings and outdated stock. Shirtmaster prides itself on its ability to respond to the demands of its small retail customers and the long-term relationships built up with these retailers. Typically, these retailers order in small quantities and want quick delivery. Shirtmaster has to introduce new shirt designs throughout the year, contrasting with the spring and autumn ranges launched by its competitors. This creates real pressure on the small design team available.

The retail side of the shirt business has undergone even more fundamental change. Though the market for branded shirts continues to exist, such shirts are increasingly sold through large departmental stores. There is increasing competition between the shirt makers for the limited shelf space available in the departmental stores. Shopping centres and malls are increasingly dominated by nationwide chains of specialist clothing retailers. They sell to the premium segment of the market and are regarded as the trendsetters for the industry. These chains can develop quickly, often using franchising to achieve rapid growth, and are increasingly international in scope. All of them require their suppliers to make their clothes under the chain's own label brand. Some have moved successfully into selling via catalogues and the Internet. Finally, the UK supermarket chains have discovered the profitability of selling nonfood goods. The shirts they sell are aimed at value for money rather than style, sourced wherever they can be made most cheaply and sold under the supermarket's own label. Small independent clothing retailers are declining both in number and market share.

The Shirtmaster division, with its continued over-reliance for its sales on these small independent retailers, is threatened by each of the retail driven changes, having neither the sales volume to compete on price nor the style to compete on fashion.

The Shirtmaster division's international strategy

Tony's answer to these changes is to make the Shirtmaster brand an international one. His initial strategy is to sell to European clothing retailers and once established, move the brand into the fast growing consumer markets in Asia and the Far East. He recognises that the division's current UK focus means that working with a European partner is a necessity. He has given the sales and marketing manager the job of finding major retailers, distributors or manufacturers with whom they can make a strategic alliance and so help get the Shirtmaster range onto the shelves of European clothing retailers.

Corporate Clothing division – operations and market environment

Corporate Clothing has in recent years implemented a major turnaround in its business as the market for corporate clothing began to grow significantly. Corporate Clothing designs, manufactures and distributes a comprehensive range of workwear for its corporate customers, sourcing much of its range from low cost foreign suppliers. It supplies the corporate clothing requirements of large customers in the private and public sectors. Major contracts have been gained with banks, airlines, airports and the police, fire and ambulance services.

The Corporate Clothing division supplies the whole range of workwear required and in the sizes needed for each individual employee. Its designers work closely with the buyers in its large customers and the division's sales benefit from the regular introduction of new styles of uniforms and workwear. Corporate employers are increasingly aware of the external image they need to project and the clothes their employees wear are the key to this image. Corporate Clothing has invested heavily in manufacturing and IT systems to ensure that it meets the needs of its demanding customers. It is particularly proud of its computer-aided design and manufacturing (CAD/CAM) systems, which can be linked to its customers and allows designs to be updated and manufacturing alterations to be introduced with its customers' approval. Much of its success can be attributed to the ability to offer a customer service package in which garments are stored by Corporate Clothing and distributed directly to the individual employee in personalized workwear sets as and when required. The UK market for corporate workwear was worth £500 million in 2005. Evidence suggests that the demand for corporate workwear is likely to continue to grow.

The Corporate Clothing division also has ambitions to enter the markets for corporate clothing in Europe and recognises that might be most easily done through using a suitable strategic partner. There is friendly rivalry between the two divisions but each operates largely independently of the other. Over the past 10 years the fortunes of the two divisions have been completely reversed. Corporate Clothing now is a modest profit maker for the group – Shirtmaster is consistently losing money.

Shirtmaster Group – future strategy

Tony is determined to re-establish Shirtmaster as a leading shirt brand in the UK and successfully launch the brand in Europe. He sees a strategic alliance with a European partner as the key to achieving this ambition. Though he welcomes the success of the Corporate Clothing division and recognises its potential in Europe, he remains emotionally and strategically committed to restoring the fortunes of the Shirtmaster division. Unfortunately, his autocratic style of leadership tends to undermine the position of the senior management team at Shirtmaster. He continues to play an active role in both the operational and strategic sides of the business and is both well known and regarded by workers in the Shirtmaster division's factory.

The initial feedback meeting with the management consultant has confirmed the concern that he is not delegating sufficiently. The consultant commented that Tony's influence could be felt throughout the Shirtmaster division. Managers either try to anticipate the decisions they think he would make or, alternatively, not take the decisions until he has given his approval. The end result is a division not able to meet the challenges of an increasingly competitive retail marketplace, and losing both money and market share.

Table 1 – Financial Information on the Shirtmaster Group (£ million)

	2003	2004	2005	2006 Budget	2007 Forecast	2008 Forecast
Total sales	25.0	23.8	21.4	23.5	24.4	26.7
UK sales	24.5	23.2	21.0	22.7	23.4	24.7
Overseas sales	0.5	0.6	0.4	0.8	1.0	2.0
Cost of sales	17.7	16.8	15.2	16.3	16.8	17.8
Gross profit	7.3	7.0	6.2	7.2	7.6	8.9
Marketing	1.7	1.5	1.2	1.7	1.9	2.2
Distribution	1.6	1.4	1.2	1.4	1.5	1.9
Administration	1.8	1.8	1.7	1.9	1.9	2.1
Net profit	2.2	2.3	2.1	2.2	2.3	2.7
Shirtmaster division						
Total sales	14.8	12.6	10.3	11.7	12.0	13.5
UK sales	14.3	12.0	9.9	10.9	11.0	11.5
Overseas sales	0.5	0.6	0.4	0.8	1.0	2.0
Cost of sales	11.1	9.8	8.2	9.1	9.4	10.1
Gross profit	3.7	2.8	2.1	2.6	2.6	3.4
Marketing	1.5	1.3	1.0	1.5	1.7	2.0
Distribution	1.2	1.0	0.8	0.9	1.0	1.3
Administration	1.3	1.2	1.1	1.2	1.2	1.3
Net profit	(0.3)	(0.7)	(0.8)	(1.0)	(1.3)	(1.2)
Stock	2.0	2.2	3.0	2.7	2.5	2.0
Employees	100	100	98	98	99	100
Corporate Clothing division						
Total sales	10.2	11.2	11.1	11.8	12.4	13.2
Cost of sales	6.6	7.0	7.0	7.2	7.4	7.7
Gross profit	3.6	4.2	4.1	4.6	5.0	5.5
Marketing	0.2	0.2	0.2	0.2	0.2	0.2
Distribution	0.4	0.4	0.4	0.5	0.5	0.6
Administration	0.5	0.6	0.6	0.7	0.7	0.8
Net profit	2.5	3.0	2.9	3.2	3.6	3.9
Stock	0.9	1.0	0.8	0.8	0.9	1.0
Employees	84	84	80	79	77	75

Required

(a)   Assess the strategic position and performance of the Shirtmaster Group and its divisions over the 2003-2005 period. Your analysis should make use of models where appropriate.   **(20 marks)**

(b)   Both divisions have recognised the need for a strategic alliance to help them achieve a successful entry into European markets.

        Critically evaluate the advantages and disadvantages of the divisions using strategic alliances to develop their respective businesses in Europe.   **(15 marks)**

(c)   The Shirtmaster division and Corporate Clothing division, though being part of the same group, operate largely independently of one another.

        Assess the costs and benefits of the two divisions continuing to operate independently of one another.

(15 marks)

(Total = 50 marks)

SECTION B – TWO questions ONLY to be attempted

Question 2

Good Sports Limited is an independent sports goods retailer owned and operated by two partners, Alan and Bob. The sports retailing business in the UK has undergone a major change over the past ten years. First of all the supply side has been transformed by the emergence of a few global manufacturers of the core sports products, such as training shoes and football shirts. This consolidation has made them increasingly unwilling to provide good service to the independent sportswear retailers too small to buy in sufficiently large quantities. These independent retailers can stock popular global brands, but have to order using the Internet and have no opportunity to meet the manufacturer's sales representatives. Secondly, UK's sportswear retailing has undergone significant structural change with the rapid growth of a small number of national retail chains with the buying power to offset the power of the global manufacturers. These retail chains stock a limited range of high volume branded products and charge low prices the independent retailer cannot hope to match.

Good Sports has survived by becoming a specialist niche retailer catering for less popular sports such as cricket, hockey and rugby. They are able to offer the specialist advice and stock the goods that their customers want. Increasingly since 2000 Good Sports has become aware of the growing impact of e-business in general and e-retailing in particular. They employed a specialist website designer and created an online purchasing facility for their customers. The results were less than impressive, with the Internet search engines not picking up the company website. The seasonal nature of Good Sports' business, together with the variations in sizes and colours needed to meet an individual customer's needs, meant that the sales volumes were insufficient to justify the costs of running the site.

Bob, however, is convinced that developing an e-business strategy suited to the needs of the independent sports retailer such as Good Sports will be key to business survival. He has been encouraged by the growing interest of customers in other countries to the service and product range they offer. He is also aware of the need to integrate an e-business strategy with their current marketing, which to date has been limited to the sponsorship of local sports teams and advertisements taken in specialist sports magazines. Above all, he wants to avoid head-on competition with the national retailers and their emphasis on popular branded sportswear sold at retail prices that are below the cost price at which Good Sports can buy the goods.

Required

(a) Provide the partners with a short report on the advantages and disadvantages to Good Sports of developing an e-business strategy and the processes most likely to be affected by such a strategy. **(15 marks)**

(b) Good Sports Limited has successfully followed a niche strategy to date.

Assess the extent to which an appropriate e-business strategy could help support such a niche strategy.

(10 marks)

(Total = 25 marks)

Question 3

Clyde Williams is facing a dilemma. He has successfully built up a small family-owned company, Concrete Solutions Ltd, manufacturing a range of concrete based products used in making roads, pavements and walkways. The production technology is very low tech and uses simple wooden moulds into which the concrete is poured. As a consequence he is able to use low skilled and low cost labour, which would find it difficult to find alternative employment in a region with high unemployment levels. The company has employed many of its workforce since its creation in 1996. The company's products are heavy, bulky and costly to transport. This means its market is limited to a 30-mile area around the small rural town where the manufacturing facility is located. Its customers are a mix of private sector building firms and public sector local councils responsible for maintaining roads and pavements. By its nature much of the demand is seasonal and very price sensitive.

A large international civil engineering company has recently approached Clyde with an opportunity to become a supplier of concrete blocks used in a sophisticated system for preventing coast and riverbank erosion. The process involves interlocking blocks being placed on a durable textile base. Recent trends in global warming and pressure in many countries to build in areas liable to flooding have created a growing international market for the patented erosion prevention system. Clyde has the opportunity to become the sole UK supplier of the blocks and to be one of a small number of suppliers able to export the blocks to Europe. To do it he will need to invest a significant amount in CAM (computer aided manufacturing) technology with a linked investment in the workforce skills needed to operate the new technology. The net result will be a small increase in the size of the labour force but redundancy for a significant number of its existing workers either unwilling or unable to adapt to the demands of the new technology. Successful entry into this new market will reduce his reliance on the seasonal low margin concrete products he currently produces and significantly improve profitability.

One further complication exists. Concrete Solutions is located in a quiet residential area of its home town. Clyde is under constant pressure from the local residents and their council representatives to reduce the amount of noise and dust created in the production process. Any move into making the new blocks will increase the pollution problems the residents face. There is a possibility of moving the whole manufacturing process to a site on a new industrial estate being built by the council in a rival town. However closure of the existing site would lead to a loss of jobs in the current location. Clyde has asked for your help in resolving his dilemma.

Required

(a) Using models where appropriate, advise Clyde on whether he should choose to take advantage of the opportunity offered by the international company. **(15 marks)**

(b) Assess the extent to which social responsibility issues could and should affect his decision to move into the new product area. **(10 marks)**

(Total = 25 marks)

Question 4

Matthew Sanders is the Operations Director of Chestlands Insurance Ltd. Chestlands is a medium-sized company, operating in a specific niche within the financial services sector. It has found a reasonably profitable segment focusing on the lower income end of the personal insurance market. Its customers are generally unskilled workers, single parent families or older people with poor pensions. The common factor is that they all have little discretionary income. Most other financial companies see this segment as being unattractive and unlikely to yield high profits and as a result Chestlands have had few competitors. By concentrating on this one segment it can obtain economies of scale, particularly in collection and administration. Furthermore it does not need to provide a wide portfolio of products as most other financial companies are obliged to.

Most of the business is for cheap insurance policies to cover future contingencies – the cost of essential household repairs, furniture and even funerals. These clients generally have insufficient money to pay for these types of bill out of current income and therefore they need to save for them. Unfortunately some of them do not have bank accounts and so savings have to be collected in a more direct manner. Others, with bank accounts, rarely use them for saving, and it is not unknown for these accounts to be mismanaged. The company uses agents who make weekly calls at the clients' homes to collect their payment. These agents also are responsible for seeking new business by following up enquiries from potential customers who have heard of Chestlands through advertising in the local newspapers or from word-of-mouth recommendations from other customers. Because the company inevitably works on low margins the payment to these agents is low and a significant proportion of it is commission based. Consequently this 'salesforce' is mainly unskilled and turnover is high.

Recently Sanders has received an increasing number of complaints from his customers and new business has been declining. Existing customer have not renewed policies and there have been fewer new customers. The complaints have centered around the sales staff, involving incomplete and unfinished documentation, missed appointments, financial irregularities and an aggressive attitude towards selling new policies. Sanders is aware that his company is only profitable because it has volume sales in a focused market. Any loss of business will damage his company's reputation and profits. He has come to the conclusion that quality is the key to recovery and so he has decided to implement a system of checking the paper work so as to ensure a more acceptable level of delivery. He feels confident that this will solve the problem.

Required

(a)   Discuss whether Sanders' proposed solution will correct the problems currently being experienced by Chestlands.   **(13 marks)**

(b)   It has been suggested to Sanders that a system of Total Quality Management should be introduced into Chestlands.

Describe the actions which must be undertaken within the organisation to ensure that this quality initiative is successfully implemented.   **(12 marks)**

(Total = 25 marks)

Answers

A plan of attack

We discussed the problem of which question to start with earlier, in 'Passing the P3 exam'. Here we will merely reiterate our view that question 1 is nearly always the best place to start and, if you do decide to start with a Section B question, **make sure that you finish your answer in no more than 45 minutes**.

Question 1 is largely straight-forward and of the type we are quite used to. The well-prepared candidate should be able to tackle it with some confidence. The only requirement that might cause some head scratching is requirement (b), which revolves around the idea of strategic alliances. This is not a very prominent topic in the syllabus and you might have some difficulty in finding enough to say about it within the rather specialised context of the scenario. Nevertheless, you should not have too much difficulty in obtaining a pass mark in this question.

Question 2 is, unfortunately, of a common type, in that requirement (b) amplifies an aspect of requirement (a). You would have to take care, therefore, that you did not steal your own thunder by dealing with the topic of requirement (b) while responding to requirement (a), thus leaving yourself with nothing to say when you come to deal with requirement (b). However, e-commerce is an important part of the syllabus and you should be well-prepared for questions dealing with it.

Question 3 is more attractive in that it is concerned with the mainstream topics of **strategic options** and **social responsibility**. The only quibble you might have is that the scenario content appears a little biased towards requirement (b), while the marks are biased towards requirement (a). This is unfortunate, but if you are confident in your basic analysis and options models, as you should be, you should not find it too much of a problem. We like this question.

Question 4 is rather specialised and requires a certain amount of analysis, particularly in requirement (a). Also, it is unusual in the order in which the requirements appear: it is more common for the theory-based part to come first and be followed by the more open-ended, judgement-based element. Despite all of that, however, this could be a good choice if you are confident in your knowledge of quality topics.

SECTION A

Question 1

Part (a)

> **Text reference.** The topics mentioned in this answer are covered in Chapter 7 of your BPP Study Text.
>
> **Top tips.** Our answer includes the figures so that we can highlight some key trends – you may not have provided this information in such a format for your answer, and indeed you would not have been expected to in the exam due to time constraints. An understanding of the key trends, however, is what the question is all about and you must be capable of analysing the separate performances of the two divisions. Your findings are likely to inform your answers to later parts of the question.

	2003	2004	2005	2006 Budget	2007 Forecast	2008 Forecast
Overall Shirtmaster Group:						
Total sales	25.0	23.8	21.4	23.5	24.4	26.7
UK sales	24.5	23.2	21.0	22.7	23.4	24.7
Trend		*-5%*	*-9%*	*8%*	*3%*	*6%*
Overseas sales	0.5	0.6	0.4	0.8	1.0	2.0
Cost of sales	17.7	16.8	15.2	16.3	16.8	17.8
Cost of sales %	*71%*	*71%*	*71%*	*69%*	*69%*	*67%*
Gross profit	7.3	7.0	6.2	7.2	7.6	8.9
Gross profit %	*29%*	*29%*	*29%*	*31%*	*31%*	*33%*
Marketing	1.7	1.5	1.2	1.7	1.9	2.2
Distribution	1.6	1.4	1.2	1.4	1.5	1.9
Administration	1.8	1.8	1.7	1.9	1.9	2.1
Other costs %	*20%*	*20%*	*19%*	*21%*	*22%*	*23%*
Net profit	2.2	2.3	2.1	2.2	2.3	2.7
Net profit %	*9%*	*10%*	*10%*	*9%*	*9%*	*10%*
Shirtmaster division:						
Total sales	14.8	12.6	10.3	11.7	12.0	13.5
UK sales	14.3	12.0	9.9	10.9	11.0	11.5
Trend		*-19%*	*-19%*	*10%*	*1%*	*5%*
Overseas sales	0.5	0.6	0.4	0.8	1.0	2.0
Cost of sales	11.1	9.8	8.2	9.1	9.4	10.1
Cost of sales %	*75%*	*78%*	*80%*	*78%*	*78%*	*75%*
Gross profit	3.7	2.8	2.1	2.6	2.6	3.4
Gross profit %	*25%*	*22%*	*20%*	*22%*	*22%*	*25%*
Marketing	1.5	1.3	1.0	1.5	1.7	2.0
Distribution	1.2	1.0	0.8	0.9	1.0	1.3
Administration	1.3	1.2	1.1	1.2	1.2	1.3
Other costs %	*27%*	*28%*	*28%*	*31%*	*33%*	*34%*
Net profit	(0.3)	(0.7)	(0.8)	(1.0)	(1.3)	(1.2)
Net profit %						
Stock	2.0	2.2	3.0	2.7	2.5	2.0
Employees	100	100	98	98	99	100

BPP
LEARNING MEDIA

	2003	2004	2005	2006 Budget	2007 Forecast	2008 Forecast
Corporate Clothing division:						
Total sales	10.2	11.2	11.1	11.8	12.4	13.2
Trend		*10%*	*-1%*	*6%*	*5%*	*6%*
Cost of sales	6.6	7.0	7.0	7.2	7.4	7.7
Cost of sales %	*65%*	*63%*	*63%*	*61%*	*60%*	*58%*
Gross profit	3.6	4.2	4.1	4.6	5.0	5.5
Gross profit %	*35%*	*38%*	*37%*	*39%*	*40%*	*42%*
Marketing	0.2	0.2	0.2	0.2	0.2	0.2
Distribution	0.4	0.4	0.4	0.5	0.5	0.6
Administration	0.5	0.6	0.6	0.7	0.7	0.8
Other costs %	*11%*	*11%*	*11%*	*12%*	*11%*	*12%*
Net profit	2.5	3.0	2.9	3.2	3.6	3.9
Net profit %	*25%*	*27%*	*26%*	*27%*	*29%*	*30%*
Stock	0.9	1.0	0.8	0.8	0.9	1.0
Employees	84	84	80	79	77	75

As demonstrated by these figures and ratios, the performance of the Shirtmaster Group is a composite of two very different performances by the totally separate divisions. These divisions are operating in very different markets, with very different strategies and very different results. For the group as a whole, sales have declined to 2005 and net margins are struggling to get into double figures.

The Shirtmaster division is **dragging down the performance of the entire group**. The overall group net profit margin of 10% in 2005 masks the fact that the Shirtmasters division suffered a net loss, while Corporate Clothing recorded a net profit margin of 26%.

Using the information from the scenario to consider the Shirtmasters value chain, for example, Tony Masters' strategy of being an integrated shirt manufacturer carrying out all the activities needed to design, manufacture and distribute its shirts is in doubt, because most of its competitors have recognised the commercial sense in **outsourcing production to cheaper and more flexible manufacturers overseas**. There is no competitive advantage in retaining production in the higher cost UK, particularly when the company has no other point of differentiation (such as recognised high style or fashion) for its products.

The premium end of the shirt market, its historical focus, has changed since the days of Shirtmasters' earlier success and the division now needs to change to respond to a new **market structure** with **new participants in the value system**. As can be seen from the above analysis, Shirtmasters' reliance on small retailers has seen the costs of its support activities (marketing, distribution and administration) take up a huge part of its turnover. Trips to buy cloth from foreign suppliers have resulted in large stocks of expensive cloth, around a month's worth of sales being held at any one time. Meeting the demands of its many small customers is therefore having a real impact on marketing, manufacturing and distribution costs.

Making reference to Porter's five competitive forces, the key ones at work are the **rivalry between the shirt makers**, and the increased **buying power of customers** in the industry – the specialist retail outlets and supermarkets. To accommodate these forces, Shirtmasters may have to consider the possibility of making own brand shirts for the supermarkets so that it can expand its market.

The effect of these problems is revealed in selected aspects of performance, when compared to the Corporate Clothing division:

	Shirtmaster division	Corporate Clothing division
Sales growth to 2005	Slowing	Increasing
Gross margin	Lower	Higher and sustained
Sales per employee	Modest	Improving
Marketing etc expenses	Out of control	Acceptable levels
Stock levels	Too high	More modest
Net margins	Negative	Positive
Market share	Minimal, stagnant	Growing
Product innovation	Nil	Customer focus
Process innovation	Nil	Investment in technology
Customer base	Declining	Growing

The measures above reflect a **balanced scorecard approach** to performance analysis. On all measures, Corporate Clothing is a stronger performer and this must be due to its **focus on the customer**, through its willingness to embrace the realities of its market, invest in appropriate technology and take close note of customer needs. The contrast with Tony's 'pet' division, Shirtmasters, could not be more stark, and should serve to impress upon the senior management of the group the need to give more strategic responsibility to managers possessing the necessary detachment to manage Shirtmasters more effectively.

Marking scheme

	Marks
Shirtmaster Group position and performance Eg Static sales; low margins; little synergy	up to 3 marks
Shirtmaster division Value chain comments Stock levels, procurement Customers segment served declining High marketing etc costs	up to 10 marks
Corporate Clothing division Better customer focus Growing market Positive margins	up to 10 marks
Use of models	up to 3 marks
	Maximum 20 marks

Part (b)

Text reference. The topics mentioned in this answer are covered in Chapter 7 of your BPP Study Text.

Top tips. Begin your answer by defining a strategic alliance, and outlining its advantages and disadvantages. We have concentrated upon the suitability of a joint venture for this answer. Apply the advantages and disadvantages to the circumstances of Shirtmakers and Corporate Clothing and use your answers to part (a) to examine the suitability of each company. You should answer large scenario questions in order, as your answers to one part may inform the content of a later part, as is the case here.

Johnson and Scholes define a strategic alliance as 'where two or more organisations share resources and activities to pursue a strategy'. Alliances can be particularly attractive to smaller firms such as Shirtmakers, or where expensive new technologies or markets are being developed and the costs can be shared. One particular form of strategic alliance is the joint venture, whereby two or more firms join forces for manufacturing, financial and marketing purposes and each has a share in both the equity and the management of the business.

Particular advantages to Shirtmakers and Corporate Clothing of the pursuit of such an alliance are the following.

(a) **Share costs**. As the capital outlay is shared, joint ventures can be especially attractive. The joint operation may lead to economies of scale that mean that costs can be reduced.

(b) **Cut risk.** A joint venture can reduce the risk of government intervention if a local firm is involved.

(c) Alliances provide **close control** over marketing and other operations, as both companies have a strong interest in ensuring that processes are effective.

(d) Overseas joint ventures provide **local knowledge**. Alliances are commonly entered into where, as in this scenario, a company is seeking to expand overseas.

(e) **Synergies.** One firm's production expertise, for example, can be supplemented by the other's marketing and distribution facility. In this way, particular competences can be exploited for the good of the whole alliance.

(f) **Learning.** Alliances can also be a learning exercise in which each partner tries to learn as much as possible from the other, particularly about local markets.

(g) **Technology.** New technology offers many uncertainties and many opportunities. Such alliances provide funds for expensive research projects, spreading risk.

(h) **The alliance itself can generate innovations** and be a learning exercise for all participants.

(i) The alliance can involve **testing the firm's core competence** in different conditions, which can suggest ways to improve it.

When choosing the type of alliance to pursue, the following factors need to be considered by Shirtmakers and Corporate Clothing.

What benefits are going to be offered by collaboration?

• Which partners should be chosen?
• Is the environment favourable to a partnership?
• What activities and processes will have to be set up?
• Are there any other alliances within the industry?

Johnson and Scholes argue that for an alliance to be successful there needs to be a **clear strategic purpose** and **senior management support**; **compatibility** between the partners; time spent defining **clear goals**, governance and other organisational arrangements; and **trust** between the partners that together they can get the job done.

The major disadvantage of joint ventures is that there can be **major conflicts of interest**. Disagreements may arise over profit shares, amounts invested, the management and control of the alliance, and overall strategy. Shirtmakers and Corporate Clothing would need to make sure that such issues are clearly set out and agreed at the beginning to avoid damaging clashes later.

The Shirtmaster and Corporate Clothing divisions have very different experience and business conditions to offer any potential partner. Shirtmaster may struggle to attract a partner with its current product and strategy, particularly its insistence on **retaining manufacture in the UK** when most competitors now source from cheaper markets in Europe and the Far East. Its dwindling network of low volume small retail customers, and the processes by which it manages its stock and designs would appear to many potential partners and European retailers to be anachronistic. By contrast, the Corporate Clothing division seems to be much more favourable as a potential partner. The market for corporate workwear is growing, and the company employs sophisticated systems coupled with a superior customer service record. This could be repeated in Europe if the right partner could be found.

	Marks
Definition of strategic alliance	1 mark
Advantages of successful strategic alliances, eg: Economies of scale Specialisation and synergies Learning from partners and developing competences	up to 6 marks
Disadvantages of strategic alliances, eg: Conflicts of interest and disagreement	up to 3 marks
Application to Shirtmasters/Corporate Clothing	up to 5 marks
	Maximum 15 marks

Part (c)

Top tips. This is a complex question. The existence of the two divisions largely reflects the origins of the two family businesses, and the divisions have grown and developed separately. Think about the advantages and disadvantages of divisionalisation and how these are currently manifested in the Shirtmasters group. Does divisionalisation make sense for the management of these businesses? Their products may be along the same lines, but their trading conditions and circumstances are very different.

Divisionalisation has some advantages, notably **focusing the attention of subordinate management** on business performance and results. It therefore can provide a good training ground for junior managers in the individual divisions. It also enables proper concentration on particular product-market areas – in this case, shirts and workwear.

Problems can arise, as in this scenario, with the **power of the head office**, and **control of resources**. It appears that Tony Masters has more emotional commitment, and presumably more management time, to devote to Shirtmaster at the expense of Corporate Clothing.

Mintzberg believes there are inherent problems in divisionalisation, many of which are actually those of conglomerate diversification. In the Shirtmaster group, it could be that each business might be better run independently. The different businesses might offer different returns for different risks which shareholders might prefer to **judge independently**.

There does not appear to be any common effort between the divisions, with no sharing of resources apparent from the scenario details. While both are in the clothing market, their respective value systems run very differently. Information systems are also likely to operate independently. This may be leading to **duplication of effort** and **waste of resources**.

If divisionalisation is to operate effectively, divisional management should be free to use their authority to do what they think is right for their part of the organisation. This is not happening in the Shirtmaster division, and the time has come for Tony Masters to allow his management team to **develop strategy** to drive the company forward, perhaps with the necessity to take some tough decisions that he appears incapable of making. Performance in both divisions needs to be clearly identified and controlled, and resources channelled to those areas showing potential.

Each division must have a potential for growth in its own area of operations. It seems that only Corporate Clothing can satisfy this test in current trading conditions.

Divisions should exist side by side with each other. If they deal with each other, it should be as an arm's length transaction. There should be no insistence on preferential treatment to be given to one particular unit. While there is no suggestion in the scenario that this is happening, Tony Masters' favouring of the Shirtmaster division in more subtle ways is having an effect upon performance.

Using the BCG matrix it is possible to classify the Shirtmaster division as a 'dog' with low market share, in a market with little growth. It needs refreshed management to take it forward and find new markets. The Corporate Clothing division, by contrast, has a small share of a growing market, and this potential also needs to close management.

Marking scheme

	Marks
Advantages of divisions operating independently: eg performance monitoring, manager training	up to 5 marks
Disadvantages of divisions operating independently: eg no sharing of resources/skills Duplicated costs	up to 5 marks
Effective divisionalisation eg management initiative encouraged not stifled	up to 5 marks
	Maximum 15 marks

SECTION B

Question 2

Text reference. The topics mentioned in this answer are covered in Chapters 6 and 10 of your BPP Study Text.

Part (a)

Top tips. This question puts e-commerce firmly into a strategic context. IT and the Internet pervade the modern business organisation and so it should be possible for you to offer sensible comments upon this basis. The main advantages and disadvantages of an e-business strategy that you put into your answer must be applicable to Good Sports' own business situation. It is not a foregone conclusion that involvement in e-commerce will be unequivocally beneficial. There a several strategic issues to consider – such as the familiar framework of 'suitability, acceptability and feasibility'. Porter's generic strategies are also brought into this question, and you should have little difficulty discussion 'niche' for the 8 available marks.

REPORT

To: Alan and Bob, Good Sports Limited
From: Strategic consultant
Date: December 20XX
Subject: E – Business strategy

Introduction

Very few businesses can afford to ignore the **potential of the Internet** for driving forward strategy and activity. The markets that Good Sports operates in are being affected by the development of e-business. Small enterprises such as this one can gain access to customers on a global scale, which only relatively recently would have been viewed as impossible. In many ways the advantages and disadvantages of e-business can be viewed from the perspective of the customer.

Advantages of an e-business strategy

Through the integration and acceleration of standard business processes via highly sophisticated IT systems (order placing, stock control, dispatch and so on), attention to customer needs, and communication with them, can be much quicker.

Although the Internet has a global reach, its benefits are not confined to large organisations. Good Sports can move into a global marketplace.

Websites can provide new channels of communication, linked with customer databases which can be analysed to provide much greater insights into consumer buying behaviour.

Increased quantities of data, and more sophisticated methods of analysing it, mean that greater attention can be paid to customising product offerings to more precisely defined **target customers**.

Disadvantages of an e-business strategy

E-commerce presents completely new problems of management and organisation, not least because it needs the **involvement of specialists**. There may be a lack of in-house expertise.

A detailed cost/benefit analysis should be undertaken. It may even be decided that costs exceed the benefits of setting up the e-business operation.

New technology installed by Good Sports will need to **link up with existing business systems**, so the resources needed (money, time and effort) should not be underestimated.

Processes

For Good Sports, e-business will probably be a **supplement** to its traditional retail operations, with the website forming a supplementary channel for communication and sales. Even so, its development is likely to have wide implications and involve and affect several functions, and so should be managed at the highest level. It is also necessary that it conform to the standard criteria for any strategic choice: suitability, acceptability and feasibility. Precise objectives for this new strategy need to be set. The company will need to go back to basics and ask itself some fundamental questions such as:

- What do customers want to buy from us?
- What business are we in?
- What kind of suppliers might we need?
- What categories of customer do we want to attract and retain?

Assuming that these questions can be answered satisfactorily, new technology can be introduced to connect electronically with employees, customers and suppliers to help drive the strategy forward.

Part (b)

With a **niche strategy**, a firm concentrates its attention on one or more particular secure segments (or niches) of the market, and does not try to serve the entire market. Good Sports has pursued such a strategy, seeking to serve a local market for less popular sports, in a way that insulates it from competition against the major high volume retailers who are concentrating on the more popular sports such as football.

In this way, Good Sports has been able to ensure that it **does not spread itself too thinly** in the market for sporting goods. There is nothing in the scenario to suggest they have reached saturation point in their chosen niche market. The question then needs to be asked whether it makes strategic sense for Good Sports to invest in online transaction capability to continue to serve (and develop) its market.

It is recognised that one of the key features of e-business is that it brings far greater **price transparency**, with customers being able to shop around for the cheapest deal using the vast information resources available on the Internet (either from other companies, or other customers). The customer has become far more powerful. There is a theory that customers expect goods and services to be discounted when sold online (and indeed, many are) since they are aware that administrative costs are likely to be lower than in more traditional forms of distribution. Good Sports will need to find out how likely this is to happen with their customers, and whether there are competitors who are offering lower prices on the same range of goods. This should be easy to find out using market research and a search of competitor sites.

Such customer involvement however could provide a mechanism for **increasing customer loyalty**, for example by targeting particular groups and finding out more about their sports activity and spending habits. This can be done via online questionnaires or surveys, and could lead to the identification of new niche markets, currently not served by any competitors, that can be developed (such as new types of sports equipment to be included in the product range; new services). As indicated in the answer to part (a), Good Sports needs to go back to basics and consider all the costs and benefits that could be associated with offering such enhanced online capability to its chosen niche market.

Marking scheme

		Marks
(a)	*Advantages of Good Sports developing an e-business strategy:* Improved processes for better customer service Global marketplace Greater communication; more information	up to 6 marks
	Disadvantages of developing an e-business strategy: Lack of in-house skills and competences Cost/benefit analysis Expensive investment	up to 6 marks
	Processes	up to 3 marks
		Maximum 15 marks
(b)	*E-strategy supporting Good Sports' niche strategy*	up to 3 1/2 per point
	Customers' own awareness New sports Better understanding of customers	**Maximum 10 marks**
		Total 25 marks

Question 3

Text reference. The topics mentioned in this answer are covered in Part A of your BPP Study Text.

Top tips. Easy marks are on offer in part (a) for application of recognised models. We have used PEST analysis in our answer, as there are several obvious 'environmental' elements pointed out in the scenario. We also consider the use of SWOT and 'suitability, feasibility and acceptability'. In part (b), use your understanding of the term 'corporate social responsibility' to frame your answer, particularly in terms of the importance of stakeholders.

Part (a)

This scenario highlights the many factors that may need to be considered when making strategic decisions. The PEST framework can be used to analyse the environment. Use of PEST will indicate to Clyde the various risks and influences upon his decision, and help him decide upon its suitability or otherwise for his business.

An initial PEST analysis would indicate the following.

Political/legal

The local council is likely to be **split** between supporting Concrete Solutions for its employment opportunities and other contributions that it makes to the local economy (such as payment of rates and supply of product) and responding to the pressure from residents who object to the noise and pollution from it activities. The council in the rival town is likely to welcome any relocation of the business to its own site, but is likely to have the same pollution concerns. Legal limits on poisonous emissions must be considered.

Economic

The decision to take up the opportunity with the new company would involve **redundancies** in the local community, which already has high unemployment levels. For Concrete Solutions, however, an entire **new market** would be opened up and would reduce the current reliance on a relatively slow and seasonal local economy.

Social

Redundancies would have an impact on the social framework of the local area.

Technology

The current processes are very low-tech, but this new opportunity would require **significant investment** in new CAM technology, with a trained workforce to operate it. This would be a fundamental change to the usual business environment that Concrete Solutions operates in. The **resource implications** of the new opportunity are therefore very significant.

Such a move can be viewed as a related diversification. A detailed SWOT is likely to be necessary, along the lines of the following.

Strengths

Familiarity and experience with basic product

Weaknesses

- Experience to manage the new (larger) operation, with international expertise and new technology required
- Low skill; low tech operation – low barriers to entry
- Small company; limited (seasonal) market
- Small margin
- Resource constraints

Opportunities

- Increased profitability with new venture
- Expanded markets and new product
- Exposure to new technology and new partners

Threats

- Development of competitor products
- Legislation against pollution

This quick initial analysis would seem to indicate that the current operations of Concrete Solutions are a source of several weaknesses that the company could start to overcome by its involvement with the new venture.

As a major strategic option there is also a need to address issues of its suitability, acceptability and feasibility.

Suitability

The opportunity seems to solve some of the problems associated with the current **product range**. The new blocks can be sold all year round and into a much wider geographical market area. This will lead to increased profitability and possible exposure to new opportunities.

Acceptability of the new venture to both Concrete Solutions and the various stakeholders involved (employees, local residents, local councilors, new venture partner) is more complicated to assess. Clyde may find stakeholder mapping and scenario building useful in coming to a decision. As the owner of the business he needs to assess the **risk** involved against the likely **returns**.

Feasibility

New resources and skills will be needed, but with the support of the partner this may not be problematic.

Part (b)

Johnson and Scholes see **corporate social responsibility** as 'concerned with the ways in which an organisation exceeds the minimum obligation to stakeholders specified through regulation and corporate governance'.

Businesses both large and small are subject to **increasing expectations** that they will exercise social responsibility. This is an ill-defined concept, but appears to focus on the fulfilment of obligations to society in general, such as (in Clyde's case) the creation or preservation of employment and the consideration of environmental improvement or maintenance. A great deal of the pressure is created by the activity of **pressure groups** and other interested stakeholders, and is aimed at businesses because they are perceived to possess the resources to solve such problems.

There is no doubt that many businesses have behaved irresponsibly in the past, and it is very likely that some continue to do so. Small firms such as Concrete Solutions are therefore not exempt from the requirement to consider issues of social responsibility when making strategic decisions. The **impact** of such decisions upon all interested parties becomes crucial up front, in order to avoid damaging a company's reputation later.

A consideration of Concrete Solutions' **stakeholders** is therefore needed. Clyde is entitled to distinguish between 'contractual' and specified stakeholders (customers, suppliers, employees) who have a legal relationship with Concrete Solutions, and 'community' stakeholders – such as local residents and councillors – who do not have the same legal status. For the latter, the trade-off between the creation of skilled jobs, the necessity for redundancies and the possibility of increased pollution in the local area will need to be made, probably after negotiations between all the parties concerned.

The decisions are not easy ones to make. A decision by Clyde to bow to pressure and not increase his investment in new operations, for example, may protect local jobs and conserve resources in the short term, but will affect the **long term ability** of Concrete Solutions to compete effectively and may hand opportunities to his competitors.

Marking scheme

		Marks
(a)	Assessing the opportunity:	
	Environmental appraisal	up to 5 marks
	SWOT analysis	up to 2 marks
	Criteria for assessing option – suitability, acceptability and feasibility	up to 3 marks each
		Maximum 15 marks
(b)	Social responsibility dimensions	up to 3 marks each
	Definition	
	Corporate social responsibility – compatibility with business strategy	
	Stakeholders	
	Short v long term	
		Maximum 10 marks
		Total 25 marks

Question 4

Text reference. The topics mentioned in this answer are dealt with in Chapter 12 of your BPP Study Text.

Top tips. This is quite a common type of question: the scenario describes a problem and a possible solution: then you are asked to comment. You need to form an opinion and be able to back it up with sensible remarks based on both theory and business reality. It will normally be fairly clear to the well-prepared student what the best solution is.

Part (a)

Easy marks. Up to half of the marks available for this part of the question were awarded for a discussion of the theoretical background to quality issues. Of the remainder, most were awarded for dealing with the HRM implications of the new policy.

A **system of checking** is an obvious measure to deal with errors, especially those of procedure, and is routinely used in tasks such as aircraft operations **where performance must be highly standardised**. A system of checking the paperwork will address some of the unsatisfactory occurrences that Chestlands Insurance has suffered. Incomplete documentation will be detected at an early stage; financial irregularities and mis-selling may also be affected for the better.

Nevertheless, simple checking is probably **not the best way** to address the current quality problems. The process of checking would not add value to correctly completed documentation but it *would* increase costs and the complexity of operations. **Checking is something to be avoided if possible**.

A more modern approach to quality would be to take steps to **eliminate the creation of errors**. This is the **quality assurance** approach, rather than the quality control approach, which depends on inspection or quality checking. Quality assurance requires that members of staff **accept responsibility for the quality of all aspects of their work**. Such an approach would address all of the problems now apparent in Chestlands Insurance's operations.

However, taking the quality control approach would require **significant changes** to the company's management of its human resources, since success would be dependent upon the motivation and skill of the individual employee.

(a) It would be necessary to review the **recruitment policy** so that only people with suitable personal qualities started work.

(b) Identifiable **poor performers** would have to go, preferably by natural wastage, but by dismissal if necessary.

(c) **Effective training** would be required, both for new recruits and for existing staff who were not working satisfactorily.

(d) The **remuneration policy** should be reviewed. There should be incentives that promote the behaviour the company needs. At the moment, the large element of commission will tend to encourage dubious selling practices and poor attention to documentation. An adjusted system, with a higher level of basic pay, would encourage sales people to take a longer-term view of their customers. A performance related bonus could include an element of penalty for inadequate documentation.

It will be difficult to strike the right balance between the need for more effective staff and the need to hold down costs, but a quality assurance approach is the best way to approach the problem.

Part (b)

Easy marks. This part of the question gives an example of a requirement that can be satisfied in several ways. One or two marks would be available for a whole range of relevant points. In addition to the matters we discuss, you might also mention the need for a training programme and the long-term commitment that would be required.

Total Quality Management (TQM) is an extension of the quality assurance approach to every activity in the organisation, with the aim of ensuring complete customer satisfaction both externally and *internally*. Quality lies in the eye of the consumer and this applies as much to those products that are consumed *within* the organisation as to those that are marketed externally. Total Quality Management thus views the organisation as an integrated whole and quality as an organisation-wide concern.

TQM is more of a philosophy of business than a collection of techniques. A high degree of commitment is necessary if it is to be implemented. Senior management, in particular, must support its introduction and promote the necessary changes. This can be a particularly difficult thing to achieve, since it demands changes of practice, not just lip service. A TQM initiative can also be expensive, especially if there is much training to undertake. It is necessary to take a long view and maintain the momentum of the programme over the longer term.

Staff at lower levels must be prepared to accept responsibility for their performance and to undergo appropriate training. A problem Mr Sanders will have to solve is the likelihood that staff will expect greater remuneration in return for improved performance and for accepting greater responsibility. In the longer term, improved productivity and quality should pay for these extra costs.

The development of a TQM programme inevitably requires the participation of the workforce. They have the greatest knowledge of the details of the work and they will see the effects of changes first. Quality circles are a possible technique for promoting their continued input. Participation in development is also likely to encourage internalisation of the principles of the new approach.

It will not be enough to rely on the positive motivational effects of participation to ensure compliance with the aims of the new approach. Work procedure should be reviewed with a view to simplification and standardisation, both of which will improve performance. Also, the philosophy must be supported by improvements in control and discipline to ensure that poor performance is checked.

ACCA
Paper P3
Business Analysis

Mock Examination 2

Question Paper	
Time allowed	
Reading and planning	15 minutes
Writing	3 hours
This paper is divided into two sections	
Section A	ONE compulsory question to be attempted
Section B	TWO questions ONLY to be attempted

During reading and planning time only the question paper may be annotated

DO NOT OPEN THIS PAPER UNTIL YOU ARE READY TO START UNDER EXAMINATION CONDITIONS

SECTION A – The one question in this section is compulsory and MUST be attempted

Question 1

The Ace Bicycle Company (ABC) is a private UK company, based within the United Kingdom and managed by Colin Doncroft, the grandson of its founder. The shares are totally owned by the family, with Colin and his wife controlling just under half of the shares, the rest being held by other members of the family. The company was started in 1935, producing bicycles for the general market. These bicycles were targeted mainly at people who could not afford to buy motor vehicles – then a relative luxury – but who needed transportation to get them to work or for local travel. Initially the company was a regional producer focusing on markets in Central England but over the next 60 years ABC transformed itself into a national company. ABC took advantage of changes in fashion and periodically introduced new models focusing on different market segments. Its first diversification was into making racing bicycles, which still account for 20% of its volume output. Most of these bicycles are very expensive to produce. They are made of specialist light-weight metals and are often custom-built for specific riders, most of the sales being made on a direct basis. Members of amateur cycling clubs contact the company directly with their orders and this minimises distribution costs, so making these machines more affordable to the customers. ABC's reputation has been enhanced by this highly profitable product. The company has seen no reason to change its branding policy and these products are still sold under the 'ABC' brand name.

During the 1980s the company responded to the demand for more sporty leisure machines. Mountain bikes had become the fashion and ABC designed and produced some models which appealed to the cheaper end of the market. These products, although robust and stylish, were relatively cheap and were aimed at families with teenage children and who could not afford to spend large sums of money on the more sophisticated models. The company is currently selling nearly 30% of its output to this market segment. Most of the sales are through specialist bicycle shops, although about 25% of these mountain bikes sales are made through a national retail chain of bicycle and motor vehicle accessories stores. Apart from those sold via this retail network, under the retail brand name, the mountain bikes were also sold under the ABC brand. With the advent of fitness clubs the company saw and opening for the provision of cycling machines for the health club and gymnasium market. These machines were sold at a premium price but they still accounted for less than 5% of total volume sales of the company. The main product group for the company was still its basic bicycle – it is the entry model for most families who are buying bicycles for teenagers and for those people who still use bicycles as a means of transportation as distinct from seeing them as entertainment or fun machines. The product is standardised, with few differentiating features, and as such can be produced relatively cheaply. About 75% of this segment is sold through the same national retail chain mentioned above with reference to mountain bike sales. These bicycles in fact are built for the retail chain and marketed under their brand name. This appears to be advantageous to ABC because it guarantees them a given level of business without their being responsible for either distribution or promotion. This segment, however, is now seeing increasing competition from cheaper overseas imports.

The company had historically made reasonable profits and most of these were re-invested in the company's production facilities, increasing capacity substantially. However, throughout the late 1990s, ABC has seen its market being eroded. Sales have fallen gradually, mainly because the total United Kingdom market for bicycles has been in decline, but also because of increased competition from foreign suppliers. The high value of sterling has encouraged imports. Surprisingly, during this period ABC actually increased its share of domestic output. This is due to the fact that it has been prepared to accept lower margins so as to maintain sales and, in addition, a few UK producers had decided to exit the market and move into other, more attractive product lines.

By early in the year 2000 the company has seen its profits continue to fall. It now has a debt to the bank of £4 million, having been unable to pay for all recent, new capital expenditure out of retained earnings. (Table I gives some financial information about the recent performance of ABC.)

There are now very few UK manufacturers of bicycles who concentrate solely on producing bicycles. Most have a diversified portfolio and can count on other product groups to support the bicycle sector when demand is poor. However, ABC has continued to focus entirely on this specialised product range. It is surviving basically because it has built up a strong reputation for reliable products and because the Doncroft family has, until recently, been content with a level of profits which would be unacceptable to a public company that had external shareholders to consider. However, it is now becoming apparent that unless some radical action is taken the company cannot hope to survive. The bank will now only make loans if ABC can find a suitable strategy to provide it with a higher and more acceptable level of profit. If the company is to retain its independence (and it is questionable whether any company will really want to acquire it in its current position) it has to consider radical change. Its only experience is within the bicycle industry and therefore it appears to be logical that it should stay in this field in some form or other.

Colin Doncroft has examined ways to improve the profitability of the company. He is of the opinion that if ABC becomes more successful it could become a desirable acquisition for other companies. However, currently the company will not attract bidders unless it is at a low price. Doncroft has looked at the profile of his products and wonders whether any rationalisation could help to improve performance. He has also decided to look at the potential for overseas marketing. Having examined statistics on current world production and sales statistics he has identified that the real growth areas for bicycles are in the Far East. China alone supports a bigger market for bicycles than the whole of Europe and North America. India and Pakistan have also developed a significant demand for bicycles. Doncroft decided to visit some of these markets and he has returned full of enthusiasm for committing ABC to operate in these Far Eastern markets or in India and Pakistan. Whilst Doncroft considers that exporting from the UK might be a viable option, he has become increasingly attracted to manufacturing in the Far East, particularly in China. He believes that transportation costs could prove to be a disadvantage to exporting for ABC. He estimates that costs for shipping and insurance could add about 15% to the final selling price. Furthermore, he is concerned about the discrepancy between labour costs in the United Kingdom and in China. Wage rates, including social costs in China appear to be about 30% of those in the UK and these costs account for approximately 25% of the total production costs.

Colin Doncroft has summoned a meeting of all the shareholders to persuade them to agree to plan to manufacture, or at least assemble bicycles in the Far East. The other shareholders are not quite so enthusiastic. They feel that this strategy is too risky. The company has never been involved in overseas business and now they are being asked to sanction a strategy which by-passes the exporting stage and commits them to significant expenditure overseas. Colin is convinced that the bank will loan them the necessary capital, given the attractiveness of these overseas markets. The other shareholders are more in favour of a gradual process. They want to improve the position within the United Kingdom market first rather than leap into the unknown. They also believe that diversification into other non-bicycle products might be less risky than venturing overseas. They know the UK market but overseas is an unknown area. Colin has decided that it is time he sought some professional advice for the company. A management consultant, Simon Gaskell, has been retained. He is a qualified accountant who also has an MBA from a prestigious business school.

Table I: Information concerning ABC's current sales and financial performance

Financial Year April/March	1998/1999	1999/2000	2000/2001 (forecast)
Mountain Bikes			
volume	18,000	17,500	16,500
direct costs £000	2,070	2,187.5	2,145
revenue £000	2,610	2,625	2,475
Standard Bicycles			
volume	27,000	26,200	25,000
direct costs £000	2,160	2,096	2,075
revenue £000	2,430	2,227	2,125
Racing Bicycles			
volume	11,000	1,500	11,750
direct costs £000	4,950	5,750	6,227.5
revenue £000	6,875	7,475	7,931.25
Exercise Bicycles			
volume	2,800	2,800	2,700
direct costs £000	756	840	837
revenue £000	910	980	945
Indirect costs £000: inc.	1,225	1,730	1,890
Distribution	175	200	250
Promotion	300	280	240
Administration and other	750	850	1,000
Interest on loan	-	400	400
Profit before tax £000	1,664	703.5	301.75

Required

Acting in the role of Simon Gaskell:

(a)   Write a report, evaluating the current strategies being pursued by the Ace Bicycle Company (ABC) for its different market segments, using appropriate theoretical models to support your analysis.   **(25 marks)**

(b)   Identify and explain the key factors which should be taken into consideration before ABC decide on developing manufacturing/assembly facilities in China.   **(13 marks)**

(c)   Using the example of the ACE Bicycle Company to support your views, identify the benefits of:

    (i)   organic growth   **(4 marks)**

    (ii)   acquisitions   **(4 marks)**

    (iii)   joint developments   **(4 marks)**

         as a preferred means of developing the business in China.

(Total = 50 marks)

SECTION B – TWO questions ONLY to be attempted

Question 2

All organisations have objectives in some form or another. The methods of setting these objectives vary depending on the nature of the organisation. After they have been set and an appropriate period of time has elapsed, organisations should assess to what extent their objectives have been achieved.

Two organisations with very different characteristics set strategic objectives and evaluate their achievement. The two organisations are

- A publicly-funded local administrative authority which provides housing, education, social and road maintenance services for an area within a country, and

- A multi-national conglomerate company (MNC).

Required

(a) Explain the differences between how the local administrative authority and the MNC should set their strategic objectives.   **(10 marks)**

(b) Discuss how each organisation should assess how well it has performed in respect of the attainment of its strategic objectives.   **(15 marks)**

(Total = 25 marks)

Question 3

Elite Fabrics (EF) is a medium-sized manufacturer of clothing fabrics. Historically, EF has built up a strong reputation as a quality fabric manufacturer with appealing designs and has concentrated mainly on the women's market, producing fabrics to be made up into dresses and suits. The designs of the fabric are mainly of a traditional nature but the fabrics, almost all woven from synthetic yarns, include all the novel features which the large yarn producers are developing.

Three years ago EF decided that more profit and improved control could be obtained by diversifying through forward integration into designing and manufacturing the end products (ie clothes) in-house rather than by selling its fabrics directly to clothing manufacturing companies.

EF's intention had been to complement its fabric design skills with the skills of both dress design and production. This had been achieved by buying a small but well-known, dress design and manufacturing company specialising in traditional products, targeted mainly at the middle-aged and middle-income markets. This acquisition appears to have been successful, with combined sales turnover during the first two years increasing to £100 million (+ 34%) with a pre-tax profit of £14 million (+ 42%). This increased turnover and profit could be attributed to two main factors: firstly the added value generated by designing and manufacturing end-products and secondly, the increased demand for fabrics as EF was more able to influence their end-users more directly.

In the last financial year, however, EF had experienced a slow down in its level of growth and profitability. EF's penetration of its chosen retail segment - the independent stores specialising in sales to the middle-class market - may well have reached saturation point. The business had also attempted to continue expansion by targeting the large multiple stores which currently dominate the retail fashion sector. Unfortunately the buying power of such stores has forced EF to accept significantly lower, and potentially unacceptable, profit margins. The management team at EF believes that the solution is to integrate even further forward by moving into retailing itself. EF is now considering the purchase of a chain of small, but geographically dispersed, retail fashion stores. At the selling price of £35 million, EF would have to borrow substantially to finance the acquisition.

Required

(a)   Consider how the EF strategy of integrating forward into dress manufacturing has affected its ability to compete. Use an accepted model as a framework for analysis. **(12 marks)**

(b)   EF's potential expansion into retailing presents both advantages and disadvantages to the company. Evaluate the consequences of such a move for the business and assess the change in competences which would be required by the newly expanded business. **(13 marks)**

(Total = 25 marks)

Question 4

Natalia Norman is a designer and manufacturer of knitwear clothing. She has based her designs on ethnic patterns, inspired by clothing she has seen in Central Asia. She has sourced her products both from these Asian regions – Uzbekistan and Kazakhstan – as well as from small factories in parts of the United Kingdom. Her products, though stylish, are relatively cheap, but her marketing strategy is totally passive. She has a web-site and most of her sales are reactive, responding to orders over the internet. The resultant sales and, in particular, profits have been disappointing and so she has hired a marketing consultant to give her some advice. The following are extracts from the consultant's report.

'Your product, although distinctive, is insufficiently unique. The designs have no patents nor copyright and because the production technology is so simple and inexpensive there are few barriers to entry. Competition is all too prevalent. Your promotion is too general. It focuses on no specific market. By relying on the internet your advertising is rather indiscriminate and you have failed to create a loyal following and your image is diffused with little opportunity for building brand awareness. There is a failure within distribution. Most consumers wish to see, handle or try on products before making a purchase, particularly if the products do not already have a well-established reputation and/or a brand name. In your case the only exposure your products have is via the world-wide web. Your pricing structure is too cost-based. You are able to source your products cheaply but your margins are too low to provide you with the necessary capital to reinvest if the business is to develop profitably in the future.

You have failed to establish yourself in the market place as a dominant player. Too many of your business decisions are reactive and often too late to have adequate impact. You are following market trends and not attempting to lead them.'

Natalia is naturally disturbed by the criticisms which this report has levelled at her company's operations and has decided that she must be more positive in her actions. In particular she has decided that her marketing efforts must be more focused and she must pursue more proactively her competitive activities.

Required

In order to focus her company's marketing efforts more precisely Natalia has decided to segment the market for knitwear products.

(a)   Suggest potential bases for segmenting this knitwear market and discuss the benefits which a more focused segmentation could bring to the company.   **(15 marks)**

(b)   Evaluate strategies which Natalia might pursue as a market follower to make her knitwear company more competitive.   **(10 marks)**

(Total = 25 marks)

Answers

A plan of attack

We discussed the problem of which question to start with earlier, in 'Passing the P3 exam'. Here we will merely reiterate our view that question 1 is nearly always the best place to start and, if you do decide to start with a Section B question, **make sure that you finish your answer in no more than 45 minutes**.

Question 1 is quite typical of the sort of thing you are likely to find in the exam. Its only unusual feature is its strong international flavour. You should not allow this to put you off, as the actual technical implications are minimal. The tabulated numerical data present two immediately obvious routes into analysis: year on year comparison and product line comparison. Five minutes calculator work along these lines will give you lots of ideas for comment in requirement (a). Twenty five marks are available for this part of the question and there is plenty to say. Note the use of the word 'report' in the requirement and act accordingly.

There are several models and theories you could make use of to help you to deal with requirement (b), including the various aspects of environmental analysis and even the suitability-acceptability-feasibility framework for assessing strategic options. However, you can produce a perfectly acceptable answer without using any of them if you can identify the relevant material in the setting.

Part (c) is heavily biased towards theory but you must relate it carefully to the circumstances of the company.

Question 2 is very easy and would make a very good choice for your first Section B question, but only if you are sufficiently knowledgeable about the general organisational background. Candidates for this exam tend to be a little unsure of themselves when dealing with questions about non-commercial organisations, but there is little here to worry about since the topic of objectives is fairly easy to discuss from a general awareness of the nature of the public sector. This question follows the usual pattern of two linked parts, with the second requirement building logically on the first. It is noteworthy that the marks are quite heavily biased towards part (b).

Question 3 needs an answer that combines a careful analysis of the detail in the setting with the ability to apply theory relating to the value system and vertical integration. There is lots of opportunity to earn good marks, but this would be a difficult question to answer well if you do not have the theory in the forefront of your mind.

Question 4, coincidentally, is also about the clothing industry but approaches it from a completely different direction. Marketing is one of the Examiner's favourite topics and this is a fairly typical question. Note the appropriate split of marks between requirement (a) and requirement (b): segmentation is a more fundamental topic that the market position strategies referred to in (b). Overall, this is probably a more accessible question than Question 3.

SECTION A

Question 1

Part (a)

> **Text reference.** The topics mentioned in this answer are discussed in Chapter 6 of your BPP Study Text.
>
> **Top tips.** Do not be daunted by a single requirement worth twenty five marks. This indicates that there is plenty to say. Work methodically and plan your answer so that if flows logically from section to section. Also, take care: the mark allocation amounts to almost a quarter of your available time. Do not get carried away and spend too long on part (a)!
>
> **Examiner's comments.** The examiner pointed out that an answer could have been based on other theoretical models, such as the product life cycle or *Ansoff's* product/market growth vector matrix. However, the BCG approach does seem particularly useful here for assessing ABC's portfolio.

REPORT

To:	Colin Doncroft, Managing Director
From:	Simon Gaskell, Management Consultant
Date:	December 2000
Subject:	Evaluation of Ace Bicycle Company strategies

Introduction

This report is designed to consider the different **strategies** that Ace Bicycle Company (ABC) is following in its different markets and to **evaluate each of these individual strategies** given the information provided for the last two years and the current year's forecast figures .

In overall terms ABC has seen a **decline in demand** for its products, with demand expected to fall by 5% over the period. Although revenue is expected to increase in 2000/01 the direct costs are an increasingly large proportion of sales revenue and are expected to reach 84% of revenue in the current year, a rise of 14% over the period. Together with a dramatic expected increase in indirect costs of 54% over the period this has caused a significant fall in profits to an expected, and unacceptable low, of just 2%.

ABC has **four distinct market sectors** – racing bicycles, mountain bikes, health clubs and basic bicycles – with distinctly different strategies being followed for each market therefore I will consider each market in turn.

Background

ABC is a private, family owned company which is now a national producer of bicycles. Some of its products are sold under its own brand name whereas others are sold through a national retail chain under its retail brand name. Over the last few years ABC has seen its **market being eroded** with **increasing competition** from cheaper overseas imports. The overall UK market for bicycles is in decline and this has been made worse by the high value of sterling encouraging imports from foreign suppliers. However during this period ABC has been able to increase its share of domestic output by accepting lower profit margins in order to maintain sales. ABC concentrates its efforts solely on the bicycle market and has a **strong reputation** for reliable products.

Each individual market that ABC operates in will now be considered in turn in the light of this background information.

Racing bicycles

ABC has been making racing bicycles for many years and this area currently accounts for approximately 20% of its volume output and almost 60% of its sales revenue. This is the only sector of ABC's business where the volume of sales is expected to **increase** this year. This sector is by far the **most profitable** of ABC's market areas, but even though anticipated revenue has increased by 15% over the period considered, the **direct costs** of production have outstripped this with an expected increase of 25%. However, this area still remains profitable and although the bicycles are expensive to produce, some being custom made, the **distribution costs** in this sector are minimised by the policy of taking direct orders from amateur cycling clubs. These racing bicycles are marketed under the ABC brand name and have enhanced ABC's reputation.

ABC appears to have followed a successful strategy of **premium pricing** in this market and has **differentiated** the product by the policy of producing custom made bicycles. Despite the cost increases, the margins in this sector are still healthy with clear potential for volume and revenue growth. Any potential for increasing UK market share in this area or diversifying into sales of racing bicycles overseas should seriously be considered as this is clearly the most successful part of the current business.

This area of the business could be described as a **cash cow** according to the BCG growth-share matrix as ABC's market share is relatively high and the market is growing slowly.

Mountain bikes

ABC moved into this fashion area in the 1980s producing relatively cheap models and currently this sector accounts for 30% of ABC's output but only 16% of revenue. The volume of **sales is expected to decline by 8%** over the period considered and **revenue to decline by 5%**. However direct costs of production have increased each year and are anticipated to be 87% of revenue for mountain bikes in the current year. Despite increases in costs and decreases in revenue this sector remains **relatively profitable** in relation to other market sectors of the business.

About 75% of these mountain bike sales are made under the ABC brand name through **specialist bicycle shops**. The remainder of the sales are made through a **national retail chain** of bicycle and motor vehicle accessories stores under the retailer's own brand name.

ABC's pricing policy of charging relatively low prices for the mountain bikes is a strategy of **penetration pricing**; however, in order for this to be successful, ABC needs to be able to **compete on costs**. The increases in direct costs will tend to invalidate this policy as ABC does not appear to have the production capacity to achieve the **economies of scale** necessary to maintain profit margins as sales volumes decline and cheaper foreign imports pose a threat.

As ABC has been so successful in its premium pricing policy in the racing bike market, and the majority of the mountain bikes are also marketed under the ABC brand name, the company should consider **moving away from the low price market** for mountain bikes. If the mountain bikes produced are promoted as being of high quality based upon the well-respected **brand name** of ABC in the racing bike market, the company may be able to attract customers prepared to pay a higher price due to the quality of the product.

This area of ABC's business certainly appears to have potential but if changes in both the stabilisation of costs and marketing and pricing policy are not made it would appear that profits from this sector will continue to decline.

Exercise bicycles

The health club market for **exercise bicycles** plays only a small part in ABC's business currently with less than 5% of total volume sales. As this is a **niche market** it is possible to have a **premium pricing policy**; this sector has been consistently profitable over the period, although margins have reduced to an expected 11% for the current year. Part of the reason for the fall in profitability is, as with other areas of the business, the **escalation of costs** which in the current year represent 88% of the sales value of the exercise bicycles.

This market sector is different from ABC's other areas as it is a **diversification** into a different line of business. The exercise bicycles will have some similarities to the other bicycles manufactured but the market characteristics are very different. Health clubs are a completely different type of customer from those for the other sectors. Sales volume is expected to show a slight fall in the current year since ABC do not produce a full range of exercise equipment, which the market seems to prefer in its suppliers. Therefore ABC might consider **diversifying** into production of **other fitness equipment** such as running machines and cross trainers. This market appears to be potentially profitable but currently ABC is too small a player to take advantage of it in full.

Basic bicycles

The main product of the group, the basic bicycle, accounts for about 45% of the output volume and is therefore still the **core of the business**. However, the **margins** in this area are the main cause of ABC's overall fall in profitability. Sales volume has decreased by 7% over the past two years but sales revenue has fallen by even more, at 12%, as a result of reducing price in an attempt to maintain sales levels in the face of **increasing competition** from cheaper overseas imports. In the current year the margin has fallen to 2.4%, a drop of almost 80% over the two years. Two years ago the production cost per bicycle was £80 but this has increased to £83 per bicycle in the current year. In addition to this the selling price has reduced from £90 two years ago to £85 currently.

About 75% of these bicycles are supplied to a national retail chain supplying bicycles and motor accessories and marketed under the chain's own brand name. As ABC is heavily dependent upon the retail chain it may be that the retailer is forcing prices down using its **buying power**.

ABC's strategy in this market appears to have been one of competing on **both cost and price**. Unfortunately, it appears not to have worked. Prices are coming down and costs are rising. This area of the business is now being **subsidised** by the other more profitable but smaller markets.

There is no real brand association with the basic bicycles as the majority are sold under the retailer's brand name. Therefore it might be difficult for ABC to disassociate itself from the retailer and sell directly, although it may be possible to build on the brand association from the racing bicycle market. According to the BCG growth-share matrix the basic bicycle market could be categorised as a **dog** as the UK market in this area does not appear to be growing and ABC appear to have a relatively low market share.

If ABC is to improve profitability in this market it must decrease costs, probably move away from dependence on the retailer and attempt to **differentiate its product** in some way. Withdrawal from this market could be considered although as it is such a significant element of the business this may be a **dangerous strategy** and should only be considered when all other options have been examined.

Indirect costs

A further worrying area of the business is in the **escalating indirect costs**. Over the two years there has been a staggering increase of 54% in total indirect costs. **Distribution costs** are up by 43% although this may be understandable given the nature of the direct sales of the racing bicycles and exercise bicycles.

Administration costs have also increased by 25% over the last two years which, given the decrease in sales volumes, appears unusual.

Promotion costs have, however, fallen and this must be **rectified** if ABC is to capitalise on its brand name and increase sales volumes.

Loan interest is unavoidable but worryingly high as in the current year **interest cover is only 1.75 times**, a potentially dangerous level.

Conclusion

ABC currently has a wide range of strategies, a premium pricing policy for racing bicycles and exercise bicycles, and an attempt to be a cost leader at the lower end of the market with its basic and mountain bikes. **Production costs** must be brought under control before any rationalisation of strategies can be considered.

It would appear that ABC's strengths lie in its **strong reputation and brand** association in the racing bicycle market. If this can be extended to the **mountain bike market** and a premium pricing policy introduced here with **market differentiation based upon the quality of the product**, then this could produce significant improvements in the mountain bike market.

A further potentially successful market is that of the **health club equipment** if the production range can be extended. The basic bicycle market could be improved with more control of direct costs but as the UK market is not expanding and the strategy has been one of cost leader, which has not succeeded, then it may be necessary to consider withdrawal from this market.

It would appear that the future of ABC lies with the **quality products** as ABC does not appear to have the production capacity to achieve the cost economies necessary for a successful cost leader strategy at the lower end of the market.

Part (b)

> **Top tips.** To some extent our answer is unstructured, addressing salient points in no particular order. If you prefer a more structured approach, you could use the PEST and five forces concepts to produce something like an environmental analysis. You would have to cover the same ground, but you may find this approach more fruitful if you are wondering just how to get started.

When considering any potential investment many factors must be taken into account but when considering such a major change in strategy as the managing director is proposing then there must be a **wide ranging review** of the key factors.

Operations

Let us first consider the **operational aspects** of the development of a manufacturing or assembly facility in China. The proposal is based upon the **large demand** for bicycles perceived in the Far East, the **cheaper labour** which would reduce **production costs** and the reduction in **transportation costs**.

As far as the demand for bicycles is concerned, the view of the market appears to be that of the managing director and there is no evidence that any **market research activities** have been carried out. What type of bicycles are in demand in China and can ABC produce bicycles that satisfy this demand? If the bicycles required are not the same as those currently manufactured by ABC there may be significant costs involved in re-design and changes to the manufacturing processes.

The **labour cost** aspect must be put into perspective. Labour costs only account for 25% of the total production cost therefore the cheaper labour would only lead to a maximum decrease in production costs of 17.5%. The labour issue should be considered further – how does the **productivity** of bicycle manufacturing employees in China compare to that in the UK. If productivity is significantly lower in China then this could **wipe out any cost benefit**.

The **transportation costs** of bicycles from the UK to China are obviously significant. However, if the proposed facility is set up in China instead there are still likely to be significant transportation costs since China covers a vast area and demand is likely to be spread widely. This internal transportation cost should not be ignored.

ABC must consider other operational aspects of setting up a manufacturing facility in China. Can the correct **components** be purchased at a competitive price and be delivered on time? What type and amount of **marketing expenses** will there be? ABC must also question its **ability to run** such an operation as it has no experience in even trading with other countries, let alone setting up a full scale operation in one, particularly one as distant and unknown as China.

Finance

ABC must also consider **financial aspects**. ABC has very low profit levels currently and a large debt outstanding. How does it propose to **raise the finance** necessary for such a major investment? Would the finance be raised in this country or in China? Are there opportunities for a UK company to raise major finance in China? Would a joint venture with a Chinese company be a viable option?

Further financial problems will concern the **remittance of funds back to the UK** and any **foreign exchange risks** that ABC may face. Many countries restrict the amount of their currency that can be taken out of the country and as ABC is so short of funds it will clearly require any profits to be remitted back to the UK. ABC should also consider the foreign exchange risks that are associated with any form of trade with foreign countries. If the Chinese currency moves against sterling then ABC could be subjected to large foreign exchange losses.

Risk

Political risk is a further important area that should be considered. How stable is the Chinese government? What is their attitude to foreign investors, are they encouraged or are there sanctions which will make operations more difficult and expensive?

Analysis

Many of the key factors involved in this proposal can be addressed through a **SLEPT analysis** (social, legal, economic, political and technological aspects). Analysis of social factors will help to define the market, determine the type of bicycle required and clarify the potential customer and method of marketing and sale. Legal factors will include dealing with suppliers, contracts for setting up a factory and employment issues. Economic factors will help to define the demand structure, inflation rates, interest rates and availability of finance. Political issues will be of great importance in a country such as China which has large state control. From the technological viewpoint, particularly if there is a demand for ABC's more high-tech products, such as the racing bicycle, does the technology exist in China or must it be exported?

Conclusion

The theory behind diversification for large companies is that there is no need for a company to do this simply to reduce the risk of just being in one industry as the shareholders are quite capable of doing this on their own behalf by owning a portfolio of shares. However for a private family owned company that is experiencing problems with profitability, a move into a new area is enticing. For ABC, given its core expertise, diversification should only be considered if it is believed that there are no future gains to be made from its current markets and that moves into non-core areas are likely to be successful.

Part (c)

> **Text reference.** The topics mentioned in this answer are discussed in Chapter 7 of your BPP Study Text.
>
> **Easy marks.** There is little in the scenario that you can use in this answer, so you may proceed more or less on a text book basis, which is generally easier than applying knowledge to scenario problems.

(a)   **Organic growth**

Organic growth means setting up the operation purely with ABC's own resources. The benefits of such an approach are:

- Since ABC would provide all of the resources for the investment, the development can be scheduled according to its **own timetable** rather than that of a partner.

- Organic growth tends to be slower than setting up a joint venture and will be less of a **drain on the resources** of ABC, since it can set its own pace.

- As ABC is setting up the venture on its own **all profits will accrue to ABC** and do not need to be shared with any partner.

- As ABC is not reliant on any other party it will be able to expand its own **competences and knowledge**.

- The development can to take place in an orderly manner with no pressures from third parties to introduce products early. ABC will be in control and can introduce its products to the market **as and when it deems appropriate**.

- There is no need for ABC to **integrate with a partner**, either organisationally or culturally.

- Organic growth is likely to mean **higher motivation for employees and managers** as they are in control of the operation without input from any other party.

(b) **Acquisition**

- A further way of setting up the operation in China would be to acquire a bicycle manufacturer in China. The benefits of this approach are:

- The project can get **started more quickly** as the acquired company will already have the infrastructure in place and the expertise and resources required.

- This approach may be **cheaper than organic growth** if the cost of setting up the operation from scratch was going to be very high. Also, an acquisition can sometimes be self-financing; this occurs if unwanted parts of the acquired entity can be sold at a profit.

- ABC has no experience of trade in China and therefore by acquiring a company already operating there they are also effectively **acquiring the knowledge and expertise required**.

- ABC may find that there are **barriers to entry into the market by organic growth** such as access to distribution outlets, building a brand name or obtaining necessary licences; by acquiring an already operational company ABC may be able to avoid these problems.

(c) **Joint developments**

A further method of entering the Chinese market is to enter into some sort of joint venture with a Chinese organisation. The benefits of such a joint development are:

- The **cost of the investment would be reduced** as it would be spread between ABC and its partner.

- The **risk would also be lower** as it would be shared with the partner – if the venture were unsuccessful ABC would have less investment to lose.

- In many countries foreign operations are **treated with suspicion** by government and customers alike – if a joint venture with a Chinese organisation is set up then this would make the operation more politically and commercially acceptable.

- ABC should be able to enter the market much more **rapidly** in a joint venture than by organic growth.

- ABC will obtain the benefit of the partner's **market knowledge** and access the partner's current customer base and supplier network.

- By entering into a joint venture the partner is **avoided as a direct competitor**.

SECTION B

Question 2

> **Text reference.** The topics mentioned in this answer are discussed in Chapter 1 of your BPP Study Text.
>
> **Top tips.** This question is not difficult in itself, but you must make sure that you clearly distinguish the two types of organisation throughout your answer. It is easy for an answer to a question like this to degenerate into an unstructured ramble. Our answer takes the rational planning model as its starting point but you could have used the emergent strategy model just as easily.
>
> **Easy marks.** The easy marks in this question are in part (a). It is obvious that public sector and private sector objectives differ: the key to understanding how the objective setting process works lies in the influence of **stakeholders**.
>
> **Examiner's comments.** The Examiner noted that there was a failure to differentiate between the environments faced by the two types of organisation, and methods of performance measurement suggested were often inappropriate. Strategic objectives and operational activities were not sufficiently distinguished.

Part (a)

The **rational planning model** of business strategy starts with the mission statement as the basis for the development of objectives. The mission statement denotes values, and the organisation's rationale for existing. Objectives are the quantified embodiments of the mission, and include measures such as profitability, timescales and deadlines. In practice, most organisations set themselves quantified objectives in order to enact the mission, using the **SMART** acronym.

The MNC will have as its main financial objective the interests of its **shareholders**, narrowly defined as **profit maximisation**, in order to reward shareholders for the risks that they take. Financial objectives would include the following.

- Profitability
- Return on investment (ROI) or return on capital employed (ROCE)
- Share price, earnings per share, dividends
- Growth

Growth in shareholder value is the yardstick by which most companies measure their success. This takes precedence over other growth objectives such as size, market share and so forth.

Private sector organisations have **other stakeholder groups**, with employees being of particular significance. However, their interests are generally subordinated to the overriding demands of commercial success and indeed, survival.

Local administrative authorities do not set objectives with the aim of achieving profit for shareholders, but they are being increasingly required to apply the same disciplines and processes as companies which are oriented towards straightforward profit goals. Business strategy issues are just as relevant to a local authority as they are for an MNC operating with a profit motive.

Having said that, whilst the basic principles are appropriate for the public sector, **differences** in how the public and private sectors apply these principles should not be forgotten.

Objectives for the local administrative authority will concentrate on achieving a particular response from target markets, and embody **social priorities**. **Efficiency** (getting the most output for the level of input) and **effectiveness** (meeting the objectives set) are particularly important in the use of public funds. Objectives related to these may even be set by central government.

There are no buyers in the public sector, or shareholders to satisfy. Instead, the local authority has a number of different **stakeholders**, particularly those in the local community who are to benefit from the housing, education, social and road maintenance services that they provide. Possible objectives for the local authority follow on from this and include the following. They are sometimes directly comparable with the objectives of an MNC.

- Surplus maximisation (equivalent to profit maximisation)
- Revenue maximisation (as for a commercial business)
- Maximising the use of facilities and services
- Matching the capacity available to the demands for it
- Cost recovery
- Satisfying staff
- Satisfying clients

Part (b)

The CIMA definition of **performance measurement** can be applied to both public and private sector organisations. It is 'the process of assessing the proficiency with which a reporting entity succeeds, by the economic acquisition of resources and their efficient and effective development, in achieving its objectives. Performance measures may be based on non-financial as well as financial information.'

Performance measurement communicates the objectives of the company and concentrates efforts towards those objectives. There are a number of key areas to consider when determining the approach to adopt towards performance evaluation in a given set of circumstances, and these can be used to discuss how the local administrative authority and the MNC should assess how well they have performed.

(a) **What is evaluated?**

This is a key question for both organisations. Some approaches concentrate on the performance of the organisation as a whole, while others look at strategic business units, divisions or functions. The local authority will want to assess the performance of its key service areas, while the MNC will be looking at profitability over a certain time period.

(b) **Who wants the evaluation?**

The MNC may base its assessment upon the viewpoint of a single group, primarily its investors and, by extension, the market. Their reactions will impact its share price. The local authority will be concerned about the maintenance of positive relations with its interested 'publics' which will include the clients for its services, the government and interest groups.

(c) **What are the objectives of the organisation?**

Is there a single goal, or many goals? Are the goals short or long term? Are they directly measurable? There is likely to be a mix of these for both organisations. The long term goal of the MNC could be to expand its operations into many more countries over the next ten years, while the local authority may be planning to open several more schools in that time. Short term objectives for the MNC may include divesting certain non-core businesses. The local authority may be trying to secure additional funding. All of these objectives will require different methods of assessment and control.

It must be remembered that objectives are likely to need revision and updating, so measurement of progress towards their attainment is an ongoing process which will need systematic reporting.

(d) **Are quantitative or qualitative measures appropriate?**

Measures must be relevant to the way that the organisation operates, and managers themselves must believe that the indicators are useful. Controlling activities is complicated for the local authority by the difficulty of judging whether non-quantitative objectives have been met. In a business such as the MNC, measures such as the level of sales, profit or ROI can indicate progress towards the achievement of objectives. This cannot be the case when the services are not sold but are provided to meet social needs. Improving services and increasing the satisfaction of those using them are likely to be important goals.

It is not always easy to measure the quality of output in public services. For example, league tables of exam results have been established to enable identification of those schools which get the best results. Housing services may be assessed by the length of waiting lists for accommodation.

(e) **What targets are used to assess performance?**

Measures are meaningless unless they are compared against something. Common sources of comparison for both organisations could include historic figures, standards/budgets, similar activities carried out by different local authorities, organisations or divisions, indices and trends over time.

Value for money audits can be seen as being of particular relevance in not-for-profit organisations. Such an audit focuses on economy, efficiency and effectiveness. These measures may be in conflict with each other. To take the example of higher education, larger class sizes may be economical in their use of teaching resources, but are not necessarily effective in creating the best learning environment.

Question 3

Part (a)

Forward integration into dress manufacture and its effect on competitive ability

Forward vertical integration is often justified as it enables the firm to do three things

(a)　Earn more of the profit available in the value chain

(b)　**Control marketing and pricing strategy** (eg Benetton) – the firm can ensure it maintains the image of quality and exclusivity

(c)　**Control usage of the product**

EF's main motivation has been to earn more profit. In this, the incorporation of an **in-house clothing design team** has enabled it to increase its profits.

EF has thus extended the value chain. Previously, the process of adding value was simply a matter of designing and producing cloth. Dressmakers then creamed off the value added from turning the cloth into dresses and suits. A consequence is that EF's customer has changed from being the trade customer to being the end consumer. The operations process in the value chain is now more complicated, because **what were previously two value chains in a value system have now become one.**

The firm's success may lead its directors to consider that vertical integration has no drawbacks, hence their suggestion to enter retailing.

The drawbacks of EF's approach

(a)　EF has **restricted its market** to the middle aged and middle income market. This is probably a sensible strategy for a clothing design company, but not for a fabric manufacturer. EF has put more eggs into one basket.

(b)　EF has **precluded the possibility of other ways of increasing fabric sales**, by exporting for example.

(c)　The **dress design company is limited** in its use of fabrics to what EF supplies. Its designers may resent the restrictions and lack of freedom.

(d)　EF has to support **two different production operations** – spinning/weaving the fabrics, on the one hand, and dress manufacture on the other. There are thus two sets of machinery and two workforces.

(e)　Capacity may not be matched properly. EF will have increased warehousing costs if it needs to manufacture cloth ahead of retail demand.

(f)　There are other minor administrative issues such as **transfer pricing**. However, it should not be too difficult to compare cloth prices with competing products on the market.

Forwards vertical integration has made it harder to compete with **other yarn manufacturers**, and EF is now competing for fickle consumers who face many other offers.

Part (b)

Forward vertical integration into retail outlets

EF is proposing copying *Laura Ashley* and *Benetton* in having exclusive outlets for its own products. The intention is to earn more of the value in the value system.

Advantages

(a)   EF would have **total control over production, pricing and marketing**. It could develop a precise marketing strategy that further differentiates the product, enabling an even more targeted focus on its desired customer base. Moreover, it will have more freedom to develop marketing messages and integrate its marketing strategy.

(b)   EF will also be able to ensure that its products are available and visible, and are not competing in the same clothes racks as other competitors – thereby **avoiding price comparisons**. In other words, EF will not depend on retailers' professional buyers to order or display its products.

EF will **become fully informed of its target market.** It may be able to make clothes to order, if customer measurements can be transmitted electronically to the factory: this would be an example of **mass customisation.**

Drawbacks

(a)   EF will acquire a range of high street properties, with management problems of their own. **Debt service** will eat into any extra profits that are made on clothing sales.

(b)   **Higher risk.** If EF's clothes go out of fashion, the stores will become an expensive liability. Owning a chain of retail outlets involves a much higher proportion of fixed costs than cloth and clothing manufacture. Much depends on the location of the shops.

(c)   If EF products are exclusively sold in its own shops, **EF may forgo the sales it would have made at the department stores**. EF might be better advised to bite the bullet and accept that it will have to accept the high customer bargaining power with the stores.

(d)   EF will need to produce a wide enough range of products to encourage customers to enter. EF may have to supplement its own wares with others by other suppliers – will it be able to do so cost-effectively?

Competences

(a)   As EF is acquiring the chain, it will inherit the many competences needed, providing both that it can keep the staff and that EF's managers integrate the acquisition in a sensitive way.

(b)   Stock management for many small retail stores will be quite complicated. EF may well inherit systems currently employed in the acquired company.

(c)   EF needs to understand high street retailing, display, and merchandising (ensuring a suitable range of clothes is available in the right volumes and at the right time).

(d)   EF needs a more responsive distribution system.

(e)   EF is now running three different types of business. To benefit from economies of scale it may need a performance monitoring system for each business.

Question 4

> **Top tips.** A common problem for candidates is the **application** of their theoretical knowledge to question scenarios. In this answer we show in *italics* those parts that constitute application of theory to the specific problems represented by the scenario.

Part (a)

> **Text reference.** The topics mentioned in this answer are discussed in Chapter 3 of your BPP Study Text.
>
> **Top tips.** The great advantage of careful market segmentation is that it permits a precise determination of the marketing mix variables. This saves money and allows the firm to make best use of its competences.
>
> **Easy marks.** Part (a) is about segmentation methods. This idea less well known than some of the strategic theory you have come across, such as, say, *Porter's* generic strategies, so there are going to be some marks simply for enumerating some suitable bases. Part (a) is worth fifteen marks overall, which can be expected to break down into seven for suggesting the bases and eight for saying why segmentation is a good idea. Thus we might expect three marks for proposing three bases and saying a little about the relevance of each, with another three (or possibly four) for deeper discussion. Our discussion of each of the bases we have chosen illustrates this approach, progressing from the name of the base through its relevance to its wider implications or applications.

Segmentation would be Natalia's first step towards a more active relationship with her existing and potential customers. If she knew who they were in more detail she could design her market offering in a way that would improve her own **efficiency** *while also providing increased* **customer satisfaction**.

The simplest form of segmentation is probably **geographical**. *Natalia's potential market could be very simply split into domestic and overseas, for instance. Indeed, she probably does this already, in a sense, since she must make appropriate arrangements for the extra complications of shipping to foreign customers. Geographical segmentation would be necessary if Natalia wished to sell in other ways than via the Internet, perhaps by issuing catalogues, since the styles of knitwear offered would have to appeal to varying local tastes.*

Geographical segmentation becomes much more useful when it is combined with demographic information. *This* **geo-demographic** *segmentation would enable Natalia to target segments defined by such variables as place, age, sex, income and social class. A consideration of these variables might for instance lead her to concentrate her marketing effort on older, affluent people in specific metropolitan areas. This would have immediate implications for design, quality, promotion, price and distribution.*

Psychographic segmentation analyses the market according to personality and lifestyle. *This might be difficult for Natalia to use, but if she could, perhaps by continuing to employ her marketing consultant, it might offer important advantages in the areas of design and promotion in particular.*

A further segmentation variable is customer **behaviour**. This includes such matters as sensitivity to changes in the marketing mix variables, purchase frequency and magnitude and how the product is used. *This approach might be useful to Natalia. For example, she might find that some of her designs are frequently bought by women for their menfolk. This might have important implications for design and sizing.*

The benefit of accurate market segmentation is that it permits a more precise specification of the marketing mix variables, so that they are shaped to conform to the needs of the target segment or segments.

Product. Different segments will probably require different products. When the size of each segment, its product requirements and their costs are known, it will be possible both to estimate the most profitable segment to attack and to specify fairly precisely the nature of the products needed to do so. *Natalia might find, for instance, that she needed to adjust her designs to make her range more recognisable and coherent.*

Price. Pricing decisions are fundamental to trade and very difficult to take. It is very easy to set prices too high, so that customers are put off, or too low, so that potential profit is lost. The problem is compounded by the complex messages about quality, exclusivity and value that can be sent by price levels and changes to them. *At the moment, Natalia's products are relatively cheap and this is preventing her from generating the funds needed for expansion: she may find that she can charge more for some of her knitwear.*

Promotion. *Natalia's consultant has identified her promotion efforts as insufficiently focused, which has led to a diffuse image and little brand awareness. Detailed knowledge of the characteristics of her target segments will allow Natalia to develop the accuracy of her promotion. She may find, for example, that a large market exists which is unwilling to use the Internet at all and so remains in ignorance of her products.*

Place. *Natalia's distribution is currently largely via her web site. This limits her potential market to those who are both confident in the use of computers and interested in original design knitwear. It is likely that a much larger market could be served through a more traditional approach using prestige clothing outlets. This could be established by careful consideration of the results of the segmentation exercise.*

Part (b)

Text reference. The topics mentioned in this answer are discussed in Chapter 6 of your BPP Study Text.

The **market follower** accepts the status quo and thus **avoids the cost and risk associated with innovation** in product, price or distribution strategy. Such a **me-too** strategy is based on the leader's approach. This can be both profitable and stable. However, it is very easy for this strategy to come to depend entirely on charging lower prices. As the follower is unlikely to have the scale economies that accrue to the market leader, this means accepting a much lower level of profit

To be consistently successful, the market follower must not simply imitate. The follower should **compete in the most appropriate segments**, maintain its **customer base** and ensure that its **turnover grows** in line with the general expansion of the market. *Natalia could attempt to do this by exploiting the originality of her designs, thus effectively differentiating her market offering and justifying higher prices. The development of her brand image will be a necessary precondition for success with this strategy.*

An important problem for the market follower is that it may constitute an **attractive target** for market challengers seeking growth by acquisition, or indeed for the market leader seeking to extend control over the market. *An agreed turnover may, in due course, be a suitable way for Natalia to realise the equity in her business; however, assuming that she wishes to maintain her independence of operations for the foreseeable future she must control her costs and exploit appropriate opportunities to achieve differentiation. Otherwise, cash flow difficulties may force her to sell out.*

ACCA
Paper P3
Business Analysis

Mock Examination 3
Pilot Paper

Question Paper	
Time allowed	**15 minutes**
Reading and planning	**3 hours**
Writing	
This paper is divided into two sections	
Section A	**ONE compulsory question to be attempted**
Section B	**TWO questions ONLY to be attempted**

During reading and planning time only the question paper may be annotated

DO NOT OPEN THIS PAPER UNTIL YOU ARE READY TO START UNDER EXAMINATION CONDITIONS

SECTION A – This question is compulsory and MUST be attempted

BPP Note. The following pages contain the pilot paper questions and answers produced by the ACCA.

Pilot paper

Paper P3

Business Analysis

Time allowed

Reading and planning: 15 minutes
Writing: 3 hours

This paper is divided into two sections:

Section A – This ONE question is compulsory and MUST be attempted

Section B – TWO questions ONLY to be attempted

Do NOT open this paper until instructed by the supervisor.

During reading and planning time only the question paper may be annotated. You must NOT write in your answer booklet until instructed by the supervisor.

This question paper must not be removed from the examination hall.

Warning

The pilot paper cannot cover all of the syllabus nor can it include examples of every type of question that will be included in the actual exam. You may see questions in the exam that you think are more difficult than any you see in the pilot paper.

Section A – The ONE question in this section is compulsory and MUST be attempted.

The following information should be used when answering question 1.

The case study of this Business Analysis pilot paper is based on the one examined in Paper 3.5 – Strategic Business Planning and Development in June 2004. Slight amendments have been made to the scenario, questions and answers to reflect the Business Analysis syllabus and emphasis.

1 Introduction

Network Management Systems (NMS) is a privately owned hi-tech business set up in a location near London in 1993. NMS is the brainchild of a Canadian computer engineer, Ray Edwards. Ray is a classic hi-tech entrepreneur, constantly searching for ways to exploit technological opportunities and unafraid to take the risks associated with high technology start-ups. NMS's first product was a digital error detection box able to 'listen' to computer signals and detect faults. The original box, designed by Ray, was built on his kitchen table and manufactured in a garage. Ray is a flamboyant character and a committed entrepreneur. In his words an entrepreneur is "someone willing to work 18 hours a day for themselves ... to avoid working eight hours a day for someone else!"

Structure of the business and key product areas

By 2006 NMS employed 75 full time employees in a new, purpose built factory and office unit. These employees were a mix of technically qualified engineers working in research and development (R&D), factory staff manufacturing and assembling the products and a small sales and service support team. In 2006, NMS had three distinct product/service areas.

One of the three products NMS produced was data communication components which it sold directly to original equipment manufacturers (OEMs) that used these components in their hardware. Both the OEMs and their customers were predominantly large international companies. NMS had established a good reputation for the quality and performance of its components, which were also competitively priced. However, NMS had less than 1% share of the UK market in this sector and faced competition from more than twenty suppliers, most of who also competed internationally. Furthermore, one of NMS's OEM customers accounted for 40% of its sales. The European market for data communications equipment had increased from $3.3 billion in 1999 to $8.0 billion in 2006. Forecasts for 2007 and beyond, predict growth from increased sales to currently installed networks rather than from the installation of new networks. The maturity of the technology means that product lifecycles are becoming shorter. Success comes from producing large volumes of relatively low priced reliable components. However, all new components have to be approved by the relevant government approval body in each country being supplied. Approval for new data communication equipment is both costly and time consuming.

NMS's second product area was network management systems – hence the name of the company. Fault detection systems were supplied directly to a small number of large end users such as banks, public utility providers and global manufacturers. NMS recognised the unique configuration of each customer and so it customised its product to meet specific needs and requirements. They have pioneered a "modular building block" design, which allows the customer to adapt standard system modules to fit their exact networking requirements. NMS products focused on solving network management problems and the success of its products was reflected in the award of the prestigious Government Award for Technology for "technological innovation in the prevention of computer data communication downtime". This was recognition of the excellence of the R&D engineers who developed the software and related hardware. It further enhanced NMS's reputation and enabled it to become a successful niche player in this low volume market with gross margins in excess of 40%. NMS only faces two or three competitors in a specialist market where there is no need to gain government approval for new products and systems.

Finally, the complexity of NMS products means that technical support is a third key business area. NMS has established a reputation for excellent technical support, reflecting Ray's continuing concern with customer care. However, it is increasingly difficult and costly to maintain this support because the company lacks a national network. All technical support is provided from its headquarters. This contrasts with the national and international distributed service structure operated by its large, international competitors.

Emerging problems

NMS's growth has made Ray increasingly concerned about the ability of NMS to identify market trends, scan its competitive environment and create marketing strategies and plans. NMS's market and sales planning only covers the year ahead. Larger competitors invest heavily in market research analysis and customer relationship marketing. Business-to-business marketing is becoming an increasingly complex and sophisticated activity in this sector.

Accurate sales forecasting is also a key input into production planning and scheduling. NMS manufactures 40% of the components used in its products. The rest of the components, including semiconductors and microprocessors, are bought in from global suppliers. Serious production problems result from periodic component shortages, creating significant delays in manufacturing, assembly, and customer deliveries. Furthermore, the growth of NMS has outstripped the largely manual control systems designed to support its production and sales operation.

Ray is acutely aware of his key role as founder and chairman of the firm. He is also finding the skills and attributes necessary for founding and growing the business are not appropriate in a mature business. He is heavily reliant on his extrovert personality and his ability to muddle through with informal, flexible systems. The limitation of this approach is now beginning to show. He is finding it increasingly difficult to cope with the day-to-day demands of running the business while at the same time planning its future. Functional departments in the shape of sales and marketing, technical (R&D), manufacturing and administration are in place but strategic planning, such as there is, is very much his responsibility.

Recruitment of high calibre staff is also a problem – NMS's small size and location means that it struggles to attract the key personnel necessary for future growth. Ray feels pressure on him to either develop the necessary skills himself, or to develop the right people with the right skills. In Ray's words, starting a business is like "building your own airplane and then teaching yourself how to fly".

One particular skill in short supply is the financial capability of dealing with growth. His negotiations with bankers and other financial intermediaries have become increasingly difficult and time consuming. The financial control information required to support growth and, more recently, to ensure survival is often inadequate. However, 2006 had started well, with NMS approached as a target for a possible acquisition by a major data communications company. The opportunity to realise some of the equity in the business had considerable appeal. Unfortunately, while protracted negotiations were taking place, a downturn in the global economy occured. Orders for NMS's products fell and the banks and venture capitalists supporting NMS through overdraft and long-term investment became much less sympathetic. The final insult occurred when Ray was approached by a venture capitalist with a management buyout proposal put together with NMS's financial director and sales manager. The value placed on the business was a derisory £50K. Ray was angry and hurt by the size of the offer and also at the disloyalty of his senior staff in seeking to buy the business. To make matters worse the uncertainty over the future of the business has led to a number of key members of staff deciding to leave the company. The financial director and sales manager are still both in post, but their future plans are uncertain. Financial data for NMS is presented in Table 1.

Ray's future at NMS
Ray is currently considering his future at NMS. He has identified three main exit options. The first is to personally lead the company out of its current problems, which he largely attributes to global economic slowdown, and to launch the business on the stock exchange as soon as its economic position improves. His second option is to sell the business for a figure which more accurately reflects its real value and to walk away and reflect on his future. His final option is to seek acquisition by one of his large customers (or competitors) and so become part of a much larger organisation. In such circumstances he would offer to stay on and develop NMS within the structures imposed by a parent organisation. By nature a fighter, the recent uncertainties over ownership and gloomy forecasts for the global economy have made him seriously reflect on his own priorities. His hands-on approach and involvement with all aspects of the business seems increasingly inappropriate for handling the problems of a hi-tech business such as NMS.

Table 1: Financial data for Network Management Systems

	2004	2005	2006	2007 (forecast)
Sales	£'000	£'000	£'000	£'000
UK sales	4,500	6,300	6,930	6,235
Export sales	300	500	650	520
Total sales	4,800	6,800	7,580	6,755
Cost of sales	2,640	3,770	4,550	4,320
Gross margin	2,160	3,030	3,030	2,435
Expenses				
Administration	500	630	700	665
Distribution	715	940	945	885
Marketing	50	60	70	70
R&D	495	590	870	690
Overheads	200	280	320	325
Operating profit	200	530	125	-200
Sales Interest paid	25	120	150	165
Net profit	175	410	-25	-365
Financing				
Long-term liabilities	160	750	1,000	1,100
Share capital and reserves	375	605	600	575
Other information				
Employees	50	60	75	60
% of orders late	5	7	10	6
Order book	4,725	4,150	3,150	2,500

Required:

(a) **Assess the macro-environment of NMS by undertaking a PESTEL analysis.**   (10 marks)

(b) **Using appropriate models and financial and quantitative data from the scenario, provide an environmental and financial analysis of NMS, highlighting problem areas.**   (25 marks)

(c) **Ray is considering three main exit options from the business as it currently exists. Assess each of the three identified exit options in terms of their ability to solve the problems highlighted in your analysis and in terms of Ray's future role in the business.**   (15 marks)

(50 marks)

Section B – TWO questions ONLY to be attempted

2   The Environment Management Society (EMS) was established in 1999 by environment practitioners who felt that environmental management and audit should have its own qualification. EMS has its own Board who report to a Council of eight members. Policy is made by the Board and ratified by Council. EMS is registered as a private limited entity.

EMS employs staff to administer its qualification and to provide services to its members. The qualification began as one certificate, developed by the original founding members of the Society. It has since been developed, by members and officers of the EMS, into a four certificate scheme leading to a Diploma. EMS employs a full-time chief examiner who is responsible for setting the certificate examinations which take place monthly in training centres throughout the country. No examinations are currently held in other countries.

If candidates pass all four papers they can undertake an oral Diploma examination. If they pass this oral they are eligible to become members. All examinations are open-book one hour examinations, preceded by 15 minutes reading time. At a recent meeting, EMS Council rejected the concept of computer-based assessment. They felt that competence in this area was best assessed by written examination answers.

Candidate numbers for the qualification have fallen dramatically in the last two years. The Board of EMS has concluded that this drop reflects the maturing marketplace in the country. Many people who were practitioners in environmental management and audit when the qualification was introduced have now gained their Diploma. The stream of new candidates and hence members is relatively small.

Consequently, the EMS Board has suggested that they should now look to attract international candidates and it has targeted countries where environmental management and audit is becoming more important. It is now formulating a strategy to launch the qualification in India, China and Russia.

However, any strategy has to recognise that both the EMS Board and the Council are very cautious and notably risk-averse. EMS is only confident about its technical capability within a restricted definition of environmental management and audit. Attempts to look at complementary qualification areas (such as soil and water conservation) have been swiftly rejected by Council as being non-core areas and therefore outside the scope of their expertise.

Required:

Internal development, acquisitions and strategic alliances are three development methods by which an organisation's strategic direction can be pursued.

(a)   **Explain the principles of internal development and discuss how appropriate this development method is to EMS.**   (8 marks)

(b)   **Explain the principles of acquisitions and discuss how appropriate this development method is to EMS.**
                                                                                          (8 marks)

(c)   **Explain the principles of strategic alliances and discuss how appropriate this development method is to EMS.**   (9 marks)

(25 marks)

3 CCT Computer Systems plc specialises in the development and implementation of software for the logistics industry. After experiencing a number of years of growth and profitability the company is continuing to report growth in turnover but, for the last five quarters, it has also reported small losses. An investigation into this has revealed that costs have risen greatly in systems development and support and consequently margins have been eroded in recently completed projects. It appears that this trend is going to continue. Many people within the company attribute this worsening financial performance to a perceived reduction in software quality. Here are three testimonies received during the investigation

Amelia Platt: Software Development Manager CCT Computer Systems plc
"You have to remember that the original logistics system was developed by Ilya Borisova (the founder of CCT) and three of his friends from university days. They did not build the software with expansion or maintenance in mind. Also, it is difficult to know what some of the programs actually do, so making changes is a nightmare. Programmers make changes to program code without really knowing what the knock-on effect will be."

Tony Osunda: General Manager QANDO logistics – a major customer
"We feel that the last project was most unsatisfactory. We specified our requirements very carefully but the delivered system did not work the way we wanted. We found it cumbersome to use and key areas of functionality were either wrong or missing altogether. After implementation, we asked for a number of changes so that the system would work as it should. We were originally asked to pay for these changes but we pointed out that they weren't really changes – they were things we had asked for all along. Eventually, CCT backed down and so we got the changes for free. The system works fine now, but it has been delivered late and we are still seeking compensation for this.

Carlos Theroux: One of the original programmers of the CCT logistics software solution: Now lead programmer CCT Computer Systems plc
"It is no fun here anymore. When we were smaller we could all dive in and solve the problems. When I joined we had three programmers, now we have one hundred and thirty. What do they all do? There is no work ethic. We all used to stay over until we got the problem solved. Now there is documentation, documentation and documentation. We have now adopted a formal project management method, more documentation! I am not sure this place suits me anymore."

Required:

(a) **A perceived reduction in software quality is blamed by many people for the decline in profitability at CCT. Discuss the importance and characteristics of software quality and explain how each of these characteristics might be measured.** (10 marks)

(b) **Explain the levels within the Capability Maturity Model Integration (CMMI) process and discuss their implications for CCT.** (15 marks)

(25 marks)

4 DRB Electronic Services operates in a high labour cost environment in Western Europe and imports electronic products from the Republic of Korea. It re-brands and re-packages them as DRB products and then sells them to business and domestic customers in the local geographical region. Its only current source of supply is ISAS electronics based in a factory on the outskirts of Seoul, the capital of the Republic of Korea. DRB regularly places orders for ISAS products through the ISAS web-site and pays for them by credit card. As soon as the payment is confirmed ISAS automatically e-mails DRB a confirmation of order, an order reference number and likely shipping date. When the order is actually despatched, ISAS send DRB a notice of despatch e-mail and a container reference number. ISAS currently organises all the shipping of the products. The products are sent in containers and then trans-shipped to EIF, the logistics company used by ISAS to distribute its products. EIF then delivers the products to the DRB factory. Once they arrive, they are quality inspected and products that pass the inspection are re-branded as DRB products (by adding appropriate logos) and packaged in specially fabricated DRB boxes. These products are then stored ready for sale. All customer sales are from stock. Products that fail the inspection are returned to ISAS.

Currently 60% of sales are made to domestic customers and 40% to business customers. Most domestic customers pick up their products from DRB and set them up themselves. In contrast, most business customers ask DRB to set up the electronic equipment at their offices, for which DRB makes a small charge. DRB currently advertises its products in local and regional newspapers. DRB also has a web site which provides product details. Potential customers can enquire about the specification and availability of products through an e-mail facility in the web site. DRB then e-mails an appropriate response directly to the person making the enquiry. Payment for products cannot currently be made through the web site.

Feedback from existing customers suggests that they particularly value the installation and support offered by the company. The company employs specialist technicians who (for a fee) will install equipment in both homes and offices. They will also come out and troubleshoot problems with equipment that is still under warranty. DRB also offer a helpline and a back to base facility for customers whose products are out of warranty. Feedback from current customers suggests that this support is highly valued. One commented that "it contrasts favourably with your large customers who offer support through impersonal off-shore call centres and a time-consuming returns policy". Customers can also pay for technicians to come on-site to sort out problems with out-of-warranty equipment.

DRB now plans to increase their product range and market share. It plans to grow from its current turnover of £5m per annum to £12m per annum in two years time. Dilip Masood, the owner of DRB, believes that DRB must change its business model if it is to achieve this growth. He believes that these changes will also have to tackle problems associated with

– Missing, or potentially missing shipments. Shipments can only be tracked through contacting the shipment account holder, ISAS, and on occasions they have been reluctant or unable to help. The trans-shipment to EIF has also caused problems and this has usually been identified as the point where goods have been lost. ISAS does not appear to be able to reliably track the relationship between the container shipment and the Waybills used in the EIF system.

– The likely delivery dates of orders, the progress of orders and the progress of shipments is poorly specified and monitored. Hence deliveries are relatively unpredictable and this can cause congestion problems in the delivery bay.

Dilip also recognises that growth will mean that the company has to sell more products outside its region and the technical installation and support so valued by local customers will be difficult to maintain. He is also adamant that DRB will continue to import only fully configured products. It is not interested in importing components and assembling them. DRB also does not wish to build or invest in assembly plants overseas or to commit to a long-term contract with one supplier.

Required:

(a) **Draw the primary activities of DRB on a value chain. Comment on the significance of each of these activities and the value that they offer to customers.** (9 marks)

(b) **Explain how DRB might re-structure its upstream supply chain to achieve the growth required by DRB and to tackle the problems that Dilip Masood has identified.** (10 marks)

(c) **Explain how DRB might re-structure its downstream supply chain to achieve the growth required.** (6 marks)

(25 marks)

Answers

**DO NOT TURN THIS PAGE UNTIL YOU HAVE
COMPLETED THE MOCK EXAM**

A plan of attack

We discussed the problem of which question to start with earlier, in 'Passing the P3'. Here we will merely reiterate our view that question 1 is nearly always the best place to start and, if you do decide to start with a Section B question, **make sure that you finish your answer in no more than 45 minutes**.

You should pay particular attention to this exam as it is the only guidance we have as to how the examiner envisages the P3 exam.

Question 1 is based on a Paper 3.5 question from 2004; requirements (b) and (c) are totally unchanged, while requirement (a) is more typical of past section A questions than the original.

Questions 2, 3 and 4 are different in type of from typical Section B questions in Paper 3.5 exams – they are narrowly focused and emphasise some very specific aspects of syllabus knowledge. This perhaps reflects the Examiner's experience of examining at the intermediate level. There is little to choose between them and your choice will depend on how well you know the various topics.

At the Professional level it is not always possible to publish a suggested answer which is fully comprehensive. Credit will be given to candidates for points not included in the suggested answers but which nevertheless, are relevant to the questions.

The suggested answers presented below give more detail than would be expected from a candidate under examination conditions. The answers are intended to provide guidance on the approach required from candidates, and on the range and depth of knowledge, which could be written by an excellent candidate.

1   (a)   The PESTEL framework may be used to explore the macro-environmental influences that might affect an organisation. There are six main influences in the framework: political, economic, social, technological, environmental and legal. However, these types are inter-linked and so, for example, political developments and environmental requirements are often implemented through enacting legislation. Candidates will be given credit for defining the main macro-environmental influences that affect NMS, rather than the classification of these influences into the PESTEL framework.

Political – NMS is situated in a country with a relatively stable political system. Like many industrialised countries, all political parties in this country appear to value and promote technology. Tax incentives and grants are often given to companies to invest in technology and research and development. These incentives are not only available to NMS, but also (in the United Kingdom) to their customers. This has helped fuel the growth in the data communications market and although evidence suggests that this growth is tailing off, investment is still significant. Government itself is a major investor in communications technology, often using such investments to facilitate economic growth in this sector. However, most governments are also anxious to set standards that any company supplying equipment that links into the national telecommunications network have to meet. There is evidence of government control in the shape of the approvals process. This may arise from fears about technical reliability and compatibility but it may also be designed to hinder competition from foreign suppliers. Finally, government may promote the recognition of technology through an awards scheme. NMS has received such recognition through a Government Award for Technology.

Economic – again a significant factor, in that the stage in the economic or business cycle can clearly affect buying decisions. The case study suggests that 2006 has seen a slight downturn in the UK and international economy and a consequent slowing down in large customers' commitment to long-term investment. The bad news is that customers can postpone such investment. The good news is that if innovation creates products and systems that bring cost and communication advantages to customers then eventually they will have to invest in them. Wage rates remain high in the United Kingdom and NMS may wish to re-consider their commitment to manufacturing 40% of their components in the United Kingdom. Labour costs (allied to compliance costs – see below) and legal obligations makes manufacturing in the UK extremely expensive. It is likely that many of their competitors source 100% of their components abroad and only assemble their products in the UK.

Social – communication and information exchange will continue to increase with consequent implications for companies supplying the products and systems to meet these growing needs. All evidence suggests that the social use of services on such networks will increase. Hence, although demand appears to be dropping off, new social uses for telecommunication networks might spark off a new wave of economic investment.

Technological – clearly a significant factor in shaping the life cycles of existing products and the introduction of new ones. The hi-tech sector is extremely innovative, with new and improved technologies constantly emerging. NMS must scan the marketplace for such technologies and identify how such they might affect the future of their products. NMS must also consider how such emergent technologies might be used in their own products.

Environmental issues – continue to have an impact on organisations. Organisations are encouraged by politicians and by legislation to reduce their emissions and improve their re-cycling. The cost of disposal of raw materials is also increasing. There is no direct evidence of such issues in the case study scenario. However, as a manufacturing company in the United Kingdom it is highly likely that NMS will be affected by such factors.

Legal – NMS operates in a country where there are many laws defining employer responsibilities and employee rights. It is likely that regulation will continue and the NMS will, like all organisations working in the European Union (EU), have to evaluate the benefits and cost of working within such legal structures. Some organisations seek to gain advantage by moving to countries where regulation is more lax and hence avoid the compliance costs incurred by their competitors. The case study scenario suggests that NMS has significant international competitors. It is likely that some of these will be based in countries where legislative requirements are less onerous.

(b)   Michael Porter provides, through his five forces model, a useful means of analysing the competitive environment. Analysis suggests the following key factors are shaping this environment.

Bargaining power of buyers
There is evidence that large industrial customers are becoming more cost conscious and this is likely to lead to increased price negotiation with their suppliers. At the same time customers are placing a premium on quality and service. Data communications products are becoming important in virtually every area of large organisations, causing greater sensitivity to price, quality and reliability. The end users of this equipment are becoming less technically proficient and more demanding, particularly in their unwillingness to adopt products that are difficult to use.

The supplying industry is relatively fragmented and so buyers have a wide choice and can compare competitors and exert buyer power on them. Information on NMS and their competitors' products and services is easily available to potential buyers. Buyer power is therefore likely to become more significant – particularly in view of the downturn in the global economy.

It is important to recognise that NMS is competing in two discrete markets. Firstly, data communications components, where with a 1% market share, they are at best a marginal supplier. The customers are OEMs who are large industrial buyers with the ability to demand a testing combination of low prices, high quality and reliability. This is expected both in terms of component performance and even more significantly, in view of recent manufacturing and assembly problems, guaranteed delivery. A combination of circumstances suggests that OEM's have significant bargaining power in this market. The OEM who accounts for 40% on the company's current sales is in a particularly strong position.

In the second market, where network management systems are supplied to large end users, buyers appear to have less bargaining power. NMS is a significant supplier in this market place with only two or three competitors. NMS is catering for each customer's specific network needs and so each solution is to some degree a bespoke solution. This makes it much harder for buyers to compare the prices of potential suppliers, particularly given the modular design of the NMS product. Furthermore, this product represents a relatively small part of the overall cost of the end user's investment in information and communication systems. This is also likely to make such products less price sensitive and hence provides an opportunity to generate good margins.

Bargaining Power of Suppliers
Evidence from the information provided gives no real insight into the bargaining power of suppliers but the purchase of components such as semiconductors and microprocessors is likely to be from major global companies such as Intel and, as a consequence, supplier power may be very significant. NMS, as a small company, will not have the power to exert buyer pressure on its suppliers, either in terms of price or delivery. Such components form 60% of current product production and problems over deliveries and scheduling are having significant impact on the company's ability to meet customer deadlines. Clearly an audit needs to be made of supplier performance and the opportunity, or otherwise, for NMS to concentrate on suppliers able to deliver on time. However, for a small company like NMS, the supplier is in an excellent bargaining position.

Threats from New Entrants
NMS is operating in an industry where the costs of entry are significant because it is capital and knowledge intensive. NMS has shown there is a place for smaller innovative companies able to identify specialist market niches. Economies of scale compel new entrants to enter at significant output levels or suffer a cost disadvantage. The products are complex and there is likely to be a significant learning curve with costs only falling as volume builds up over time. Large international customers (such as OEMs, banks, public utilities) are likely to be cautious in moving to new suppliers.

The need for government approval of new data communications equipment creates a process that is both lengthy and expensive and this creates a significant barrier to entry. New entrants may be discouraged by the considerable uncertainty surrounding the industry – both in terms of technology, user acceptance and the R&D investment necessary to create components and systems compatible with the OEM's equipment and end user systems. Furthermore, the need to offer comprehensive support, although something of a problem to a small company such as NMS, does also create a significant barrier to new entrants.

Evidence suggests that market knowledge as an input into product design and delivery is becoming more critical and NMS's ability to create a recognised brand with its end users is creating a competitive advantage. Finally, the barriers to exit from the industry in the shape of knowledge, skills and assets which are very industry specific also reduces the attractiveness of the market place to new entrants.

Rivalry among Competitors
Very different levels of competition are being experienced in the two market places NMS is operating in. Unfortunately the financial data given does not separate out the results from each market but it is clear that the high-volume, low-margin component business offers intense competition with buyers who are able to use their size to extract favourable prices. The ability of NMS to generate better market share and margins through product innovation in this market seems highly unlikely.

Intensity of rivalry in the network management systems market is significantly less because there are only two or three competitors in this specialist market. NMS is dealing with a small number of large end users and designing products specific to their needs. In Porter's terms, NMS are adopting a focused differentiation strategy. In these low-volume, high-margin markets the emphasis has to be on increasing the volume side of the business, but at the same time making sure they have the resources to handle new customers.

Threats from Substitutes
High-tech industries are, almost by their very nature, prone to new technologies emerging that threaten and then eventually replace the established technology. Hence it is important that companies in the industry have scanning systems in place to warn of such threats. NMS will need to ensure that it has innovative new products under development which incorporate any significant technological change. There is evidence that suggests that large successful, high-tech companies are particularly vulnerable to ignoring the challenge coming from disruptive new technologies. However, NMS being small may have a competitive advantage in its ability to respond quickly and flexibly to such change.

Financial Analysis
The significant slowdown in sales growth and its predicted decline in 2007 is a major cause for concern. The extent to which this is externally determined through the economic downturn, as opposed to internal management, product and sales force failings is difficult to determine. It would be useful to compare the performance of NMS with its competitors and the market place as a whole. Export sales continue to form less than 10% of total sales and this is worrying for a company operating in a global industry. It appears from the 2007 forecast, which predicts a more significant decline in export sales than home sales

that nothing is being done to address this. Equally concerning is the upward drift in the cost of sales over the 2004–2006 period. Evidence from the case suggests that supplier performance and consequent production scheduling problems needs to be investigated. The inevitable result of these revenue and cost trends is a falling gross margin.

Expenses do not seem to have been controlled, increasing at a faster rate than turnover. The impact of this on net profit is all too obvious. Failure to control expenses in a period of reduced growth suggests poor management control systems and inadequate management response. The forecast for 2007 suggests an increase in overhead expenses despite the decline in sales.

Commitment to research and development (R&D) in a hi-tech business is crucial to continued product innovation and NMS have maintained an R&D:Total sales ratio of 10% or more each year. However, R&D is notoriously difficult to predict in terms of its success and the timing of breakthroughs. The commitment of NMS should be applauded, but funding it from borrowing, as is increasingly occurring, could explain some of the problems the company is having with the banks and other financial intermediaries. Again, not untypical in a hi-tech business, there is little spending on marketing, perhaps because the company is under the impression that the products sell themselves. However, NMS could point out that the marketing spend was also relatively low at a time that they were relatively successful.

Perhaps one of the most worrying performance features is the slowing down in new business being generated. In 2004 unfulfilled orders virtually matched total sales but the forecast for 2007 sees that key ratio fall to barely one-third of total sales. This issue clearly has to be addressed.

Finally, in terms of measuring performance, the balanced scorecard could be used to good effect. Financially, the current position does not augur well – growth in turnover is slowing down, profitability is falling, the debt ratio is high and stock levels are worrying.

Customer measures are mixed – the company's products are well regarded but production scheduling problems are leading to increasing waiting time for customers. Market share in data communications is small and measuring the market share in network management systems is difficult because of the bespoke nature of the product. Technical support to customers is perceived as a key business area and NMS still has an excellent reputation for customer care.

There is a mixture of signals in terms of the progress being made with internal processes. Products are innovative and the ability to tailor the network management system means that end user needs are met. However, operational and management control processes appear weak – flexible but informal. Operations have a need for more sophisticated planning and scheduling systems and although post-sales performance in the shape of technical support looks good, this appears to be expensive to maintain.

Finally, from the perspective of learning/innovation, NMS has recognised the need to grow people in order to develop the business, but seems unable to recruit and retain the right calibre of people. Failure to do so will prevent Ray from being able to delegate to subordinates and focus his energies on the strategic threats to the survival of the company. Evidence suggests that a number of key personnel have left the company, hopefully not the innovative R&D engineers who gained the company its Government Award for Technology.

(c)   The decision of the founding owner-manager to leave the business is clearly a critical one, particularly in terms of a company such as NMS where the value of the business is very much linked to the founder's vision.

Any exit strategy must be carefully planned so as to not jeopardise the future of the business. In the strategy literature, considerable attention is paid to the entry barriers that do or do not discourage the entrance of new competitors. Exit barriers receive far less attention but are very relevant to an owner-manager such as Ray looking to leave the business as a going/growing concern and realising a return on their personal investment – financial and emotional – in the business. As identified above there are barriers to entry into the industry but unfortunately for Ray there are significant barriers to exit as well – exit in this case referring to him rather than the business. The assets of the business are not easily put to alternative use. Alternative markets for the company's products are difficult to find. Above all in knowledge based, R&D intensive businesses such as NMS, these less tangible assets are very specific to the products, markets and customers that the firm currently has.

Johnson, Scholes and Whittington offer what is now regarded as the classic framework for choosing between strategic options or in their terms determining the 'success criteria' of suitability, acceptability and feasibility in choosing between options. Using their language – 'suitability is concerned with whether a strategy addresses the circumstances in which a company is operating (its environment, its resources/competences and the expectations of its stakeholders) – the strategic position or rationale of a strategy and whether it makes sense'. Alternative options can be ranked, decision trees drawn up or scenarios used to compare the relative suitability of each option in achieving a desired position. 'Acceptability is concerned with the expected performance outcomes of a strategy', where acceptability is measured against the rewards, risk and anticipated stakeholder reactions to the chosen option. 'Feasibility is concerned with whether the organisation has the resources and competencies to deliver a strategy' – and in particular the funding flows and resource deployment capabilities associated with each option.

The three identified exit strategies and an assessment of each option against the three success criteria is given below. Comparing the three options shows the inevitable uncertainties and trade-offs associated with having to make a choice. Ray will face an opportunity cost (the value of the best alternative option not chosen) whichever option he chooses. Such choices are particularly hard in the owner-managed business where there is a need to reconcile personal goals with the well-being of the business. Essentially Ray faces a difficult choice as to when he leaves the business and his degree of involvement in helping solve its current problems – is his presence a cost or benefit to the business?

Option 1: Turnaround and going public Suitability
This is clearly an ambitious long-term strategy, which will require significant time and effort to turn the company round. It is difficult to see who else could achieve this, other than Ray, and the retention of Ray's know-how may be crucial to success. Ray will need to address how he transfers that knowledge to key managers in the business.

Acceptability

This appears to be a relatively high risk and return option, which prolongs Ray's role in the business. The reactions of customers may be favourable, the reactions of the bank and venture capitalist less so, particularly as Ray has no track record in this area. He has no experience of floating a company on a stock exchange and of meeting shareholder expectations.

Feasibility

The willingness of the financial agencies to provide the necessary funding to support the recovery is open to question and may be a function of developing a coherent recovery plan including a phased withdrawal of Ray and the identification of able managers to succeed him.

Option 2: Outright sale
Suitability

This option depends on the ability to identify a suitable buyer able to put in the necessary resources to turn the company round. Selling out is not really a strategy for recovery, as it does not address the initial strategic problems identified in the analysis. It just transfers the problems to someone else.

Acceptability

This can be seen as a medium risk-low return option, but one which allows Ray to make a reasonably swift and clean exit from the business. The reaction of Ray's customers will be crucial to the success of this strategy. Given Ray's recognition of his management limitations in a mature company, banks and other financial stakeholders might find this approach very acceptable.

Feasibility

This depends on the ability to obtain a fair price for the business and for the new owners to have the necessary funds to carry out the necessary changes to NMS and the necessary resources to cope with Ray's departure from the firm. Failure to find a buyer may mean this is not the short-term solution that Ray is looking for. The (low) valuation of their companies is always an issue for entrepreneurs. Perhaps this is what was behind the protracted negotiations with a potential suitor in 2006?

Option 3: Friendly acquisition
Suitability

The support and resources of a large customer (or competitor) company may be just what NMS needs. Ray's expertise and technical knowledge could be useful to the new holding company and so he could therefore be retained in this business for an agreed length of time. This option should address the identified weaknesses regarding staff, systems and structure if the acquisition is properly implemented.

Acceptability

This is likely to be a medium risk and return strategy with any price premium for NMS dependent on the value placed on Ray's continued contribution. Its acceptability to Ray depends on his willingness to give up control. It is likely to find favour with the financial stakeholders. The problem may be Ray's ability to work in a corporate structure, particularly in the light of his declaration that an entrepreneur is "someone willing to work 18 hours a day for themselves.... to avoid working eight hours a day for someone else!"

Feasibility

Funding issues should not be a problem given the resources of the acquirer. The key problem will be in integrating Ray and the firm into a large company environment.

Clearly this is a complex set of options for Ray to consider, and it requires him to be clear about his personal goals and objectives and how far any strategy is either helped or hindered by his presence in the firm. Each option will have a different timescale for achieving Ray's goal of exiting from the business.

2 Context

The decline in the number of people taking the qualification appears to be a reflection of the maturity of the marketplace. The large pool of unqualified environmental managers and auditors that existed when the qualification was launched has now been exploited. There are now fewer candidates taking the examinations and fewer members joining the EMS. The organisation's response to this has been to look for international markets where it can promote the qualifications it currently offers. It hopes to find large pools of unqualified environmental managers and auditors in these markets.

The scenario suggests that EMS currently has relatively limited strategic ambitions. There is no evidence that EMS plans to develop new qualifications outside its current portfolio. Indeed, attempts to look at complementary qualifications (such as soil and water conservation) have been rejected by Council. Hence, expansion into new strategic business markets does not appear to be an option.

Strategy Development

(a) Internal development

Internal development takes place when strategies are developed by building on or developing the organisation's own capabilities. It is often termed organic growth. This is how EMS has operated up to now. The original certificates were developed by the founders of the Society. Since then, additional certificates have been added and the Diploma programme developed at the instigation of members and officers of the Society.

In many ways this type of organic growth is particularly suited to the configuration of the organisation, one where there is a risk-averse and cautious culture. The organic approach spreads cost and risk over time and growth is much easier to control and manage. However, growth can be slow and indeed, as in the case of EMS, may have ceased altogether. Growth is also restricted by the breadth of the organisation's capabilities. For example, EMS has not been able to develop (or indeed even consider developing) any products outside of its fairly restricted product range. Furthermore, although internal development may be a reasonable strategy for developing a home market it maybe an inappropriate strategy for breaking into new market places and territories. This is particularly true when, as it appears in the case of the EMS, internal resources have no previous experience of developing products in overseas markets.

In summary, internal growth has been the method of strategy development at EMS up to now, based on a strategic direction of consolidation and market penetration. There is no evidence that EMS is considering developing new products to arrest the fall in qualification numbers. However, the Board has suggested developing new markets for the current qualification range and India, China and Russia have been identified as potential targets. It seems unlikely that internal development will be an appropriate method of pursuing this strategic direction.

(b) Mergers and Acquisitions
A strategy of acquisition is one where one organisation (such as EMS) takes ownership of other existing organisations in the target countries. One of the most compelling reasons for acquisition is the speed it allows an organisation to enter a new product or market area. EMS might look to acquire organisations already offering certification in its target markets. These organisations would then become the mechanism for launching EMS qualifications into these markets. In addition, it is likely that these organisations will have qualifications that the EMS does not currently offer. These qualifications could then be offered, if appropriate, in EMS's home market. This arrangement would provide EMS with the opportunity to quickly offer its core competences into its target markets, as well as gaining new competencies which it could exploit at home.

However, acquisitions usually require considerable expenditure at some point in time and evidence suggests that there is a high risk that they will not deliver the returns that they promised. It is unlikely that the EMS will have enough money to fund such acquisitions and its status as a private limited entity means that it cannot currently access the markets to fund such growth. Any acquisitions will have to be funded from its cash reserves or from private equity investment groups. Furthermore, acquisitions also bring political and cultural issues which evidence suggests the organisation would have difficulty with. Under achievement in mergers and acquisitions often results from problems of cultural fit. This can be particularly problematic with international acquisitions, which is exactly the type of acquisition under consideration here. So, although acquisitions are a popular way of fuelling growth it is unlikely that EMS will have either the cash or the cultural will to pursue this method of strategy development. There is no evidence that EMS has any expertise in acquiring organisations in it home market and so such acquisitions overseas would be extremely risky.

(c) Strategic Alliances
A strategic alliance takes place when two or more organisations share resources and activities to pursue a particular strategy. This approach has become increasingly popular for a number of reasons. In the context of EMS it would allow the organisation to enter into a marketplace without the large financial outlay of acquiring a local organisation. Furthermore, it would avoid the cultural dislocation of either acquiring or merging with another organisation. The motive for the alliance would be co-specialisation with each partner concentrating on the activities that best match their capabilities. Johnson, Scholes and Whittington suggest that co-specialisation alliances "are used to enter new geographic markets where an organisation needs local knowledge and expertise". This fits the EMS requirement exactly.

The exact nature of the alliance would require much thought and indeed different types of alliance might be forged in the three markets targeted by EMS. A joint venture is where a new organisation is set up jointly owned by the parents. This is a formal alliance and will obviously take some time to establish. EMS will have to contribute cost and resources to the newly established company, but such costs and resources should be much less than those incurred in an acquisition. However, joint ventures take time to establish and it may be not be an option if EMS wants to quickly move into a target marketplace to speedily arrest its falling numbers. A licence agreement could be an alternative where EMS licenses the use of its qualification in the target market. This could be organised in a number of ways. For example, a local organisation could market the EMS qualification as its own and pay EMS a fee for each issued certificate and diploma. Alternatively, the qualification may be marketed by the local organisation as an EMS qualification and EMS pays this organisation a licence fee for every certificate and diploma it issues in that country. This requires less commitment from EMS but it is likely to bring in less financial returns, with less control over how the qualification is marketed. Furthermore, if the qualification is successful, there is the risk that the local organisation will develop its own alternative so that it gains all the income from the transaction, not just a percentage of the transaction fee.

At first sight, the strategic alliance appears very appropriate to EMS's current situation. The licensing approach is particularly attractive because it seems to offer very quick access to new markets without any great financial commitment and without any cultural upheaval within EMS itself. However, the uptake of the qualification is unpredictable and the marketing and promotion of the qualification is outside the control of EMS. EMS may find this difficult to accept. Furthermore, the EMS will only be receiving a fraction of the income and so it must ensure that this fraction is sufficient to fuel growth expectations and service the newly qualified members in other countries. Finally, there is often a paradox in organisations where internal development has been the strategic method adopted so far. An organisation used to internal development and control often finds it difficult to trust partners in an alliance. Yet trust and cooperation is probably the most important ingredient of making such strategic alliances work.

3 **(a)** Software quality is notoriously difficult to define, but at least four issues deserve consideration.

Conformity to requirements

This is concerned with the software performing business functions correctly. It does what the user expects it to do and does not do what it is not expected to do. This issue is about meeting expectations. The conformity to requirements might be measured by the number of change requests submitted immediately after the system has gone live. If the system performs to requirements then there should be very few change requests until the system has been in operation for some time. Evidence at CCT suggests that this is a major issue. These problems are highlighted by Tony Osunda. He states that "the delivered system did not work the way we wanted" and that "key areas of functionality were either wrong or missing altogether". The fact that changes were subsequently made for free indicates why margins are falling. Doing these would have significantly eroded into the projected profitability of the project.

Reliability

The software behaves consistently and reliably and so is available for the user. The reliability of software can be measured by availability and downtime. Indeed, reliability is often defined within service level agreements (SLAs). For example; the software must be available for 99% of the agreed service time, where service time is defined as 07.00 – 22.00, Monday to Friday. Reliability is relatively easy to measure because it concerns the availability of the software. There is no evidence at CCT that their software has reliability problems.

Usability

The ease of use of software is a major issue in software delivery and e-business development. The usability of software may be assessed in a number of ways. For example;
*   By logging the nature and number of calls to a HELP desk. This should be relatively low if the software is easy to use.
*   By observing users actually using the software and recording the problems and difficulties they encounter.
*   By using questionnaires to ask users how easy they have found the system to use.

There is some evidence that CCT software has usability problems. Crispin Peters-Ward stated that "We found (the system) cumbersome to use."

Degree of excellence

The software should exhibit elements of good build, such as maintainability, flexibility and expandability. This software quality is about long-term design potential. This is quite difficult to measure. However, there are technical measures which allow the modularity of the software to be assessed. If the modularity of the software is low then the software is likely to be easy to maintain and test. There is evidence that the CCT software has long-term design problems. Amelia Platt comments that the software was not built "with expansion in mind. Also, it is difficult to know what some of the programs actually do, so making changes is a nightmare. Programmers make changes to program code without really knowing what the knock-on effect will be." There are now one hundred and thirty programmers in the company. It is unlikely that they all understand how the software has been constructed. Hence, there is ample opportunity for introducing faults into the system.

Software quality is extremely important to end users. Users expect systems to perform functions correctly and reliably. They expect systems to be easy to use. Failure to fulfil these expectations may lead to frustration with the product, inefficient use of systems and the under-performance of organisations. In the extreme it may lead to organisational collapse and, where safety-critical software fails, to loss of life. The elements of product quality (degree of excellence) may not be immediately obvious to an end user. However, high maintenance costs become very clear to organisations over time, as they increasingly consume a company's operational budget.

(b) The Capability Maturity Model Integration (CMMI) is a process improvement approach that provides organisations with the essential elements of effective processes. It can be used to guide process improvement across a project, a division, or an entire organisation. It has five levels of capability. Organisations are encouraged to move up the levels and to eventually achieve capability level 5. A successful appraisal at this level would assist CCT in delivering quality software as well as publicly demonstrating their competence to do so. Many customers mandate that suppliers should be at a certain level in the CMMI assessment.

Capability level 0 is where there is an incomplete process which is either not performed at all or is partially performed. One or more of the specific goals of the process area are not satisfied. There is no evidence of such a process at CCT. Capability Level 1 is defined as performed. A performed process is a process that satisfies all of the specific goals of a process area such as software development. At this level the processes are performed informally, without following a documented process description or plan. The rigour with which these practices are performed depends on the individuals managing and performing the work and the quality of the outcomes may vary considerably. Successful outcomes for an organisation operating at level 1 depend upon the heroic efforts of individuals. Carlos Theroux alludes to these days at CCT; "when we were smaller we could all dive in and solve the problems. We all used to stay over until we got the problem solved".

A capability level 2 process is characterized as a managed process. A managed process is a performed (capability level 1) process that is also planned and executed in accordance with a defined procedure. A critical distinction between a performed process and a managed process is the extent to which the process is actually managed! A managed process is planned (the plan may be part of a more encompassing plan) and the performance of the process is managed against the plan. Corrective actions are taken when the actual results and performance deviate significantly from the plan. A managed process achieves the objectives of the plan and is documented as a standard for consistent performance. Carlos Theroux has alluded to the introduction of a project management methodology and its adoption will assist CCT to achieve capability level 2.

A capability level 3 process is characterized as a "defined process." A defined process is a managed (capability level 2) process that is tailored from the organisation's set of standard processes according to the organisation's tailoring guidelines.

It contributes work products, measures, and other process-improvement information to the organisational process. A critical distinction between a managed process and a defined process is the scope of the process descriptions, standards, and procedures. In software terms, capability level 3 is achieved when a defined engineering process is in place so that the process of software development (not just its management) is consistent and standard. At this level of capability, the organisation is interested in deploying standard processes that are proven and that therefore take less time and money than continually writing and deploying new processes. Another critical distinction is that a defined process is described in more detail and performed more rigorously than a managed process. CCT does not appear to be at this level at the moment. It could be argued that the problems in requirements functionality highlighted by Tony Osunda would not happen in a defined process.

A capability level 4 process is characterized as a "quantitatively managed process." A quantitatively managed process is a defined (capability level 3) process that is controlled using statistical and other quantitative techniques. Quantitative objectives for quality and process performance are established and used as criteria in managing the process. The quality and process performance are understood in statistical terms and are managed throughout the life of the process. A critical distinction between a defined process and a quantitatively managed process is the predictability of the process performance. A defined process only provides qualitative predictability. Clearly, CCT is not at this level yet. However, statistical analysis of faults, perhaps using Six Sigma principles, could deliver important quality improvements. The measurement of quality is fundamental to this level. Hence, the organisation must consider some of the issues raised in the answer to part a) of this question.

A capability level 5 process is characterized as an "optimizing process." An optimizing process is a quantitatively managed (capability level 4) process that is changed and adapted to meet relevant current and projected business objectives. An optimizing process focuses on continually improving the process performance through both incremental and innovative technological improvements. A critical distinction between a quantitatively managed process and an optimizing process is that the optimizing process is continuously improved by addressing common causes of process variation. In a process that is optimized, common causes of process variation are addressed by changing that process. The process of continuous process improvement through quantitative feedback from the process itself is clearly not happening in CCT at present.

4 **(a)** A simple value chain of the primary activities of DRB is shown below.

Handling and storing inbound fully configured equipment Quality inspection	Re-branding of products Re-packaging of products	Customer collection Technician delivery and installation	Local advertising Web based enquiries	On-site technical support Back to base support
Inbound logistics	**Operations**	**Outbound Logistics**	**Marketing and sales**	**Service**

Comments about value might include:

Inbound logistics: Excellent quality assurance is required in inbound logistics. This is essential for pre-configured equipment where customers have high expectations of reliability. As well as contributing to customer satisfaction, high quality also reduces service costs.

Operations: This is a relatively small component in the DRB value chain and actually adds little value to the customer. It is also being undertaken in a relatively high cost country. DRB might wish to re-visit the current arrangement.

Outbound logistics: Customer feedback shows that this is greatly valued. Products can be picked up from stock and delivery and installation is provided if required. Most of the company's larger competitors cannot offer this service. However, it is unlikely that this value can be retained when DRB begins to increasingly supply outside the geographical region it is in.

Marketing and sales: This is very low-key at DRB and will have to be developed if the company is to deliver the proposed growth. The limited functionality of the web site offers little value to customers.

Service: Customer feedback shows that this is greatly valued. Most of the company's competitors cannot offer this level of service. They offer support from off-shore call centres and a returns policy that is both time consuming to undertake and slow in rectification. However, it is unlikely that this value can be retained when DRB begins to increasingly supply outside the geographical region it is in.

(b) DRB has already gained efficiencies by procuring products through the supplier's web-site. However, the web site has restricted functionality. When DRB places the order it is not informed of the expected delivery date until it receives the confirmation e-mail from ISAS. It is also unable to track the status of their order and so it is only when it receives a despatch email from ISAS that it knows that it is on its way. Because DRB is not the owner of the shipment, it is unable to track the delivery and so the physical arrival of the goods cannot be easily predicted. On occasions where shipments have appeared to have been lost, DRB has had to ask ISAS to track the shipment and report on its status. This has not been very satisfactory and the problem has been exacerbated by having two shippers involved. ISAS has not been able to reliably track the transhipment of goods from their shipper to EIF, the logistics company used to distribute their products in the country. Some shipments have been lost and it is time-consuming to track and follow-up shipments which are causing concern. Finally, because DRB has no long term contract with ISAS, it has to pay when it places the order through a credit card transaction on the ISAS website.

DRB has stated that it wishes to continue importing fully configured products. It is not interested in importing components and assembling them. It also does not wish to build or invest in assembly plants in other countries. However, it may wish to consider the following changes to its upstream supply chain:

- Seek to identify a wider range of suppliers and so trade through other sell-side web sites. Clearly there are costs associated with this. Suppliers have to be identified and evaluated and financial and trading arrangements have to be established. However, it removes the risk of single-sourcing and other suppliers may have better systems in place to support order and delivery tracking.
- Seek to identify suppliers who are willing and able to re-brand and package their products with DRB material at the production plant. This should reduce DRB costs as this is currently undertaken in a country where wage rates are high.
- Re-consider the decision not to negotiate long-term contracts with suppliers (including ISAS) and so explore the possibility of more favourable payment terms. DRB has avoided long-term contracts up to now. It may also not be possible to enter into such contracts if DRB begins to trade with a number of suppliers.
- Seek to identify suppliers (including ISAS) who are able to provide information about delivery dates prior to purchase and who are able to provide internet-based order tracking systems to their customers. This should allow much better planning.
- Consider replacing the two supplier shippers with a contracted logistics company which will collect the goods from the supplier and transport the goods directly to DRB. This should reduce physical transhipment problems and allow seamless monitoring of the progress of the order from despatch to arrival. It will also allow DRB to plan for the arrival of goods and to schedule its re-packaging.

DRB might also wish to consider two other procurement models; buy-side and the independent marketplace.

In the buy-side model DRB would use its web site to invite potential suppliers to bid for contract requirements posted on the site. This places the onus on suppliers to spend time completing details and making commitments. It should also attract a much wider range of suppliers than would have been possible through DRB searching sell-side sites for potential suppliers. Unfortunately, it is unlikely that DRB is large enough to host such a model. However, it may wish to prototype it to see if it is viable and whether it uncovers potential suppliers who have not been found in sell-side web sites searches.

In the independent marketplace model, DRB places its requirements on an intermediary web site. These are essentially B2B electronic marketplaces which allow, on the one hand, potential customers to search products being offered by suppliers and, on the other hand, customers to place their requirements and be contacted by potential suppliers. Such marketplaces promise greater supplier choice with reduced costs. They also provide an opportunity for aggregation where smaller organisations (such as DRB) can get together with companies that have the same requirement to place larger orders to gain cheaper prices and better purchasing terms. It is also likely that such marketplaces will increasingly offer algorithms that automatically match customers and suppliers, so reducing the search costs associated with the sell-side model. The independent marketplace model may be a useful approach for DRB. Many of the suppliers participating in these marketplaces are electronics companies.

(c) DRB's downstream supply chain is also very simple at the moment. It has a web-site that shows information about DRB products. Customers can make enquiries about the specification and availability of these products through an e-mail facility. Conventional marketing is undertaken through local advertising and buyers either collect their products or they are delivered and installed by a specialist group of technicians. DRB could tune its downstream supply chain by using many of the approaches mentioned in the previous section. For example:
- Developing the web site so that it not only shows products but also product availability. Customers would be able to place orders and pay for them securely over the web site. The site could be integrated with a logistics system so that orders and deliveries can be tracked by the customer. DRB must recognise that most of its competitors already have such systems. However, DRB will have to put a similar system in place to be able to support its growth plans.
- Participating in independent marketplace web sites as a supplier. DRB may also be able to exploit aggregation by combining with other suppliers in consortia to bid for large contracts.
- DRB may also consider participating in B2C marketplaces such as e-bay. Many organisations use this as their route to market for commodity products.

DRB may also wish to consider replacing its sales from stock approach with sales from order. In the current approach, DRB purchases products in advance and re-packages and stores these products before selling them to customers. This leads to very quick order fulfilment but high storage and financing costs. These costs will become greater if the planned growth occurs. DRB may wish to consider offering products on its website at a discount but with specified delivery terms. This would allow the company to supply to order rather than supply from stock.

1   **(a)**   1 mark for identifying an appropriate macro-environmental influence in each of the PESTEL areas – even if it is justifying the lack of influence. A further 4 marks are available for given credit to candidates who have extended their argument in selected areas of the framework. It must be accepted that each area of the PESTEL will have a differential effect.   (10 marks).

    (b)   1 mark for each relevant point made in the competitive analysis of NMS (up to a maximum of 13 marks) and 1 mark for each relevant point made in the financial analysis of NMS (up to a maximum of 9 marks). A further 3 professional marks are available for such aspects as the structure, presentation and logical flow of the answer.   (25 marks)

    (c)   1 mark for each relevant point up to a maximum of 5 marks for each of the three exit strategies.   (15 marks)

                                                                                                                (50 marks)

2   The question asks for principles and suitability.

    1 mark for each relevant point up to a maximum of 8 marks for internal development. There is a maximum of 4 marks for points relating to principles.   (8 marks)

    1 mark for each relevant point up to a maximum of 8 marks for acquisitions. There is a maximum of 4 marks for points relating to principles.   (8 marks)

    1 mark for each relevant point up to a maximum of 9 marks for strategic alliances. There is a maximum of 5 marks for points relating to principles.   (9 marks)

                                                                                                                (25 marks)

3   **(a)**   1 mark for each relevant point up to a maximum of 5 marks for identifying and discussing software quality. 1 mark for each relevant point up to a maximum of 5 marks for identifying appropriate measures.   (10 marks)

    (b)   1 mark for each relevant point up to a maximum of 2 marks for introducing the CMMI concept. 1 mark for each relevant point up to a maximum of 2 marks for a description of each capability level (five levels)

            1 mark for each relevant point up to a maximum 3 marks for applying CMMI to the CCT scenario.   (15 marks)

                                                                                                                (25 marks)

4   **(a)**   1 mark for each relevant point up to a maximum of 3 marks for the value chain
            1 mark for each relevant point up to a maximum of 6 marks for the significance and value of the primary activities.
                                                                                                                (9 marks)

    (b)   1 mark for each relevant point up to a maximum of 6 marks for identifying upstream changes.

            1 mark for each relevant point up to a maximum of 4 marks for identifying how these changes address problems experienced by DRB.   (10 marks)

    (c)   1 mark for each relevant point up to a maximum of 6 marks for identifying upstream changes.   (6 marks)

                                                                                                                (25 marks)

Review Form & Free Prize Draw – Paper P3 Business Analysis (6/07)

All original review forms from the entire BPP range, completed with genuine comments, will be entered into one of two draws on 31 July 2007 and 31 January 2008. The names on the first four forms picked out on each occasion will be sent a cheque for £50.

Name: _____

Address: _____

_____

_____

How have you used this Kit?
(Tick one box only)

☐ Home study (book only)

☐ On a course: college _____

☐ With 'correspondence' package

☐ Other _____

Why did you decide to purchase this Kit?
(Tick one box only)

☐ Have used the complementary Study text

☐ Have used other BPP products in the past

☐ Recommendation by friend/colleague

☐ Recommendation by a lecturer at college

☐ Saw advertising

☐ Other _____

During the past six months do you recall seeing/receiving any of the following?
(Tick as many boxes as are relevant)

☐ Our advertisement in *Student Accountant*

☐ Our advertisement in *Pass*

☐ Our advertisement in *PQ*

☐ Our brochure with a letter through the post

☐ Our website www.bpp.com

Which (if any) aspects of our advertising do you find useful?
(Tick as many boxes as are relevant)

☐ Prices and publication dates of new editions

☐ Information on product content

☐ Facility to order books off-the-page

☐ None of the above

Which BPP products have you used?

Text	☐	Success CD	☐	Learn Online	☐
Kit	☑	i-Learn	☐	Home Study Package	☐
Passcard	☐	i-Pass	☐	Home Study PLUS	☐

Your ratings, comments and suggestions would be appreciated on the following areas.

	Very useful	Useful	Not useful
Passing ACCA exams	☐	☐	☐
Passing P3	☐	☐	☐
Planning your question practice	☐	☐	☐
Questions	☐	☐	☐
Top Tips etc in answers	☐	☐	☐
Content and structure of answers	☐	☐	☐
'Plan of attack' in mock exams	☐	☐	☐
Mock exam answers	☐	☐	☐

Overall opinion of this Kit   Excellent ☐   Good ☐   Adequate ☐   Poor ☐

Do you intend to continue using BPP products?   Yes ☐   No ☐

The BPP author of this edition can be e-mailed at: glennhaldane@bpp.com

Please return this form to: Nick Weller, ACCA Publishing Manager, BPP Learning Media Ltd, FREEPOST, London, W12 8BR

Review Form & Free Prize Draw (continued)

TELL US WHAT YOU THINK

Please note any further comments and suggestions/errors below.

Free Prize Draw Rules

1 Closing date for 31 July 2007 draw is 30 June 2007. Closing date for 31 January 2008 draw is 31 December 2007.

2 Restricted to entries with UK and Eire addresses only. BPP employees, their families and business associates are excluded.

3 No purchase necessary. Entry forms are available upon request from BPP Learning Media Ltd. No more than one entry per title, per person. Draw restricted to persons aged 16 and over.

4 Winners will be notified by post and receive their cheques not later than 6 weeks after the relevant draw date.

5 The decision of the promoter in all matters is final and binding. No correspondence will be entered into.